IMPERIALISM

A Study

IMPERIALISM

A Study

Third Edition

J. A. HOBSON

with an Introduction by J. Townshend
Manchester Polytechnic

London
UNWIN HYMAN
Boston   **Sydney**   **Wellington**

Published by the Academic Division of
Unwin Hyman Ltd
15/17 Broadwick Street, London W1V 1FP, UK

Allen & Unwin (Australia) Ltd,
8 Napier Street, North Sydney, NSW 2060, Australia

Allen & Unwin (New Zealand) Ltd in association with the
Port Nicholson Press Ltd,
60 Cambridge Terrace, Wellington, New Zealand

First published in 1902
Second edition 1905
Third entirely revised and reset edition 1938
First published in paperback in 1988

British Library Cataloguing in Publication Data

Hobson, J.A.
   Imperialism : a study.
1.   Economics — Great Britain — History
2.   Imperialism — History — 3. Great
Britain — Colonies — Economic
conditions
I.   Title
        325'.32'01   HC255
        ISBN 0-04-325019-X

Printed in Great Britain by
Billing and Sons Ltd., Worcester.

CONTENTS

INTRODUCTION
BY J. TOWNSHEND

Few classics of political literature are written with immortality in mind. They are usually passionate, partisan pieces that aim to explain and resolve pressing political problems. They are often fragmentary, inconsistent and ambiguous. Hobson's *Imperialism, A Study*, published in 1902, was no exception. It was a collection of loosely connected magazine articles covering a variety of imperial issues which faced Britain at the turn of the century.[1] Nevertheless, an anonymous reviewer quickly spotted Hobson's intellectual achievement. *Imperialism* was described as 'the first sustained attempt to fix the underlying principles of the most powerful force of modern times' (*Review of Reviews*, November 1902). Today, *Imperialism* is rightly celebrated as one of the classics of modern political writing (Butler, 1968, p. 17; Gollwitzer, 1969, p. 189). It created a new genre of intellectual inquiry, the study of 'economic imperialism' (Koebner, 1949, pp. 3–4).

Hobson explored more comprehensively and systematically than any other writer of his time the political, economic and social interconnections between capitalism and imperialism, the effects of imperialism on the conquering and conquered peoples, and its legitimating arguments.[2] Indeed, *Imperialism* was the first attempt to understand the politics of Western capitalism as it entered the twentieth century. It took account of the growing part that monopoly and finance played within the economic and political systems. It noted the internationalization of capital that gave rise to a 'world politics' of competing empires. It analysed the transformation of the political processes of

[9]

advanced capitalist states. These were characterized by the increased power and centralization of government and the emergence of large electorates influenced by the new phenomenon of mass circulation newspapers.

Even today some of *Imperialism*'s root concepts, filtered through the prism of Lenin and his followers, can be seen in explorations of contemporary international politics (Baran and Sweezy, 1966, 1968, *passim*, Brewer, 1980, p. 133). Whilst in the post-1945 era the West's empires have been formally eclipsed, the imperialist imperative, defined as unequal international political and economic relations, continues to flourish in ways that Hobson would have instantly recognized and explained. On a more specific and substantive issue his message concerning Britain's economic future, that 'quantitative' imperial expansion would be ultimately self-defeating, has proved prophetic. Britain has lost its empire and may, in order to survive economically, be forced down the road he advocated, taken by Switzerland and by Scandinavian countries. This was the path of 'qualitative' and 'scientific' development.

The book's classic stature is reinforced by its broad intellectual appeal. It covers a number of domains within the social and historical sciences. Hobson lived in a world where territorial and intellectual frontiers could be crossed without hindrance. He recognized neither the sovereignty nor autonomy of any particular discipline. *Imperialism*, a great work of synthesis, is a testament to Hobson's intellectual versatility. It embraces economic theory, political sociology, social psychology, international relations and cultural analysis. Further, it has excited the interest of historians wishing to refute or defend (albeit in modified form) his explanation of late-nineteenth-century imperialism. It has attracted the attention of intellectual historians seeking to understand, first, the origins of the anti-imperialist movement, especially since it is the acknowledged precursor of Lenin's theory of imperialism, and, secondly, the transformation of *laissez-faire* liberalism into its modern collectivist mode.

Finally, *Imperialism* is unique in the annals of modern political thought in achieving, quite paradoxically, acclaim from upholders of competing ideologies, for example, from liberals such as Campbell-Bannerman, from socialists such as H. N. Brailsford, Leonard Woolf and John Strachey, and from Marxists such as Lenin.[3]

A BRIEF BIOGRAPHICAL
SKETCH

Hobson was an intellectual, political campaigner and a prolific writer and journalist. He was a pivotal figure, along with his friend L. T. Hobhouse, in recasting British liberal ideology into a form of collectivism.[4]

His life began in Derby in 1858. His father, a Liberal, was an important figure in local politics, as a proprietor of the *Derbyshire and North Staffordshire Advertiser* and as town mayor on two occasions. Hobson went to Derby Grammar School and eventually became head boy. He obtained a classics scholarship to Lincoln College, Oxford, and finished with a second class degree in Greats and Classical Moderations. After teaching at two public schools, he moved to London in 1887 to take up journalism and university extension lecturing. The most politically and intellectually formative decade in Hobson's life began. With businessman and famous mountaineer A. F. Mummery he co-authored, as junior partner, *The Physiology of Industry*, which was published in 1889. Maynard Keynes magnanimously noted that the book marked 'an epoch in economic thought' (Keynes, 1936, p. 365). It also marked the beginning of an epoch in Hobson's life. The book outraged academic orthodoxy by arguing that economic depressions were caused by oversaving. Hobson and Mummery challenged a a central tenet of the Protestant ethic — thrift — and its economic defence in Say's Law. This suggested that production created its own demand and that therefore, all things being equal, capitalism was a self-equilibriating system. Consequently, Hobson was prevented from giving extension lectures in Political Economy at the University of London. So began, almost unwittingly, Hobson's career as a courageous intellectual non-conformist, and his curious love-hate relationship with British academia. He wanted academic recognition and an academic post. But his radical propensities and critical broadsides against conventional economic theory and its practitioners alienated him from university establishments which claimed to be above class partisanship.

He was a founder member of the 'Rainbow Circle' in 1893. The circle, which met for the next thirty years, did much to inspire the Liberal reforms of 1906–14. Its membership consisted of Liberals, non-aligned socialists, Fabians, Marxists, imperialists and anti-imperialists. It was devoted to formulating a coherent rationale for increasing the social and economic functions of the state.[5] Much of Hobson's subsequent writing was concerned with bringing this project to fruition.

In addition Hobson played a significant part in the 'South Place Ethical Society'. He joined the society in 1896 and became one of its permanent lecturers, a post he held until 1934 (MacKillop, 1986, p. 70). The society represented the progressive, collectivist wing of the Victorian ethical movement that rejected Christianity, but needed a surrogate religion. Membership of this society was strongly reflected in Hobson's work, which even at its most 'scientific' was underpinned by powerful ethical commitment.

His political debut came in 1899 with the outbreak of the Boer War. L. T. Hobhouse, possibly on the strength of reading his article, 'Free trade and foreign policy', published a year earlier, suggested to C. P. Scott, the illustrious editor of the *Manchester Guardian*, that Hobson be sent to South Africa as a special correspondent (Clarke, 1978, p. 90). His dispatches, giving an eye-witness account of the unfolding prewar drama, were compiled in a book, *The War in South Africa* (1900a). It excited a great deal of public interest and controversy. On his return from South Africa he became prominent in the anti-war opposition. He spoke at public meetings, frequently broken up by jingoists. Out of these experiences, and the theoretical framework he had developed before and during the war, *Imperialism* was born.

Before the First World War Hobson was a notable figure in a number of progressive political and intellectual movements. He also joined the staff of *The Nation* in 1907 under H. W. Massingham's editorship. The journal was an important intellectual force behind the 1906–14 Liberal reforms. Hobson was known as the 'jester-in-chief' at the famous *Nation* lunches (Nevinson, 1925, p. 217). His 'formidable gift for irony and satire' (Brailsford, 1948, p. 4) scarcely surfaced in print, with the notable exception of *1920: Dips into the Near Future* ('Lucian', 1918), which contained striking anticipations of Orwell's *1984* (1949).

During the First World War he was an active peace campaigner and became significant in the movement that established the League of Nations. He left the Liberal Party in 1916 partly as a result of its lurch towards protectionism. In this period he was a member of a couple of government-sponsored bodies: the Whitley Committee on the reform of industrial relations and the Reconstruction Subcommittee on trusts. He joined the Labour Party in 1924 and contributed to a document entitled 'The living wage', which contained his underconsumptionist analysis. It was debated and ultimately rejected at the 1927 Labour Party Conference.

His engagement with social and economic reform has to be seen against the background of his constant pre-occupation with literary activity. He wrote thirty-seven books and published over six hundred reviews and articles on a huge variety of economic, political, philosophical and literary topics. In the last decade of his life, when he was over 70 years of age, he wrote nine books and over a hundred reviews and articles. He displayed this literary energy throughout his life although he was physically frail. He suffered from numerous bouts of insomnia and neuritis. H. W. Nevinson wrote poignantly, 'I suppose that for forty years at least, the stupefying sword of death has been hanging over him by a cobweb', and he wondered, 'Is it that unmoving peril which has driven him to produce more work and finer work than almost any healthy man I have known?' (Nevinson, 1925, p. 217). Hobson probably surprised himself by living to the ripe age of 82. He died in 1940.

IMPERIALISM: THE CONTEXT

Imperialism should be understood as a response by Hobson to the challenges posed by the interconnected issues of imperialism and social reform to liberalism, and its organized expression, the Liberal Party, in the late nineteenth and early twentieth centuries. These challenges amounted to a demand for the redefinition of the nature and scope of state activity.[6]

Hobson and his progressive colleagues firmly believed that the mid-Victorian *laissez-faire* liberalism, if not strictly adhered to in practice, had become a suffocating shibboleth for the Liberal Party. They saw this position as irrelevant to an electorate that increasingly demanded social reform: the alleviation of poverty, poor housing, health, working conditions, education, low pay and unemployment, recently 'discovered' by the new breed of social reformers. The question no longer seemed to be whether the state should intervene to promote social improvement, but how and to what extent? And in so far as these reforms entailed financial support, how were they to be funded? Equally important, Hobson recognized that the growth of monopoly had undermined the fundamental premiss of liberal political economy — perfect competition. Monopolies created a maldistribution of income, which according to Hobson was primarily responsible for poverty, economic depression and imperialism. These problems, he argued, could only be solved through state intervention.

Abroad, Britain encountered increasingly acute economic and political problems with which Hobson felt he had to grapple. The first stemmed from Britain's acquisition since the 1880s of huge imperial 'responsibilities' in the tropics and subtropics. The Cobdenite solution, colonial separation, even for followers of Cobden, such as Hobson, no longer seemed feasible or desirable in the short term. Thus greater saliency was given to the question of how these new colonies were to be administered. Perhaps even more important issues for ruling circles were posed by growing economic and political pressures from abroad that put in doubt Britain's continued imperial pre-eminence.

First, there was conflict with France over the headwaters of the Nile which culminated in the showdown at Fashoda in 1898. Secondly, Germany, a rapidly industrializing power, seemed to threaten not only the British economy but, through its naval build-up, the empire's life-support mechanism, the fleet. The United States, under Theodore Roosevelt's presidency, had also entered the imperialist game by the turn of the century. It had absorbed many of Spain's colonial possessions and had begun to quarrel with Britain over Venezuela.

This growing insecurity was matched by an increasing pride in empire, or 'jingoism' as it was called, amongst the mass of the population. It started as a response to the abortive Jameson Raid of 1895. Later it was manifested by the celebrations that surrounded Queen Victoria's Diamond Jubilee of June 1897, and the battle of Omdurman in the following year, which was seen as avenging General Gordon's death at Khartoum.

The ultimate climax of this mixture of triumphalism and insecurity came during the Boer War (1899-1902). The hysterical demonstrations that accompanied the lifting of the Boer siege of the British army at Mafeking in May 1900 were against a background of Britain's diplomatic isolation and its difficulty in defeating the Boer guerrillas. The war, therefore, starkly questioned Britain's continued existence as a major military and imperial power.

Hobson and his co-thinkers felt compelled to tackle these domestic and imperial problems at a time when what they regarded as 'non-progressive' solutions were gaining ascendency. Socialists, although profoundly divided over imperialism, were united in demanding wide-ranging state control of the economy to remedy the multiplicity of social problems. The Liberal imperialists, led by Lord Rosebery, briefly Gladstone's successor in the 1892−5 Liberal administration, were the strongest advocates of what has been termed 'social imperialism'. They saw social reform and imperialism as interdependent. A strong and growing empire was vital to Britain's future economic prosperity, which was necessary to pay for social improvements. In turn social reform by generating social cohesion and a healthy and educated population, thereby enhancing Britain's 'national' or 'social' efficiency, was seen as crucial to Britain's survival as a major imperial power. The Liberal Unionists, under the leadership of Joseph Chamberlain, Colonial Secretary until 1903, shared this perspective, but differed over the issue of free trade. Whilst Rosebery, in part reflecting the financial interests of the City of London, supported free trade, Chamberlain championed a form of protectionism called 'Tariff Reform'. He advocated an imperial *Zollverein* in 1896 as a means of defending manufacturing interests, especially those of the Midlands. Such an imperial customs union would also, he thought, have the convenient virtue of broadening the fiscal base deemed necessary to finance social reform, especially old age pensions, and growing arms expenditure. In addition,

Chamberlain hoped that by implementing social welfare measures he would 'dish' the socialists, who were experiencing astounding electoral success on the continent.

For Hobson, the social imperialist formula was unworkable and undesirable. There could be a welfare state or a warfare state, but not both. A warfare state, which highlighted militarism and international questions, marginalized the issue of social reform and diverted resources away from social improvement. Conversely, social reform and free trade would eliminate the necessity for an imperialist warfare state. Social reform would dissipate the economic 'surplus', which was in Hobson's eyes the root cause of imperialism. Free trade would reduce international tension and the need for colonial acquisition. But Hobson also wanted to meet the socialist threat of wholesale statism. He sought to stake out a new intellectual and political middle ground that would reconcile certain types of individual economic liberty essential to economic progress, with a 'collectivist' solution to the problems of poverty, monopoly and imperialism that did not entail complete state control of industry.[7] Secondly, this middle ground was designed to promote social reform that did not require funding by revenues generated by protectionism. *Imperialism* aimed, therefore, to advance a strategy that would redirect British politics towards social reform without having to pay the price of imperialism or state socialism.

Developing a new Liberal strategy was one problem. The instrument for its realization, the Liberal Party, was quite another. By the mid-1890s the party appeared to Hobson and many others to be in a terminal state.[8] A mood of *fin de siècle* pessimism translated itself into a *fin de partie* fatalism. The party had collapsed at the 1895 elections. Its representation in parliament fell from 273 to 177. It was left leaderless, as a result of the conflict between the imperialist Lord Rosebery and the Gladstonian wing led by Lord Harcourt. The party rank and file was also riven with dissension, divided between imperialists and anti-imperialists, old-style *laissez-faire* radicals and new-style social reformers. There were also specific interest groups within the party, who often put their interests before those of the party: Lib-Labs, Non-conformists, the Welsh, the Scottish and the Irish. Hobson and many of his Rainbow Circle colleagues believed that the party was in disarray and decline because of its attitude towards social reform. They wished to revitalize the party by formulating a radical and coherent programme of social reform that would unite the disparate reform groups within the party and appeal to the working-class electorate, whilst simultaneously isolating the imperialists.

However, the demise of the Liberal Party seemed almost certain to Hobson during the Boer War. Divisions between the imperialists and anti-imperialists came to a head. Rosebery was a strong, if not always totally enthusiastic, supporter of the government during the war, while Lloyd George and John Morley led the Liberal opposition. Campbell-Bannerman, the party leader, attempted to hold the party together by steering a middle course, although his sympathies lay with the 'Pro-Boers'. But in June 1901 he came off the fence. In his 'methods of barbarism' speech he denounced the means by which the war was being pursued, particularly the use of concentration camps. It looked as though the Liberal imperialists were contemplating leaving the party. Hobson and others saw the party as finished and openly toyed with the idea of forming a new party, consisting of middle-class progressives and organized labour, which had consistently opposed the war. Hobson observed in September 1901, 'If ever the time was ripe for an effective Labour Party, it is now. The old Liberal Party is rotten to its core, divided in just as many separate ways as there are separate issues' (Hobson, 1901a, p. 617).[9] What followed was a public discussion about the establishment of a new party initiated by Hobson through the pages of the *Echo* and the *Labour Leader*, to which leaders of the Independent Labour

[18]

Party and trade unions contributed.[10] Hobson's attempt to bring about some form of Lib-Lab coalition is also reflected in *Imperialism* (p. 145). He was in effect telling socialists, trade unionists, anti-imperialists and middle-class social reformers that they had a common cause in the removal of the 'unproductive' or 'unearned' surplus that produced the maladies of militarism, imperialism, economic depression and poverty.

KEY ARGUMENTS AND EXPLANATIONS AND THEIR GENESIS

Readers coming fresh to *Imperialism* with a preconception that Hobson was an anti-imperialist *per se* will become puzzled as they progress through the book. They will discover that he metes out commendation and condemnation for different *forms* of imperialism: 'sane' (p. 246) and 'legitimate' (p. 23) imperialism on the one hand, and 'insane' (p. 246) and 'aggressive' (pp. 11, 55, 65, 200) imperialism on the other. Hobson identifies only certain types of imperialism for hostile treatment. They were included under the generic term 'New Imperialism', a global phenomenon that started approximately in 1870. The New Imperialism was characterized by the existence of: (1) competing empires, rather than all-embracing single empires of the past (pp. 8, 304); (2) the dominance of financial or investment capital over mercantile interests (p. 304); and (3) the absorption of new territories populated by culturally unassimilable peoples for whom self-government was not intended (pp. 6, 37, 124). This contrasted sharply with the previous colonialism, which he regarded as legitimate, because it constituted a 'natural outflow of nationality' to sparsely populated areas and was marked by the evolution of self-governing institutions (p. 7).

The arguments, explanations and remedies in *Imperialism* were not forged *de novo* by Hobson. He borrowed from the liberal tradition, especially in its Cobdenite form, as did many of the 'pro-Boer' opposition.[11] He also added insights and perspectives which he had developed in the 1890s and earlier, and which resulted from his contact with liberal and socialist intellectuals. If there was any one individual above others who inspired Hobson in his anti-imperialist writings, it was probably William Clarke.[12]

There are five separate motifs in *Imperialism*, discussed below.

1 The Cobdenite Tradition

Hobson and many other so-called 'Little Englanders' employed many of Cobden's free trade and anti-imperialist arguments. His own summary of his imperialism-does-not-pay position could have come straight from Cobden:

> the new Imperialism . . . consumes to an illimitable extent the financial resources of a nation by military preparation . . . burdening posterity with heavy loads of debt.[13] Absorbing the public money, time, interest and energy on costly and unprofitable work of territorial aggrandisement, it thus wastes those energies of public life in the governing classes and the nations which are needed for internal reforms and for the cultivation of the arts of material and intellectual progress at home.[14] Finally, the spirit, the policy and the methods of imperialism are hostile to the institutions of popular self-government, favouring forms of political tyranny and social authority which are the deadly enemies of effective liberty and equality (p. 152).[15]

Hobson embellished the last point by demonstrating the incompatibility of imperialism and democracy in Britain. The growth of the military was inimical to democratic citizenship. Good soldiers did not make good citizens, because they were not encouraged to develop moral sensibilities and socially responsible attitudes (p. 133). The empire also spawned a new stratum of colonial administrators imbued with an autocratic spirit, adding to the weight of reaction when they returned from the imperial outposts (p. 150). Indeed, the 'burdens' of empire and the international conflicts engendered by imperial questions had produced a large and highly centralized bureaucracy that, along with the Cabinet, was not subject to proper parliamentary control. This loss of parliamentary efficacy was matched by a decline decline in the party system. It had previously flourished on the basis of party divisions arising from differences on domestic issues. Because imperial questions now predominated on the parliamentary agenda, such conflicts were supplanted by an unhealthy consensus (pp. 145−8).

Another Cobdenite cost he added to the debit side of the ledger was the possibility of retribution, although Hobson argued this not in theological but biological terms. Imperialism was akin to parasitism, and parasites inevitably decayed in nature (p. 367) (Cobden, 1886, p. 458; Hobson, 1938a, pp. 367−8). He also followed Cobden in stressing the costs of colonization, as well as the pacific and economic benefits of free trade (Cobden, 1886, pp. 24, 36−8; Hobson, 1938a, pp. 68−9, 362). In refuting the imperialist position he strongly denied that trade followed the flag (pp. 33−40). Yet he departed from the spirit of the free trade position by asserting that foreign trade was diminishing in relation to Britain's total industrial activity and that dependence on it could be reduced further if income was more equitably distributed (pp. 28−31).[16]

Hobson was at one with Cobden in noting the harmful and despotic nature of British rule in India and, implicitly at least, in his advocacy of Indian self-government, a principle which he extended to China, but not to Africa (p. 285).

In his mode of explanation Hobson partly relied on the liberal conspiracy theory of 'sinister interests'. Cobden had singled out the landed aristocracy and the suppliers to the armed forces as the beneficiaries and, *therefore*, as the proponents of aggressive international posturing (Hobson,

1919, pp. 10, 211). This *cui bono* explanation figured prominently in *Imperialism* (p. 55). But Hobson, in the light of his interpretation of the origins of the Boer War, which he argued was caused by finance capitalists, changed the central *dramatis personae*: plutocrats were substituted for aristocrats, who were left with the occasional walk-on part (p. 50).[17]

Hobson's ideal of a pacific world polity of democratic self-governing states, based upon free trade, international arbitration and minimal intergovernmental relations, was also powerfully advanced by Cobden (Morley, 1881, Vol. I, pp. 230−1; Cobden, 1886, pp. 36, 78; Hobson, 1938a, p. 363). For Hobson 'genuine democracy' was the key political solution to imperialism, by making foreign policy accountable to the people, whose real interests lay in peaceful relations with other peoples.[18]

2 *Organicism*

Whether used in a metaphorical, or in a genuinely explanatory, sense, Hobson's biological, 'organicist' perspective was the linchpin of his social philosophy. It was inspired by Herbert Spencer, who not only applied scientific methods to social understanding, but also saw human society as an organism moving from a simple to a more complex 'individuated' form (Hobson, 1904, pp. 49−55). This reached its apotheosis in modern industrial civilization, which engendered a favourable environment for maximum individual liberty. Hobson differed in rejecting the need to create competitive conditions in the realm of physical survival, which Spencer saw as essential to human progress. Instead, he postulated that as human knowledge and sensibilities advanced, society would be subject to greater collective rational and ethical control, which would enable 'individuation' and human progress to take place on a more intellectual and cultural level.

The biological conception of society was extremely popular in the 1880s and 1890s amongst intellectuals of different political persuasions (Muirhead, 1942, p. 87).[19] In coming to terms with their loss of Christian faith they, in part, replaced theology with biology. They used evolutionary concepts to understand the trajectory of modern society and to justify their respective political and ethical positions. To this form of evolutionary positivism Hobson added a humanism derived from Ruskin, whose writings in the 1890s had acquired cult status. Hobson made Ruskin's saying, 'There is no wealth but life', into his own personal slogan (Hobson, 1938b, p. 39). In particular, he used it to attack the modern obsession with quantitative, as opposed to qualitative, values, as expressed in economics and implicit in the justification of imperialism. He additionally employed in a slightly modified form Ruskin's stern remonstration against parasitism: 'Whosoever will not work, neither *can* he eat' (Hobson, 1901b, p. 118, original emphasis).[20]

Imperialism revealed Hobson's organic perspective in a number of ways. First, he saw imperialism as a form of parasitism. Retribution would surely fall on the imperialist powers, as all parasites inevitably perished in nature (p. 367). Secondly, his organic conception emphasized the fundamentally co-operative and interdependent nature of society in its national and international dimensions. This reinforced his Cobdenite belief in the benefits of free trade and lent support to his own brand of 'sane' imperialism (pp. 225, 363). Neither states nor individuals had absolute rights. Thirdly, his form of organicism enabled him to combat the Social Darwinist, 'scientific defence' of imperialism, upheld by Kidd, Giddings and Pearson. Human evolution had reached a stage where it was no longer necessary to compete for physical survival in order to stimulate progress. Instead this could be achieved through the application of scientific methods to production and the creation of better human 'stock'. Hobson took eugenics seriously in order to combat the survival-of-the-fittest arguments. Indeed, he advocated the application of eugenics on an international scale (pp. 190–1). Thus, competition in promoting human progress

[23]

could be elevated from the quantitative and physical to the qualitative, aesthetic and intellectual plane (pt 2, ch. 2, *passim*)[21]. Imperialism was regressive because it signified the exaltation of quantitative over qualitative values (pp. 92, 180, 368). Fourthly, he used evolutionary concepts to explain imperialism as a regressive phenomenon, as a form of atavism, a view that had something in common with Schumpeter in his *Imperialism and Social Classes*, a collection of essays, the first of which was written in 1919. The masses in supporting imperialism displayed primitive feelings that were necessary only for physical survival in the past, but were now redundant (p. 213)[22].

3 *Underconsumption*

The most original and famous part of *Imperialism* is Hobson's underconsumptionist explanation. He first applied his theory of underconsumption to imperialism in an article, 'Free trade and foreign policy', in 1898. He did not, however, originate the surplus capital theory of imperialism. Businessmen in the 1890s employed it to *justify* imperialism (Langer, 1935, Vol. I, p. 74; Porter, 1968, ch. 2, pt 1; Etherington, 1984, pp. 44—6). His originality lay in his explanation for this glut of capital. His earliest formulation of underconsumption in *The Physiology of Industry* (1889) was a psychological one, in terms of an individual's habit of saving, which when aggregated to the same propensities of other individuals caused oversaving (Mummery and Hobson, 1889, pp. iv, 97—8). Later, he saw the growth of machine production as accentuating the resulting economic disequilibrium. (Hobson, 1894, ch. 7, *passim*). By the time he came to write *Imperialism*, monopolies were also seen as responsible for generating the 'unproductive' surplus, as he called it, which created an imbalance between production and consumption (p. 85). In *The Economics of Distribution* this surplus was explained in terms of the superior bargaining power of the monopoly capitalist *vis-à-vis* the worker (Hobson, 1900c, p. 219). This surplus was created by force and had a double significance. Morally, it was the tangible sign of parasitism, of an unearned income not gained by honest effort. Economically, this unearned surplus represented a loss of consuming power required to absorb current production. Moreover, such a surplus because it was gained by force did not act as an incentive to produce. Here Hobson extended the Ricardian theory of rent, as the Fabians had done, to cover not only land, but the other factors of production (Hobson, 1890−1, p. 265; Ricci, 1969, pp. 105−21). A crucial implication, although not fully elaborated in *Imperialism*, was that this 'unproductive' surplus which Hobson saw as the 'taproot' of imperialism could be diverted into higher wages, or social reform, without harmfully affecting production (Hobson, 1901b, p.162).

4 *The Psychology and Ideology of Imperialism*

Hobson's faith in growing human rationality was severely shaken by the Boer War. The verbal and physical abuse he and his anti-war comrades-in-arms received on public platforms, the beer-sodden triumphalism of Mafeking night in May 1900 and the results of the 'khaki' elections in the same year, seemed to demonstrate all too clearly that imperialism had mass support. Hobson had sought to explain this 'social pathology' in *The Psychology of Jingoism* (1901c) which was based partly on articles already published in *The Ethical World*. He incorporated its key ideas into *Imperialism* (pt 2, ch. 3, *passim*). He relied heavily, if not uncritically, on Gustav Le Bon's book, *The Crowd* (1896). He also may have been influenced by William Clarke's earlier attempt to explain the phenomenon in his article, 'The genesis of jingoism' (Burrows and Hobson, 1908, pp. 108−17). In addition, he may have gained something from his Oxford friend and fellow member of the South Place Ethical Society, Graham Wallas, who later made a significant contribution to understanding the psychological bases of political processes in *Human Nature and Politics* (1908).

Hobson saw the 'mob mind' of jingoism as a result of trends in urban industrial civilization. These impaired the capacity for independent rational thinking amongst the masses, by subjecting them to mechanical and uniform work operations, overcrowding, superficial and homogeneous leisure pursuits (Hobson, 1901c, pp. 6–7). The music hall, and especially the 'yellow press', much of which was controlled by finance capitalists, stirred up primitive lusts, which were reinforced by the growth of passive spectator sports (Hobson, 1901c, pp. 9–10; *Imperialism*, pp. 214–15).

This outburst of irrationality entailed the debasement of thought and language. Hobson was strikingly modern in the way in which he analysed imperialist 'ideology'; although he did not use the term *Imperialism*, it has now become a common coin of intellectual exchange. He postulated that the connection between self-interest and the justification of imperialism was obscure even to the beneficiaries themselves, apart from the finance capitalists. The ideological defence of imperialism was the result of self-deception (pp. 197–8). People blinded themselves to what was really happening in the world of imperialism through inconsistent thinking and 'masked words' (Ruskin's phrase). He paid particular attention to the claim that the 'lower races' were ruled as a 'trust for civilisation'. White colonists in reality used these races as 'live tools', and irresponsibly extracted natural resources from their lands (p. 246). Hobson also observed how the 'educated classes' had become imbued with imperialist ideology: 'the church, the press, the schools and colleges, the political machine, the four chief instruments of popular education are accommodated to [imperialism's] service' (p. 216).

5 *Trusteeship*
One of Hobson's biggest departures from the Cobdenite tradition of non-intervention lay in his advocacy of trusteeship over the 'lower races' (although not over India and China, whose civilizations he saw as different from but

equal to those of the West) by an 'organised representation of civilised humanity' (p. 285). This pre-figured the mandate system of the League of Nations. He argued for practical and moral reasons that the 'lower races' could not be left to themselves (pp. 223–32). The idea of trusteeship went back at least as far as Edmund Burke in the eighteenth century and was widely current in the 1900s, possible as a result of Britain's recent acquisition of a greatly enlarged empire with commensurate 'responsibilities' (Porter, 1968, p. 20). Hobson accepted many of the arguments in favour of trusteeship advanced by Kidd, Giddings and the Fabians (pp. 227–8). The real issues were those of 'safeguards, of motives and of methods' (p. 229). Genuine disinterest by the Western powers could only be guaranteed by an 'organised representation of civilized humanity', a kind of international welfare state. Although he believed that the material interests of the West should ultimately predominate, he maintained that the 'character' and 'condition' of the subject nation must also be improved (pp. 229–30, 235). This could be done by studying their culture in its totality (p. 243). His attitude towards indigenous cultures had already developed by the time he wrote *Imperialism*. In *The Social Problem* he referred to civilization as 'multi-form', implying that there should be a mutual respect between different cultures (Hobson, 1901b, p. 276).[23] Although he did not fully extend this conclusion to African peoples, this perspective at least implied that they did have a culture, which had to be studied if it was to be transformed. Hobson may also have gained something from Le Bon's *Psychology of Peoples* (1899), which he had reviewed in *The Social Problem* (Hobson, 1901b, p. 276). Le Bon emphasized the existence of powerful racial characteristics, not susceptible to quick transformation by external forces. Finally, this line of thought may have been suggested to him by Mary Kingsley, a keen student of African culture, and Professor William Knight, who both gave talks to the South Place Ethical Society between 1895 and 1897 (Porter, 1968, p. 182).

AFTER *IMPERIALISM*

Although Hobson made few significant changes to the texts of subsequent editions of *Imperialism*, he did reformulate some of his arguments elsewhere.[24] In effect, he recognized that there were tensions and problems that he had not resolved in *Imperialism*. They stemmed from his under consumptionist analysis and his updating of the Cobdenite tradition, especially from his portrayal of the plutocracy rather than the aristocracy as imperialism's sinister interest-in-chief.

The first problem that underconsumptionism created was a vulnerability to the charge of economic determinism. In fact, he was aware of this danger both before and after *Imperialism*. At the time of the Boer War he acknowledged the case 'of Capitalism issuing Imperialism is of necessity imperfect. No play of historical forces is so simple as this' (Hobson, 1900b, p. 15). In his autobiography he wrote in self-criticism that *Imperialism* contained 'an excessive and too simple advocacy of the economic determination of history' (Hobson, 1938b, p. 63). Critics such as Norman Angell insisted that psychological factors were more important in explaining imperialism than economic ones (Porter, 1968, p. 222). Yet although he made concessions on this score, Hobson held fast to the primacy of economics, which determined the 'concrete application' of power politics, or was in the final analysis the 'dominant directive motive' (Hobson, 1926, p. 192; Hobson 1938a, p. v). Here, Hobson probably had the conspiratorial methods of the financial magnates very much in mind.

Hobson, though, recognized very real problems resulting from his reconstituted Cobdenism. The implication of his underconsumptionist analysis was that imperialism was the necessary outcome of an unreformed capitalism, the creation of the 'unproductive' surplus, generated mainly by monopoly. This was a 'systemic', functional, or economic determinist explanation, which suggested that finance capitalists, other capitalists and investors had a strong interest in imperialism because they required an outlet as a result of 'unproductive' surplus.

The implications of Cobdenism pointed in another direction. Capitalism and capitalists, apart from arms manufacturers and other suppliers to the forces, were benign influences. They developed world resources and fostered world peace. Since they wanted a peaceful environment for their efforts to come to fruition, war was irrational. The economic solution to international conflict lay in free trade, which would create an international mutuality of interest in the avoidance of war. The political solution lay in democracy, which would remove aristocratic, or, in Hobson's case, plutocratic control over foreign policy.

Both sets of explanations were somewhat detached in *Imperialism*.[25] In formal terms he attempted to combine both in the 1906 revised edition of *The Evolution of Modern Capitalism*. As a result of excess profits derived from monopolistic combination in the domestic market 'a swelling stream of investors' savings is constantly pressing into the banking and financial system, which [the financier] controls; in order to keep it flowing he must find or fashion fresh investments'. Consequently, the financier was prompted to look to 'new and [politically] unsettled areas' (Hobson, [1894] 1906, pp. 264–6). Hobson's explanatory framework kept both 'structure' (i.e. underconsumption) and 'agency' (i.e. finance capitalists) in play, a position he continued to maintain to the end of his life.[26]

A more substantial puzzle emerged when his agency/structure explanation was mixed with his Cobdenite inheritance. He had difficulty in working out a coherent position towards finance capital. At one level he maintained a consistently positive position: international investment was crucial to world economic development. This view is evident in *Imperialism* if only by implication. In justifying his 'sane' imperialism, he stated: 'It is the great practical business of the country to explore and develop, by every method which science can devise, the hidden natural and human resources of the globe'(p. 229). This objective would necessitate foreign investment. He was more explicit in *An Economic Interpretation of Investment*. He said: 'finance capital provided through joint stock companies is now the great fertilising stream in world industry' (Hobson, 1911a, p. 19).[27]

Yet at another level he was decidedly unsure about finance capital's bellicose propensities. In *Imperialism* he was manifestly contradictory. Finance capital was the 'governor of the imperial engine' and 'imperialism . . . implies militarism now and ruinous war in future' (pp. 59, 130, 131). But he also held the opposite view, which paralleled Karl Kautsky's theory of 'ultra-imperialism' (Kautsky, 1970, pp. 39—46): 'the rapid growth of effective internationalism in the financial and great industrial magnates, who seem destined more and more to control national politics, may in the near future render such [imperialist] wars impossible' (p. 311). In a similar vein he stated nine years later: 'modern finance is the great sympathetic system in an economic organism in which political divisions are of constantly diminishing importance' (Hobson, 1911a, p. 113; cf. Hobson, 1911b, p. 242).

This element in his Cobdenite perspective died with the Great War, whose advent he had considered a 'surprise' (Hobson, 1920, p. 337):

It is important to recognise that a fundamental assumption of Cobdenism, and of liberalism to which it appertained, that war and militarism were doomed to disappear with the advance of industry and commerce, is definitely false. Indeed, a large part of the analysis upon which we are engaged is devoted to showing how modern capitalism, both in its structure and its operations, requires, feeds and utilizes militarism. (Hobson, 1917, p. 27)

Henceforth he stressed his systemic, underconsumptionist analysis, which suggested that an unreformed capitalism was inherently antagonistic on an international scale (Hobson, 1938a, p. xxii).

By the same token Hobson was uncertain whether other investors and capitalists, apart from finance capitalist suppliers to the armed forces, were in favour of war or peace. He exonerated the rank-and-file investors, yet he could also see their interests lying in imperial expansion (pp. 55–6, 359). He revealed a similar attitude to manufacturers. Sometimes they were accused of belligerency because they needed outlets for their surplus goods, whilst at others they were seen as essentially non-imperialist (pp. 55, 95–6). By 1938 he had clarified his attitude towards manufacturers in a way that was consistent with his underconsumptionist explanation. Exporters of goods were much more strongly featured as a force for imperialism, in contrast to his original position (Hobson, 1938a, pp. v–vi).

A final problem that surfaced as a result of his attempt to marry underconsumptionism with Cobdenism was spotted by his friend and collaborator on *The Nation*, H. N. Brailsford. He noted that Hobson had argued that imperialism could not be eliminated until 'the axe is laid at the economic root of the tree', and yet had simultaneously attempted to lay down the foundations of international government (Brailsford, 1948, p. 26). In the 1930s he recognized this problem, but contended that options should be kept open. He recommended a policy of 'wise opportunism' (Hobson, 1934, pp. 135, 152). By 1938, however, he abandoned this position, and 'privileged' domestic reform, possibly in the light of the League of Nations' failure to prevent the drift towards war:

The great lesson of the War and the even more important lesson of the Peace thus brought home to me the truth that justice as well as charity begins at home. It is impracticable to hope for international peace and justice in international affairs unless the conditions for international peace and justice within the nations have already been substantially obtained. (Hobson, 1938b, p. 113)

Hobson then finally chose to emphasize domestic reform in resolving international conflict. A symmetry thus emerged in the evening of his life between this strategy for international reform and the primacy he gave to his underconsumptionist explanation of imperialism.

FRIENDS AND CRITICS

Imperialism shares the fate of all political classics. Its very power and partisanship invite criticism and counter-criticism. Its immediate impact was small and its reception mixed. One anonymous commentator drew parallels with Mill's *On Liberty* (*Birmingham Gazette*, 21 November 1902). Many reviewers disliked the superior tone of the book, to the point of ridicule: 'Doubtless he is quite convinced that the audience he addresses is a kingdom of the blind; though he is not its king, he is yet a one-eyed man' (*Glasgow Herald*, 17 October 1902). A strong and common criticism of his imperialism-does-not-pay argument was that Hobson ignored the future benefits in trade that the newly acquired colonies would bring.[28] It was summed up in the oft-used contemporary vindication of imperialism: 'A field of corn does not ripen in a day' (*Spectator*, 31 January 1903). Critics also rejected his semi-autarkic proposal that sought to minimize, first, the value of foreign trade in a statistically misleading fashion, and secondly, the advantages of the international division of labour (Courtney, 1903, pp.

806—12). Another probing comment was that Hobson should have found more evidence for the finance capitalists' conspiratorial activities (Reinsch, 1903, pp. 531—3).[29] Finally, there was a basic criticism already noted, by Norman Angell, advanced against Hobson's economic determinism, which gave greater saliency to non-rational psychological factors.[30]

Imperialism did not at the time it was published enjoy the popularity of Angell's own later work on this subject, *The Great Illusion*.[31] Yet interest in it has been far more sustained, partly because sections of the Labour movement in the 1920s and 1930s embraced his ideas on imperialism (Hobson was for a time a member of the Labour Party Advisory Committee on International Questions). But more significantly *Imperialism*'s reputation was greatly enhanced by Lenin's handsome acknowledgements to Hobson in *Imperialism, The Highest Stage of Capitalism* (1917). Recently, curiosity in the work has been prompted by Third World liberation struggles, which have revived interest in the study of imperialism in general.

Lenin was perhaps Hobson's greatest admirer and critic. Estimations of Hobson's theoretical impact on Lenin vary wildly.[32] Let us confine ourselves mainly to what Lenin *said* he gained from *Imperialism*, and what he rejected.

He was clearly impressed by Hobson's definition of the New Imperialism, which he had characterized by competing empires and the pre-eminence of financial and investing capital over mercantile capital. Lenin used his definition to expose the limitations of Kautsky's definition of it as industrial nations seeking to annex agrarian territories. Hobson's definition was superior because it emphasized general economic and political competition between the imperial powers, which was not confined to the agrarian zones. Secondly, it stressed the importance of finance capital in fostering imperial expansion (Lenin, [1917] 1966, pp. 84—6).

In addition Lenin adopted Hobson's observation of the

trend towards parasitism, as manifested by Britain's becoming a rentier state, living off overseas investments and employing native armies to fight its battles. This seemed to demonstrate to Lenin how advanced capitalism had inevitably become non-progressive (Lenin, [1917] 1966, ch. 8, *passim*). Lenin also made extensive use of Hobson's statistics on British trade, investment and imperial expansion, as well as finding support for his theory of the labour aristocracy, a working-class elite bribed into acquiescence through profits derived from the colonies (Lenin, 1968, p. 420).

Lenin, however, was characteristically unambiguous about his differences with Hobson. Lenin saw himself as a revolutionary Marxist. He maintained that imperialism and violence were inevitable under capitalism and that the First World War was both an expression of, and a crucial factor in, its demise. Hence, he rejected Hobson's underconsumptionism which implied that imperialism could be abolished through the reform of capitalism.[33] The masses' lack of consuming power was an ineradicable feature of imperialism (Lenin, [1917] 1966, p. 58). Secondly, Lenin's theory of uneven development led him to dismiss the possibility of inter-imperialist co-operation (Lenin, 1968, p. 431). Lenin further held that Hobson's political solution to imperialism, 'genuine democracy', was not possible (Lenin, 1968, p. 432). A final ironic difference was that Lenin, following Hilferding, explained imperialism partly in terms of finance capital's need to control supplies of raw materials (Lenin, 1968, pp. 338–9). Hobson, though, rather than seeing this as a cause of imperialism, sought to justify the annexation of areas not developing their potential for producing raw material, albeit under the control of a 'representation of civilised humanity' (Lenin, [1917] 1966, p. 114).

Academic critics have on the whole been less generous to Hobson. Whilst recognizing his importance as the principal architect of the theory of economic, or capitalist, imperialism, economic and political historians see him as a poor historian of post-1870 imperialism, methodologically simplistic and empirically impoverished. His theory of investment-led imperialism in explaining everything explained nothing. Hobson did not do what historians do, namely look at specific acts of annexation and their consequences. His *a priori* position predetermined the answer. Historians tend to proceed by detailed case studies and build up, if at all possible, inductively based generalizations (Fieldhouse, 1967, p. 193).

After a close study of the facts and figures of late-nineteenth-century imperial expansion, many historians conclude that there is little left of Hobson's thesis. The principal and most repeated criticism is that he failed to demonstrate a decisive link between capital export and annexation (Taylor, 1967, p. 127; Fieldhouse, 1967, p. 189; Mommsen, 1981, p. 18; Baumgart, 1982, p. 109; Brown, 1970, p. 93). Evidence shows that insignificant amounts of capital, relatively and absolutely, went to the newly acquired tropical and subtropical areas after annexation. It is claimed that Hobson should have employed a little economic logic and realized that investment went to those countries with which Britain traded heavily to meet its growing demand for food and raw material (Nurske, 1967, p. 162). British investment went primarily to the non-colonized Americas and to parts of the old empire, Canada and Australia, with South Africa the exception. Moreover, critics argue that it is difficult to generalize Hobson's theory. Not all imperialist countries, such as Japan, Russia, Italy and Portugal, had large amounts of surplus capital (Baumgart, 1982, p. 110; Gann and Duignan, 1968, p. 44).

A major criticism is that an analysis of annexation decisions by imperial statesmen reveals that the chief motive in most cases was political and not economic. Many, but not all, critics see the colonies acquired after 1870 as newly fashioned pieces for the European diplomatic chess-board, and the game played for essentially non-economic purposes.

For France national prestige, after defeat by Germany in 1870, was the main impulse for imperial expansion (Brunschwig, 1964, p. 117). Strategic motives could not be discounted, as, for example, Britain's occupation of Egypt in 1882 (Baumgart, 1982, p. 131; Robinson and Gallagher, 1961, ch. 15, *passim*). Indeed, economic arguments were often used by statesmen to support their strategy for politically motivated expansion (Koebner, 1949, p. 22). And paradoxically, rather than being the puppets of investors, they used them in many instances to strengthen their diplomatic claims (Taylor, 1967, p. 127; Staley, 1967, p. 148; Frankel, 1967, pp. 152−3; Baumgart, 1982, p. 131). Where pressure groups were effective, they did not always get enthusiastic government backing. British imperial expansion in the 1880s was carried out reluctantly by the governments of the time (Koebner, 1949, pp. 7−8). Crucially, the key pressure group for Hobson, finance capital, was much less interested in conquest than various parts of industry (Mommsen, 1981, p. 18). The City of London was in favour of free trade and was opposed to imperial expansion because of the burdens it imposed (Baumgart, 1982, p. 126). In addition, investors did not want to go as far as war (Staley, 1967, pp. 147−8). Critics in fact have rejected Hobson's proposition that imperialism and foreign investment benefited only specific groups, but not the nation as a whole. Foreign investments gave everyone the benefit of cheap food and a buoyant export market (Baumgart, 1982, p. 125; Cairncross, 1967, p. 159).

Finally, Hobson ignored the central continuity of British imperial policy before and after 1870. Annexations occurred before this date, during the period of 'anti-imperialism', and arguably more significantly, prior to 1870 Britain was building up an 'informal' empire that stopped short of outright annexation. After 1870 there was merely a change in the method of control (Robinson and Gallagher, 1953, pp. 1−15). A key but not exclusive factor in the spate of annexations after 1870 was the pressure from the peripheries of empire, especially as a result of the breakdown of law and order in areas contiguous to British colonies. The annexationist impulse was not therefore necessarily Eurocentric in origin as Hobson had assumed.

Economists have challenged the theoretical core of his explanation of imperialism – underconsumption. The theory assumed that economic equilibrium would be maintained only if a 'right' amount was saved out of a given income (Nemmers, 1967, pp. 120–3). This was at variance with the Keynesian understanding of the trade cycle, because the role of liquidity preference and of interest rates in matching saving, investment and consumption was not taken into account by Hobson. In addition he saw all investment as capital 'widening' and not as capital 'deepening' (that is, invested in technological innovation), which helped to dissipate 'surplus' investment through increasing the rate of depreciation. Moreover, Hobson mistakenly saw investment only as a means to the production of consumption goods, and not as a form of consumption in its own right (Bleaney, 1976, p. 180). Lastly, his analogy between extensive or 'quantitative' farming and imperialism, and his rejection of the latter in favour of intensive or 'qualitative' farming on the grounds of greater economic benefit, was unsound. Only marginal analysis could decide the issue, that is whether marginal gains were greater through quantitative or qualitative development (Nemmers, 1967, pp. 123–4; Winslow, 1931, p. 736).

Intellectual historians have noted other difficulties in Hobson's thinking on imperialism. Bernard Porter has discovered a tension between his conspiracy explanation and his underconsumptionist model. Furthermore, the singling out of finance capitalists as the major motive force behind imperialism was not 'empirically deduced', but was derived from his 'intellectualist assumption' that since

[37]

imperialism was irrational for the nation as a whole, someone was benefiting from it and had the capacity to get their own way (Porter, 1968, pp. 215, 225).[34]

The sustained assault of modern academic artillery seems to have left little of the Hobsonian edifice standing. Unfortunately, a full-scale discussion of the viability of Hobson's theory cannot be essayed here, since many of the fundamental issues of method in the social and historical sciences are posed. Certainly, economic and diplomatic historians have demonstrated the imperfections of Hobson's theory of investment-led imperialism as a general and all-embracing explanation of late-nineteenth-century European and American expansion. Yet two obdurate questions remain. Have his critics chosen the relevant criteria to falsify his theory?

Before an answer can be given, a prior question has to be addressed. Have Hobson's critics correctly identified his theory of imperialism? As Bernard Porter has suggested, refutation is made difficult because there are two theories at work in *Imperialism*, conspiratorial and under-consumptionist. Hobson did not have to maintain that a large and growing proportion of overseas investment went to newly colonized countries. He acknowledged that it did not (Porter, 1968, pp. 216–17). He could contend that the imperialist impulse was orchestrated by a small group of finance capitalists, something which was harder to prove or disprove. In fact, as Trevor Lloyd has indicated, there is nothing implausible in assuming that investment-minded capitalists exercised an important influence over British policy in Africa out of all proportion to their relative economic weight (Lloyd, 1972, p. 141). Another valuable point made by Lloyd, which lends support to Hobson's thesis, is that in the African example the political requirements, especially of law and order, often entailing outright annexation, changed as the needs of investment began to predominate over those of trade (Lloyd, 1972, p. 143).

Hobson's critics by concentrating almost exclusively on his explanation of imperialism also miss his political purpose. He was far less concerned with describing the exact mechanisms of annexation than he was to alert the British public to the new plutocratic phenomenon that was hijacking British foreign policy. Precisely because he recognized that most investments went outside the empire, Hobson declared the finance capitalists a threat, since in protecting their investments, or as a result of speculating, they put illegitimate expansionist pressure on government (pp. 357–8).

Even if we accept that Hobson's critics have identified Hobson's theory correctly as one in which under-consumption and investment have causal primacy, should it be rejected? Have his critics chosen the appropriate criteria to disprove his theory? The figures showing that substantial investment did not go to the newly acquired territories do not necessarily refute his theory.[35] The object of annexation does not have to be immediate investment. Both statesmen and businessmen can have a longer-term conception of their interests, such as the desire not to be excluded by rival imperialist powers and enterprises from a potential field of investment.[36] Indeed, defenders of imperialism often used the justification already noted: 'A field of corn does not ripen in a day.' Politicians and capitalists may also favour annexation for speculative reasons, since the take-over of the African continent was relatively easy in military terms. Indeed, if little or no investment took place subsequently, all that is proved is that they incorrectly speculated.

The refutation of Hobson's thesis through the citation of diplomatic texts to demonstrate that the primary impulse for annexation came from the state, which on occasion used investors to support its territorial claims, and that therefore the motivation was political or strategic, rather than economic, raises two general considerations. First, there is the question of unstated assumptions. What may appear as a 'political' or 'strategic' motive for annexation may have a powerful and profound economic content. For example, the British occupation of Egypt in 1882 was for a strategic purpose, to protect communications with India, rather than to safeguard the interests of the bond-holders. Yet in another sense the motive was clearly economic, since Britain derived enormous wealth from India through trade and investment and therefore required secure communications with this sub continent. Thus, the distinction between the 'political' and 'strategic', on the one hand, and the 'economic', on the other, whilst useful for analytical purposes, may not be accorded such a separation in real life where political and economic institutions formally interact and are connected informally through the ties of family and class. Indeed, Hobson's objective was not to explain every detail of contemporary diplomatic history. Rather, he was attempting to comprehend the underlying dynamics that worked themselves out in military and political conflict. Methodologically, Hobson offered what might be called an 'economic sociology' of imperialism.[37]

A second consideration is that if we depart from a mechanistic, economic determinist account of the relation of the state to economic interests and activity, which Hobson himself began to do at least indicatively, towards the end of his life, and conceive of this relationship in a looser and more reciprocal way, his position is considerably strengthened (Hobson, 1938b, p. 63).[38] Statesmen can be interpreted as taking a broader view of economic interests that may not correspond with the immediate short-term interests of capitalist profit-making. Equally, economic interests can limit what imperialist politicians may attempt, in that annexations could not be sustained without their support.

The questions and hypotheses raised here are not intended to imply that Hobson had no case to answer, but to suggest that further research is needed. This entails greater methodological sophistication and conceptual clarity before the facts can be put to work in proving or refuting his thesis. In a sense, Hobson has provided us with the foundations of a research programme. He has indicated the road to travel, but has not taken us to our ultimate destination. In all probability, his arguments and ideas are unlikely to be laid to rest as long as capitalism and imperialism continue to exist.

J. TOWNSHEND

1987

PREFACE TO THE FIRST EDITION

THIS study of modern Imperialism is designed to give more precision to a term which is on everybody's lips and which is used to denote the most powerful movement in the current politics of the Western world. Though Imperialism has been adopted as a more or less conscious policy by several European States and threatens to break down the political isolation of the United States, Great Britain has travelled so much faster and farther along this road as to furnish in her recent career the most profitable guidance or warning.

While an attempt is made to discover and discuss the general principles which underlie imperialist policy, the illustration of that policy is mainly derived from the progress of British Imperialism during the last generation, and proceeds rather by diagnosis than by historical description.

In Part I the economic origins of Imperialism are traced, with such statistical measurements of its methods and results as are available.

Part II investigates the theory and the practice of Imperialism regarded as a "mission of civilization," in its effects upon "lower" or alien peoples, and its political and moral reactions upon the conduct and character of the Western nations engaging in it.

The book is addressed to the intelligence of the minority who are content neither to float along the tide of political opportunism nor to submit to the shove of some blind "destiny," but who desire to understand political forces in order that they may direct them.

PREFACE

Those readers who hold that a well-balanced judgment consists in always finding as much in favour of any political course as against it will be discontented with the treatment given here. For the study is distinctively one of social pathology, and no endeavour is made to disguise the nature of the disease.

The statistics given in Part I are derived, when the source is not stated, from the "Statistical Abstracts" published by the Government, reinforced in some instances, by figures derived from the *Statesman's Year Book*.

I am indebted to the editor of the *Financial Reform Almanac* for permission to reproduce the valuable diagram illustrative of British expenditure from 1870, and to the editors of the *Speaker*, the *Contemporary Review*, the *Political Science Quarterly*, and the *British Friend* for permission to embody in chapters of this volume articles printed in these magazines.

I desire also to express my gratitude to my friends Mr. Gilbert Murray and Mr. Herbert Rix for their assistance in reading most of the proof-sheets and for many valuable suggestions and corrections.

JOHN A. HOBSON.

August, 1902.

In this revised edition, facts and figures have been, as far as possible, brought up to date, a number of additions and deletions have been made, and in some instances the line of argument has been recast.

J. A. H.

September, 1905.

INTRODUCTION TO THE 1938 EDITION

SO momentous have been the occurrences in world history during the past thirty years, so numerous the changes in national policies and sentiments that it may seem an act of impertinence to republish a book dealing with these issues as they presented themselves at the opening of the century. Nevertheless it may be worth while showing that the chief perils and disturbances associated with the aggressive nationalism of to-day, though visibly inflamed and accelerated by the Great War and the Bad Peace, were all latent and discernible in the world of a generation ago, and find their economic, political and moral roots in the foreign policy of the governments of the advanced industrial nations. Recent events have, indeed, done much to clarify the respective parts played in modern Imperialism by the interactions and conjunctions of the different theories, interests and emotions that inspire aggressive national activities.

Before proceeding to make good this statement it may be convenient here to rehearse in bare terms the main argument of this book, and then to discuss such changes and modifications of the earlier argument as the current of recent history appears to demand.

That argument was to the effect that whereas various real and powerful motives of pride, prestige and pugnacity, together with the more altruistic professions of a civilising mission, figured as causes of imperial expansion, the dominant directive motive was the demand for markets and for profitable investment by the exporting and financial classes within each imperialist regime. The urgency of this economic demand was attributed to the growing tendency of industrial productivity, under the new capitalist technique of machinery and power, to exceed the effective demand of the national markets, the rate of production to outrun the rate of home consumption. This was not, of course, the whole story. The rising productivity of industry required larger imports of some forms of raw materials, more imported foods for larger urban populations, and a great variety of imported consumption goods for a rising standard of living. These imports could only be purchased by a corresponding expansion of exports, or else by the incomes derived from foreign investments which implied earlier exports of capital goods.

But with these qualifications in mind, it is nevertheless true that the most potent drive towards enlarged export trade was the excess of capitalist production over the demands of the home market. Now, since it is manifest that everything that is produced belongs to someone connected with its production, who can either consume it or exchange it for some other consumable goods, it seems at first sight unreasonable to expect that an excess of goods requires a foreign market, unless some error has taken place in the apportionment of producing power as between the different industries. But when we find that at frequent intervals there is a general excess of production beyond the current demands of the home and foreign markets, it becomes manifest that the productive power of capital has been excessively fed. This in its turn means that the processes of saving and investment have proceeded too rapidly. In other words, there has been over-saving and under-spending. For while a certain and a growing quantity of saving and production of more and better capital goods belongs to every progressive national economy, there exists at any given time, having regard to the arts of industry, on the one hand, and the arts of consumption, on the other, a right balance or equilibrium between spending and saving. It has been held by the classical school of economists that this equilibrium was necessarily maintained by the free play of natural economic laws, which would check any such tendency to over-save and over-invest as appears actually to take place. But a closer scrutiny of the motives which actuate saving show that they do not conform to the ordinary price-law. A rise or fall in the price of saving, i.e. rate of interest, though serving to distribute saving properly among the several channels of investment, does not operate to any appreciable extent to increase or diminish the total volume of saving. There is a check upon saving, but it comes too late, after a wasteful trade depression has occurred. For most saving comes from profits, dividends, rents of the owning well-to-do classes. When a trade depression is in actual course, these sources of saving are greatly diminished and though for a time some actual over-saving lies idle in banks waiting an opportunity for favourable investment, the period of bad trade is soon attended by a fall in the rate of saving below the level which a normal trade condition would justify.

Now this argument signifies that the constant impulse to push for overseas markets in normal times and the periodic slumps of national trade in the home markets, are due to a chronic tendency to try to save a larger proportion of the national income than can find a useful expression in new capital. This is not due to the folly of individual savers, but to a distribution of the general income which puts too small a share in the hands of the working-classes, too large a share in the hands of the employing and owning classes. For it is to the latter that over-saving is attributable.

Now we are not here concerned with the important

problems of equity and humanity involved in a maldistribution of income which places the vast bulk of purchasing
power beyond the requirements of a bare living in the
possession of a small proportion of the population in Great
Britain, the United States and other advanced industrial
countries. Our concern here is with the urgent drive this
situation impels towards the acquisition of foreign markets
and areas of lucrative overseas investment. Here we are
confronted with the question to what extent this need for
increased foreign markets and investment is a true cause of
Imperialism. Now it may be admitted at the outset of
any discussion of this question that other motives than
trade-profits consciously occupy the mind of the statesmen
who pursue an imperial policy, and that the term Empire
does not connote commercial gain to the mind of the rank
and file of imperialists. Power, pride, prestige are prevailing
sentiments in an imperialist policy. Territorial expansion,
the control over backward peoples, the mission of civilisation,
the safe-guarding of existing colonial possessions, are not
indeed dissociated from the belief that " trade follows the
flag " and that by helping to establish order and develop
the resources of the peoples and countries which come under
our rule, we shall increase our trade and enlarge our national
income. Indeed, the history of our empire, acquired, as
Sir John Seeley once stated, " in a fit of absence of mind,"
attests clearly enough the confused sentiments and the
opportunism which underlie the process of acquisition.
But, when we study the particulars of the process, we
recognise that " mind " in the sense of conscious motive
was not entirely absent, and that trade played an important
part in most of the early acquisitions. For though it is
true that we do not need to own a country in order to
trade with its people, the establishment of permanent
trading arrangements with primitive or backward peoples

generally involves some territorial holding which is likely to expand with the expanding importance of that trade. The rise and growth of our great Empire in India furnish the crucial example. The East India Company, a purely trading concern in origin and motive, actually carried out the great imperial process of expansion until the middle of the nineteenth century, and in the early days of territorial acquisition the South Sea Company and other private groups of trade adventurers were authorised by the State to conduct their distinctively commercial missions. If several advanced countries engage upon the same process, as in India, collisions of interest, partly political, partly commercial, are likely to arise in which the competing groups enlist native forces in their cause, and conduct a conflict which leads to the supremacy of that commercial group which can rally to its profitable cause the largest governmental and native support. It is a confused procedure widely differing in the older and populous civilisations of Asia and the more primitive and thinly peopled areas of Africa and North America. But, in nearly all cases where white peoples have brought under their sway lands peopled by coloured races, the earliest contacts have been of a commercial nature, and though considerations of political acquisition, colonial settlement and missionary services have been conscious supports, economic motives of trade and the exploitation of natural resources have been the dominant urges. Nor has this aggressive Imperialism been confined to the acquisition of backward countries. When this book was written the conquest of the Boer Republics and the incorporation of those territories in our South African Dominion furnished the latest and most striking example of the imperialist process. Here the directly economic factor was paramount over all the political and humanitarian considerations invoked to justify the forceful seizure. The mine-owners of the Transvaal had a definite interest in transferring the country from Boer to British rule, and the press and other political propaganda which secured this end were owned or controlled by these financial and industrial groups.

It will be said by those who controvert this economic causation of Imperialism that the Boer War was an exceptional case, and that the causation of the Great War lay outside the economic purview. It was power politics, not profit politics. But I am not here arguing the case for an exclusively or even a mainly economic causation of modern Wars. It is not yet clear how far and in what sense the enlargement of national territory or external control underlay the policy of Germany, Russia, or France, in loosing the forces of war. Still less is it reasonable to suppose that calculations of economic gains resulting from territorial changes governed the minds of the statesmen who were responsible for their country entering the war. But in the Peace arrangements the insane mentality of Versailles carried various illusions of an economic character. That annexation was profitable to the annexing country, that the extortion of huge reparation payments was possible and advantageous to the recipients, that national economic self-sufficiency, aided by tariffs and embargoes, was not only strategically but economically gainful—these and other related fallacies flowed from the heated atmosphere of a poisoned nationalism. Nor can it be held that the experience of the post-war period has altogether exploded these fallacies, and that we now know that territorial expansion does not increase the trade gains and the average wealth of the people of the imperialist power.

If we turn to the three Powers which by their professed policies are the chief disturbers of world-peace at the present time, Italy, Germany and Japan, we perceive that each of them pleads economic necessities of territorial expansion as a justification for its actual or intended imperial aggression. In each case there is a growth of population needing more land for its employment and maintenance. In order to be economically effective that increase of land must be under the national flag. For though in the pre-war era freedom of emigration into the United States, Canada and other foreign countries prevailed, such outlets are now closed. It is held to be not only politically humiliating but economically unsafe that a nation should be dependent for its foods and raw materials upon the arbitrary changeful policies of foreign countries. For though it is evident that these foreign countries are not merely willing but eager to sell abroad their abounding supplies of these necessaries of life and industry, the countries needing them can only obtain supplies by selling abroad the surpluses of their own products, and these are now kept out or closely rationed by most foreign governments. Why? Because under the urge of nationalist sentiment, supported by appeals to self-sufficiency for purposes of defence, most nations conserve their own markets for their own producers, or for producers in their colonies or allied countries. For in almost all branches of production, agricultural, mining, manufacturing, the technical advances have been so great that each country is afraid of being flooded by foreign goods in its own markets and of being excluded from foreign markets for the sale of its own export goods. It is idle to urge that such fears and the policies of restriction and aggression which they stimulate are unreasonable, and that the removal of all barriers to international trade and migration would at once assuage hostilities and restore prosperity. Those who hold this view either assume and assert that the political sentiments of nationalism are the real sources of the economic policy they hold to be irrational, or else that certain monetary disturbances are responsible for the unemployment, closing of markets and other interferences with the natural forces of free exchange. In fact we are confronted with three sorts of foolishness, the political illusions of which Sir Norman Angell gives such an able exposition, the financial fears and mistrusts which prevent sane monetary arrangements for internal and external marketing, and the tragic absurdity summarised as " poverty in plenty," the refusal to make full use of existing or attainable productive resources. It is the contest for priority in these three fields of causation that here concerns us. For each of them evidently figures in the process of imperialism. It may well be admitted that each disturbing factor has its own illusions and its own sentimental urges. The distinctively political passion for greatness of territory acquired by a strong right hand is a manifestly potent driving force in all imperialisms, though it is not always openly avowed. To extend the area of national ownership by seizure of neighbouring land or of distant colonies has a sentimental appeal which cannot be dispelled by citing the human or financial costs and risks of such virile procedure. The sort of patriotism that can be evoked in Italy, Germany or Japan for such aggression does not really proceed from the economic necessities cited in its defence. It is rooted in some ineradicable pugnacity and predacity of the animal man, intensified by herd appeals that repress any doubts or qualms of reason and humanity. But, though this patriotism has its own basic instinctive origins, it is fed and directed in its activities by economic motives. Are these economic motives equally irrational and based on miscalculations of business interests ?

My contention is that the system prevailing in all developed countries for the production and distribution of wealth has reached a stage in which its productive powers are held in leash by its inequalities of distribution ; the excessive share that goes to profits, rents and other surpluses impelling a chronic endeavour to oversave in the sense of trying to provide an increased productive power without a corresponding outlet in the purchase of consumable goods. This drive towards oversaving is gradually checked by the inability of such saving to find any profitable use in the provision of more plant and other capital. But it also seeks to utilise political power for outlets in external markets, and as foreign independent markets are closed or restricted, the drive to the acquisition of colonies, protectorates and other areas of imperial development becomes a more urgent and conscious national policy. If this reasoning is correct, capitalism to maintain its profitable character, by utilising its new productive powers as fully as possible, is impelled to seek the help of the State in the various ways that are now so much in evidence, tariffs, embargoes, subsidies, and the acquisition or retention of colonies where the home capitalist can have advantages both for his import and export trade, with such securities in monetary matters as can be provided by imperial control.

In such a policy the trades directly or indirectly connected with the production of armaments have a twofold function. On the one hand, they batten upon the public expenditure needed to sustain a spirited foreign policy. On the other hand, they evoke a corresponding " defensive " policy in other countries to which they contribute by profitable supplies of arms and ammunition—thus producing a growing competition in costs of " defence." It is sheer effrontery for well-informed officials and directors of armament firms to deny that pressure is exerted by these firms in political quarters for the enlargement of their profitable operations, and that the employment by these firms of retired army and navy officials has not a definitely business motive.

But though it is incontestible that the armaments trades are naturally disposed to an international competition in the instruments of war which is itself provocative of war, it is often contended that actual war is detrimental to their interests, as it is to Capitalism in general. Sir Norman Angell states this wider issue in the following terms :—

" That Capitalism as an economic system neither needs nor benefits by war ; that it cannot use successful war in the modern world as a means of disposing of the surplus of its production, acquiring new markets, increasing its profits ; that, on the contrary—as the position of the victorious capitalist states after a completely victorious war ·abundantly demonstrated—Capitalism has suffered disastrously and been incalculably weakened by war, and that another like the last will, as enlightened Capitalists are aware, probably destroy it altogether."[1]

Now, though war, with its revolutionary aftermath, may well seem dangerous to the capitalist system, it is open to argument whether such risks may not appear worth running in view of the alternative piling up of unsaleable surpluses which the extension and improved methods of modern capitalism involve. For though war is the most wasteful and foolish way of disposing of the actual and potential surpluses which maldistribution of income involves, it does for the time being rectify the balance between pro-ductivity and consumption and give prosperity alike to capital and labour in the uninvaded and the neutral countries. During the Great War and for a few years after when the let-down-part of Capitalism was in course of restoration, both workers and capitalists were profitably employed in most of the affected countries. There has been, of course, a terrible aftermath with an unprecedented amount of unemployment and misery. But up to the disastrous

[1] *Preface to Peace*, p. 196.

slump of 1929–30 there is no ground for holding that capitalism in this country, America, and even in France, Germany and Italy, was not earning good profits in most industries. The dislocation and shrinkage of foreign markets, due to the redistribution of territories under the Peace Treaties, the new economic barriers and the monetary disturbances, did grave damage to certain industries and markets, and involved attempts at national self-sufficiency very wasteful from the standpoint of " division of labour." But in spite of these obstacles post-war capitalism did not " suffer disastrously " until the rapid growth of its new productivity, with a rise of profits faster than the rise of wages, brought once again the fatal disequilibrium between production and consumption now seen to be the world's economic peril.

But in arguing the case for maldistribution as the main cause of Imperialism and of the wars which accompany that policy, it is not necessary to contend that capitalism as " an economic system " benefits by war, but only that certain sections of capitalism with political influence at their disposal favour pushful foreign policies that involve the risk of war. This applies not merely to the armaments industries but to most other industries dependent largely upon export and import trades. While it remains true that we do not need to own a country in order to trade with it, the flag still carries certain trading advantages. And those advantages have grown with our new imperial policy of protection and preference, a policy directly due to our recognition of the insufficiency of markets. So long as our wide-flung Empire presented free markets to the traders of foreign nations, the advantages enjoyed by members of the imperial power, by way of contracts for developmental work and official emoluments, were not causes of strong discontent. But the new restrictive preferential policy applied to a picked quarter of the globe by Great Britain and her Dominions has a natural reaction upon other countries which have entered on a capitalist career. It stimulates them to seek territorial expansion for themselves with a view to exclusive markets and areas for planting their surplus labour and capital, while feeding a dangerous resentment against the satisfied or glutted countries which have pre-empted the most desirable territories. The peril which confronts the world to-day arises manifestly from the new passion for imperial growth on the part of the great unsatisfied Powers and the conscious avowal of their aggressive intentions. This peril has been increased by the annexation of the German colonies under the Peace Treaty. For though the tangible value of these colonies to Germany either in terms of trade or as an outlet for her surplus population was extremely small, their seizure and transfer to the various Allies under the title of Mandatory territories has been a natural source of grievance to Germany. The air of hypocrisy which attended this power of transfer, the secret haggling of the Allies, solemnly endorsed later on by these same Allies acting as Council of the League, did not help to make this seizure more palatable.

It may be true that the capitalist system in Italy, as a whole and in the long run, stands to lose rather than to gain by its costly seizure of Ethiopia. It may be true that Japan would have been economically wiser to have pursued a policy of peaceful penetration in Manchuria and North China instead of the expensive military operations upon which she has embarked. But it is wrong to exclude capitalist and business motives from the play of such imperialism and to impute it to the arrogance of political magalomania. Certain important organised business interests in Italy and in Japan have stood to gain out of the expenses of this imperialism. Political realism must reckon with this fact. While therefore Sir Norman Angell may be right in holding that capitalism as a whole system and in the long run is weakened and imperilled by such operations, it must be borne in mind that capitalism does not work as a single profitable system, and that capitalists often prefer a short to a long run in the pursuit of profit.

But there remains a wider issue for our consideration. Suppose it to be the case that the education of the workers in most capitalist countries has been bringing into the forefront of their consciousness the injustices, the wastes, the cruelties of the current economic system in its effects on the production and distribution of wealth. Suppose some demand for a new economic system that shall displace the imperfectly competitive capitalism, and shall organise the available human and material resources of production on a conscious basis of the satisfaction of human needs— suppose that such a demand is visibly seeking expression through the democratic machinery of popular self-government, is it not reasonable to expect that strong capitalist interests would seek methods of repressing these thoughts and designs of the workers ?

For though capitalism might hope to maintain some of its supremacy by such concessions to labour and such extensions of social services as would buy off the organised resentment of the workers, the results of such a concession policy might be inadequate to meet the actual economic pressure. For the larger working class and public consumption involved in this policy might be conducive to an increased efficiency of labour and advance of productive technique great enough to keep capitalism upon a basis so profitable that the disequilibrium between production and consumption continues as a disturbing influence in industry. This issue of the sufficiency of this concession policy is, indeed, being worked out in Britain to-day, and the United States is making some attempt at its application in America. Its success would seem to imply a formal retention of capitalism as the directive power of industry, working in closely organized relations with the employees in the several industries and the consumer as the co-ordinative factor in the relations of the several industries. Some such alteration in the form and functions of capitalism is also apparent in the Italian and the German schemes for a Corporative State. But in all these cases of public planning two difficulties have to be confronted. First, the question how far large personal gains are a necessary stimulus to the creative work of men responsible for rapid and advantageous improvements in technique and organization. Routine workers necessarily tend to overlook the enormous productive importance of such creative activities, or to think that they can always be secured by departments of technical research attached to each industry. It may, therefore, be desirable to leave outside any scheme of public planning those newer industries where rapid improvements of technique may be expected and those industries most susceptible to changes in the demand for the goods they supply.

But important as this question may be of securing the best inventive and administrative services by adequate incentives of gain, there remains another question of still greater importance, viz. the utilization or the displacement of that financial control over big industry which is the latest fruit of capitalist evolution. The closest study of this financial control has been made by the American economist Thorstein Veblen who examines the relations which exist in the United States between the manipulations of credit and prices and the industrial management. Whereas the latter aims at the highest technical and working efficiency in producing the maximum output, the former pay exclusive regard to the regulation and limitation of that output so as to maintain a price level which shall yield the largest aggregate profit. In many standard industries for the production of the necessaries and conventional comforts of life, it may pay the financiers and investors to market a limited quantity of goods at a higher price. Hence the tendency of the bankers and other organizers of finance to promote cartels, trusts and other amalgamations which shall enable them to control the aggregate output, closing down superfluous plant and reducing the volume of employment. Though America with her highly organized money-power and her protective system has taken the lead in this financial dominion, other capitalist countries, Germany and Britain in particular, have made considerable advances in the same direction. In Germany the banks have for a long time past devoted themselves to these profitable restrictions of industry, and more recently the textile, metal, mining, milling and other standard industries in Great Britain have been seeking similar organization for the profitable regulation of output.

This analysis of the various attempts to escape from the perils of excessive productivity shows that they fall under three heads. One consists in the policy of organized labour and the State, aiming to secure a more equal and equitable distribution of the money and real income of the community, by higher wages, shorter hours and other betterment of working and living conditions. The second consists in the business policy of restricted output just described, involving a close financial control of the major businesses in specified national or international industries, accompanied by a regulation of their markets and, when deemed desirable, by quotas and tariffs. The third method, and that most relevant to our present subject of Imperialism, is the combined or separate action of capital to obtain the help, financial, diplomatic, military, of the national government so as to secure preferential access to foreign markets and foreign areas of development by colonies, protectorates, spheres of preferential trade and other methods of a pushful economic foreign policy. It may be true that the people of the imperialist state are in the long, or even the short, run losers by a policy so costly in money and in lives. But if, as is normally the case, the larger part of this expense falls upon the public as a whole, it may still be advantageous to those capitalist interests engaged in foreign trade and investments to promote a policy that is to their profit. Even if, as Sir Norman Angell contends, such imperialism involves war-making and with it the perils of a domestic revolution fatal to the capitalist regime, the risks of such an issue may either be unrealised, or may be disregarded in view of the immediate gains which imperialism brings to favoured industries. If, as many close investigators of the business world appear to hold, the capitalism which has prevailed for the past few centuries is in any case destined to disappear, it may seem better for its defenders to endeavour to prolong its life by political pressure for external markets than to succumb without a struggle to the popular demand for state socialism or a policy of social services, the expenses of which shall consume the whole of surplus profits. There still remain large fields for capitalist exploitation. The largest of these, China, appears to be marked down for Japanese exclusive exploitation. But this appearance is deceptive, for the task of Chinese development far exceeds the national resources of Japan. If capitalists in the several Western Powers were capable of intelligent co-operation, instead of wrangling among themselves for separate national areas of exploitation, they would have combined for a joint international enterprise in Asia, a project which might have given the whole of Western capitalism another generation military rulers who in Japan, as in Germany, conduct the territorial aggressions, and the capitalists who must help to finance them. But the clearer-sighted capitalists perceive that dictatorships and their imperial enterprises, expensive as they may be, are preferable to the more revolutionary courses to which democracies are now committed. Imperialism thus figures as an important and imposing feature of neo-capitalism, seeking to avert internal democratic struggles for economic equalitarianism by providing outlets for surplus goods and surplus population together with emotional appeals to the combatant predacity which animates a spirited foreign policy. It may be true that Imperialism in its competitive aspect carries within itself the seeds of its own demise, leading, as it must, to conflicts ever more destructive to life and property. Indeed, its competition for an ever shrinking area of profitable acquisition may so intensify the struggle between the possessing and the non-possessing nations as to destroy the fabric of civilization. Whether the slowly evolving rationality and sociability of man have advanced sufficiently to furnish a strong enough safeguard against this imperial predacity is the question that confronts the world to-day.

. . . .

Though the general trend of Imperialism in its economic and political character has not changed within the past thirty years, the attitude of many countries towards Imperialism has undergone considerable changes, chiefly, though not entirely, as a result of post-war policies. It may be well, briefly, to cite the nature of these changes. The Peace Treaties, by removing from Germany and Turkey large areas of imperial control and placing them as mandated territories under the control of victorious allies, chiefly Britain, her Dominions and France, enlarged considerably of active profitable survival. Such a scheme of economic Interimperialism may now no longer be possible, for though Japan cannot perform her self-imposed task without financial assistance from the wealthier West, she may be able to obtain this assistance by making the financiers of several Western countries compete with one another for the provision of the required finance, without allowing their governments any real share in the accompanying political control over China.

From the standpoint of the defence of capitalism it is not necessary to show that imperialism is profitable in the long run to the general body of the owning and exploiting class within a capitalist country, but only that it enables the members of that class concerned with foreign trade and investment to utilize the political and financial resources of their State to extend the area of such trade and investment or to retain and develop the colonies, protectorates and other portions of the existing empire.

It is such considerations that bring out the conflict of imperialism with democracy. For a political democracy, in which the interests and will of the whole people wield the powers of the State, will actively oppose the whole process of imperialism. Such a democracy has now learnt the lesson that substantial economic equality in income and ownership of property is essential to its operation. The defence of capitalism is, therefore, bound up in every country with the destruction or enfeeblement of the popular franchise and representative government. If the forms of such democracy are still retained, they are reduced to the automatic or compulsory registration of the will of a dictator or a ruling caste. The cases above cited suffice to show the place which Imperialism occupies as an ingredient in the capitalist-military nationalism of the age. There is, of course, some division of interest and policy between the

the portion of the backward countries which came under the sway of the allies, and roused a lasting resentment in Germany and Turkey, especially against the British Empire.

The feebleness revealed in the League of Nations, designed originally as a growing instrument of political and economic internationalism, has served to aggravate the sense of injury in Germany from the seizure of her colonies, for League control is rightly felt to be a fiction, save in the matter of a trade equality only operative in certain mandates. The passion of German imperialism thus inflamed has been rivalled in intensity by Italian resentment against the insufficiency of her share of the lands disposed of under the Peace Treaties and her sentimental revival of a Roman Empire which should own the Mediterranean and large portions of North Africa. In Asia the centres of disturbance are India and the Far East. The latter is due to the conscious and avowed Imperialism of Japan, seeking her early prey in Manchuria and North China, but only limited in her further control of Asia by her straitened financial national resources and the possible intervention of Britain and America. Imperialism in India is seeking a new basis which shall reconcile a large measure of democratic self-government with two British requirements, a safeguarding of the large investment interests in Indian railways and industrial undertakings and a retention of the foreign policy of India, its internal order and protection against foreign aggression. It is too early to say how this new Constitution is likely to work, but the experiment is an important contribution to a limited Imperialism.

The most momentous of post-war events has been the Communist experiment in Russia, in its bearing upon the Imperialism of European countries. Though the Soviet Government harbours no aggressive designs upon lands outside the Russian boundaries, and is more and more occupied in the development of its own economic resources, it has from the beginning sought to promote the growth of Communism in other countries by an active subsidised propaganda. The Marxist doctrines which Lenin imposed upon the Russian revolution demanded an international Communism as an essential, and though Stalin appears to have withdrawn any immediate extra-national policy, the Comintern, an international propagandist body, still operates from Moscow, presumably with the consent and assistance of the Soviet Government. It was the fear of this Communism issuing from Russia, and spreading among the working classes of Germany that frightened the upper owning classes into the substitution of a thinly-disguised, but very real, autocracy for the shallow democracy of the post-war era. Though Russian propaganda played a smaller part in Italy, it was the same fear and the same revolutionary movement that enabled Mussolini to rally the owning classes to his flag and to establish his political domination. In later cases prestige and power-politics combined with the economic interests of certain capitalist groups to stimulate a colonial policy of aggression associated with an inter-nationalism of counter-revolution which calls for active intervention wherever Bolshevism appears to raise its head. Thus the isolated economic nationalism of tariffs, embargoes and other customs is found in active and combined collusion with an external policy of imperialism and of possible interference with the liberty of weaker nations to settle their own political and economic affairs.

The one apparent exception to the general trend of Imperialism is the United States. After the Spanish war had left her in possession of Cuba and other colonies she seemed committed to a genuine though limited Imperialism as distinct from the sort of protectorate over mid and south America conveyed by the Monroe Doctrine. But the lasting shock made to public opinion in America by her temporary entanglement with Europe during the latter years of the Great War brought on a strong wave of political isolation which found expression not merely in a refusal to join the League of Nations but in her withdrawal from active control over her colonies, and, still more important, the placing of her relations with the Monroe States upon a formal basis of equal co-operation. How far this political isolation will be found compatible with the trading and credit relations with the outside world which her rapid industrial development makes inevitable, is one of the great speculative problems of the near future.

IMPERIALISM: A STUDY

NATIONALISM AND IMPERIALISM

AMID the welter of vague political abstractions to lay one's finger accurately upon any " ism " so as to pin it down and mark it out by definition seems impossible. Where meanings shift so quickly and so subtly, not only following changes of thought, but often manipulated artificially by political practitioners so as to obscure, expand, or distort, it is idle to demand the same rigour as is expected in the exact sciences. A certain broad consistency in its relations to other kindred terms is the nearest approach to definition which such a term as Imperialism admits. Nationalism, internationalism, colonialism, its three closest congeners, are equally elusive, equally shifty, and the changeful overlapping of all four demands the closest vigilance of students of modern politics.

During the nineteenth century the struggle towards nationalism, or establishment of political union on a basis of nationality, was a dominant factor alike in dynastic movements and as an inner motive in the life of masses of population. That struggle, in external politics, sometimes took a disruptive form, as in the case of Greece, Servia, Roumania, and Bulgaria breaking from Ottoman rule, and the detachment of North Italy from her unnatural alliance with the Austrian Empire. In other cases it was a unifying or a centralising force, enlarging the area of nationality, as in the case of Italy and the Pan-Slavist movement in

Russia. Sometimes nationality was taken as a basis of federation of States, as in United Germany and in North America.

It is true that the forces making for political union sometimes went further, making for federal union of diverse nationalities, as in the cases of Austria-Hungary, Norway and Sweden, and the Swiss Federation. But the general tendency was towards welding into large strong national unities the loosely related States and provinces with shifting attachments and alliances which covered large areas of Europe since the break-up of the Empire. This was the most definite achievement of the nineteenth century. The force of nationality, operating in this work, is quite as visible in the failures to achieve political freedom as in the successes; and the struggles of Irish, Poles, Finns, Hungarians, and Czechs to resist the forcible subjection to or alliance with stronger neighbours brought out in its full vigour the powerful sentiment of nationality.

The middle of the century was especially distinguished by a series of definitely "nationalist" revivals, some of which found important interpretation in dynastic changes, while others were crushed or collapsed. Holland, Poland, Belgium, Norway, the Balkans, formed a vast arena for these struggles of national forces.

The close of the third quarter of the century saw Europe fairly settled into large national States or federations of States, though in the nature of the case there can be no finality, and Italy continued to look to Trieste, as Germany still looks to Austria, for the fulfilment of her manifest destiny.

This passion and the dynastic forms it helped to mould and animate are largely attributable to the fierce prolonged resistance which peoples, both great and small, were called on to maintain against the imperial designs of Napoleon.

The national spirit of England was roused by the tenseness of the struggle to a self-consciousness it had never experienced since " the spacious days of great Elizabeth." Jena made Prussia into a great nation ; the Moscow campaign brought Russia into the field of European nationalities as a factor in politics, opening her for the first time to the full tide of Western ideas and influences.

Turning from this territorial and dynastic nationalism to the spirit of racial, linguistic, and economic solidarity which has been the underlying motive, we find a still more remarkable movement. Local particularism on the one hand, vague cosmopolitanism upon the other, yielded to a ferment of nationalist sentiment, manifesting itself among the weaker peoples not merely in a sturdy and heroic resistance against political absorption or territorial nationalism, but in a passionate revival of decaying customs, language, literature and art ; while it bred in more dominant peoples strange ambitions of national " destiny " and an attendant spirit of Chauvinism.

The true nature and limits of nationality have never been better stated than by J. S. Mill.

" A portion of mankind may be said to constitute a nation if they are united among themselves by common sympathies which do not exist between them and others. This feeling of nationality may have been generated by various causes. Sometimes it is the effect of identity of race and descent. Community of language and community of religion greatly contribute to it. Geographical limits are one of the causes. But the strongest of all is identity of political antecedents, the possession of a national history and consequent community of recollections, collective pride and humiliation, pleasure and regret, connected with the same incidents in the past."[1]

[1] *Representative Government*, chap. xvi.

It is a debasement of this genuine nationalism, by attempts to overflow its natural banks and absorb the near or distant territory of reluctant and unassimilable peoples, that marks the passage from nationalism to a spurious colonialism on the one hand, Imperialism on the other.

Colonialism, where it consists in the migration of part of a nation to vacant or sparsely peopled foreign lands, the emigrants carrying with them full rights of citizenship in the mother country, or else establishing local self-government in close conformity with her institutions and under her final control, may be considered a genuine expansion of nationality, a territorial enlargement of the stock, language and institutions of the nation. Few colonies in history have, however, long remained in this condition when they have been remote from the mother country. Either they have severed the connexion and set up for themselves as separate nationalities, or they have been kept in complete political bondage so far as all major processes of government are concerned, a condition to which the term Imperialism is at least as appropriate as colonialism. The only form of distant colony which can be regarded as a clear expansion of nationalism is the self-governing British colony in Australasia and Canada, and even in these cases local conditions may generate a separate nationalism based on a strong consolidation of colonial interests and sentiments alien from and conflicting with those of the mother nation. In other " self-governing " colonies, as in Cape Colony and Natal, where the majority of whites are not descended from British settlers, and where the presence of subject or " inferior " races in vastly preponderating numbers, and alien climatic and other natural conditions, mark out a civilization distinct from that of the " mother country," the conflict between the colonial and the imperial ideas has long been present in

6

the forefront of the consciousness of politicians. When Lord Rosmead spoke of the permanent presence of the imperial factor as "simply an absurdity," and Mr. Rhodes spoke of its "elimination," they were championing a "colonialism" which is more certain in the course of time to develop by inner growth into a separate "nationalism" than in the case of the Australasian and Canadian colonies, because of the wider divergence, alike of interests and radical conditions of life, from the mother nation. Our other colonies are plainly representative of the spirit of Imperialism rather than of colonialism. No considerable proportion of the population consists of British settlers living with their families in conformity with the social and political customs and laws of their native land : in most instances they form a small minority wielding political or economic sway over a majority of alien and subject people, themselves under the despotic political control of the Imperial Government or its local nominees. This, the normal condition of a British colony, was well-nigh universal in the colonies of other European countries. The "colonies" which France and Germany established in Africa and Asia were in no real sense plantations of French and German national life beyond the seas ; nowhere, not even in Algeria, did they represent true European civiliza- tion ; their political and economic structure of society is wholly alien from that of the mother country.

Colonialism, in its best sense, is a natural overflow of nationality ; its test is the power of colonists to transplant the civilization they represent to the new natural and social environment in which they find themselves. We must not be misled by names ; the "colonial" party in Germany and France is identical in general aim and method with the "imperialist" party in England, and the latter is the truer title. Professor Seeley well marked the nature of

7

Imperialism. "When a State advances beyond the limits of nationality its power becomes precarious and artificial. This is the condition of most empires, and it is the condition of our own. When a nation extends itself into other territories the chances are that it cannot destroy or completely drive out, even if it succeeds in conquering, them. When this happens it has a great and permanent difficulty to contend with, for the subject or rival nationalities cannot be properly assimilated, and remain as a permanent cause of weakness and danger."[1]

The novelty of recent Imperialism regarded as a policy consists chiefly in its adoption by several nations. The notion of a number of competing empires is essentially modern. The root idea of empire in the ancient and mediæval world was that of a federation of States, under a hegemony, covering in general terms the entire known recognized world, such as was held by Rome under the so-called *pax Romana*. When Roman citizens, with full civic rights, were found all over the explored world, in Africa and Asia, as well as in Gaul and Britain, Imperialism contained a genuine element of internationalism. With the fall of Rome this conception of a single empire wielding political authority over the civilized world did not disappear. On the contrary, it survived all the fluctuations of the Holy Roman Empire. Even after the definite split between the Eastern and Western sections had taken place at the close of the fourth century, the theory of a single State, divided for administrative purposes, survived. Beneath every cleavage or antagonism, and notwithstanding the severance of many independent kingdoms and provinces, this ideal unity of the empire lived. It formed the conscious avowed ideal of Charlemagne, though as a practical ambition confined to Western Europe. Rudolph of Habsburg not

[1] " Expansion of England," lect. iii.

merely revived the idea, but laboured to realize it through Central Europe, while his descendant Charles V gave a very real meaning to the term by gathering under the unity of his imperial rule the territories of Austria, Germany, Spain, the Netherlands, Sicily, and Naples. In later ages this dream of a European Empire animated the policy of Peter the Great, Catherine, and Napoleon. Nor is it impossible that Kaiser Wilhelm III held a vision of such a world-power.

Political philosophers in many ages, Vico, Machiavelli, Dante, Kant, have speculated on an empire as the only feasible security for peace, a hierarchy of States conforming on the larger scale to the feudal order within the single State.

Thus empire was identified with internationalism, though not always based on a conception of equality of nations. The break-up of the Central European Empire, with the weakening of nationalities that followed, evoked a new modern sentiment of internationalism which, through the eighteenth century, was a flickering inspiration in the intellectual circles of European States. "The eve of the French Revolution found every wise man in Europe— Lessing, Kant, Goethe, Rousseau, Lavater, Condorcet, Priestley, Gibbon, Franklin—more of a citizen of the world than of any particular country. Goethe confessed that he did not know what patriotism was, and was glad to be without it. Cultured men of all countries were at home in polite society everywhere. Kant was immensely more interested in the events of Paris than in the life of Prussia. Italy and Germany were geographical expressions ; those countries were filled with small States in which there was no political life, but in which there was much interest in the general progress of culture. The Revolution itself was at bottom also human and cosmopolitan. It is, as Lamartine said, ' a date in the human mind,' and it is because of that fact that all the carping of critics like Taine cannot prevent us from seeing that the character of the men who led the great movements of the Revolution can never obliterate the momentous nature of the Titanic strife. The soldiers of the Revolution who, barefooted and ragged, drove the insolent reactionaries from the soil of France were fighting not merely for some national cause, but for a cause dimly perceived to be the cause of general mankind. With all its crudities and imperfections, the idea of the Revolution was that of a conceived body of Right in which all men should share."[1]

This early flower of humane cosmopolitanism was destined to wither before the powerful revival of nationalism which marked the next century. Even in the narrow circles of the cultured classes it easily passed from a noble and a passionate ideal to become a vapid sentimentalism, and after the brief flare of 1848 among the continental populace had been extinguished, little remained but a dim smouldering of the embers. Even the Socialism which upon the continent retains a measure of the spirit of internationalism is so tightly confined within the national limits, in its struggle with bureaucracy and capitalism, that " the international " expresses little more than a holy aspiration, and has little opportunity of putting into practice the genuine sentiments of brotherhood which its prophets have always preached.

Thus the triumph of nationalism seems to have crushed the rising hope of internationalism. Yet it would appear that there is no essential antagonism between them. A true strong internationalism in form or spirit would rather imply the existence of powerful self-respecting nationalities which seek union on the basis of common national needs and interests. Such a historical development would be far

[1] W. Clarke, *Progressive Review*, February, 1897.

more conformable to laws of social growth than the rise of anarchic cosmopolitanism from individual units amid the decadence of national life.

Nationalism is a plain highway to internationalism, and if it manifests divergence we may well suspect a perversion of its nature and its purpose. Such a perversion is Imperialism, in which nations trespassing beyond the limits of facile assimilation transform the wholesome stimulative rivalry of varied national types into the cutthroat struggle of competing empires.

Not only does aggressive Imperialism defeat the movement towards internationalism by fostering animosities among competing empires : its attack upon the liberties and the existence of weaker or lower races stimulates in them a corresponding excess of national self-consciousness. A nationalism that bristles with resentment and is all astrain with the passion of self-defence is only less perverted from its natural genius than the nationalism which glows with the animus of greed and self-aggrandisement at the expense of others. From this aspect aggressive Imperialism is an artificial stimulation of nationalism in peoples too foreign to be absorbed and too compact to be permanently crushed. We welded Africanderdom into just such a strong dangerous nationalism, and we joined with other nations in creating a resentful nationalism until then unknown in China. The injury to nationalism in both cases consists in converting a cohesive, pacific internal force into an exclusive, hostile force, a perversion of the true power and use of nationality. The worst and most certain result is the retardation of internationalism. The older nationalism was primarily an inclusive sentiment ; its natural relation to the same sentiment in another people was lack of sympathy, not open hostility ; there was no inherent antagonism to prevent nationalities from growing and thriving side by side. Such in the main was the nationalism of the earlier nineteenth century, and the politicians of Free Trade had some foundation for their dream of a quick growth of effective, informal internationalism by peaceful, profitable intercommunication of goods and ideas among nations recognizing a just harmony of interests in free peoples.

The overflow of nationalism into imperial channels quenched all such hopes. While co-existent nationalities are capable of mutual aid involving no direct antagonism of interests, co-existent empires following each its own imperial career of territorial and industrial aggrandisement are natural necessary enemies. The full nature of this antagonism on its economic side is not intelligible without a close analysis of those conditions of modern capitalist production which compel an ever keener " fight for markets," but the political antagonism is obvious.

The scramble for Africa and Asia virtually recast the policy of all European nations, evoked alliances which cross all natural lines of sympathy and historical association, drove every continental nation to consume an ever-growing share of its material and human resources upon military and naval equipment, drew the great new power of the United States from its isolation into the full tide of competition ; and, by the multitude, the magnitude, and the suddenness of the issues it had thrown on to the stage of politics, became a constant agent of menace and of perturbation to the peace and progress of mankind. The new policy exercised the most notable and formidable influence upon the conscious statecraft of the nations which indulge in it. While producing for popular consumption doctrines of national destiny and imperial missions of civilization, contradictory in their true import, but subsidiary to one another as supports of popular Imperialism, it evoked a calculating, greedy type of Machiavellianism, entitled " real-politik " in Germany, where it was made, which remodelled the whole art of diplomacy and erected national aggrandisement without pity or scruple as the conscious motive force of foreign policy. Earth hunger and the scramble for markets were responsible for the openly avowed repudiation of treaty obligations which Germany, Russia, and England had not scrupled to defend. The sliding scale of diplomatic language, hinterland, sphere of interest, sphere of influence, paramountcy, suzerainty, protectorate, veiled or open, leading up to acts of forcible seizure or annexation which sometimes continue to be hidden under " lease," " rectification of frontier," " concession," and the like, was the invention and expression of this cynical spirit of Imperialism. While Germany and Russia were perhaps more open in their professed adoption of the material gain of their country as the sole criterion of public conduct, other nations were not slow to accept the standard. Though the conduct of nations in dealing with one another has commonly been determined at all times by selfish and shortsighted considerations, the conscious, deliberate adoption of this standard at an age when the intercourse of nations and their interdependence for all essentials of human life grow ever closer, is a retrograde step fraught with grave perils to the cause of civilization.

PART I

THE ECONOMICS OF IMPERIALISM

CHAPTER I

THE MEASURE OF IMPERIALISM

QUIBBLES about the modern meaning of the term Imperialism are best resolved by reference to concrete facts in the history of the last sixty years. During that period a number of European nations, Great Britain being first and foremost, annexed or otherwise asserted political sway over vast portions of Africa and Asia, and over numerous islands in the Pacific and elsewhere. The extent to which this policy of expansion was carried on, and in particular the enormous size and the peculiar character of the British acquisitions, were not adequately realized even by those who pay some attention to Imperial politics.

The following lists, giving the area and, where possible, the population of the new acquisitions, are designed to give definiteness to the term Imperialism. Though derived from official sources, they do not, however, profess strict accuracy. The sliding scale of political terminology along which no-man's land, or hinterland, passes into some kind of definite protectorate is often applied so as to conceal the process ; " rectification " of a fluid frontier is continually taking place ; paper " partitions " of spheres of influence or protection in Africa and Asia are often obscure, and in some cases the area and the population are highly speculative.

In a few instances it is possible that portions of territory put down as acquired after 1870 may have been ear-marked by a European Power at some earlier date. But care is taken to include only such territories as have come within this period under the definite political control of the Power to which they are assigned. The figures in the case of Great Britain are so startling as to call for a little further interpretation. I have thought it right to add to the recognized list of colonies and protectorates[1] the " veiled Protectorate " of Egypt, with its vast Soudanese claim, the entire territories assigned to Chartered Companies, and the native or feudatory States in India which acknowledged our paramountcy by the admission of a British Agent or other official endowed with real political control.

All these lands are rightly accredited to the British Empire, and if our past policy is still pursued, the intensive as distinct from the extensive Imperialism will draw them under an ever-tightening grasp.[2]

In a few other instances, as, for example, in West Africa, countries are included in this list where some small dominion had obtained before 1870, but where the vast majority of the present area of the colony is of more recent requisition. Any older colonial possession thus included in Lagos or Gambia is, however, far more than counter-balanced by the increased area of the Gold Coast Colony, which is not included in this list, and which grew from 29,000 square miles in 1873 to 39,000 square miles in 1893.

The list is by no means complete. It takes no account of several large regions which passed under the control of our Indian Government as native or feudatory States, but of which no statistics of area or population, even approximate were available. Such are the Shan States, the Burma Frontier, and the Upper Burma Frontier, the districts of Chitral, Bajam, Swat, Waziristan, which came under our

[1] The Statistical Abstract for British Empire in 1903 (Cd. 2395, pub. 1905), gives an area of 9,631,100 sq. miles and a population of 360,646,000.
[2] The situation is that of 1905. The transfer of large regions from the control of our Foreign Office to that of our Colonial Office is a register of the tightening process. Northern and Southern Nigeria underwent this change in 1900, the E. African Protectorate, Uganda, and Somaliland in 1904.

	Date of Acquisition.	Area Square Miles.	Population.
EUROPE—			
Cyprus	1878	3,584	237,022
AFRICA—			
Zanzibar and Pemba . .	1888 ⎫	1,000,000	⎧ 200,000
East Africa Protectorate .	1895 ⎭		⎩ 2,500,000
Uganda Protectorate .	1894–1896	140,000	3,800,000
Somali Coast Protectorate .	1884–1885	68,000	(?)
British Central Africa Pro-			
tectorate . . .	1889	42,217	688,049
Lagos	to 1899	21,000	3,000,000
Gambia	to 1888	3,550	215,000
Ashantee	1896–1901	70,000	2,000,000
		⎧ 400,000	25,000,000
Niger Coast Protectorate .	1885–1898	⎨ to	to
		⎩ 500,000	40,000,000
Egypt	1882	400,000	9,734,405
Egyptian Soudan . .	1882	950,000	10,000,000
Griqualand West . .	1871–1880	15,197	83,373
Zululand	1879–1897	10,521	240,000
British Bechuanaland .	1885	51,424	72,736
Bechuanaland Protectorate	1891	275,000	89,216
Transkei	1879–1885	2,535	153,582
Tembuland . . .	1885	4,155	180,130
Pondoland . . .	1894	4,040	188,000
Griqualand East . .	1879–1885	7,511	152,609
British South Africa Charter	1889	750,000	321,000
Transvaal . . .	1900	117,732	1,354,200
Orange River Colony .	1900	50,000	385,045
ASIA—			
Hong Kong (littoral) .	1898	376	102,284
Wei-hai-wei . . .	—	270	118,000
Socotra	1886	1,382	10,000
Upper Burma . . .	1887	83,473	2,046,933
Baluchistan . . .	1876–1889	130,000	500,000
Sikkim	1890	2,818	30,000
Rajputana (States) . ⎫		⎧ 128,022	12,186,352
Burma (States) . . ⎬	since 1881	⎨ 62,661	785,800
Jammu and Kashmir . ⎭		⎩ 80,000	2,543,952
Malay Protected States .	1883–1895	24,849	620,000
North Borneo Co. . .	1881	31,106	175,000
North Borneo Protectorate.	1888	—	—
Sarawak	1888	50,000	500,000
British New Guinea . .	1888	90,540	350,000
Fiji Islands . . .	1874	7,740	120,124

" sphere of influence " in 1893, and have been since taken under a closer protectorate. The increase of British India itself between 1871 and 1891 amounted to an area of 104,993 square miles, with a population of 25,330,000, while no reliable measurement of the formation of new native States within that period and since is available. Many of the measurements here given are in round numbers, indicative of their uncertainty, but they are taken, wherever available, from official publications of the Colonial Office, corroborated or supplemented from the *Statesman's Year Book*. They will by no means comprise the full tale of our expansion during the thirty years, for many enlargements made by the several colonies themselves are omitted. But taken as they stand they make a formidable addition to the growth of an Empire whose nucleus is only 120,000 square miles, with 40,000,000 population.

For so small a nation to add to its domains in the course of a single generation an area of 4,754,000 square miles[1] with an estimated population of 88,000,000, is a historical fact of great significance.

Accepting Sir Robert Giffen's estimate[2] of the size of our Empire (including Egypt and the Soudan) at about 13,000,000 square miles, with a population of some 400 to 420 millions (of whom about 50,000,000 are of British race and speech), we find that one-third of this Empire, containing quite one-fourth of the total population of the Empire, was acquired within the last thirty years of the nineteenth century. This is in tolerably close agreement with other independent estimates.[3]

---

[1] Sir R. Giffen gives the figures as 4,204,690 square miles for the period 1870–1898.

[2] " The Relative Growth of the Component Parts of the Empire," a paper read before the Colonial Institute, January, 1898.

[3] See table, " British Colonies and Dependencies," on page 20.

The character of this Imperial expansion is clearly exhibited in the list of new territories.

Though, for convenience, the year 1870 has been taken as indicative of the beginning of a conscious policy of Imperialism, it will be evident that the movement did not attain its full impetus until the middle of the eighties. The vast increase of territory, and the method of wholesale partition which assigned to us great tracts of African land, may be dated from about 1884. Within fifteen years some three and three-quarter millions of square miles were added to the British Empire.[1]

Nor did Great Britain stand alone in this enterprise. The leading characteristic of that modern Imperialism, the competition of rival Empires, was the product of this same period. The close of the Franco-German war marked the beginning of a new colonial policy in France and Germany, destined to take effect in the next decade. It was not unnatural that the newly-founded German Empire, surrounded by powerful enemies and doubtful allies, and perceiving its more adventurous youth drawn into the United States and other foreign lands, should form the idea of a colonial empire. During the seventies a vigorous literature sprang up in advocacy of the policy[2] which took shape a little later in the powerful hands of Bismarck. The earliest instance of official aid for the promotion of German commerce abroad occurred in 1880 in the Government aid granted to the " German Commercial and Plantation Association of the Southern Seas." German connexion with Samoa dates from the same year, but the definite advance of Germany upon its Imperialist career began in 1884, with a policy of African protectorates and annexations

[1] *Liberalism and the Empire*, p. 341.
[2] Fabri's *Bedarf Deutschland der Colonien* was the most vigorous and popular treatise.

BRITISH COLONIES AND DEPENDENCIES, 1900.[2]

	Area Square Miles.	Estimated Population.
EUROPEAN DEPENDENCIES . . .	119	204,421
ASIATIC DEPENDENCIES—		
India (1,800,258 square miles, 287,223,431 inhabitants)	} 1,827,579	291,586,688
Others (27,321 square miles, 4,363,257 inhabitants)		
AFRICAN COLONIES	535,398	6,773,360
AMERICAN COLONIES	3,952,572	7,260,169
AUSTRALASIAN COLONIES . . .	3,175,840	5,009,281
Total	9,491,508	310,833,919
PROTECTORATES—		
Asia	120,400	1,200,000
Africa (including Egypt, Egyptian Soudan)	3,530,000	54,730,000
Oceania	800	30,000
Total Protectorates . . .	3,651,200	55,960,000
Grand total	13,142,708	366,793,919

of Oceanic islands. During the next fifteen years she brought under her colonial sway about 1,000,000 square miles, with an estimated population of 14,000,000. Almost the whole of this territory was tropical, and the white population formed a total of a few thousands.

Similarly in France a great revival of the old colonial spirit took place in the early eighties, the most influential of the revivalists being the eminent economist, M. Paul Leroy-Beaulieu. The extension of empire in Senegal and Sahara in 1880 was followed next year by the annexation of Tunis, and France was soon actively engaged in the scramble for Africa in 1884, while at the same time she was fastening her rule on Tonking and Laos in Asia. Her

[1] Compiled from Morris' *History of Colonization*, vol. ii, p. 87, and *Statesman's Year Book*, 1900. Figures for 1933-4 are given in the Appendix, p. 369.

acquisitions between 1880 and 1900 (exclusive of the extension of New Caledonia and its dependencies) amounted to an area of over three and a half million square miles, with a native population of some 37,000,000, almost the whole tropical or sub-tropical, inhabited by lower races and incapable of genuine French colonization.

Italian aspirations took similar shape from 1880 onwards, though the disastrous experience of the Abyssinian expeditions gave a check to Italian Imperialism. Her possessions in East Africa are confined to the northern colony of Eritrea and the protectorate of Somaliland.[1]

Of the other European States, two only, Portugal[2] and Belgium, enter directly into the competition of this new Imperialism. The African arrangements of 1884–6 assigned to Portugal the large district of Angola on the Congo Coast, while a large strip of East Africa passed definitely under her political control in 1891. The anomalous position of the great Congo Free State, ceded to the King of Belgium in 1883, and growing since then by vast accretions, must be regarded as involving Belgium in the competition for African empire.

Spain may be said to have definitely retired from imperial competition. The large and important possessions of Holland in the East and West Indies, though involving her in imperial politics to some degree, belong to older colonialism : she takes no part in the new imperial expansion.

Russia, the only active expansionist country of the North, stood alone in the character of her imperial growth, which differed from other Imperialism in that it was principally Asiatic in its achievements and proceeded by direct extension of imperial boundaries, partaking to a

[1] In the year 1905.

[2] Portugal's true era of Imperialism in Africa, however, dates back two centuries. See Theal's fascinating story of the foundation of a Portuguese Empire in *Beginnings of South African History* (Fisher Unwin).

larger extent than in the other cases of a regular colonial policy of settlement for purposes of agriculture and industry. It is, however, evident that Russian expansion, though of a more normal and natural order than that which characterises the new Imperialism, came definitely into contact and into competition with the claims and aspirations of the latter in Asia, and was advancing rapidly during the period which is the object of our study.

The entrance of the powerful and progressive nation of the United States of America upon Imperialism by the annexation of Hawaii and the taking over of the relics of ancient Spanish empire not only added a new formidable competitor for trade and territory, but changed and complicated the issues. As the focus of political attention and activity shifted more to the Pacific States, and the commercial aspirations of America were more and more set upon trade with the Pacific islands and the Asiatic coast, the same forces which were driving European States along the path of territorial expansion seemed likely to act upon the United States, leading her to a virtual abandonment of the principle of American isolation which hitherto dominated her policy.

The comparative table of colonisation (page 369), compiled from the *Statesman's Year Book* for 1900 by Mr. H. C. Morris,[1] marked the expansion of the political control of Western nations in 1905.[2]

The political nature of British Imperialism may be authoritatively ascertained by considering the governmental relations which the newly annexed territories have held with the Crown.

Officially,[3] British " colonial possessions " fall into three

---

[1] *Cf.* his *History of Colonization*, vol. ii, p. 318 (Macmillan & Co.).
[2] Figures for the years 1934–5 are given in the Appendix, p. 369.
[3] See the " Colonial Office List."

	Number of Colonies.	Area. Square Miles.		Population.	
		Mother Country.	Colonies, &c.	Mother Country.	Colonies, &c.
United Kingdom	50	120,979	11,605,238	40,559,954	345,222,239
France . .	33	204,092	3,740,756	38,517,975	56,401,860
Germany . .	13	208,830	1,027,120	52,279,901	14,687,000
Netherlands .	3	12,648	782,862	5,074,632	35,115,711
Portugal . .	9	36,038	801,100	5,049,729	9,148,707
Spain . .	3	197,670	243,877	17,565,632	136,000
Italy . .	2	110,646	188,500	31,856,675	850,000
Austria-Hungary	2	241,032	23,570	41,244,811	1,568,092
Denmark . .	3	15,289	86,634	2,185,335	114,229
Russia . .	3	8,660,395	255,550	128,932,173	15,684,000
Turkey . .	4	1,111,741	465,000	23,834,500	14,956,236
China . .	5	1,336,841	2,881,560	386,000,000	16,680,000
U.S.A. . .	6	3,557,000	172,091	77,000,000	10,544,617
Total . .	136	15,813,201	22,273,858	850,103,317	521,108,791

classes—(1) "Crown colonies, in which the Crown has the entire control of legislation, while the administration is carried on by public officers under the control of the Home Government ; (2) colonies possessing representative institutions, but not responsible government, in which the Crown has no more than a veto on legislation, but the Home Government retains the control of public affairs ; (3) colonies possessing representative institutions and responsible government, in which the Crown has only a veto on legislation, and the Home Government has no control over any officer except the Governor."

Now, of the thirty-nine separate areas which were annexed by Great Britain after 1870 as colonies or protectorates, not a single one ranks in class 3 and the Transvaal alone in class 2.

The new Imperialism established no single British colony endowed with responsible self-government. Nor, with the

exception of the three new States in South Africa, where white settlers lived in some numbers, is it seriously pretended that any of these annexed territories was being prepared and educated for representative, responsible self-government; and even in these South African States there is no serious intention, either on the part of the Home Government or of the colonists, that the majority of the inhabitants shall control the government.

It is true that some of these areas enjoy a measure of self-government, as protectorates or as feudatory States, under their own native princes. But all these in major matters of policy are subject to the absolute rule of the British Government, or of some British official, while the general tendency is towards drawing the reins of arbitrary control more tightly over protectorates, converting them into States which are in substance, though not always in name, Crown colonies. With the exception of a couple of experiments in India, the tendency everywhere has been towards a closer and more drastic imperial control over the territories that have been annexed, transforming protectorates, company rule, and spheres of influence into definite British States of the Crown colony order.

This is attributable, not to any greed of tyranny on the part of the Imperial Government, but to the conditions imposed upon our rule by considerations of climate and native population. Almost the whole of this new territory is tropical, or so near to the tropics as to preclude genuine colonisation of British settlers, while in those few districts where Europeans can work and breed, as in parts of South Africa and Egypt, the preoccupation of the country by large native populations of " lower races " precludes any considerable settlement of British workers and the safe bestowal of the full self-government which prevails in Australasia and Canada.

The same is true to an even more complete extent of the Imperialism of other continental countries. The new Imperialism nowhere extended the political and civil liberties of the mother country to any part of the vast territories which, after 1870, fell under the government of Western civilized Powers. Politically, the new Imperialism was an expansion of autocracy.

Taking the growth of Imperialism as illustrated in the expansion of Great Britain and of the chief continental Powers, we find the distinction between Imperialism and colonisation closely borne out by facts and figures, and warranting the following general judgments :—

First—Almost the whole of this imperial expansion was occupied with the political absorption of tropical or sub-tropical lands in which white men will not settle with their families.

Second—Nearly all the lands were thickly peopled by " lower races."

Thus this recent imperial expansion stands entirely distinct from the colonization of sparsely peopled lands in temperate zones, where white colonists carry with them the modes of government, the industrial and other arts of the civilization of the mother country. The " occupation " of these new territories was comprised in the presence of a small minority of white men, officials, traders, and industrial organisers, exercising political and economic sway over great hordes of population regarded as inferior and as incapable of exercising any considerable rights of self-government, in politics or industry.

CHAPTER II

THE COMMERCIAL VALUE OF IMPERIALISM

THE absorption of so large a proportion of public interest, energy, blood and money in seeking to procure colonial possessions and foreign markets would seem to indicate that Great Britain obtained her chief livelihood by external trade. Now this was not the case. Large as was our foreign and colonial trade in volume and in value, essential as was much of it to our national well-being, nevertheless it furnished a small proportion of the total industry of the nation.

According to the conjectural estimate of the Board of Trade " the proportion of the total labour of the British working classes which was concerned with the production of commodities for export (including the making of the instruments of this production and their transport to the ports) was between one-fifth and one-sixth of the whole."[1]

If we suppose the profits, salaries, etc., in connexion with export trade to be at the same level with those derived from home trade, we may conclude that between one-fifth and one-sixth of the income of the nation comes from the production and carriage of goods for export trade.

Taking the higher estimate of the magnitude of foreign trade, we should conclude that it furnished employment to one-fifth of our industrial factors, the other four-fifths being employed in supplying home markets.

But this must not be taken as a measure of the net value

[1] Cd. 1761, p. 361.

of foreign trade to our nation, or of the amount of loss that would have been sustained by a diminution of our foreign markets. We are not entitled to assume that a tariff-policy or some other restrictive policy on the part of foreign nations which gradually reduced our export trade would imply an *equivalent* loss of national income, and of employment of capital and labour in Great Britain. The assumption, sometimes made, that home demand is a fixed amount, and that any commodities made in excess of this amount must find a foreign market, or remain unsold, is quite unwarranted. There is no necessary limit to the quantity of capital and labour that can be employed in supplying the home markets, provided the effective demand for the goods that are produced is so distributed that every increase of production stimulates a corresponding increase of consumption.

Under such conditions a gradual loss of foreign markets would drive more capital and labour into industries supplying home markets ; the goods this capital and labour produced would be sold and consumed at home. Under such circumstances some loss would normally be sustained, because it could be reasonably assumed that the foreign market that was lost was a more profitable one than the new home market which took its place ; but that loss would certainly be much smaller than the aggregate of the value of trade thus transferred ; it would, in fact, be measured by the reduction in profit, and perhaps in wages, attending the substitution of a less remunerative home market for a more remunerative foreign market.

This argument, of course, does not imply that Great Britain could dispense with her external markets, and be no great sufferer in trade and income. Some considerable foreign markets, as we know, are an economic necessity to her, in order that by her exports she may purchase foods and materials which she cannot produce, or can only produce at a great disadvantage.

This fact makes a considerable external market a matter of vital importance to us. But outside the limit of this practical necessity the value of our foreign markets must rightly be considered to be measured, not by the aggregate value of the goods we sell abroad, but by the superior gain from selling them abroad as compared with selling them (or corresponding quantities of other goods) at home. To assume that if these goods are not sold abroad, neither they nor their substitutes could be sold, even at lower prices, in the home market, is quite unwarranted. There is no natural and necessary limit to the proportion of the national product which can be sold and consumed at home. It is, of course, preferable to sell goods abroad where higher profit can be got by doing so, but the net gain to national industry and income must be measured not by the value of the trade done, but by its more profitable nature.

These reflections are required to make us realize (1) that the importance of external trade is not rightly measured by the proportion its volume and value bear at any given time to those of home trade ; and (2) that it is by no means essential to the industrial progress of a nation that her external trade should under all conditions keep pace with her home trade.

When a modern nation has attained a high level of development in those industrial arts which are engaged in supplying the first physical necessaries and conveniences of the population, an increasing proportion of her productive energies will begin to pass into higher kinds of industry, into the transport services, into distribution, and into professional, official and personal services, which produce goods and services less adapted on the whole for international trade than those simpler goods which go to build the lower

Year.	Trade (in Millions).	Value per Head of Population.			Year.	Trade (in Millions).	Value per Head of Population.		
		£	s.	d.			£	s.	d.
1870 .	547				1885 .	642			
1871 .	615				1886 .	619			
1872 .	669				1887 .	643			
1873 .	682				1888 .	686			
1874 .	668				1889 .	743			
Average .	636	**19**	**19**	**3**	Average .	666	18	4	5
1875 .	655				1890 .	749			
1876 .	632				1891 .	744			
1877 .	647				1892 .	715			
1878 .	616				1893 .	682			
1879 .	612				1894 .	682			
Average .	632	18	16	6	Average .	715	18	14	10
1880 .	697				1895 .	703			
1881 .	694				1896 .	738			
1882 .	720				1897 .	745			
1883 .	732				1898 .	764			
1884 .	686				1899 .	805			
Average .	706	20	1	3	Average .	753	**18**	**15**	**6**

Figures for the years 1910-1934 are given in the Appendix, p. 370.

stages of a civilization.[1]   If this is true, it would appear that, whereas up to a certain point in the development of national life foreign trade will grow rapidly, after that point a decline, not in absolute size or growth but in relative size and growth, will take place.

There is some reason to hold that Great Britain had, in 1905, reached an industrial level where external trade, though still important, will be relatively less important in her national economy.

Between 1870 and 1900, as the above table shows, the

[1] See *Contemporary Review*, August, 1905, in which the author illustrates this tendency by the statistics of occupations in various nations.

value of our foreign trade had not grown so fast as our population. Whereas upon the generally accepted estimate the growth of the income of the nation during these three decades was from about £1,200,000,000 to £1,750,000,000, yielding an increase of about 10 per cent. in the income per head of the population, the value of foreign trade per head had positively shrunk.

Although the real increase in volume of external trade was considerable when the general fall of prices after 1870 is taken into account, it remains quite evident that neither volume nor value of external trade had kept pace during this period with volume and value of internal trade.[1]

Next, let us inquire whether the vast outlay of energy and money upon imperial expansion was attended by a growing trade within the Empire as compared with foreign trade. In other words, does the policy tend to make us more and more an economically self-sufficing Empire ? Does trade follow the flag ?

The figures in the table facing represent the proportion which our trade with our colonies and possessions bears to our foreign trade during the last half of the nineteenth century.

A longer period is here taken as a basis of comparison in order to bring out clearly the central truth, viz., that Imperialism had no appreciable influence whatever on the determination of our external trade until the protective and preferential measures taken during and after the Great War. Setting aside the abnormal increase of exports to our colonies in 1900–1903 due to the Boer War, we perceive that the proportions of our external trade had changed

---

[1] The four years subsequent to 1899 show a considerable increase in value of foreign trade, the average value per head for 1900–1903 working out at £21 2s. 5d. But this is abnormal, due partly to special colonial and foreign expenditure in connexion with the Boer War, partly to the general rise of prices as compared with the earlier level.

PERCENTAGES OF TOTAL VALUES.

Annual Averages.	Imports into Great Britain from		Exports from Great Britain to	
	Foreign Countries.	British Possessions.	Foreign Countries.	British Possessions.
1855–1859	76·5	23·5	68·5	31·5
1860–1864	71·2	28·8	66·6	33·4
1865–1869	76·0	24·0	72·4	27·6
1870–1874	78·0	22·0	74·4	25·6
1875–1879	77·9	22·1	67·0	33·0
1880–1884	76·5	23·5	65·5	34·5
1885–1889	77·1	22·9	65·0	35·0
1890–1894	77·1	22·9	66·5	33·5
1895–1899	78·4	21·6	66·0	34·0
1900–1903	77·3	20·7	63·0	37·0

This table (Cd. 1761 p. 407) refers to merchandise only, excluding bullion. From the export trade, ships and boats (not recorded prior to 1897) are excluded. In exports British produce alone is included. Figures for the years up to 1934 are given in the Appendix, p. 371.

very little during the half century; colonial imports slightly fell, colonial exports slightly rose, during the last decade, as compared with the beginning of the period. Although since 1870 such vast additions have been made to British possessions, involving a corresponding reduction of the area of " Foreign Countries," this imperial expansion was attended by no increase in the proportions of intra-imperial trade as represented in the imports and exports of Great Britain during the nineteenth century.

From the standpoint of the recent history of British trade there is no support for the dogma that " Trade follows the Flag." So far we have examined the question from the point of view of Great Britain. But if we examine the commercial connexion between Great Britain and the colonies from the colonial standpoint, asking whether the external trade of our colonies tends to a closer union with the mother country what result do we reach ?

The elaborate statistical investigation of Professor Alleyne Ireland into the trade of our colonial possessions strikes a still heavier blow at the notion that trade follows the flag. Taking the same period, he establishes the following two facts :—

" The total import trade of all the British colonies and possessions has increased at a much greater rate than the imports from the United Kingdom." " The total exports of all the British colonies and possessions have increased at a much greater rate than the exports to the United Kingdom."[1]

The following table[2] shows the gradual decline in the importance to the colonies of the commercial connexion with Great Britain since 1872–75, as illustrated in the proportion borne in the value of their exports from and their imports to Great Britain as compared with the value of the total imports and exports of the British colonies and possessions :—[1]

Four-Yearly Averages.	Percentages of Imports into Colonies, &c., from Great Britain.	Percentages of Exports from Colonies, &c., into Great Britain.
1856–1859	**46.5**	**57.1**
1860–1863	41·0	65·4
1864–1867	38·9	57·6
1868–1871	**39.8**	**53.5**
1872–1875	43·6	54·0
1876–1879	41·7	50·3
1880–1883	42·8	48·1
1884–1887	38·5	43·0
1888–1891	36·3	39·7
1892–1895	32·4	36·6
1896–1899	**32.5**	**34.9**

[1] *Tropical Colonization*, Page 125.

[2] Founded on the tables of Professor Ireland (*Tropical Colonization*, pp. 98–101), and revised up to date from figures in the Statistical Abstract of Colonial Possessions, Cd. 307.

[1] Figures for the years 1913–4, 1924–9, 1933–4 are given in the Appendix, pp. 372–3.

In other words, while Great Britain's dependence on her Empire for trade was stationary, the dependence of her Empire upon her for trade was rapidly diminishing.

The actual condition of British trade with foreign countries and with the chief groups of the colonies respectively may be indicated by the following statement[1] for the year ending December, 1901 :—

	Imports from.		Exports to.	
	Value.	Percentage.	Value.	Percentage.
	£		£	
Foreign Countries . . .	417,615,000	80	178,450,000	63½
British India	38,001,000	7	39,753,000	14
Australasia	34,682,000	7	26,932,000	9½
Canada	19,775,000	4	7,797,000	3
British South Africa . .	5,155,000	1	17,006,000	6
Other British Possessions . .	7,082,000	1	10,561,000	4
Total	522,310,000	100	280,499,000	100

It is thus clearly seen that while imperial expansion was attended by no increase in the value of our trade with our colonies and dependencies, a considerable increase in the value of our trade with foreign nations had taken place. Did space permit, it could be shown that the greatest increase of our foreign trade was with that group of industrial nations whom we regard as our industrial enemies, and whose political enmity we were in danger of arousing by our policy of expansion—France, Germany, Russia, and the United States.

One more point of supreme significance in its bearing on the new Imperialism remains. We have already drawn

[1] " Cobden Club Leaflet," 123, by Harold Cox. Figures for the year 1934–5 are given in the Appendix, p. 371.

attention to the radical distinction between genuine colonialism and Imperialism. This distinction is strongly marked in the statistics of the progress of our commerce with our foreign possessions.

The results of an elaborate investigation by Professor Flux[1] into the size of our trade respectively with India, the self-governing colonies and the other colonies may be presented in the following simple table :—[2]

	Percentages of imports from Great Britain.		Percentage of Exports to Great Britain.	
	1867–71.	1892–96.	1867–71.	1892–96.
India	69·2	71·9	52·6	33·2
Self-governing Colonies . .	57·5	59·2	55·4	70·3
Other Colonies . . .	34·3	26·4	46·4	29·3

Professor Flux thus summarises the chief results of his comparisons : " The great source of growth of Britain's colonial trade is very clearly shown to be the growth of trade with the colonies to which self-government has been granted. Their foreign trade has nearly doubled, and the proportion of it which is carried on with the mother country has increased from about 56½ per cent. to 65 per cent.

Later statistics[3] distinguishing British trade with India, the self-governing colonies and other colonies and possessions impress the same lesson from the standpoint of Great Britain in an even more striking manner.

[1] " The Flag and Trade," *Journal of Statistical Society*, September, 1899. Vol. lxii, pp. 496–98.

[2] Figures for the years 1913–4, 1924–9 and 1933–4 are given in the Appendix, p. 371.

[3] Statistical Abstract for the British Empire from 1889 to 1903. (Cd. 2395 pp. 25–28). Full tables of the Export and Import trade of Great Britain with the several parts of the Empire for the years 1904 to 1934, are given in the Appendix, pp. 372–3.

VALUE OF IMPORTS INTO GREAT BRITAIN FROM THE SEVERAL PARTS OF THE
EMPIRE (000,000 OMITTED).

	1889	1890	1891	1892	1893	1894	1895	1896	1897	1898	1899	1900[1]	1901	1902	1903
Self-governing Colonies	51	52	57	58	58	62	67	64	77	80	80	69	68	71	84
India . . .	37	33	33	34	28	31	29	27	26	29	29	31	34	32	37
Other possessions .	15	15	16	15	15	17	16	16	16	16	18	19	17	19	16

VALUE OF EXPORTS FROM GREAT BRITAIN INTO THE SEVERAL PARTS OF THE
EMPIRE

	1889	1890	1891	1892	1893	1894	1895	1896	1897	1898	1899	1900	1901	1902	1903
Self-governing Colonies . .	48	44	45	39	37	35	43	47	45	44	48	55	59	68	66
India . . .	40	45	39	37	38	36	31	38	37	38	40	41	46	42	45
Other possessions .	15	17	15	14	14	15	14	13	13	15	17	18	18	17	18

These tables show that whereas the import and the export trade with our self-governing colonies exhibited a large advance, our import trade alike with India and the "other possessions" was virtually stagnant, while our export trade with these two parts shows a very slight and very irregular tendency to increase.

Now the significance of these results for the study of modern Imperialism consists in the fact that the whole trend of this movement was directed to the acquisition of lands and populations belonging not to the self-governing order but to the "other possessions." Our expansion was almost wholly concerned with the acquisition of tropical and sub-tropical countries peopled by races to whom we have no serious intention of giving self-government. With the exception of the Transvaal and the Orange River

[1] Fall-off in imports from self-governing colonies 1900-2 is due entirely to stoppage in gold imports from South Africa.

37

Colony, none of our acquisitions since 1870 belonged, even prospectively, to the self-governing group, and even in the case of the two South African states, the prospective self-government was confined to a white minority of the population. The distinctive feature of modern Imperialism, from the commercial standpoint, is that it adds to our empire tropical and sub-tropical regions with which our trade is small, precarious and unprogressive.

The only considerable increase of our import trade since 1884 is from our genuine colonies in Australasia, North America, and Cape Colony; the trade with India has been stagnant, while that with our tropical colonies in Africa and the West Indies has been in most cases irregular and dwindling. Our export trade exhibits the same general character, save that Australia and Canada show a growing resolution to release themselves from dependence upon British manufactures; the trade with the tropical colonies, though exhibiting some increase, is very small and very fluctuating.

As for the territories acquired under the new Imperialism, except in one instance, no serious attempt to regard them as satisfactory business assets is possible.

The following table (page 39) gives the official figures of the value of our import and export trade with our tropical and sub-tropical possessions for the beginning of the present century. Bullion and specie are included in both accounts.

The entire volume of our export trade with our new protectorates in Africa, Asia and the Pacific amounted to not more than some nine millions sterling, of which more than six millions took place with the Malay Protected States, and was largely through traffic with the Far East. The entire volume of the import trade consisted of about eight millions sterling, half of which is with the same Malay States. At whatever figure we estimate the profits in this

British Trade with New Possessions.[1]	Imports from	Exports to
	£	£
Cyprus	83,842	132,445
Zanzibar Protectorate . .	114,088	88,777
British East Africa Protectorate (including Uganda) . . .	123,006	17,274
Somaliland	389,424[2]	333,842[2]
Southern Nigeria Protectorate . .	1,228,959	922,657
Northern Nigeria Protectorate . .	240,110	68,442
Lagos	641,203	366,171
Gambia	142,560	15,158
British North Borneo . . .	275,000	368,000
Malay Protected States . . .	4,100,000	6,211,000
Fiji	30,567	10,161
British Solomon Islands Protectorate	—	32,203
Gilbert and Ellice Islands Protectorate	20,359	21,502
British New Guinea . . .	—	62,891
Leeward Islands . . .	168,700	67,178
Windward Islands	739,095	305,224

trade, it forms an utterly insignificant part of our national income, while the expenses connected directly and indirectly with the acquisition, administration and defence of these possessions must swallow an immeasurably larger sum.

Apart from its quantity, the quality of the new tropical export trade was of the lowest, consisting for the most part, as the analysis of the Colonial Office shows, of the cheapest textile goods of Lancashire, the cheapest metal goods of Birmingham and Sheffield, and large quantities of gunpowder, spirits, and tobacco.

Such evidence leads to the following conclusions bearing upon the economics of the new Imperialism. First, the external trade of Great Britain bore a small and diminishing proportion to its internal industry and trade. Secondly, of the external trade, that with British possessions bore a diminishing proportion to that with foreign countries.

[1] Cd. 2395 and Cd. 2337.
[2] Trade with British possessions as well as with Great Britain is here included.

Thirdly, of the trade with British possessions the tropical trade, and in particular the trade with the new tropical possessions, was the smallest, least progressive, and most fluctuating in quantity, while it is lowest in the character of the goods which it embraces.

CHAPTER III

IMPERIALISM AS AN OUTLET
FOR POPULATION

THERE is a widely prevalent belief that imperial expansion is desirable, or even necessary, in order to absorb and utilize the surplus of our ever-growing population. "The reproductive powers of nature," runs the argument, "brook no restraint: the most dominant force in history is the tendency of population to overflow its ancient banks, seeking fuller and easier subsistence. Great Britain is one of the most congested areas in the world; her growing population cannot find enough remunerative occupation within these islands; professional and working-classes alike find it more and more difficult to earn a decent and secure living, every labour market is overstocked, emigration is a prime economic necessity. Now, those who under such pressure leave our shores consist largely of the strongest and most energetic stuff the nation contains. Many of these people, whose permanent alienation would be a heavy loss, have been saved to the Empire by the policy of imperial expansion : they have settled either in vacant places of the earth which they have seized and kept under British rule, or in places where they have set up a definitely British supremacy over lower races of existing inhabitants. (It is our most urgent national interest that this surplus emigrant population shall settle in lands which are under the British flag, and we must therefore maintain a constant policy of extending the political control of Great Britain so as to cover the new homes to which these people betake themselves in pursuit of employment." This motive is closely linked with other economic motives relating to trade and investments. The establishment of British trade, and especially of British capital, in foreign lands naturally attracts a certain British population; traders, engineers, overseers, and mechanics are needed as entrepreneurs and managers. So wherever a new area was opened up to our trade and capital the nucleus of an outlander population was formed. Hence, of necessity, sprang up a crop of political issues, an outlander problem: the British outlanders, not satisfied with the foreign rule, demanded the intervention of their home Government. Thus the duty of protecting British subjects in a foreign country has been identified with the duty of protecting British property, not merely the personal property of the outlanders, often a trivial matter, but the far larger stakes of the home investors. But apart from these cases of special interest, wherever any considerable number of British subjects settles in a savage or semi-civilized country they have a " right " to British protection, and since that protection can seldom be made effective without the exercise of direct British authority, the imperial ægis of Great Britain must be spread over all such areas, when a convenient occasion for such expansion should present itself.

Such has been the accepted theory and practice. What validity did it possess as an argument for imperial expansion ? Let me first ask: Was England over-populated, and was the prospect of further increase such as to compel us to " peg out claims for posterity " in other parts of the world ? The facts are these. Great Britain is not and was not so thickly populated as certain prosperous industrial areas in Germany, the Netherlands, and China : along with every recent growth of population has come a far greater growth of wealth and of the power to purchase food and other subsistence. The modern specialization of industry has caused a congestion of population upon certain spots which may be injurious in some ways to the well-being of the nation, but it cannot be regarded as over-population in the sense of a people outgrowing the means of subsistence. Nor have we reason to fear such over-population in the future. It is true that our manufactures and commerce may not continue to grow as rapidly as in the past, though we have no clear warrant from industrial statistics for this judgment : but if this be so, neither is our population likely to increase so fast. Of this we have clear statistical evidence : the diminution of the rate of growth of our population, as disclosed by the recent censuses, is such as to justify the conclusion that, if the same forces continue to operate, the population of Great Britain will be stationary by the middle of the century.

There exists, then, no general necessity for a policy of expansion in order to provide for over-population, present or prospective. But supposing it had been necessary for an increasing surplus of our population to emigrate, was it necessary for us to spend so large a part of our national resources, and to incur such heavy risks, in seizing new territory for them to settle upon ?

The total emigration of Britons represents no large proportion of the population ; that proportion during the years of imperial expansion perceptibly diminished : of the emigrants less than one-half settled in British possessions, and an infinitesimally small fraction settled in the countries acquired under the new Imperialism. These most instructive facts are established by the following official table, giving the statistics of emigration from 1884 to 1903, the year from which the full tide of imperial expansion is to be dated :—

NUMBER OF OUTWARD BOUND PASSENGERS OF BRITISH AND IRISH ORIGIN, FROM
THE UNITED KINGDOM TO COUNTRIES OUT OF EUROPE.[1]

Year.	Passengers to					Total.
	United States.	British North America.	Australia and New Zealand.	Cape of GoodHope and Natal.	Other Places.	
1884	155,280	31,134	44,255	—	11,510	242,179
1885	137,687	19,828	39,395	—	10,724	207,644
1886	152,710	24,745	43,076	3,897	8,472	232,900
1887	201,526	32,025	34,183	4,909	8,844	281,487
1888	195,986	34,853	31,127	6,466	11,496	279,928
1889	168,771	28,269	28,294	13,884	14,577	253,795
1890	152,413	22,520	21,179	10,321	11,683	218,116
1891	156,395	21,578	19,547	9,090	11,897	218,507
1892	150,039	23,254	15,950	9,891	10,908	210,042
1893	148,949	24,732	11,203	13,097	10,833	208,814
1894	104,001	17,459	10,917	13,177	10,476	156,030
1895	126,502	16,622	10,567	20,234	11,256	185,181
1896	98,921	15,267	10,354	24,594	12,789	161,925
1897	85,324	15,571	12,061	21,109	12,395	146,460
1898	80,494	17,640	10,693	19,756	12,061	140,644
1899	92,482	16,410	11,467	14,432	11,571	146,362
1900	102,797	18,443	14,922	20,815	11,848	168,825
1901	104,195	15,757	15,350	23,143	13,270	171,715
1902	108,498	26,293	14,345	43,206	13,370	205,662
1903	123,663	59,652	12,375	50,206	14,054	259,950

Regarded as a measure of the outflow of " surplus "
population, even these figures are excessive in two ways.
In the first place, they include considerable numbers of
travellers and casual visitors who were not real emigrants,
Secondly, to measure aright the net emigration, we must
set against these figures the immigration figures. The net
reduction of our population by emigration is thus reduced
to an average, during the years 1895–1900 to 31,474 per
annum.

The " boom " in North-West Canada and in the colonies

[1] Number of passengers for the years 1912–1934 are given in the Appendix,
p. 374.

of South Africa perceptibly increased the flow at the turn of the century. But the rest of our Empire has absorbed a very small proportion of our emigrants. The number sailing for " other parts " of the Empire in 1903 was 8,719, and of these the number of actual settlers in the new tropical dominions would be a mere handful.

A certain quantity of military and official employment is afforded by the new Imperialism to the influential upper classes, a few engineers, missionaries, prospectors, and overseers of trading and industrial undertakings get temporary posts, but as a contribution towards the general field of employment the new Imperialism is an utterly insignificant factor.

No substantial settlement of Britons was taking place in 1905 upon any of the areas of the Empire acquired since 1870, excepting the Transvaal and the Orange River Colony, nor was it likely that any such settlement would take place. The tropical character of most lands acquired under the new Imperialism renders genuine colonisation impossible : there was no true British settlement in these places ; a small number of men spent a short broken period in precarious occupations. The new Empire was even more barren for settlement than for profitable trade.

CHAPTER IV

ECONOMIC PARASITES OF IMPERIALISM

I

SEEING that the Imperialism of the last six decades is clearly condemned as a business policy, in that at enormous expense it has procured a small, bad, unsafe increase of markets, and has jeopardised the entire wealth of the nation in rousing the strong resentment of other nations, we may ask, " How is the British nation induced to embark upon such unsound business ? " The only possible answer is that the business interests of the nation as a whole are subordinated to those of certain sectional interests that usurp control of the national resources and use them for their private gain. This is no strange or monstrous charge to bring ; it is the commonest disease of all forms of government. The famous words of Sir Thomas More are as true now as when he wrote them : " Everywhere do I perceive a certain conspiracy of rich men seeking their own advantage under the name and pretext of the commonwealth."

Although the new Imperialism has been bad business for the nation, it has been good business for certain classes and certain trades within the nation. The vast expenditure on armaments, the costly wars, the grave risks and embarrassments of foreign policy, the checks upon political and social reforms within Great Britain, though fraught with great injury to the nation, have served well the present business interests of certain industries and professions.

It is idle to meddle with politics unless we clearly recognise this central fact and understand what these sectional interests are which are the enemies of national safety and the commonwealth. We must put aside the merely sentimental diagnosis which explains wars or other national blunders by outbursts of patriotic animosity or errors of statecraft. Doubtless at every outbreak of war not only the man in the street but the man at the helm is often duped by the cunning with which aggressive motives and greedy purposes dress themselves in defensive clothing. There is, it may be safely asserted, no war within memory, however nakedly aggressive it may seem to the dispassionate historian, which has not been presented to the people who were called upon to fight as a necessary defensive policy, in which the honour, perhaps the very existence, of the State was involved.

The disastrous folly of these wars, the material and moral damage inflicted even on the victor, appear so plain to the disinterested spectator that he is apt to despair of any State attaining years of discretion, and inclines to regard these natural cataclysms as implying some ultimate irrationalism in politics. But careful analysis of the existing relations between business and politics shows that the aggressive Imperialism which we seek to understand is not in the main the product of blind passions of races or of the mixed folly and ambition of politicians. It is far more rational than at first sight appears. Irrational from the standpoint of the whole nation, it is rational enough from the standpoint of certain classes in the nation. A completely socialist State which kept good books and presented regular balance-sheets of expenditure and assets would soon discard Imperialism ; an intelligent *laissez-faire* democracy which gave duly proportionate weight in its policy to all economic interests alike would do the same. But a State in which certain well-organised business interests are able to outweigh the weak, diffused interest of the community is bound to pursue a policy which accords with the pressure of the former interests.

In order to explain Imperialism on this hypothesis we have to answer two questions. Do we find in Great Britain any well-organised group of special commercial and social interests which stand to gain by aggressive Imperialism and the militarism it involves ? If such a combination of interests exists, has it the power to work its will in the arena of politics ?

What is the direct economic outcome of Imperialism ? A great expenditure of public money upon ships, guns, military and naval equipment and stores, growing and productive of enormous profits when a war, or an alarm of war, occurs ; new public loans and important fluctuations in the home and foreign Bourses ; more posts for soldiers and sailors and in the diplomatic and consular services ; improvement of foreign investments by the substitution of the British flag for a foreign flag ; acquisition of markets for certain classes of exports, and some protection and assistance for British trades in these manufactures ; employment for engineers, missionaries, speculative miners, ranchers and other emigrants.

Certain definite business and professional interests feeding upon imperialistic expenditure, or upon the results of that expenditure, are thus set up in opposition to the common good, and, instinctively feeling their way to one another, are found united in strong sympathy to support every new imperialist exploit.

If the £60,000,000[1] which may now be taken as a minimum expenditure on armaments in time of peace were subjected to a close analysis, most of it would be traced directly to

[1] In 1905; now, in 1938, £200,000,000.

the tills of certain big firms engaged in building warships and transports, equipping and coaling them, manufacturing guns, rifles, ammunition, 'planes and motor vehicles of every kind, supplying horses, waggons, saddlery, food, clothing for the services, contracting for barracks, and for other large irregular needs. Through these main channels the millions flow to feed many subsidiary trades, most of which are quite aware that they are engaged in executing contracts for the services. Here we have an important nucleus of commercial Imperialism. Some of these trades, especially the shipbuilding, boilermaking, and gun and ammunition making trades, are conducted by large firms with immense capital, whose heads are well aware of the uses of political influence for trade purposes.

These men are Imperialists by conviction ; a pushful policy is good for them.

With them stand the great manufacturers for export trade, who gain a living by supplying the real or artificial wants of the new countries we annex or open up. Manchester, Sheffield, Birmingham, to name three representative cases, are full of firms which compete in pushing textiles and hardware, engines, tools, machinery, spirits, guns, upon new markets. The public debts which ripen in our colonies, and in foreign countries that come under our protectorate or influence, are largely loaned in the shape of rails, engines, guns, and other materials of civilization made and sent out by British firms. The making of railways, canals, and other public works, the establishment of factories, the development of mines, the improvement of agriculture in new countries, stimulate a definite interest in important manufacturing industries which feeds a very firm imperialist faith in their owners.

The proportion which such trade bears to the total industry of Great Britain is not great, but some of it is extremely influential and able to make a definite impression upon politics, through chambers of commerce, Parliamentary representatives, and semi-political, semi-commercial bodies like the Imperial South African Association or the China Society.

The shipping trade has a very definite interest which makes for Imperialism. This is well illustrated by the policy of State subsidies now claimed by shipping firms as a retainer, and in order to encourage British shipping for purposes of imperial safety and defence.

The services are, of course, imperialist by conviction and by professional interest, and every increase of the army, navy and air force enhances the political power they exert. The abolition of purchase in the army, by opening the profession to the upper middle classes, greatly enlarged this most direct feeder of imperial sentiment. The potency of this factor is, of course, largely due to the itch for glory and adventure among military officers upon disturbed or uncertain frontiers of the Empire. This has been a most prolific source of expansion in India. The direct professional influence of the services carries with it a less organised but powerful sympathetic support on the part of the aristocracy and the wealthy classes, who seek in the services careers for their sons.

To the military services we may add the Indian Civil Service and the numerous official and semi-official posts in our colonies and protectorates. Every expansion of the Empire is also regarded by these same classes as affording new openings for their sons as ranchers, planters, engineers, or missionaries. This point of view is aptly summarised by a high Indian official, Sir Charles Crossthwaite, in discussing British relations with Siam. " The real question was who was to get the trade with them, and how we could make the most of them, so as to find fresh markets for our goods and also employment for those superfluous articles of the present day, our boys."

From this standpoint our colonies still remain what James Mill cynically described them as being, "a vast system of outdoor relief for the upper classes."

In all the professions, military and civil, the army, diplomacy, the church, the bar, teaching and engineering, Greater Britain serves for an overflow, relieving the congestion of the home market and offering chances to more reckless or adventurous members, while it furnishes a convenient limbo for damaged characters and careers. The actual amount of profitable employment thus furnished by our recent acquisitions is inconsiderable, but it arouses that disproportionate interest which always attaches to the margin of employment. To extend this margin is a powerful motive in Imperialism.

These influences, primarily economic, though not unmixed with other sentimental motives, are particularly operative in military, clerical, academic, and Civil Service circles, and furnish an interested bias towards Imperialism throughout the educated circles.

II

By far the most important economic factor in Imperialism is the influence relating to investments. The growing cosmopolitanism of capital has been the greatest economic change of recent generations. Every advanced industrial nation has been tending to place a larger share of its capital outside the limits of its own political area, in foreign countries, or in colonies, and to draw a growing income from this source.

No exact or even approximate estimate of the total amount of the income of the British nation derived from foreign investments is possible. We possess, however, in the income tax assessments an indirect measurement of certain large sections of investments, from which we can form some judgment as to the total size of the income from foreign and colonial sources, and the rate of its growth.

These returns give us a measure of the amount and growth of the investments effected by British citizens in foreign and colonial stocks of a public or semi-public character, including foreign and colonial public securities, railways, etc. The income from these sources is computed as follows :—[1]

	£
1884	33,829,124
1888	46,978,371
1892	54,728,770
1896	54,901,079
1900	60,266,886
1903	63,828,715

From this table it appears that the period of energetic Imperialism coincided with a remarkable growth in the income for foreign investments.

These figures, however, only give the foreign income which can be identified as such. The closer estimates made by Sir R. Giffen and others warrant the belief that the actual income derived from foreign and colonial investments amounted to not less than £100,000,000, the capital value of the same reaching a sum of about £2,000,000,000.[2]

Income tax returns and other statistics descriptive of the growth of these investments indicate that the total amount of British investments abroad at the end of the nineteenth century cannot be set down at a lower figure

[1] Figures for the years 1929–1933 are given in the Appendix, p. 375
[2] See Appendix, p. 375.

than this. Considering that Sir R. Giffen regarded as "moderate" the estimate of £1,700,000,000 in 1892, the figure here named is probably below the truth.

Now, without placing any undue reliance upon these estimates, we cannot fail to recognise that in dealing with these foreign investments we are facing the most important factor in the economics of Imperialism. Whatever figures we take, two facts are evident. First, that the income derived as interest upon foreign investments enormously exceeded that derived as profits upon ordinary export and import trade. Secondly, that while our foreign and colonial trade, and presumably the income from it, were growing but slowly, the share of our import values representing income from foreign investments was growing very rapidly.

In a former chapter I pointed out how small a proportion of our national income appeared to be derived as profits from external trade. It seemed unintelligible that the enormous costs and risks of the new Imperialism should be undertaken for such small results in the shape of increase to external trade, especially when the size and character of the new markets acquired were taken into consideration. The statistics of foreign investments, however, shed clear light upon the economic forces which dominate our policy. While the manufacturing and trading classes make little out of their new markets, paying, if they knew it, much more in taxation than they get out of them in trade, it is quite otherwise with the investor.

It is not too much to say that the modern foreign policy of Great Britain has been primarily a struggle for profitable markets of investment. To a larger extent every year Great Britain has been becoming a nation living upon tribute from abroad, and the classes who enjoy this tribute have had an ever-increasing incentive to employ the public policy, the public purse, and the public force to extend the field of their private investments, and to safeguard and improve their existing investments. This is, perhaps, the most important fact in modern politics, and the obscurity in which it is wrapped has constituted the gravest danger to our State.

What was true of Great Britain was true likewise of France, Germany, the United States, and of all countries in which modern capitalism had placed large surplus savings in the hands of a plutocracy or of a thrifty middle class. A well-recognised distinction is drawn between creditor and debtor countries. Great Britain had been for some time by far the largest creditor country, and the policy by which the investing classes used the instrument of the State for private business purposes is most richly illustrated in the history of her wars and annexations. But France, Germany, and the United States were advancing fast along the same path. The nature of these imperialist operations is thus set forth by the Italian economist Loria :

" When a country which has contracted a debt is unable, on account of the slenderness of its income, to offer sufficient guarantee for the punctual payment of interest, what happens ? Sometimes an out-and-out conquest of the debtor country follows. Thus France's attempted conquest of Mexico during the second empire was undertaken solely with the view of guaranteeing the interest of French citizens holding Mexican securities. But more frequently the insufficient guarantee of an international loan gives rise to the appointment of a financial commission by the creditor countries in order to protect their rights and guard the fate of their invested capital. The appointment of such a commission literally amounts in the end, however, to a veritable conquest. We have examples of this in Egypt, which has to all practical purposes become a British province, and in Tunis, which has in like manner become a dependency of France, who supplied the greater part of the loan. The Egyptian revolt against the foreign domination issuing from the debt came to nothing, as it met with invariable opposition from capitalistic combinations, and Tel-el-Kebir's success bought with money, was the most brilliant victory wealth has ever obtained on the field of battle."[1]

But, though useful to explain certain economic facts, the terms " creditor " and " debtor," as applied to countries, obscure the most significant feature of this Imperialism. For though, as appears from the analysis given above, much, if not most, of the debts were " public," the credit was nearly always private, though sometimes, as in the case of Egypt, its owners succeeded in getting their Government to enter a most unprofitable partnership, guaranteeing the payment of the interest, but not sharing in it.

Aggressive Imperialism, which costs the taxpayer so dear, which is of so little value to the manufacturer and trader, which is fraught with such grave incalculable peril to the citizen, is a source of great gain to the investor who cannot find at home the profitable use he seeks for his capital, and insists that his Government should help him to profitable and secure investments abroad.

If, contemplating the enormous expenditure on armaments, the ruinous wars, the diplomatic audacity or knavery by which modern Governments seek to extend their territorial power, we put the plain, practical question, *Cui bono ?* the first and most obvious answer is, the investor.

The annual income Great Britain derives from commissions on her whole foreign and colonial trade, import and export, was estimated by Sir R. Giffen[2] at £18,000,000 for 1899, taken at 2½ per cent., upon a turnover of £800,000,000.

---

[1] Loria, *The Economic Foundations of Politics*, p. 273 (George Allen & Unwin).
[2] *Journal of the Statistical Society*, vol. xlii, p. 9.

This is the whole that we are entitled to regard as profits on external trade. Considerable as this sum is, it cannot serve to yield an economic motive-power adequate to explain the dominance which business considerations exercise over our imperial policy. Only when we set beside it some £90,000,000 or £100,000,000, representing pure profit upon investments, do we understand whence the economic impulse to Imperialism is derived.

Investors who have put their money in foreign lands, upon terms which take full account of risks connected with the political conditions of the country, desire to use the resources of their Government to minimise these risks, and so to enhance the capital value and the interest of their private investments. The investing and speculative classes in general have also desired that Great Britain should take other foreign areas under her flag in order to secure new areas for profitable investments and speculation.

III

If the special interest of the investor is liable to clash with the public interest and to induce a wrecking policy, still more dangerous is the special interest of the financier, the general dealer in investments. In large measure the rank and file of the investors are, both for business and for politics, the cat'spaws of the great financial houses, who use stocks and shares not so much as investments to yield them interest, but as material for speculation in the money market. In handling large masses of stocks and shares, in floating companies, in manipulating fluctuations of values, the magnates of the Bourse find their gain. These great businesses—banking, broking, bill discounting, loan floating, company promoting—form the central ganglion of international capitalism. United by the strongest bonds of organisation, always in closest and quickest touch with one another, situated in the very heart of the business capital of every State, controlled, so far as Europe is concerned, chiefly by men of a single and peculiar race, who have behind them many centuries of financial experience, they are in a unique position to manipulate the policy of nations. No great quick direction of capital is possible save by their consent and through their agency. Does any one seriously suppose that a great war could be undertaken by any European State, or a great State loan subscribed, if the house of Rothschild and its connexions set their face against it ?

Every great political act involving a new flow of capital, or a large fluctuation in the values of existing investments, must receive the sanction and the practical aid of this little group of financial kings. These men, holding their realised wealth and their business capital, as they must, chiefly in stocks and bonds, have a double stake, first as investors, but secondly and chiefly as financial dealers. As investors, their political influence does not differ essentially from that of the smaller investors, except that they usually possess a practical control of the businesses in which they invest. As speculators or financial dealers they constitute, however, the gravest single factor in the economics of Imperialism.

To create new public debts, to float new companies, and to cause constant considerable fluctuations of values are three conditions of their profitable business. Each condition carries them into politics, and throws them on the side of Imperialism.

The public financial arrangements for the Philippine war put several millions of dollars into the pockets of Mr. Pierpont Morgan and his friends ; the China-Japan war, which saddled the Celestial Empire for the first time with a public debt, and the indemnity which she

will pay to her European invaders in connexion with the
recent conflict, bring grist to the financial mills in Europe ;
every railway or mining concession wrung from some
reluctant foreign potentate means profitable business in
raising capital and floating companies. A policy which
rouses fears of aggression in Asiatic states, and which
fans the rivalry of commercial nations in Europe, evokes
vast expenditure on armaments, and ever-accumulating
public debts, while the doubts and risks accruing from
this policy promote that constant oscillation of values of
securities which is so profitable to the skilled financier.
There is not a war, a revolution, an anarchist assassination,
or any other public shock, which is not gainful to these
men ; they are harpies who suck their gains from every
new forced expenditure and every sudden disturbance of
public credit. To the financiers " in the know " the
Jameson raid was a most advantageous coup, as may be
ascertained by a comparison of the " holdings " of these
men before and after that event ; the terrible sufferings
of England and South Africa in the war, which was a sequel
of the raid, has been a source of immense profit to the big
financiers who have best held out against the uncalculated
waste, and have recouped themselves by profitable war
contracts and by " freezing out " the smaller interests in
the Transvaal. These men are the only certain gainers
from the war, and most of their gains are made out of
the public losses of their adopted country or the private
losses of their fellow-countrymen.

The policy of these men, it is true, does not necessarily
make for war ; where war would bring about too great and
too permanent a damage to the substantial fabric of industry,
which is the ultimate and essential basis of speculation, their
influence is cast for peace, as in the dangerous quarrel
between Great Britain and the United States regarding

Venezuela. But every increase of public expenditure, every oscillation of public credit short of this collapse, every risky enterprise in which public resources can be made the pledge of private speculations, is profitable to the big money-lender and speculator.

The wealth of these houses, the scale of their operations, and their cosmopolitan organisation make them the prime determinants of imperial policy. They have the largest definite stake in the business of Imperialism, and the amplest means of forcing their will upon the policy of nations.

In view of the part which the non-economic factors of patriotism, adventure, military enterprise, political ambition, and philanthropy play in imperial expansion, it may appear that to impute to financiers so much power is to take a too narrowly economic view of history. And it is true that the motor-power of Imperialism is not chiefly financial: finance is rather the governor of the imperial engine, directing the energy and determining its work : it does not constitute the fuel of the engine, nor does it directly generate the power. Finance manipulates the patriotic forces which politicians, soldiers, philanthropists, and traders generate; the enthusiasm for expansion which issues from these sources, though strong and genuine, is irregular and blind; the financial interest has those qualities of concentration and clear-sighted calculation which are needed to set Imperialism to work. An ambitious statesman, a frontier soldier, an overzealous missionary, a pushing trader, may suggest or even initiate a step of imperial expansion, may assist in educating patriotic public opinion to the urgent need of some fresh advance, but the final determination rests with the financial power. The direct influence exercised by great financial houses in " high politics " is supported by the control which they exercise over the body of public opinion through the Press, which, in every " civilised " country, is becoming more and more their obedient instrument. While the specifically financial newspaper imposes " facts " and " opinions " on the business classes, the general body of the Press comes more and more under the conscious or unconscious domination of financiers. The case of the South African Press, whose agents and correspondents fanned the martial flames in this country, was one of open ownership on the part of South African financiers, and this policy of owning newspapers for the sake of manufacturing public opinion is common in the great European cities. In Berlin, Vienna, and Paris many of the influential newspapers have been held by financial houses, which used them, not primarily to make direct profits out of them, but in order to put into the public mind beliefs and sentiments which would influence public policy and thus affect the money market. In Great Britain this policy has not gone so far, but the alliance with finance grows closer every year, either by financiers purchasing a controlling share of newspapers, or by newspaper proprietors being tempted into finance. Apart from the financial Press, and financial ownership of the general Press, the City has notoriously exercised a subtle and abiding influence upon leading London newspapers, and through them upon the body of the provincial Press, while the entire dependence of the Press for its business profits upon its advertising columns has involved a peculiar reluctance to oppose the organised financial classes with whom rests the control of so much advertising business. Add to this the natural sympathy with a sensational policy which a cheap Press always manifests, and it becomes evident that the Press has been strongly biased towards Imperialism, and has lent itself with great facility to the suggestion of financial or political Imperialists who have desired to work up patriotism for some new piece of expansion.

Such is the array of distinctively economic forces making for Imperialism, a large loose group of trades and professions seeking profitable business and lucrative employment from the expansion of military and civil services, and from the expenditure on military operations, the opening up of new tracts of territory and trade with the same, and the provision of new capital which these operations require, all these finding their central guiding and directing force in the power of the general financier.

The play of these forces does not openly appear. They are essentially parasites upon patriotism, and they adapt themselves to its protecting colours. In the mouth of their representatives are noble phrases, expressive of their desire to extend the area of civilisation, to establish good government, promote Christianity, extirpate slavery, and elevate the lower races. Some of the business men who hold such language may entertain a genuine, though usually a vague, desire to accomplish these ends, but they are primarily engaged in business, and they are not unaware of the utility of the more unselfish forces in furthering their ends. Their true attitude of mind was expressed by Mr. Rhodes in his famous description of "Her Majesty's Flag" as "the greatest commercial asset in the world."[1]

APPENDIX

Sir R. Giffen estimated the income derived from foreign sources as profit, interest and pensions in 1882 at £70,000,000, and in a paper read before the Statistical Society in March, 1899 he estimated the income from the same sources for the

[1] It will be observed that this, like not a few other words of revelation, has been doctored in the volume, *Cecil Rhodes : his Political Life and Speeches*, by "Vindex" (p. 823).

current year at £90,000,000. It is probable that this last figure is an underestimate, for if the items of foreign income not included as such under the income-tax returns bear the same proportion to those included as in 1882, the total of income from foreign and colonial investments should be £120,000,000 rather than £90,000,000. Sir R. Giffen hazarded the calculation that the new public investments abroad in the sixteen years 1882–1898 amounted to over £800,000,000, " and though part of the sum may have been nominal only, the real investment must have been enormous."

Mr. Mulhall gave the following estimate of the size and growth of our foreign and colonial investments after 1862 :

Year.				Amount.	Annual Increase.
				£	Per cent.
1862	.	.	.	.	144,000,000	—
1872	.	.	.	.	600,000,000	45·6
1882	.	.	.	.	875,000,000	27·5
1893	.	.	.	.	1,698,000,000	74·8

This last amount is of especial interest, because it represents the most thorough investigation made by a most competent economist for the *Dictionary of Political Economy*. The investments included under this figure may be classified under the following general heads :—

Loans.	Million £.	Railways.	Million £.	Sundries.	Million £.
Foreign .	525	U.S.A. .	120	Banks .	50
Colonial .	225	Colonial .	140	Lands .	100
Municipal .	20	Various .	128	Mines, &c. .	390
	770		388		540

In other words, in 1893 the British capital invested abroad represented about 15 per cent. of the total wealth of the United Kingdom; nearly one-half of this capital was in the form of loans to foreign and colonial Governments; of the rest a large proportion was invested in railways, banks, telegraphs, and other public services, owned, controlled, or vitally affected by Governments, while most of the remainder was placed in lands and mines, or in industries directly dependent on land values.[1]

[1] Total (Nominal) British investments overseas for the years 1929–1933 are given in the Appendix, p. 375.

CHAPTER V

IMPERIALISM BASED ON PROTECTION

A BUSINESS man estimating the value of an extension of his business will set the increased costs against the increased takings. Is it unreasonable that a business nation should adopt the same course? From this standpoint our increased military and naval expenditure during recent years may be regarded primarily as insurance premiums for protection of existing colonial markets and current outlay on new markets.

In order to test the finance of the new Imperialism, let us compare the growth of expenditure on armaments and wars since 1884 with the increased value of colonial trade[1] (page 65).

Now, though there are no means of ear-marking the expenditure which might rank as insurance upon old markets or that which is spent upon acquiring new markets, it is not unreasonable to saddle the new Imperialism with the whole of the increase and to set against it the value of the trade of the new acquisitions. For though it might be claimed that the aggressive commercialism of rival European States raised the insurance rate upon the old markets, it cannot be contended that Great Britain's expenditure on armaments need have increased had she adopted firmly and consistently the full practice of Cobdenism, a purely defensive attitude regarding her existing Empire and a total abstinence from acquisition of new territory. The increased hostility of foreign nations towards us in the last thirty

[1] Figures for the years 1904–1931 are given in the Appendix, p. 376.

Year.	Armaments and War.	Colonial Trade. Import and Export Trade with Possessions.
	£	£
1884	27,864,000	184,000,000
1885	30,577,000	170,000,000
1886	39,538,000	164,000,000
1887	31,768,000	166,000,000
1888	30,609,000	179,000,000
1889	30,536,000	188,000,000
1890	32,772,000	191,000,000
1891	33,488,000	193,00,0000
1892	33,312,000	179,000,000
1893	33,423,000	170,000,000
1894	33,566,000	172,000,000
1895	35,593,000	172,000,000
1896	38,334,000	184,000,000
1897	41,453,000	183,000,000
1898	40,395,000	190,000,000
1899	64,283,000	201,000,000
1900	69,815,000	212,000,000
1901	121,445,000	219,000,000
1902	123,787,000	223,000,000
1903	100,825,000	232,000,000

years of the nineteenth century may be regarded as entirely due to the aggressive Imperialism of those years, and the increased expenditure on armaments may, therefore, reasonably rank in a business balance-sheet as a cost of that policy.

So, taken, this new expenditure was nothing else than a huge business blunder. An individual doing business in this fashion could not avoid bankruptcy, and a nation, however rich, pursuing such a policy is loaded with a millstone which must eventually drag her down.

In total contravention of our theory that trade rests upon a basis of mutual gain to the nations that engage in it, we undertook enormous expenses with the object of " forcing " new markets, and the markets we forced were small, precarious, and unprofitable. The only certain and palpable result of the expenditure was to keep us continually embroiled with the very nations that were our best customers, and with whom, in spite of everything, our trade made the most satisfactory advance.

Not only were these markets not worth what they cost us, but the assumption that our trade would have been proportionately less had they fallen into the hands of rival and Protectionist nations is quite groundless. If, instead of squandering money upon these territorial acquisitions, we had let any or all of them pass into the possession of France, Germany, or Russia, in order that these countries might spend their money, instead of us spending our money, in acquiring and developing them, is it certain that our foreign trade would not have grown by at least as much as our colonial trade might have shrunk ? The assumption that there is only a given quantity of trade, and that if one nation gets any portion of it another nation loses just so much, shows a blind ignorance of the elements of international trade. It arises from a curiously perverse form of separatism which insists upon a nation keeping a separate account with every other nation, and ignoring altogether the roundabout trade which is by far the most important business of an advanced industrial nation.

France seizing Madagascar practically extirpated direct British trade with the Malagasy ; Germany, by her occupation of Shan-tung, deprived us of all possibility of trade with this Chinese province. But it by no means followed that France and Germany could or would keep to themselves the whole advantage of these new markets. To make any such supposition implies a complete abandonment of the principles of Free Trade. Even were the whole of China portioned out among the other industrial nations, each imposing tariffs which virtually prohibited direct trade between Great Britain and China—the most extreme assumption of a hostile attitude—it by no means follows that England would not reap enormous benefits from the expansion of her foreign trade, attributable in the last resort to the opening up of China. Even the feeblest recognition of the intricacies of foreign trade should make us aware that an increased trade with France, Germany, or Russia, either directly or through other nations trading with them might have given us our full share of the wealth of Chinese trade, and proved as beneficial as any direct share of trade with China which at great expense and peril we might have secured. The assignment of spheres of influence in China or in Africa to France, Germany, or Russia, which they might have sought to monopolise for purposes of trade, does not imply, as seems to be believed, a corresponding loss of markets to England. The intricate and ever-growing industrial co-operation of the civilized nations through trade does not permit any nation to keep to herself the gain of any market she may hold. It is not difficult to conceive cases where another nation might enjoy a larger share of the results of a trade than the nation which owned the private markets of this trade.

These were the commonplaces of the economics of Free Trade, the plainest lessons of enlightened common sense. Why were they forgotten ?

The answer is that Imperialism repudiates Free Trade, and rests upon an economic basis of Protection. Just in so far as an Imperialist is logical does he become an open and avowed Protectionist.

If the fact of France or Germany seizing for its exclusive use a market which we might have seized necessarily reduces our aggregate external trade by the amount of this market, it is only reasonable that when we seize a territory we should take the same means to keep its market for ourselves.

F

Imperialism, when it shakes off the " old gang " of politicians who had swallowed Free Trade doctrine when they were young, openly adopts the Protectionism required to round off this policy.

Imperialism naturally strives to fasten to the mother country the markets of each new territorial acquisition, convinced that only by such separate increments can the aggregate of our trade grow; and by the success of this policy it must justify the enormous national outlay which Imperialism involves. Free Trade trusts for the increase of our foreign trade to the operation of the self-interest of other trading nations. Her doctrine is that, though it were better for us and for them that they should give us free admission to their colonial and home markets, their protective tariff, even though it prohibits us from trading directly with their colonies, does not shut us out from all the benefits of their colonial development. Through the ordinary operation of competition in European markets the rubber trade which France does in East Africa helps to increase the supply and to keep down the price of rubber for English consumers, just as the bounties which continental countries pay to sugar producers enable British boys and girls to enjoy cheap sweets.

There is, then, nothing vaguely hypothetical about these indirect gains. Every business man can trace certain concrete advantages of goods and prices which come to us from the development of colonies by Protectionist countries. The " open door " is an advantage to our trade, but not a necessity. If we have to spend vast sums and incur vast risks in keeping " doors open " against the wishes of our best customers, it is more profitable to let them close these doors and take our gain by the more indirect but equally certain processes of roundabout trade. At present Great Britain is in a stronger position than any other nation to practise this policy of abstinence, because she possesses in her carrying trade by sea a most effective guarantee that she will obtain an adequate share of the net gains from new markets opened up by foreign nations. Though no complete statistics are available, it is known that a very large proportion of the trade, not only between England and foreign countries, but between foreign countries trading among themselves and with their possessions, is carried by British ships. So long as this continues, England, apart from her share obtained in roundabout trade, must participate directly and in a most important manner in the trade advantages of foreign markets belonging to our European trade competitors.

These considerations ought to make us willing that other nations should do their share of expansion and development, well contented to await the profit which must accrue to us from every increase of world-wealth through ordinary processes of exchange. We have done our share, and more, of the costly, laborious, and dangerous work of opening up new countries to the general trade of Western industrial nations ; our later ventures were more expensive and less profitable to us than the earlier ones, and further labours of expansion seemed to conform to a law of diminishing returns, yielding smaller and more precarious increments of trade to a larger outlay of material and intellectual capital. Had we not reached, or even passed, the limit of the most profitable outlay of our national energy and resources ? Will not enlightened self-interest impel us to leave to other active and ambitious nations—France, Russia, Germany, Japan—the work of developing new tropical or sub-tropical countries ? If it is necessary that Western industrial civilization shall undertake the political and commercial management of the whole world, let these nations take their share. Why should we do all the work and get so little from it ? On the assumption that backward countries must be developed by foreign countries for the general good, a reasonable economy of power will apportion the work which remains to the " Imperialism " of other nations. Even if these other nations were disposed to shirk their share, it would pay us better to persuade them to undertake it rather than further to load our overladen shoulders. Since these other nations are not only eager to do their share, but by their jealousy at our undertaking their work continually threaten to wreck the peace of Europe, it seems sheer madness for Great Britain to weaken herself politically and financially by any further process of expansion.

CHAPTER VI

THE ECONOMIC TAPROOT OF IMPERIALISM

NO mere array of facts and figures adduced to illustrate the economic nature of the new Imperialism will suffice to dispel the popular delusion that the use of national force to secure new markets by annexing fresh tracts of territory is a sound and a necessary policy for an advanced industrial country like Great Britain.[1] It has indeed been proved that recent annexations of tropical countries, procured at great expense, have furnished poor and precarious markets, that our aggregate trade with our colonial possessions is virtually stationary, and that our most profitable and progressive trade is with rival industrial nations, whose territories we have no desire to annex, whose markets we cannot force, and whose active antagonism we are provoking by our expansive policy.

But these arguments are not conclusive. It is open to Imperialists to argue thus : " We must have markets for our growing manufactures, we must have new outlets for the investment of our surplus capital and for the energies of the adventurous surplus of our population : such expansion is a necessity of life to a nation with our great and growing powers of production. An ever larger share of our population is devoted to the manufactures and commerce of towns, and is thus dependent for life and work upon food and raw

[1] Written in 1905.

materials from foreign lands. In order to buy and pay for these things we must sell our goods abroad. During the first three-quarters of the nineteenth century we could do so without difficulty by a natural expansion of commerce with continental nations and our colonies, all of which were far behind us in the main arts of manufacture and the carrying trades. So long as England held a virtual monopoly of the world markets for certain important classes of manufactured goods, Imperialism was unnecessary. After 1870 this manufacturing and trading supremacy was greatly impaired: other nations, especially Germany, the United States, and Belgium, advanced with great rapidity, and while they have not crushed or even stayed the increase of our external trade, their competition made it more and more difficult to dispose of the full surplus of our manufactures at a profit. The encroachments made by these nations upon our old markets, even in our own possessions, made it most urgent that we should take energetic means to secure new markets. These new markets had to lie in hitherto undeveloped countries, chiefly in the tropics, where vast populations lived capable of growing economic needs which our manufacturers and merchants could supply. Our rivals were seizing and annexing territories for similar purposes, and when they had annexed them closed them to our trade. The diplomacy and the arms of Great Britain had to be used in order to compel the owners of the new markets to deal with us: and experience showed that the safest means of securing and developing such markets is by establishing 'protectorates' or by annexation. The value in 1905 of these markets must not be taken as a final test of the economy of such a policy; the process of educating civilized needs which we can supply is of necessity a gradual one, and the cost of such Imperialism must be regarded as a capital outlay, the fruits of which posterity would reap. The new markets might not be large, but they formed serviceable outlets for the overflow of our great textile and metal industries, and, when the vast Asiatic and African populations of the interior were reached, a rapid expansion of trade was expected to result.

" Far larger and more important is the pressure of capital for external fields of investment. Moreover, while the manufacturer and trader are well content to trade with foreign nations, the tendency for investors to work towards the political annexation of countries which contain their more speculative investments is very powerful. Of the fact of this pressure of capital there can be no question. Large savings are made which cannot find any profitable investment in this country; they must find employment elsewhere, and it is to the advantage of the nation that they should be employed as largely as possible in lands where they can be utilized in opening up markets for British trade and employment for British enterprise.

" However costly, however perilous, this process of imperial expansion may be, it is necessary to the continued existence and progress of our nation;[1] if we abandoned it we must be content to leave the development of the world to other nations, who will everywhere cut into our trade, and even impair our means of securing the food and raw materials we require to support our population. Imperialism is thus seen to be, not a choice, but a necessity."

The practical force of this economic argument in politics is strikingly illustrated by the later history of the United States. Here is a country which suddenly broke through a conservative policy, strongly held by both political parties,

---

[1] " And why, indeed, are wars undertaken, if not to conquer colonies which permit the employment of fresh capital, to acquire commercial monopolies, or to obtain the exclusive use of certain highways of commerce ? " (Loria, *Economic Foundations of Society*, p. 267).

bound up with every popular instinct and tradition, and flung itself into a rapid imperial career for which it possessed neither the material nor the moral equipment, risking the principles and practices of liberty and equality by the establishment of militarism and the forcible subjugation of peoples which it could not safely admit to the condition of American citizenship.

Was this a mere wild freak of spread-eaglism, a burst of political ambition on the part of a nation coming to a sudden realization of its destiny? Not at all. The spirit of adventure, the American " mission of civilization," were as forces making for Imperialism, clearly subordinate to the driving force of the economic factor. The dramatic character of the change is due to the unprecedented rapidity of the industrial revolution in the United States from the eighties onwards. During that period the United States, with her unrivalled natural resources, her immense resources of skilled and unskilled labour, and her genius for invention and organization, developed the best equipped and most productive manufacturing economy the world has yet seen. Fostered by rigid protective tariffs, her metal, textile, tool, clothing, furniture, and other manufactures shot up in a single generation from infancy to full maturity, and, having passed through a period of intense competition, attained, under the able control of great trust-makers, a power of production greater than has been attained in the most advanced industrial countries of Europe.

An era of cut-throat competition, followed by a rapid process of amalgamation, threw an enormous quantity of wealth into the hands of a small number of captains of industry. No luxury of living to which this class could attain kept pace with its rise of income, and a process of automatic saving set in upon an unprecedented scale. The investment of these savings in other industries helped to bring these under the same concentrative forces. Thus a great increase of savings seeking profitable investment is synchronous with a stricter economy of the use of existing capital. No doubt the rapid growth of a population, accustomed to a high and an always ascending standard of comfort, absorbs in the satisfaction of its wants a large quantity of new capital. But the actual rate of saving, conjoined with a more economical application of forms of existing capital, exceeded considerably the rise of the national consumption of manufactures. The power of production far outstripped the actual rate of consumption, and, contrary to the older economic theory, was unable to force a corresponding increase of consumption by lowering prices.

This is no mere theory. The history of any of the numerous trusts or combinations in the United States sets out the facts with complete distinctness. In the free competition of manufactures preceding combination the chronic condition is one of " over-production," in the sense that all the mills or factories can only be kept at work by cutting prices down towards a point where the weaker competitors are forced to close down, because they cannot sell their goods at a price which covers the true cost of production. The first result of the successful formation of a trust or combine is to close down the worse equipped or worse placed mills, and supply the entire market from the better equipped and better placed ones. This course may or may not be attended by a rise of price and some restriction of consumption : in some cases trusts take most of their profits by raising prices, in other cases by reducing the costs of production through employing only the best mills and stopping the waste of competition.

For the present argument it matters not which course is taken ; the point is that this concentration of industry in " trusts," " combines," etc., at once limits the quantity of capital which can be effectively employed and increases the share of profits out of which fresh savings and fresh capital will spring. It is quite evident that a trust which is motived by cut-throat competition, due to an excess of capital, cannot normally find inside the " trusted " industry employment for that portion of the profits which the trust-makers desire to save and to invest. New inventions and other economies of production or distribution within the trade may absorb some of the new capital, but there are rigid limits to this absorption. The trust-maker in oil or sugar must find other investments for his savings : if he is early in the application of the combination principles to his trade, he will naturally apply his surplus capital to establish similar combinations in other industries, econo-mising capital still further, and rendering it ever harder for ordinary saving men to find investments for their savings.

Indeed, the conditions alike of cut-throat competition and of combination attest the congestion of capital in the manufacturing industries which have entered the machine economy. We are not here concerned with any theoretic question as to the possibility of producing by modern machine methods more goods than can find a market. It is sufficient to point out that the manufacturing power of a country like the United States would grow so fast as to exceed the demands of the home market. No one acquainted with trade will deny a fact which all American economists assert, that this is the condition which the United States reached at the end of the century, so far, as the more developed industries are concerned. Her manufactures were saturated with capital and could absorb no more. One after another they sought refuge from the waste of competition in " combines " which secure a measure of profitable peace by restricting the quantity of operative capital. Industrial and financial princes in oil, steel, sugar, railroads, banking, etc., were faced with the dilemma of either spending more than they knew how to spend, or forcing markets outside the home area. Two economic courses were open to them, both leading towards an abandonment of the political isolation of the past and the adoption of imperialist methods in the future. Instead of shutting down inferior mills and rigidly restricting output to correspond with profitable sales in the home markets, they might employ their full productive power, applying their savings to increase their business capital, and, while still regulating output and prices for the home market, may "hustle" for foreign markets, dumping down their surplus goods at prices which would not be possible save for the profitable nature of their home market. So likewise they might employ their savings in seeking investments outside their country, first repaying the capital borrowed from Great Britain and other countries for the early development of their railroads, mines and manufactures, and afterwards becoming themselves a creditor class to foreign countries.

It was this sudden demand for foreign markets for manufactures and for investments which was avowedly responsible for the adoption of Imperialism as a political policy and practice by the Republican party to which the great industrial and financial chiefs belonged, and which belonged to them. The adventurous enthusiasm of President Theodore Roosevelt and his " manifest destiny " and " mission of civilization " party must not deceive us. It was Messrs. Rockefeller, Pierpont Morgan, and their associates who needed Imperialism and who fastened it upon the shoulders of the great Republic of the West. They needed Imperialism because they desired to use the public resources of their country to find profitable employment for their capital which otherwise would be superfluous.

It is not indeed necessary to own a country in order to do trade with it or to invest capital in it, and doubtless the United States could find some vent for their surplus goods, and capital in European countries. But these countries were for the most part able to make provision for themselves : most of them erected tariffs against manufacturing imports, and even Great Britain was urged to defend herself by reverting to Protection. The big American manufacturers and financiers were compelled to look to China and the Pacific and to South America for their most profitable chances ; Protectionists by principle and practice, they would insist upon getting as close a monopoly of these markets as they can secure, and the competition of Germany, England, and other trading nations would drive them to the establishment of special political relations with the markets they most prize. Cuba, the Philippines, and Hawaii were but the *hors d'œuvre* to whet an appetite for an ampler banquet. Moreover, the powerful hold upon politics which these industrial and financial magnates possessed formed a separate stimulus, which, as we have shown, was operative in Great Britain and elsewhere ; the public expenditure in pursuit of an imperial career would be a separate immense source of profit to these men, as financiers negotiating loans, shipbuilders and owners handling subsidies, contractors and manufacturers of armaments and other imperialist appliances.

The suddenness of this political revolution is due to the rapid manifestation of the need. In the last years of the nineteenth century the United States nearly trebled the value of its manufacturing export trade, and it was to be expected that, if the rate of progress of those years continued, within a decade it would overtake our more slowly advancing export trade, and stand first in the list of manufacture-exporting nations.[1]

This was the avowed ambition, and no idle one, of the keenest business men of America; and with the natural resources, the labour and the administrative talents at their disposal, it was quite likely they would achieve their object.[2] The stronger and more direct control over politics exercised in America by business men enabled them to drive more quickly and more straightly along the line of their economic interests than in Great Britain. American Imperialism was the natural product of the economic pressure of a sudden advance of capitalism which could not find occupation at home and needed foreign markets for goods and for investments.

The same needs existed in European countries, and, as is

[1] EXPORT TRADE OF UNITED STATES, 1890-1900.

Year.					Agriculture.	Manufactures.	Miscellaneous.
					£	£	£
1890	.	.	.	.	125,756,000	31,435,000	13,019,000
1891	.	.	.	.	146,617,000	33,720,000	11,731,000
1892	.	.	.	.	142,508,000	30,479,000	11,660,000
1893	.	.	.	.	123,810,000	35,484,000	11,653,000
1894	.	.	.	.	114,737,000	35,557,000	11,168,000
1895	.	.	.	.	104,143,000	40,230,000	12,174,000
1896	.	.	.	.	132,992,000	50,738,000	13,639,000
1897	.	.	.	.	146,059,000	55,923,000	13,984,000
1898	.	.	.	.	170,383,000	61,585,000	14,743,000
1899	.	.	.	.	156,427,000	76,157,000	18,002,000
1900	.	.	.	.	180,931,000	88,281,000	21,389,000

[1] Post-war conditions, with the immense opportunities afforded for exports of American goods and capital brought a pause and a temporary withdrawal from imperialist policy.

[2] " We hold now three of the winning cards in the game for commercial greatness, to wit—iron, steel and coal. We have long been the granary of the world, we now aspire to be its workshop, then we want to be its clearing-house." (The President of the American Bankers' Association at Denver, 1898.)

admitted, drove Governments along the same path. Over-production in the sense of an excessive manufacturing plant, and surplus capital which could not find sound investments within the country, forced Great Britain, Germany, Holland, France to place larger and larger portions of their economic resources outside the area of their present political domain, and then stimulate a policy of political expansion so as to take in the new areas. The economic sources of this movement are laid bare by periodic trade-depressions due to an inability of producers to find adequate and profit-able markets for what they can produce. The Majority Report of the Commission upon the Depression of Trade in 1885 put the matter in a nutshell. " That, owing to the nature of the times, the demand for our commodities does not increase at the same rate as formerly ; that our capacity for production is consequently in excess of our require-ments, and could be considerably increased at short notice ; that this is due partly to the competition of the capital which is being steadily accumulated in the country." The Minority Report straightly imputed the condition of affairs to " over-production." Germany was in the early 1900's suffering severely from what is called a glut of capital and of manufacturing power : she had to have new markets ; her Consuls all over the world were " hustling " for trade ; trading settlements were forced upon Asia Minor ; in East and West Africa, in China and elsewhere the German Empire was impelled to a policy of colonization and protectorates as outlets for German commercial energy.

Every improvement of methods of production, every concentration of ownership and control, seems to accentuate the tendency. As one nation after another enters the machine economy and adopts advanced industrial methods, it becomes more difficult for its manufacturers, merchants, and financiers to dispose profitably of their economic resources, and they are tempted more and more to use their Governments in order to secure for their particular use some distant undeveloped country by annexation and protection.

The process, we may be told, is inevitable, and so it seems upon a superficial inspection. Everywhere appear excessive powers of production, excessive capital in search of investment. It is admitted by all business men that the growth of the powers of production in their country exceeds the growth in consumption, that more goods can be produced than can be sold at a profit, and that more capital exists than can find remunerative investment.

It is this economic condition of affairs that forms the taproot of Imperialism. If the consuming public in this country raised its standard of consumption to keep pace with every rise of productive powers, there could be no excess of goods or capital clamorous to use Imperialism in order to find markets : foreign trade would indeed exist, but there would be no difficulty in exchanging a small surplus of our manufactures for the food and raw material we annually absorbed, and all the savings that we made could find employment, if we chose, in home industries.

There is nothing inherently irrational in such a supposition. Whatever is, or can be, produced, can be consumed, for a claim upon it, as rent, profit, or wages, forms part of the real income of some member of the community, and he can consume it, or else exchange it for some other consumable with some one else who will consume it. With everything that is produced a consuming power is born. If then there are goods which cannot get consumed, or which cannot even get produced because it is evident they cannot get consumed, and if there is a quantity of capital and labour which cannot get full employment because its products cannot get consumed, the only possible explanation of this paradox is the refusal of owners of consuming power to apply that power in effective demand for commodities.

It is, of course, possible that an excess of producing power might exist in particular industries by misdirection, being engaged in certain manufactures, whereas it ought to have been engaged in agriculture or some other use. But no one can seriously contend that such misdirection explains the recurrent gluts and consequent depressions of modern industry, or that, when over-production is manifest in the leading manufactures, ample avenues are open for the surplus capital and labour in other industries. The general character of the excess of producing power is proved by the existence at such times of large bank stocks of idle money seeking any sort of profitable investment and finding none.

The root questions underlying the phenomena are clearly these : " Why is it that consumption fails to keep pace automatically in a community with power of production ? " " Why does under-consumption or over-saving occur ? " For it is evident that the consuming power, which, if exercised, would keep tense the reins of production, is in part withheld, or in other words is " saved " and stored up for investment. All saving for investment does not imply slackness of production ; quite the contrary. Saving is economically justified, from the social standpoint, when the capital in which it takes material shape finds full employment in helping to produce commodities which, when produced, will be consumed. It is saving in excess of this amount that causes mischief, taking shape in surplus capital which is not needed to assist current consumption, and which either lies idle, or tries to oust existing capital from its employment, or else seeks speculative use abroad under the protection of the Government.

But it may be asked, " Why should there be any tendency

to over-saving ? Why should the owners of consuming power withhold a larger quantity for savings than can be serviceably employed ? " Another way of putting the same question is this, " Why should not the pressure of present wants keep pace with every possibility of satisfying them ? " The answer to these pertinent questions carries us to the broadest issue of the distribution of wealth. If a tendency to distribute income or consuming power according to needs were operative, it is evident that consumption would rise with every rise of producing power, for human needs are illimitable, and there could be no excess of saving. But it is quite otherwise in a state of economic society where distribution has no fixed relation to needs, but is determined by other conditions which assign to some people a consuming power vastly in excess of needs or possible uses, while others are destitute of consuming power enough to satisfy even the full demands of physical efficiency. The following illustration may serve to make the issue clear. " The volume of production has been constantly rising owing to the development of modern machinery. There are two main channels to carry off these products— one channel carrying off the product destined to be consumed by the workers, and the other channel carrying off the remainder to the rich. The workers' channel is in rockbound banks that cannot enlarge, owing to the competitive wage system preventing wages rising *pro rata* with increased efficiency. Wages are based upon cost of living, and not upon efficiency of labour. The miner in the poor mine gets the same wages per day as the miner in the adjoining rich mine. The owner of the rich mine gets the advantage —not his labourer. The channel which conveys the goods destined to supply the rich is itself divided into two streams. One stream carries off what the rich ' spend ' on themselves for the necessities and luxuries of life. The other is simply an 'overflow' stream carrying off their 'savings.' The channel for spending, i.e. the amount wasted by the rich in luxuries, may broaden somewhat, but owing to the small number of those rich enough to indulge in whims it can never be greatly enlarged, and at any rate it bears such a small proportion to the other channel that in no event can much hope of avoiding a flood of capital be hoped for from this division. The rich will never be so ingenious as to spend enough to prevent over-production. The great safety overflow channel which has been continuously more and more widened and deepened to carry off the ever-increasing flood of new capital is that division of the stream which carried the savings of the rich, and this is not only suddenly found to be incapable of further enlargement, but actually seems to be in the process of being dammed up."[1]

Though this presentation over-accentuates the cleavage between rich and poor and over-states the weakness of the workers, it gives forcible and sound expression to a most important and ill-recognised economic truth. The " overflow " stream of savings is of course fed not exclusively from the surplus income of " the rich "; the professional and industrial middle classes, and to some slight extent the workers, contribute. But the " flooding " is distinctly due to the automatic saving of the surplus income of rich men. This is of course particularly true of America, where multi-millionaires rise quickly and find themselves in possession of incomes far exceeding the demands of any craving that is known to them. To make the metaphor complete, the overflow stream must be represented as re-entering the stream of production and seeking to empty there all the " savings " that it carries. Where competition remains free, the result is a chronic congestion of productive

[1] *The Significance of the Trust*, by H. G. Wilshire.

power and of production, forcing down home prices, wasting large sums in advertising and in pushing for orders, and periodically causing a crisis followed by a collapse, during which quantities of capital and labour lie unemployed and unremunerated. The prime object of the trust or other combine is to remedy this waste and loss by substituting regulation of output for reckless over-production. In achieving this it actually narrows or even dams up the old channels of investment, limiting the overflow stream to the exact amount required to maintain the normal current of output. But this rigid limitation of trade, though required for the separate economy of each trust, does not suit the trust-maker, who is driven to compensate for strictly regulated industry at home by cutting new foreign channels as outlets for his productive power and his excessive savings. Thus we reach the conclusion that Imperialism is the endeavour of the great controllers of industry to broaden the channel for the flow of their surplus wealth by seeking foreign markets and foreign investments to take off the goods and capital they cannot sell or use at home.

The fallacy of the supposed inevitability of imperial expansion as a necessary outlet for progressive industry is now manifest. It is not industrial progress that demands the opening up of new markets and areas of investment, but mal-distribution of consuming power which prevents the absorption of commodities and capital within the country. The over-saving which is the economic root of Imperialism is found by analysis to consist of rents, monopoly profits, and other unearned or excessive elements of income, which, not being earned by labour of head or hand, have no legitimate *raison d'être*. Having no natural relation to effort of production, they impel their recipients to no corresponding satisfaction of consumption : they form a surplus wealth, which, having no proper place in the normal economy of production and consumption, tends to accumulate as excessive savings. Let any turn in the tide of politico-economic forces divert from these owners their excess of income and make it flow, either to the workers in higher wages, or to the community in taxes, so that it will be spent instead of being saved, serving in either of these ways to swell the tide of consumption— there will be no need to fight for foreign markets or foreign areas of investment.

Many have carried their analysis so far as to realise the absurdity of spending half our financial resources in fighting to secure foreign markets at times when hungry mouths, ill-clad backs, ill-furnished houses indicate countless unsatisfied material wants among our own population. If we may take the careful statistics of Mr. Rowntree[1] for our guide, we shall be aware that more than one-fourth of the population of our towns is living at a standard which is below bare physical efficiency. If, by some economic readjustment, the products which flow from the surplus saving of the rich to swell the overflow streams could be diverted so as to raise the incomes and the standard of consumption of this inefficient fourth, there would be no need for pushful Imperialism, and the cause of social reform would have won its greatest victory.

It is not inherent in the nature of things that we should spend our natural resources on militarism, war, and risky, unscrupulous diplomacy, in order to find markets for our goods and surplus capital. An intelligent progressive community, based upon substantial equality of economic and educational opportunities, will raise its standard of consumption to correspond with every increased power of production, and can find full employment for an un-

[1] *Poverty : A Study of Town Life.*

limited quantity of capital and labour within the limits of the country which it occupies. Where the distribution of incomes is such as to enable all classes of the nation to convert their felt wants into an effective demand for commodities, there can be no over-production, no under-employment of capital and labour, and no necessity to fight for foreign markets.

The most convincing condemnation of the current economy is conveyed in the difficulty which producers everywhere experience in finding consumers for their products : a fact attested by the prodigious growth of classes of agents and middlemen, the multiplication of every sort of advertising, and the general increase of the distributive classes. Under a sound economy the pressure would be reversed : the growing wants of progressive societies would be a constant stimulus to the inventive and operative energies of producers, and would form a constant strain upon the powers of production. The simultaneous excess of all the factors of production, attested by frequently recurring periods of trade depression, is a most dramatic exhibition of the false economy of distribution. It does not imply a mere miscalculation in the application of productive power, or a brief temporary excess of that power ; it manifests in an acute form an economic waste which is chronic and general throughout the advanced industrial nations, a waste contained in the divorcement of the desire to consume and the power to consume.

If the apportionment of income were such as to evoke no excessive saving, full constant employment for capital and labour would be furnished at home. This, of course, does not imply that there would be no foreign trade. Goods that could not be produced at home, or produced as well or as cheaply, would still be purchased by ordinary process of international exchange, but here again the pressure would be the wholesome pressure of the consumer anxious to buy abroad what he could not buy at home, not the blind eagerness of the producer to use every force or trick of trade or politics to find markets for his " surplus " goods.

The struggle for markets, the greater eagerness of producers to sell than of consumers to buy, is the crowning proof of a false economy of distribution. Imperialism is the fruit of this false economy; " social reform " is its remedy. The primary purpose of " social reform," using the term in its economic signification, is to raise the wholesome standard of private and public consumption for a nation, so as to enable the nation to live up to its highest standard of production. Even those social reformers who aim directly at abolishing or reducing some bad form of consumption, as in the Temperance movement, generally recognise the necessity of substituting some better form of current consumption which is more educative and stimulative of other tastes, and will assist to raise the general standard of consumption.

There is no necessity to open up new foreign markets; the home markets are capable of indefinite expansion. Whatever is produced in England can be consumed in England, provided that the " income " or power to demand commodities, is properly distributed. This only appears untrue because of the unnatural and unwholesome specialisation to which this country has been subjected, based upon a bad distribution of economic resources, which has induced an overgrowth of certain manufacturing trades for the express purpose of effecting foreign sales. If the industrial revolution had taken place in an England founded upon equal access by all classes to land, education and legislation, specialisation in manufactures would not have gone so far (though more intelligent progress would have been made, by reason of a widening of the area of selection of inventive and organising talents); foreign trade would have been less important, though more steady; the standard of life for all portions of the population would have been high, and the present rate of national consumption would probably have given full, constant, remunerative employment to a far larger quantity of private and public capital than is now employed.[1] For the over-saving or wider consumption that is traced to excessive incomes of the rich is a suicidal economy, even from the exclusive standpoint of capital; for consumption alone vitalises capital and makes it capable of yielding profits. An economy that assigns to the " possessing " classes an excess of consuming power which they cannot use, and cannot convert into really serviceable capital, is a dog-in-the-manger policy. The social reforms which deprive the possessing classes of their surplus will not, therefore, inflict upon them the real injury they dread; they can only use this surplus by forcing on their country a wrecking policy of Imperialism. The only safety of nations lies in removing the unearned increments of income from the possessing classes, and adding them to the wage-income of the working classes or to the public income, in order that they may be spent in raising the standard of consumption.

Social reform bifurcates, according as reformers seek to achieve this end by raising wages or by increasing public taxation and expenditure. These courses are not essentially

[1] The classical economists of England, forbidden by their theories of parsimony and of the growth of capital to entertain the notion of an indefinite expansion of home markets by reason of a constantly rising standard of national comfort, were early driven to countenance a doctrine of the necessity of finding external markets for the investment of capital. So J. S. Mill : " The expansion of capital would soon reach its ultimate boundary if the boundary itself did not continually open and leave more space " (*Political Economy*). And before him Ricardo (in a letter to Malthus) : " If with every accumulation of capital we could take a piece of fresh fertile land to our island, profits would never fall."

contradictory, but are rather complementary. Working-class movements aim, either by private co-operation or by political pressure on legislative and administrative government, at increasing the proportion of the national income which accrues to labour in the form of wages, pensions, compensation for injuries, etc. State Socialism aims at getting for the direct use of the whole society an increased share of the " social values " which arise from the closely and essentially co-operative work of an industrial society, taxing property and incomes so as to draw into the public exchequer for public expenditure the " unearned elements " of income, leaving to individual producers those incomes which are necessary to induce them to apply in the best way their economic energies, and to private enterprises those businesses which do not breed monopoly, and which the public need not or cannot undertake. These are not, indeed, the sole or perhaps the best avowed objects of social reform movements. But for the purposes of this analysis they form the kernel.

Trade Unionism and Socialism are thus the natural enemies of Imperialism, for they take away from the " imperialist " classes the surplus incomes which form the economic stimulus of Imperialism.

This does not pretend to be a final statement of the full relations of these forces. When we come to political analysis we shall perceive that the tendency of Imperialism is to crush Trade Unionism and to " nibble " at or parasitically exploit State Socialism. But, confining ourselves for the present to the narrowly economic setting, Trade Unionism and State Socialism may be regarded as complementary forces arrayed against Imperialism, in as far as, by diverting to working-class or public expenditure elements of income which would otherwise be surplus savings, they raise the general standard of home consumption and abate the pressure for foreign markets. Of course, if the increase of working-class income were wholly or chiefly "saved," not spent, or if the taxation of unearned incomes were utilised for the relief of other taxes borne by the possessing classes, no such result as we have described would follow. There is, however, no reason to anticipate this result from trade-union or socialistic measures. Though no sufficient natural stimulus exists to force the well-to-do classes to spend in further luxuries the surplus incomes which they save, every working-class family is subject to powerful stimuli of economic needs, and a reasonably governed State would regard as its prime duty the relief of the present poverty of public life by new forms of socially useful expenditure.

But we are not here concerned with what belongs to the practical issues of political and economic policy. It is the economic theory for which we claim acceptance—a theory which, if accurate, dispels the delusion that expansion of foreign trade, and therefore of empire, is a necessity of national life.

Regarded from the standpoint of economy of energy, the same "choice of life" confronts the nation as the individual. An individual may expend all his energy in acquiring external possessions, adding field to field, barn to barn, factory to factory—may "spread himself" over the widest area of property, amassing material wealth which is in some sense "himself" as containing the impress of his power and interest. He does this by specialising upon the lower acquisitive plane of interest at the cost of neglecting the cultivation of the higher qualities and interests of his nature. The antagonism is not indeed absolute. Aristotle has said, "We must first secure a livelihood and then practise virtue." Hence the pursuit of material property as a reasonable basis of physical comfort would be held true economy by the wisest men ; but the absorption of time, energy, and interest upon such quantitative expansion at the necessary cost of starving the higher tastes and faculties is condemned as false economy. The same issue comes up in the business life of the individual : it is the question of intensive *versus* extensive cultivation. A rude or ignorant farmer, where land is plentiful, is apt to spread his capital and labour over a large area, taking in new tracts and cultivating them poorly. A skilled, scientific farmer will study a smaller patch of land, cultivate it thoroughly, and utilise its diverse properties, adapting it to the special needs of his most remunerative markets. The same is true of other businesses ; even where the economy of large-scale production is greatest there exists some limit beyond which the wise business man will not go, aware that in doing so he will risk by enfeebled management what he seems to gain by mechanical economies of production and market.

Everywhere the issue of quantitative *versus* qualitative growth comes up. This is the entire issue of empire. A people limited in number and energy and in the land they occupy have the choice of improving to the utmost the political and economic management of their own land, confining themselves to such accessions of territory as are justified by the most economical disposition of a growing population ; or they may proceed, like the slovenly farmer, to spread their power and energy over the whole earth, tempted by the speculative value or the quick profits of some new market, or else by mere greed of territorial acquisition, and ignoring the political and economic wastes and risks involved by this imperial career. It must be clearly understood that this is essentially a choice of alternatives ; a full simultaneous application of intensive and extensive cultivation is impossible. A nation may either, following the example of Denmark or Switzerland, put brains into agriculture, develop a finely varied system of public education, general and technical, apply the ripest science to its special manufacturing industries, and so support in progressive comfort and character a considerable population upon a strictly limited area ; or it may, like Great Britain, neglect its agriculture, allowing its lands to go out of cultivation and its population to grow up in towns, fall behind other nations in its methods of education and in the capacity of adapting to its uses the latest scientific knowledge, in order that it may squander its pecuniary and military resources in forcing bad markets and finding speculative fields of investment in distant corners of the earth, adding millions of square miles and of unassimilable population to the area of the Empire.

The driving forces of class interest which stimulate and support this false economy we have explained. No remedy will serve which permits the future operation of these forces. It is idle to attack Imperialism or Militarism as political expedients or policies unless the axe is laid at the economic root of the tree, and the classes for whose interest Imperialism works are shorn of the surplus revenues which seek this outlet.

CHAPTER VII

IMPERIALIST FINANCE

THE analysis of economic forces in the foregoing chapter explains the character which public finance assumes in States committed to an imperialist policy. Imperialism, as we see, implies the use of the machinery of government by private interests, mainly capitalists, to secure for them economic gains outside their country. The dominance of this factor in public policy imposes a special character alike upon expenditure and taxation.

The accompanying diagram[1] brings into clear light the main features of the national expenditure of Great Britain during the last three decades of the nineteenth century.

The first feature is the rate of growth of national expenditure taken as a whole. This growth has been far faster than the growth of foreign trade. For whereas the average yearly value of our foreign trade for 1870–75, amounting to £636,000,000, increased in the period 1895–1903 to £868,000,000, the average public expenditure advanced over the same period from £63,160,000 to £155,660,000. It is far faster than the growth of the aggregate national income, which, according to the rough estimates of statisticians, advanced during the same period from about £1,200,000,000, to £1,750,000,000. The rate of growth has greatly quickened during the latter half of the period in question, for, leaving out of consideration war expenditure, the rise of ordinary imperial expenditure has been from £87,423,000 in 1888 to £128,600,000 in 1900.

[1] Appendix, p. 379.

The most salient feature of the diagram is the small and diminishing proportion of the national revenue expended for what may be regarded as directly productive purposes of government. Roughly speaking, over two-thirds of the money goes for naval and military expenditure, and for the payment of military debts, about six shillings in the pound being available for education, civil government, and the dubious policy of grants in aid of local taxation.[1]

The only satisfactory incident disclosed by the table was the growing amount and proportion of public money spent on education. A substantial part of the sum expended as aid to local taxation has simply gone as a dole to landowners.

The direct military and naval expenditure during the period has increased faster than the total expenditure, the growth of trade, of national income, or any other general indication of national resources. In 1875 the army and navy cost less than 24½ millions out of a total expenditure of 65 millions ; in 1903 they cost nearly 79 millions out of a total of 140 millions.

The enormous expenditure upon the South African war was followed by a large permanent increase in these branches of expenditure, amounting to an addition of not less than £32,000,000 per annum.

This growth of naval and military expenditure from about 25 to 79 millions in a little over a quarter of a century is the most significant fact of imperialist finance. The financial, industrial, and professional classes, who, we have shown, form the economic core of Imperialism, have used their political power to extract these sums from the nation in order to improve their investments and open up new fields for capital, and to find profitable markets for their

[1] A portion of the money expended under the head National Debt should, however, be regarded as productively expended, since it has gone towards reduction of the debt. Between 1875 and 1900 a reduction of £140,000,000, equal to about £5,800,000 per annum, has been effected.

surplus goods, while out of the public sums expended on these objects they reap other great private gains in the shape of profitable contracts, and lucrative or honourable employment.

The financial and industrial capitalists who have mainly engineered this policy, employing their own genuine convictions to conceal their ill-recognised business ends, have also made important bribes or concessions to other less directly benefited interests in order to keep their sympathy and ensure their support.

This explains the large and growing grants in aid of local taxation, almost the whole of which, interpreted by a scientific regard to incidence of taxation, must be considered as a subsidy to landowners. The support of the Church and of the liquor trade has been more cheaply purchased ; the former by relief of rates on tithes and increased grants for Church schools, the latter by a policy of masterly inaction in the matter of temperance reforms and special consideration in regard to taxation.

In making the capitalist-imperialist forces the pivot of financial policy, I do not mean that other forces, industrial, political, and moral, have no independent aims and influences, but simply that the former group must be regarded as the true determinant in the interpretation of actual policy.

We have identified almost all the organised interests, commonly summed under the head of Capitalism, including land-capital, with Imperialism. Most of them participate directly in one or other of the two sorts of gain which attend this policy : the interest, trade profits, or employment furnished by the imperialist policy, or the interest, profit, or employment connected with military and civil expenditure itself.

It cannot be too clearly recognised that increasing public

expenditure, apart from all political justification, is a direct source of gain to certain well-organised and influential interests, and to all such Imperialism is the chief instrument of such increasing expenditure.

While the directors of this definitely parasitic policy are capitalists, the same motives appeal to special classes of the workers. In many towns most important trades are dependent upon Government employment or contracts; the Imperialism of the metal and shipbuilding centres is attributable in no small degree to this fact. Members of Parliament freely employ their influence to secure contracts and direct trade to their constituents, and every growth of public expenditure enhances this dangerous bias.

The clearest significance of imperialist finance, however, appears on the side, not of expenditure, but of taxation. The object of those economic interests which use the public purse for purposes of private gain is in large measure defeated if they have first to find the money to fill that purse. To avert the direct incidence of taxation from their own shoulders on to those of other classes or of posterity is a natural policy of self-defence.

A sane policy of taxation would derive the whole or the main part of the national revenue from unearned increments of land values and from profits in trades which, by virtue of some legal or economic protection screening them from close competition, are able to earn high rates of interest or profit. Such taxation would be borne most easily, falling upon unearned elements of incomes, and would cause no disturbance of industry. This, however, would imply the taxation of precisely those elements which constitute the economic taproot of Imperialism. For it is precisely the unearned elements of income which tend towards an automatic process of accumulation, and which, by swelling the stream of surplus capital seeking markets of investment or markets for the surplus goods it helps to make, direct political forces into Imperialism. A sound system of taxation would, therefore, strike at the very root of the malady.

On the other hand, were the capitalist-imperialist forces openly to shift the burden of taxation on to the shoulders of the people, it would be difficult under popular forms of government to operate such an expensive policy. The people must pay, but they must not know they are paying, or how much they are paying, and the payment must be spread over as long a period as possible.

To take a concrete example. The medley of financial and political interests which inveigled Great Britain into spending some two hundred millions of public money, in order to obtain for them control of the land and mineral resources of the South African Republics, could not possibly have achieved their object if they had been compelled to raise the money by sending round a tax-gatherer to take from every citizen in hard cash the several pounds which constituted his share of the taxes—the share which by more crooked ways was to be got out of him.

To support Imperialism by direct taxation of incomes or property would be impossible. Where any real forms of popular control existed, militarism and wars would be impossible if every citizen was made to realise their cost by payments of hard cash. Imperialism, therefore, makes everywhere for indirect taxation ; not chiefly on grounds of convenience, but for purposes of concealment. Or perhaps it would be more just to say that Imperialism takes advantage of the cowardly and foolish preference which the average man everywhere exhibits for being tricked out of his contribution to the public funds, using this common folly for its own purposes. It is seldom possible for any Government, even in the stress of some grave emergency, to impose an income-tax ; even a property-tax is commonly evaded in cases of personal property, and is always unpopular. The case of England is an exception which really proves the rule.

The repeal of import duties and the establishment of Free Trade marked the political triumph of the new manufacturing and commercial plutocracy over the land-owning aristocracy. Free Trade was so profitable to the former classes in securing cheap importation of raw materials, and in cheapening the subsistence of labour at a time when England's priority in new industrial methods offered an indefinitely rapid expansion of trade, that they were willing to support the reimposition of the income-tax which Peel proposed in 1842 in order to enable him to repeal or reduce the import duties. When the sudden financial stress of the Crimean war came on the country the Free Trade policy was in the prime of its popularity and success, and a Liberal ministry, in preference to a reversion to Protection which would otherwise have been inevitable, gave permanency to the tax, extending the area of its application and making its removal more difficult by further repeals of import duties. No Government could now remove it, for the new unpopularity caused by finding adequate substitutes would have outweighed the credit gained by its removal, while its productivity and calculability are advantages shared in an equal degree by no other mode of taxation.

Some allowance may also be made for the principles and personal convictions of political financiers trained in the English science of political economy, and still more for the temptation of competing parties to seek the favour of the newly enfranchised populace by a well-paraded policy of class taxation. The seething revolutionism of the mid-century throughout Europe, the rapid growth of huge industrial centres throughout England, with their masses of ill-explored poverty and their known aptitude for ignorant

H   99

agitation, made the establishment of formal democracy seem a most hazardous experiment, and both parties were in a mood to conciliate the new monster by doles or bribery. When the break-up of the old Liberal party in 1885–86 had for the first time thrown the vast preponderance of personal property on to the same side as real property, a genuinely democratic budget with a progressive income-tax and a substantial death duty became possible and seemed expedient. It is not necessary to deny that Sir William Harcourt and his colleagues were sincerely convinced of the justice as well as the expediency of this policy; but it must be remembered that no alternative was open, in face of the need of increased funds for Imperialism and education, except a *volte face* upon the Free Trade principles they had most stoutly championed, and a dangerous attack upon trade interests which might recoil upon the working classes, whose cause they were anxious to espouse. The financial attack on " property," embodied in the progressive income tax and death duties, must be regarded, then, as an exceptional policy, due mainly to a combination of two causes— the difficulty of reverting suddenly to the abandoned practice of Protection, and the desire to conciliate the favour of the new unknown democracy.

Hence the anomaly of Imperialism attended by direct taxation. In no other country have the political conditions operated so. Upon the Continent Militarism and Imperialism have thriven upon indirect taxation, and have enabled the agricultural and manufacturing interests to defeat easily any movement towards Free Trade by urging the needs of revenue through tariffs. In Great Britain it seems unlikely that the policy of direct taxation upon property and income for imperial purposes will be carried any further. The Government of the propertied classes has shaken itself free from the traditions of Free Trade;

the leaders and the overwhelming majority of the rank and file are avowed Protectionists so far as agriculture and certain staple industries are concerned. They are no longer seriously frightened by the power of the people as implied by a popular franchise, nor are they prepared to conciliate it by further taxes upon property; they have experimented with the temper of "the monster," and they think that by the assistance of "the trade" and the Church he is quite manageable, and can be cajoled into paying for Imperialism through protective duties. "Panem et circenses" interpreted into English means cheap booze and Mafficking. Popular education, instead of serving as a defence, is an incitement towards Imperialism; it has opened up a panorama of vulgar pride and crude sensationalism to a great inert mass who see current history and the tangled maze of world movements with dim, bewildered eyes, and are the inevitable dupes of the able organised interests who can lure, or scare, or drive them into any convenient course.

Had the Liberal party stood by the principles of peace, retrenchment, and reform, refusing to go beyond the true "colonialism" of such men as Molesworth, and rejecting the temptations to a "spirited foreign policy" dictated by bond-holders, they might have been able to resist the attack upon Free Trade. But a Liberal party committed to a militant Imperialism whose rapidly growing expense is determined chiefly by the conduct of foreign Powers and the new arts of scientific warfare was in a hopeless dilemma. Its position as a buffer party between the propertied classes organised as Conservatism and the unorganised pressure of a loose set of forces striving to become a Socialist labour party dictated moderation, and the personnel of its leaders, still drawn from the propertied classes, prevented it from making any bold attempt to work Imperialism upon a basis of direct taxation upon property, raising the income and proper taxes to cover every increasing need of imperialist finance. It had neither the pluck nor the principle to renounce Imperialism or to insist that the classes who seek to benefit by it shall pay for it.

There is then no reason to impute to Liberalism either the desire or the power to defray the expenses of militant Imperialism by a further pursuance of progressive taxation of incomes and property. While the conveniences of finance may have prevented the repeal of taxation which was so productive, it would not be carried further; when expenditure is placed again upon a normal footing the income-tax would be reduced and all increase of normal expenditure (estimated by a statistical authority at £20,000,000 for military services alone) will be defrayed by indirect taxation.

Now any considerable calculable increase of revenue by indirect taxation means the abandonment of Free Trade. A large steady income of such a kind can only be raised by duties upon imports of necessaries and prime conveniences of life and trade. It is of course quite immaterial to urge that taxation for revenue is not Protection. If import duties are raised on sugar and tea, if they are imposed upon wheat and flour, foreign meat and raw materials of our staple manufactures, or upon finished manufactured goods competing in our market, it matters not that the object be revenue, the economic effect is Protection.

It is probable that imperialist finance is not yet prepared to admit the name or the full economic policy of Protection.[1] The preparatory steps can find other names. A countervailing duty upon beet-sugar poses as an instrument of Free Trade: once admitted, it introduces a whole train of countervailing duties by parity of reasoning. A tax on

[1] The ensuing discussion of Protection relates to the probabilities of the year of this study, 1905.

prison-made goods, on the ground that they are subsidised and so produced under " cost " price, is logically followed by similar protection against all products of " sweated " foreign industry. An export duty upon coal may well be followed by similar duties on the export of engines and machinery, which similarly aid the growth of our manu- facturing rivals. But the most formidable mask of Protection will take the shape of military necessity. A military nation surrounded by hostile empires must have within her boundaries adequate supplies of the sinews of war, efficient recruits, and a large food supply. We cannot safely rely upon the fighting capacities of a town-bred population, or upon food supplies from foreign lands. Both needs demand that checks be set upon the excessive concentration of our population in towns, and that a serious attempt be made to revive agriculture and restore the people to the soil.

There are two methods which seem possible. The one is a large radical scheme of land reform interfering with the rights of landowners by compulsory purchase or leasing on the part of public bodies, with powers to establish large numbers of small farmers on the soil with loans of capital sufficient to enable them to live and work upon the soil. The other method is Protection, the re-imposition of taxes on imported grain, cattle, fruit, and dairy produce, with the object of stimulating agriculture and keeping the population on the soil.

Given the political sway of the possessing classes, it is certain that the latter course will be preferred. The land- owning and the industrial interests are now sufficiently blended to render it impossible for the town industrialist to refuse assistance to the rural landowner. The dole in relief of rates is a convincing testimony to this truth. Political economists may prove that the chief result of " Protection," in as far as it protects, is to raise the rent of land, that a corn tax will raise the price of bread, and by raising real wages injure profits, and that if the tax really succeeded in stimulating intensive cultivation and self sufficiency for food supply it would not assist the revenue. The Protectionist will not be dismayed by the contradictory positions he is required to hold, for he will be aware that the people whose votes he craves cannot hold two arguments in their heads at the same time for purposes of comparison.

The demand for agricultural protection in order to keep upon the soil a peasantry with sound physique and military aptitudes is likely to outweigh all economic objections in the near future, and it is quite possible that Protection may here be tempered by such carefully devised land reforms as shall place a new " yeoman " class upon British soil, and a substantial sum as purchase money plus compensation for disturbance in the pockets of British landlords.

One other secret avenue to Protection is through the shipbuilding trade. Here is a case not for taxation but for bounties. If England is to be strong for contest in war and trade she must keep open for herself the highways of commerce, and must own ships and men adaptable for purposes of defence. England's great foreign trade was undoubtedly built up in the first instance by the aid of the navigation laws, and the same combination of political exigencies and commercial interests will make towards a revival of this policy. Such are the main streams of tendency towards Protection. But there is no reason to suppose that the policy will be confined to agriculture, sugar and other subsidised imports, export duties upon coal, and bounties on shipbuilding. The leading branches of the textile, metal, and other staple manufactures whose monopoly even in the home market is threatened by the progressive industries of Germany, Holland, and the United States had long lost that confident reliance on Free Trade which they entertained when England's paramountcy in the manufacturing arts was unquestioned. The local specialization of industries places a most formidable weapon in the hands of the protectionist politician. In spite of the financial and intellectual aid given to the Free Trade movement by certain manufacturing interests, Protection stands as the producer's policy, Free Trade as the consumer's. The specialization of localities enables a politician to appeal to the separate trade interests of a single town or neighbourhood, and to convince not only its capitalists but its workers of the gain that would accrue to them if their trade was protected against what is termed unfair competition of foreigners : nothing is said about what they will lose as consumers in the diminished purchasing power of their profits and wages, the result of Protection to the trades of other localities. This appeal made to the separate interests of producers is almost certain to be successful in a people of low education and intelligence. Any attempt to put the other side by representing the result of Protection to be a general rise of prices is commonly met by a confident denial that this result will follow, though it is commonly admitted that wages and profits will rise in the particular local trade to whose self-interest the protectionist appeal is addressed.

It is, however, probable that an attempt will be made to conceal the whole character of the protectionist policy by a misty atmosphere of Imperialism. Protection will not be Protection, but Free Trade within the Empire ; a protectionist tariff will hide its exclusive side and masquerade as an Imperial Zollverein. Great economic changes, requiring the use of political machinery, invent that machinery. The Imperialism of England, essentially though not exclusively an economic thing, will strive to cover the protective system of finance it favours, by a great political achievement, entitled Federation of the Empire. This avenue to Protection would in any case have been essayed by Imperialism, as indeed the curious attempt of Mr. Chamberlain in 1897 testifies. The abnormally rapid swelling of financial needs due to the disastrous policy in South Africa merely precipitates this policy and gives it political occasion. It will be sought to exploit the enthusiastic loyalty of the colonists exhibited in their rally round the mother country in the South African war for purposes of formal federation on a basis which shall bind them to contribute money and men to the protection and expansion of the Empire. The probability of success in this attempt to secure imperial federation is a matter for separate consideration. It is here named as one of the avenues to Protection.

In many ways it thus appears that Protection is the natural ally of Imperialism.

The economic root of Imperialism is the desire of strong organized industrial and financial interests to secure and develop at the public expense and by the public force private markets for their surplus goods and their surplus capital. War, militarism, and a " spirited foreign policy " are the necessary means to this end. This policy involves large increase of public expenditure. If they had to pay the cost of this policy out of their own pockets in taxation upon incomes and property, the game would not be worth the candle, at any rate as far as markets for commodities are concerned. They must find means of putting the expense upon the general public. But in countries where a popular franchise and representative government exist this cannot be successfully done in an open manner. Taxation must be indirect and must fall upon such articles of consumption or general use as are part of the general standard of consumption and will not shrink in demand or give way to substitutes under the process of taxation. This protection not only serves the purposes of imperial finance, taxing the impotent and ignorant consumer for the imperial gains of the influential economic interests, but it seems to furnish them a second gain by securing to them as producers their home market which is threatened by outside competition, and enabling them to raise their prices to the home consumers and so reap a rise of profits. To those who regard foreign trade in its normal condition as a fair interchange of goods, and services, it may seem difficult to understand how these economic interests expect to exclude foreign goods from their market, while at the same time pushing their goods in foreign markets. But we must remind such economists that the prime motive force here is not trade but investment: a surplus of exports over imports is sought as the most profitable mode of investment, and when a nation, or more strictly its investing classes, is bent on becoming a creditor or parasitic nation to an indefinite extent, there is no reason why its imports and exports should balance even over a long term of years. The whole struggle of so-called Imperialism upon its economic side is towards a growing parasitism, and the classes engaged in this struggle require Protection as their most serviceable instrument.

The nature and object of Protection as a branch of imperialist finance is best illustrated in the case of Great Britain, because the necessity of subverting an accepted Free Trade policy lays bare the different methods of Protection and the forces upon which it relies. In other nations committed to or entering upon an imperialist career with the same ganglia of economic interests masquerading as patriotism, civilization, and the like, Protection has been the traditional finance, and it has only been necessary to extend it and direct it into the necessary channels.

Protection, however, is not the only appropriate financial method of Imperialism. There is at any given time some limit to the quantity of current expenditure which can be met by taxing consumers. The policy of Imperialism to be effective requires at times the outlay of large unforeseen sums on war and military equipment. These cannot be met by current taxation. They must be treated as capital expenditure, the payment of which may be indefinitely deferred or provided by a slow and suspensible sinking fund.

The creation of public debts is a normal and a most imposing feature of Imperialism. Like Protection, it also serves a double purpose, not only furnishing a second means of escaping taxation upon income and property otherwise inevitable, but providing a most useful form of investment for idle savings waiting for more profitable employment. The creation of large growing public debts is thus not only a necessary consequence of an imperialist expenditure too great for its current revenue, or of some sudden forced extortion of a war indemnity or other public penalty. It is a direct object of imperialist finance to create further debts, just as it is an object of the private money-lender to goad his clients into pecuniary difficulties in order that they may have recourse to him. Analysis of foreign investments shows that public or State-guaranteed debts are largely held by investors and financiers of other nations; and history shows, in the cases of Egypt, Turkey, China, the hand of the bond-holder, and of the potential bond-holder, in politics. This method of finance is not only profitable in the case of foreign nations, where it is a chief instrument or pretext for encroachment. It is of service to the financial classes to have a large national debt of their own. The floating of and the dealing in such public loans are a profitable business, and are means of exercising important political influences at critical junctures. Where floating capital constantly tends to excess, further debts are serviceable as a financial drainage scheme.

Imperialism with its wars and its armaments is undeniably responsible for the growing debts of the continental nations, and while the unparalleled industrial prosperity of Great Britain and the isolation of the United States have enabled these great nations to escape this ruinous competition during recent decades, the period of their immunity is over ; both, committed as they seem to an Imperialism without limit, will succumb more and more to the moneylending classes dressed as Imperialists and patriots.[1]

[1] The later passages of this chapter describing the probable plunge towards Protection are left as written in 1901, two years before Mr. Chamberlain's dramatic espousal of a full Protection.

PART II

THE POLITICS OF IMPERIALISM

CHAPTER I

THE POLITICAL SIGNIFICANCE
OF IMPERIALISM

I

THE curious ignorance which prevails regarding the political character and tendencies of Imperialism cannot be better illustrated than by the following passage from a learned work upon " The History of Colonization "[1] : " The extent of British dominion may perhaps be better imagined than described, when the fact is appreciated that, of the entire land surface of the globe, approximately one-fifth is actually or theoretically under that flag, while more than one-sixth of all the human beings living in this planet reside under one or the other type of English colonization. The names by which authority is exerted are numerous, and processes are distinct, but the goals to which this mani-fold mechanism is working are very similar. According to the climate, the natural conditions and the inhabitants of the regions affected, procedure and practice differ. The means are adapted to the situation ; there is not any irrevo-cable, immutable line of policy ; from time to time, from decade to decade, English statesmen have applied different treatments to the same territory. Only one fixed rule of action seems to exist ; it is to promote the interests of the colony to the utmost, to develop its scheme of government as rapidly as possible, and eventually to elevate it from the position of inferiority to that of association. Under the charm of this beneficent spirit the chief colonial establish-

[1] Morris, vol. ii, p. 80.

ments of Great Britain have already achieved substantial freedom, without dissolving nominal ties; the other subordinate possessions are aspiring to it, while, on the other hand, this privilege of local independence has enabled England to assimilate with ease many feudatory States into the body politic of her system." Here then is the theory that Britons are a race endowed, like the Romans, with a genius for government, that our colonial and imperial policy is animated by a resolve to spread throughout the world the arts of free self-government which we enjoy at home,[1] and that in truth we are accomplishing this work.

Now, without discussing here the excellencies or the defects of the British theory and practice of representative self-government, to assert that our "fixed rule of action" has been to educate our dependencies in this theory and practice is quite the largest misstatement of the facts of our colonial and imperial policy that is possible. Upon the vast majority of the populations throughout our Empire we have bestowed no real powers of self-government, nor have we any serious intention of doing so, or any serious belief that it is possible for us to do so.

Of the three hundred and sixty-seven millions of British subjects outside these isles, not more than eleven millions, or one in thirty-four, have any real self-government for purposes of legislation and administration.[2]

Political freedom, and civil freedom, so far as it rests upon the other, are simply non-existent for the overwhelming majority of British subjects. In the self-governing colonies of Australasia and North America alone is responsible representative government a reality, and even there considerable populations of outlanders, as in West Australia,

---

[1] "The British Empire is a galaxy of free States," said Sir W. Laurier in a speech, July 8, 1902.

[2] Figures for the period of this study, ca. 1903.

or servile labour, as in Queensland, have tempered the genuineness of democracy. In Cape Colony and Natal events testify how feebly the forms and even the spirit of the free British institutions have taken root in States where the great majority of the population were always excluded from political rights. The franchise and the rights it carries remain virtually a white monopoly in so-called self-governing colonies, where the coloured population was, in 1903, to the white as four to one and ten to one respectively.

In certain of our older Crown colonies there exists a representative element in the government. While the administration is entirely vested in a governor appointed by the Crown, assisted by a council nominated by him, the colonists elect a portion of the legislative assembly. The following colonies belong to this order : Jamaica, Barbados, Trinidad, Bahamas, British Guiana, Windward Islands, Bermudas, Malta, Mauritius, Ceylon.

The representative element differs considerably in size and influence in these colonies, but nowhere does it out-number the non-elected element. It thus becomes an advisory rather than a really legislative factor. Not merely is the elected always dominated in numbers by the non-elected element, but in all cases the veto of the Colonial Office is freely exercised upon measures passed by the assemblies. To this it should be added that in nearly all cases a fairly high property qualification is attached to the franchise, precluding the coloured people from exercising an elective power proportionate to their numbers and their stake in the country.

The entire population of these modified Crown colonies amounted to 5,700,000 in 1898.[1]

The overwhelming majority of the subjects of the British

[1] In all essential features India and Egypt are (1903) to be classed as Crown colonies.

Empire are under Crown colony government, or under protectorates.[1] In neither case do they enjoy any of the important political rights of British citizens; in neither case are they being trained in the arts of free British institutions. In the Crown colony the population exercises no political privileges. The governor, appointed by the Colonial Office, is absolute, alike for legislation and administration; he is aided by a council of local residents usually chosen by himself or by home authority, but its function is merely advisory, and its advice can be and frequently is ignored. In the vast protectorates we have assumed in Africa and Asia there is no tincture of British representative government; the British factor consists in arbitrary acts of irregular interference with native government. Exceptions to this exist in the case of districts assigned to Chartered Companies, where business men, animated avowedly by business ends, are permitted to exercise arbitrary powers of government over native populations under the imperfect check of some British Imperial Commissioner.

Again, in certain native and feudatory States of India our Empire is virtually confined to government of foreign relations, military protection, and a veto upon grave internal disorder, the real administration of the countries being left in the hands of native princes or headmen. However excellent this arrangement may be, it lends little support to the general theory of the British Empire as an educator of free political institutions.

Where British government is real, it does not carry freedom or self-government; where it does carry a certain amount of freedom and self-government, it is not real. Not five per cent. of the population of our Empire are possessed of any appreciable portion of the political and civil liberties which are the basis of British civilization.

[1] Situation in 1903.

Outside the eleven millions of British subjects in Canada, Australia, and New Zealand, no considerable body is endowed with full self-government in the more vital matters, or being "elevated from the position of inferiority to that of association."[1]

This is the most important of all facts for students of the present and probable future of the British Empire. We have taken upon ourselves in these little islands the responsibility of governing huge aggregations of lower races in all parts of the world by methods which are antithetic to the methods of government which we most value for ourselves.

The question just here is not whether we are governing these colonies and subject races well and wisely, better than they could govern themselves if left alone, or better than another imperial European nation could govern them, but whether we are giving them those arts of government which we regard as our most valuable possessions.

The statement in the passage which we quoted, that underneath the fluctuations of our colonial policy throughout the nineteenth century lay the " fixed rule " of educating the dependencies for self-government, is so totally and manifestly opposed to historical records and to the testimony of loyal colonial politicians in all our colonies as to deserve no further formal refutation. The very structure of our party government, the ignorance or open indifference of colonial ministers of the elder generations, the biassed play of colonial cliques and interests, reduced the whole of our colonial government for many decades to something between a see-saw and a game of chance : the nearest approach to any " fixed rule " was the steady prolonged pressure of some commercial interest whose political aid was worth purchase. That any such " beneficent spirit " as is recorded

[1] All the facts and figures given here and elsewhere relate to the period of this study, 1903.

consciously presided over the policy applied to any class of colonies during the larger half of the nineteenth century is notoriously false. To those statesmen to whom the colonies were not a tiresome burden, they were a useful dumping-ground for surplus population, including criminals, paupers and ne'er-do-weels, or possible markets for British trade. A few more liberal-minded politicians, such as Sir W. Molesworth and Mr. Wakefield, regarded with sympathetic interest the rising democracies of Australasia and Canada. But the idea of planning a colonial policy inspired by the motive of teaching the arts of free representative self-government not merely was not the " fixed rule," but was not present as a rule at all for any responsible Colonial Secretary in Great Britain.

When the first dawn of the new Imperialism in the seventies gave fuller political consciousness to " empire," it did indeed become a commonplace of Liberal thought that England's imperial mission was to spread the arts of free government, and the examples of Australia and Canada looming big before all eyes suggested that we were doing this. The principles and practices of representative government were " boomed "; Liberal pro-consuls set on foot imposing experiments in India and in the West Indies; the progress of the South African colonies suggested that by fairly rapid degrees the various populations of the Empire might attain substantial measures of self-government; and the larger vision of a British Empire, consisting in the main or altogether of a union of self-governing States, began to dazzle politicians.

Some persons—though a · diminishing number—still entertain these notions and believe that we are gradually moulding the British Empire into a set of substantially self-governing States. Our position in India is justified, they think, by the training we are giving the natives in good government, and when they hear of " representative " elements in the government of Ceylon or of Jamaica they flatter themselves that the whole trend of imperial government is directed to this end. Admitting the facts regarding the small proportion of present political liberty throughout the Empire, they urge that this arises from the necessary regard we have to the mode of educating lower races : the vast majority of our subjects are " children " and must be trained slowly and carefully in the arts of responsible self-government.

Now such persons are suffering from a great and demonstrable delusion if they suppose that any appreciable number of the able energetic officials who practically administer our Empire from Downing Street, or on the spot, either believe that the populations which they rule are capable of being trained for effective free self-government, or are appreciably affected in their policy by any regard to such a contingency in the near or remote future. Very few British officials any longer retain the notion that we can instruct or are successfully instructing the great populations of India in the Western arts of government. The general admission or conviction is that experiments in municipal and other government conducted under British control on British lines are failures. The real success of our Indian Government admittedly consists in good order and justice administered autocratically by able British officials. There is some training of native officials for subordinate, and in rare instances for high offices, but there is no pretence that this is the chief or an important aim or end, nor is there the least intention that these native officials shall in the future become the servants of the free Indian nation rather than of the bureaucratic Imperial Government.

In other instances, as in Egypt, we have used natives for certain administrative work, and this training in lower offices is doubtless not without its value. Our practical success in preserving order, securing justice and developing the material resources of many of our colonies has been largely due to the fact that we have learnt to employ native agents wherever possible for detailed work of administration, and to adapt our government, where it can be safely done, to native conditions. The retention of native laws and customs or of the foreign system of jurisprudence imposed by earlier colonists of another race,[1] while it has complicated government in the final court of the Privy Council, has greatly facilitated the detailed work of administration upon the spot.

Indeed the variety, not only of laws but of other modes of government in our Empire, arouses the enthusiastic admiration of many students of its history. " The British Empire," we are told, " exhibits forms and methods of government in almost exuberant variety. The several colonies at different times of their history have passed through various stages of government, and in 1891 there are some thirty or forty different forms operating simultaneously within our Empire alone. At this moment there are regions where government of a purely despotic kind is in full exercise, and the Empire includes also colonies where the subordination of the colonial government has become so slight as to be almost impalpable."[2]

---

[1] " Every country conquered or ceded to the Crown of England retains such laws and such rules of law (not inconsistent with the general law of England affecting dependencies) as were in force at the time of the conquest or cession, until they are repealed by competent authority. Now, inasmuch as many independent States and many dependent colonies of other States have become English dependencies, many of the English dependencies have retained wholly or in part foreign systems of jurisprudence. Thus Trinidad retains much of the Spanish law ; Demarara, Cape of Good Hope, and Ceylon retain much of the Dutch law ; Lower Canada retains the French civil law according to the " coutume de Paris " ; St. Lucia retains the old French law as it existed when the island belonged to France " (Lewis, *Government of Dependencies*, p. 198).

[2] Caldecott, *English Colonization and Empire*, p. 121.

Whether this is a striking testimony to the genius for "elasticity" of our colonial policy, or an instance of haphazard opportunism, one need not here discuss.[1]

The point is that an examination of this immense variety of government disposes entirely of the suggestion that by the extension of our Empire we have been spreading the type of free government which is distinctively British.

The present condition of the government under which the vast majority of our fellow-subjects in the Empire live is eminently un-British in that it is based, not on the consent

[1] What "elasticity" actually signifies in Colonial Office government may be illustrated by the following testimony of Miss Kingsley in regard to West Africa. "Before taking any important steps the West African governor is supposed to consult the officials at the Colonial Office, but as the Colonial Office is not so well informed as the governor himself is, this can be no help to him if he is a really able man, and no check on him if he is not an able man. For, be he what he may, he is the representative of the Colonial Office ; he cannot, it is true, persuade the Colonial Office to go and involve itself in rows with European continental Powers, because the Office knows about them ; but if he is a strong-minded man with a fad, he can persuade the Colonial Office to let him try that fad on the natives or the traders, because the Colonial Office does not know the natives nor the West African trade. You see, therefore, you have in the governor of a West African possession a man in a bad position. He is aided by no council worth having, no regular set of experts ; he is held in by another council equally non-expert, except in the direction of continental politics. . . . In addition to the governor there are the other officials, medical, legal, secretarial, constabulary, and customs. The majority of them are engaged in looking after each other and clerking. Clerking is the breath of the Crown colony system, and customs what it feeds on. Owing to the climate it is practically necessary to have a double staff in all these departments—that is what the system would have if it were perfect ; as it is, some official's work is always being done by a subordinate ; it may be equally well done, but it is not equally well paid for, and there is no continuity in policy in any department, except those which are entirely clerk, and the expense of this is necessarily great. The main evil of this want of continuity is, of course, in the governors—a governor goes out, starts a new line of policy, goes home on furlough leaving in charge the colonial secretary, who does not by any means always feel enthusiastic towards that policy, so it languishes. The governor comes back, goes at it again like a giant refreshed, but by no means better acquainted with local affairs for having been away ; then he goes home again or dies, or gets a new appointment ; a brand-new governor comes out, he starts a new line of policy, perhaps has a new colonial secretary into the bargain : anyhow the thing goes on wavering, not advancing. The only description I have heard of our policy in West African colonies that seems to me to do it justice is that given by a medical friend of mine, who said it was a coma accompanied by fits."—(*West African Studies*, pp. 328–330).

of the governed, but upon the will of imperial officials; it does indeed betray a great variety of forms, but they agree in the essential of un-freedom. Nor is it true that any of the more enlightened methods of administration we employ are directed towards undoing this character. Not only in India, but in the West Indies, and wherever there exists a large preponderance of coloured population, the trend, not merely of ignorant, but of enlightened public opinion, is against a genuinely representative government on British lines. It is perceived to be incompatible with the economic and social authority of a superior race.

When British authority has been forcibly fastened upon large populations of alien race and colour, with habits of life and thought which do not blend with ours, it is found impossible to graft the tender plants of free representative government, and at the same time to preserve good order in external affairs. We are obliged in practice to make a choice between good order and justice administered autocratically in accordance with British standards, on the one hand, and delicate, costly, doubtful, and disorderly experiments in self-government on British lines upon the other, and we have practically everywhere decided to adopt the former alternative. A third and sounder method of permitting large liberty of self-government under a really loose protectorate, adopted in a few instances, as in Basutoland, part of Bechuanaland, and a few Indian States, meets with no great favour and in most instances seems no longer feasible. It cannot be too clearly recognised that the old Liberal notion of our educating lower races in the arts of popular government is discredited, and only survives for platform purposes when some new step of annexation is urged upon the country.

The case of Egypt is a *locus classicus*. Here we entered the country under the best auspices, as deliverers rather than as conquerors; we undoubtedly conferred great economic benefits upon large sections of the people, who are not savages, but inheritors of ancient civilised traditions. The whole existing machinery of government is virtually at our disposal, to modify it according to our will. We have reformed taxation, improved justice, and cleansed the public services of many corruptions, and claim in many ways to have improved the condition of the fellaheen. But are we introducing British political institutions in such wise as to graft them on a nation destined for progress in self-government ?

The following statement of Lord Milner may be regarded as typical, not of the fossilised, old-world official, but of the modern, more enlightened, practical Imperialist :—

" I attach much more importance, in the immediate future of Egypt, to the improvement of the character and intelligence of the official class than I do to the development of the representative institutions with which we endowed the country in 1883. As a true born Briton (*sic!*), I, of course take off my hat to everything that calls itself Franchise, Parliament, Representation of the People, the Voice of the Majority, and all the rest of it. But, as an observer of the actual condition of Egyptian society, I cannot shut my eyes to the fact that popular government, as we understand it, is for a longer time than any one can foresee at present out of the question. The people neither comprehend it nor desire it. They would come to singular grief if they had it. And nobody, except a few silly theorists, thinks of giving it to them."[1]

Yet here we went into this country upon the express understanding that we should do precisely what Lord Milner says we have no intention of doing, viz. teach the

[1] *England in Egypt*, pp. 378, 379.

people to govern themselves within the space of a few years and then leave them to work their government.

I am not here, however, concerned to discuss either the value of the governmental work which we are doing or our right to impose our authority upon weaker populations. But the fact is plain that the British Empire is not to any appreciable extent a training ground in the British arts of free government.

In the light of this inquiry, directed to the Empire as a whole, how do we regard the new Imperialism ? Almost the whole of it, as we have seen, consists of tropical or sub-tropical territory, with large populations of savages or " lower races " ; little of it is likely, even in the distant future, to increase the area of sound colonial life. In the few places where English colonists can settle, as in parts of the South African States, they will be so largely outnumbered by dark populations as to render the adoption of free representative government impracticable.

In a single word, the New Imperialism has increased the area of British despotism, far outbalancing the progress in population and in practical freedom attained by our few democratic colonies.

It has not made for the spread of British liberty and for the propagation of our arts of government. The lands and populations which we have annexed we govern, in so far as we govern them at all, by distinctively autocratic methods, administered chiefly from Downing Street, but partly from centres of colonial government, in cases where self-governing colonies have been permitted to annex.

II

Now this large expansion of British political despotism is fraught with reactions upon home politics which are deserving of most serious consideration. A curious blindness seems to beset the mind of the average educated Briton when he is asked to picture to himself our colonial Empire. Almost instinctively he visualises Canada, Australasia, and South Africa—the rest he virtually ignores. Yet the Imperialism which is our chief concern, the expansion of the last quarter of the nineteenth century, has nothing in common with Canada and Australasia, and very little with " white man's Africa."

When Lord Rosebery uttered his famous words about " a free, tolerant and unaggressive Empire," he can scarcely have had in mind our vast encroachments in West and Central Africa, in the Soudan, on the Burmese frontier, or in Matabeleland. But the distinction between genuine Colonialism and Imperialism, important in itself, is vital when we consider their respective relations to domestic policy.

Modern British colonialism has been no drain upon our material and moral resources, because it has made for the creation of free white democracies, a policy of informal federation, of decentralisation, involving no appreciable strain upon the governmental faculties of Great Britain. Such federation, whether it remains informal with the slight attachment of imperial sovereignty which now exists, or voluntarily takes some more formal shape, political or financial, may well be regarded as a source of strength, political and military.

Imperialism is the very antithesis of this free, wholesome colonial connection, making, as it ever does, for greater complications of foreign policy, greater centralisation of power, and a congestion of business which ever threatens to absorb and overtax the capacity of parliamentary government.

The true political nature of Imperialism is best seen

by confronting it with the watchwords of progress accepted in the middle of the nineteenth century by moderate men of both great parties in the State, though with interpretations, varying in degree—peace, economy, reform, and popular self-government. Even now we find no formal abandonment of the principles of government these terms express, and a large section of professed Liberals believe or assert that Imperialism is consistent with the maintenance of all these virtues.

This contention, however, is belied by facts. The decades of Imperialism have been prolific in wars ; most of these wars have been directly motived by aggression of white races upon " lower races," and have issued in the forcible seizure of territory. Every one of the steps of expansion in Africa, Asia, and the Pacific has been accompanied by bloodshed ; each imperialist Power keeps an increasing army available for foreign service ; rectification of frontiers, punitive expeditions, and other euphemisms for war have been in incessant progress. The *Pax Britannica*, always an impudent falsehood, has become a grotesque monster of hypocrisy ; along our Indian frontiers, in West Africa, in the Soudan, in Uganda, in Rhodesia fighting has been[1] well-nigh incessant. Although the great imperialist Powers kept their hands off one another, save where the rising empire of the United States found its opportunity in the falling empire of Spain, the self-restraint has been costly and precarious. Peace as a national policy is antagonized not merely by war, but by militarism, an even graver injury. Apart from the enmity of France and Germany, the main cause of the vast armaments which have drained the resources of most European countries is their conflicting interests in territorial and commercial expansion. Where thirty years ago there existed one sensitive spot in our

[1] The situation in 1903.

relations with France, or Germany, or Russia, there are a dozen now ; diplomatic strains are of almost monthly occurrence between Powers with African or Chinese interests, and the chiefly business nature of the national antagonisms renders them more dangerous, inasmuch as the policy of Governments passes under the influence of distinctively financial juntos.

The contention of the *si pacem vis para bellum* school, that armaments alone constitute the best security for peace, is based upon the assumption that a genuine lasting antagonism of real interests exists between the various peoples who are called upon to undergo this monstrous sacrifice.

Our economic analysis has disclosed the fact that it is only the interests of competing cliques of business men— investors, contractors, export manufacturers, and certain professional classes—that are antagonistic ; that these cliques, usurping the authority and voice of the people, use the public resources to push their private interests, and spend the blood and money of the people in this vast and disastrous military game, feigning national antagonisms which have no basis in reality. It is not to the interest of the British people, either as producers of wealth or as tax-payers, to risk a war with Russia and France in order to join Japan in preventing Russia from seizing Corea ; but it may serve the interests of a group of commercial politicians to promote this dangerous policy. The South African war, openly fomented by gold speculators for their private purposes, will rank in history as a leading case of this usurpation of nationalism.

War, however, represents not the success, but the failure of this policy ; its normal and most perilous fruit is not war, but militarism. So long as this competitive expansion for territory and foreign markets is permitted to misrepresent itself as " national policy " the antagonism of interests seems real, and the peoples must sweat and bleed and toil to keep up an ever more expensive machinery of war.

Were logic applicable in such cases, the notion that the greater the preparation for war the smaller the probability of its occurrence might well appear a *reductio ad absurdum* of militarism, implying, as it does, that the only way to secure an eternal world peace is to concentrate the entire energy of all nations upon the art of war, which is thus rendered incapable of practice.

With such paradoxes, however, we need not concern ourselves. The patent admitted fact that, as a result of imperial competition, an ever larger proportion of the time, energy, and money of " imperialist " nations is absorbed by naval and military armaments, and that no check upon further absorption is regarded as practicable by Imperialists, brings " militarism " into the forefront of practical politics. Great Britain and the United States, which have hitherto congratulated themselves on escaping the militarism of continental Europe, are now rapidly succumbing. Why ? Does any one suggest that either nation needs a larger army for the protection of its own lands or of any of its genuine white settlements in other lands ? Not at all. It is not pretended that the militarization of England is required for such protective work. Australia and New Zealand are not threatened by any power, nor could a British army render them adequate assistance if they were ; equally impotent would British land forces be against the only Power which could conceivably attack our Canadian Dominion ; even South Africa, which lies on the borderland between colony and tropical dependency, cannot ultimately be secured by the military power of England. It is our mistaken annexation of tropical and sub-tropical territories, and the attempt to govern "lower races," that is driving us down the steep road to militarism.

If we are to hold all that we have taken since 1870 and to compete with the new industrial nations in the further partition of empires or spheres of influence in Africa and Asia, we must be prepared to fight. The enmity of rival empires, openly displayed throughout the South African war, is admittedly due to the policy by which we have forestalled, and are still seeking to forestall, these rivals in the annexation of territory and of markets throughout the world. The theory that we may be compelled to fight for the very existence of our Empire against some combination of European powers, which is now used to scare the nation into a definite and irretrievable reversal of our military and commercial policy, signifies nothing else than the intention of the imperialist interests to continue their reckless career of annexation. In 1896 Lord Rosebery gave a vivid description of the policy of the last two decades of the century, and put forth a powerful plea for peace.

"The British Empire . . . needs peace. For the last twenty years, still more during the last twelve, you have been laying your hands, with almost frantic eagerness, on every tract of territory adjacent to your own or desirable from any other point of view which you thought it desirable to take. That has had two results. I daresay it has been quite right, but it has had two results. The first result is this, that you have excited to an almost intolerable degree the envy of other colonizing (sic !) nations, and that, in the case of many countries, or several countries rather, which were formerly friendly to you, you can reckon—in consequence of your colonial policy, whether right or wrong— not on their active benevolence, but on their active malevolence. And, secondly, you have acquired so enormous a mass of territory that it will be years before you can settle it or control it, or make it capable of defence or make it amenable to the acts of your administration. . . . In twelve years you have added to the Empire, whether in the shape of actual annexation or of dominion, or of what is called a sphere of influence, 2,600,000 square miles of territory . . . to the 120,000 square miles of the United Kingdom, which is part of your Empire, you have added during the last twelve years twenty-two areas as large as that United Kingdom itself. I say that that marks out for many years a policy from which you cannot depart if you would. You may be compelled to draw the sword—I hope you may not be; but the foreign policy of Great Britain, until its territory is consolidated, filled up, settled, civilized, must inevitably be a policy of peace."[1]

After these words were uttered, vast new tracts of un-digested empire were added in the Soudan, in East Africa, in South Africa, while Great Britain was busily entangling herself in obligations of incalculable magnitude and peril in the China seas, and the prophet who spoke this warning was himself an active instrument in the furtherance of the very folly he denounced.

Imperialism—whether it consists in a further policy of expansion or in the rigorous maintenance of all those vast tropical lands which have been ear-marked as British spheres of influence—implies militarism now and ruinous wars in the future. This truth is now for the first time brought sharply and nakedly before the mind of the nation. The kingdoms of the earth are to be ours on condition that we fall down and worship Moloch.

Militarism approaches Great Britain with the following dilemma. If the army needed for defence of the Empire is to remain upon a voluntary basis, consisting of selected material obtained by application of economic inducements,

[1] Edinburgh, October 9, 1896.

a considerable increase either of the regular forces or the militia can only be obtained by a rise of pay so large as to tempt men, not from the unskilled labour market or the agricultural districts as heretofore, but from the skilled artisan classes of the towns. It requires but slight consideration to perceive that every fresh increment of the army will involve an appeal to a class accustomed to a higher standard of wage, and that the pay for the entire army must be regulated by the rate of pay needed to secure this last increment. Recruiting in time of war is always brisker than in time of peace, other motives blending with the distinctly economic motive. Every increase of our forces on a peace footing will involve a far more than proportionate increase in the rate of pay—how large an increase experiment alone can teach. It seems quite likely that in a period of normally good trade our voluntary army could only be increased 50 per cent. by doubling the former rate of pay, or by other improved conditions of employment involving an equivalent rise of cost, and that, if we required to double the size of our standing army, we should have to treble the rate of pay. If, on the other hand, the prospect of some such enormous increase of military expenditure should lead us to abandon the purely voluntary basis, and have recourse to conscription or some other form of compulsory service, we could not fail to suffer in average fighting calibre. Such selection of physique and morale as prevailed under the voluntary system would now disappear, and the radical unfitness of a nation of town-dwellers for arduous military service would be disclosed. The fatuous attempt to convert ineffective slum-workers and weedy city clerks into tough military material, fit for prolonged foreign service, or even for efficient home defence, would be detected, it may be hoped, before the trial by combat with a military Power drawing its soldiers from the soil. A nation, 70 per cent. of whose inhabitants are denizens of towns, cannot afford to challenge its neighbours to trials of physical force, for in the last resort war is determined neither by generalship nor superiority of weapons, but by those elements of brute endurance which are incompatible with the life of industrial towns.

The full danger of the dilemma of militarism is only perceived when the indirect is added to the direct expenditure. An army, volunteer or conscript, formed out of town material would take longer training or more frequent exercise than a peasant army; the waste of labour power, by withdrawing the youth of the nation from their early training in the productive arts in order to prepare them for the destructive art, would be greater, and would impair more grievously the skilled industries than in nations less advanced in the specialized trades and professions. The least of these economic injuries would be the actual loss of labour time involved in the withdrawal; far graver would be the damage to industrial skill and character by withdrawing youths at the period of best docility and aptitude for skilled work and subjecting them to a distinctively mechanical discipline, for though the slum-dweller and the clodhopper may gain in smartness and alertness by military training, the skilled labouring classes will lose more by the crushing of individual initiative which professional militarism always involves.

At a time when the call for free, bold initiative and individual enterprise and ingenuity in the assimilation of the latest scientific and technical knowledge for the arts of industry, for improved organization and methods of business, becomes most urgent to enable us to hold our own in the new competition of the world—at such a time to subject the youth of our nation to the barrack system, or to any form of effective military training, would be veritable suicide. It is to no purpose to reply that some of our keen commercial competitors, notoriously Germany, are already saddled with this burden; the answer is that, if we can hardly hold our own with Germany while she bears this burden, we shall hand over to her an easy victory if we assume a still heavier one.[1] Whatever virtues are attributed to military discipline by its apologists, it is admitted that this training does not conduce to industrial efficiency. The economic cost of militarism is therefore twofold; the greatly increased expense of the army must be defrayed by an impoverished people.

So far, I have regarded the issue on its narrowly economic side. Far more important are the political implications of militarism. These strike at the very root of popular liberty and the ordinary civic virtues. A few plain reflections serve to dispel the sophistical vapours which are used to form a halo round the life of the soldier. *Respice finem*. There exists an absolute antagonism between the activity of the good citizen and that of the soldier. The end of the soldier is not, as is sometimes falsely said, to die for his country; it is to kill for his country. In as far as he dies he is a failure; his work is to kill, and he attains perfection as a soldier when he becomes a perfect killer. This end, the slaughter of one's fellow-men, forms a professional character, alien from, and antagonistic to, the character of our ordinary citizen, whose work conduces to the preservation of his fellow-men. If it be contended that this final purpose, though informing and moulding the structure and functions of an army, operates but seldom and slightly upon the consciousness of the individual soldier, save upon the battlefield, the answer is that, in the absence from consciousness of this end, the entire routine of the soldier's life, his drill, parades, and whole

[1] Refers, of course, to the situation in 1903.

military exercise, is a useless, purposeless activity, and that these qualities exercise a hardly less degrading influence on character than the conscious intention of killing his fellow-men.

The psychical reactions of military life are indeed notorious ; even those who defend the utility of an army do not deny that it unfits a man for civil life. Nor can it be maintained that a shorter general service, such as suffices for a citizen army, escapes these reactions. If the service is long and rigorous enough to be effective, it involves these psychical reactions, which are, indeed, part and parcel of military efficiency. How clearly this is set forth by Mr. March-Phillips in his admirable appreciation of the common soldier's life !

" Soldiers as a class (I take the town-bred, slum-bred majority, mind) are men who have discarded the civil standard of morality altogether. They simply ignore it. This is, no doubt, why civilians fight shy of them. In the game of life they don't play the same rules, and the consequence is a good deal of misunderstanding, until finally the civilian says he won't play with the Tommy any more. In soldiers' eyes lying, theft, drunkenness, bad language, etc., are not evils at all. They steal like jackdaws. As to language, I used to think the language of a merchant ship's fo'c'sle pretty bad, but the language of Tommies, in point of profanity, quite equals, and, in point of obscenity, beats it hollow. This department is a speciality of his. Lying he treats with the same large charity. To lie like a trooper is quite a sound metaphor. He invents all sorts of elaborate lies for the mere pleasure of inventing them. Looting, again, is one of his perpetual joys. Not merely looting for profit, but looting for the sheer fun of the destruction, etc."[1] The fidelity of this description is attested by the

[1] *With Remington*, by L. March-Phillips, pp. 131, 132.

sympathy which the writer displays with the soldierly attributes that accompany, and, in his opinion, atone for, these breaches of the civilian rules.

" Are thieving and lying and looting and bestial talk very bad things ? If they are, Tommy is a bad man. But, for some reason or other, since I got to know him, I have thought rather less of the iniquity of these things than I did before."

This judgment is itself a striking comment on militarism. The fact that it should be given by a man of sterling character and culture is the most convincing testimony to the corrupting influence of war.

To this informal witness may be added the significant evidence of Lord Wolseley's *Soldier's Pocket-book*.

" As a nation, we are brought up to feel it a disgrace to succeed by falsehood ; the word ' spy ' conveys in it something as repulsive as slave. We will keep hammering away with the conviction that honesty is the best policy, and that truth always wins in the long run. These pretty little sentences do well enough for a child's copy-book, but the man who acts upon them in war had better sheathe his sword for ever."

The order and progress of Great Britain during the nineteenth century was secured by the cultivation and practise of the ordinary civic and industrial virtues, assisted by certain advantages of natural resources and historical contingencies. Are we prepared to substitute the military code of ethics or to distract the national mind and conduct by a perpetual conflict of two warring principles, the one making for the evolution of the good citizen, the other for the evolution of the good soldier ?

Ignoring, for the present, distinctively moral degradation of this reversion from industrial to military ethics, we cannot but perceive that the damage done to commercial morality must react disastrously upon the wealth-producing power of the nation, and sap the roots of imperial expenditure.

But one loophole of escape from this dilemma presents itself, an escape fraught with still graver peril. The new Imperialism has been, we have seen, chiefly concerned with tropical and sub-tropical countries where large "lower races" are brought under white control. Why should Englishmen fight the defensive or offensive wars of this Empire, when cheaper, more numerous, and better-assimilated fighting material can be raised upon the spot, or transferred from one tropical dominion to another? As the labour of industrial development of tropical resources is put upon the "lower races" who reside there, under white superintendence, why should not militarism be organized upon the same basis, black or brown or yellow men, to whom military discipline will be "a wholesome education," fighting for the British Empire under British officers? Thus can we best economize our own limited military material, keeping most of it for home defence. This simple solution—the employment of cheap foreign mercenary armies—is no new device. The organization of vast native forces, armed with "civilized" weapons, drilled on "civilized" methods, and commanded by "civilized" officers, formed one of the most conspicuous features of the latest stages of the great Eastern Empires, and afterwards of the Roman Empire. It has proved one of the most perilous devices of parasitism, by which a metropolitan population entrusts the defence of its lives and possessions to the precarious fidelity of "conquered races," commanded by ambitious pro-consuls.

One of the strangest symptoms of the blindness of Imperialism is the reckless indifference with which Great Britain, France, and other imperial nations embarked on this perilous dependence. Great Britain has gone farthest. Most of the fighting by which we have won our Indian Empire was done by natives; in India, as later in Egypt, great standing armies were placed under British commanders; almost all the fighting associated with our African dominions, except in the southern part, was done for us by natives. How strong the pressure was to reduce the proportion of British soldiers employed in these countries to a bare minimum of safety is amply illustrated in the case of India, when the South African emergency drove us to reduce the accepted minimum by more than fifteen thousand men, while in South Africa itself we established a dangerous precedent by employing large numbers of armed natives to fight against another white race.

Those best acquainted with the temper of the British people and of the politicians who have the direct determination of affairs will understand how readily we may be drawn along this perilous path. Nothing short of the fear of an early invasion of these islands will induce the British people to undergo the onerous experience of a really effective system of compulsory military service; no statesman except under the shadow of a serious menace of invasion will dare to press such a plan. A regular provision for compulsory foreign service will never be adopted when the alternative of mercenary native armies remains. Let these " niggers " fight for the empire in return for the services we render them by annexing and governing them and teaching them " the dignity of labour," will be the prevailing sentiment, and " imperialist " statesmen will be compelled to bow before it, diluting with British troops ever more thinly the native armies in Africa and Asia.

This mode of militarism, while cheaper and easier in the first instance, implies less and less control from Great Britain. Though reducing the strain of militarism upon the population at home, it enhances the risks of wars, which become more frequent and more barbarous in proportion as they involve to a less degree the lives of Englishmen. The expansion of our Empire under the new Imperialism has been compassed by setting the " lower races " at one another's throats, fostering tribal animosities and utilising for our supposed benefit the savage propensities of the peoples to whom we have a mission to carry Christianity and civilization.

That we do not stand alone in this ignominious policy does not make it better, rather worse, offering terrible prophetic glimpses into a not distant future, when the horrors of our eighteenth century struggle with France in North America and India may be revived upon a gigantic scale, and Africa and Asia may furnish huge cock-pits for the struggles of black and yellow armies representing the imperialist rivalries of Christendom. The present tendencies of Imperialism plainly make in this direction, involving in their recoil a degradation of Western States and a possible *débâcle* of Western civilization.

In any event Imperialism makes for war and for militarism, and has brought a great and limitless increase of expenditure of national resources upon armaments. It has impaired the independence of every nation which has yielded to its false glamour. Great Britain no longer possesses a million pounds which it can call its own ; its entire financial resources are mortgaged to a policy to be dictated by Germany, France, or Russia. A move from any of these Powers can force us to expend upon more battleships and military preparations the money we had designed to use for domestic purposes. The priority and reckless magnitude of our imperial expansion has made the danger of an armed coalition of great Powers against us no idle chimera. The development of their resources along the lines of the new industrialism, on the one hand, by driving them to seek foreign markets, brings them in all parts of the world against the vexatious barriers of British possessions ; on the other, has furnished them with ample means of public expenditure. The spread of modern industrialism tends to place our " rivals " on a level with ourselves in their public resources. Hence, at the very time when we have more reason to fear armed coalition than formerly, we are losing that superiority in finance which made it feasible for us to maintain a naval armament superior to any European combination.

All these perils in the present and the future are the fruits of the new Imperialism, which is thus exposed as the implacable and mortal enemy of Peace and Economy. How far the military aspect of Imperialism has already eaten into the resources of modern European States may be judged by the following table showing the growth of expenditure of the various great European States on military equipment in the last generation :—

MILITARY EXPENDITURE OF GREAT EUROPEAN POWERS.[1]

	1869–1870.	1897–1898.
	£	£
Great Britain	22,440,000	40,094,000
France	23,554,000	37,000,000
Russia	15,400,000	35,600,000
Germany	11,217,000	32,800,000
Austria	9,103,000	16,041,000
Italy	7,070,000	13,510,000
Totals	88,784,000	175,045,000

For the whole body of European States the increase has been from £105,719,000 in 1869–1870 to £208,877,000 in 1897–1898.

[1] See Appendix, p. 378, for expenditure of the Powers on Defence in 1934.

III

There are those who deny the antagonism of Imperialism and social reform. " The energy of a nation like ours, they urge, is not to be regarded as a fixed quantity, so that every expenditure upon imperial expansion implies a corresponding restriction for purposes of internal progress ; there are various sorts of energy demanding different outlets, so that the true economy of British genius requires many domestic and external fields of activity ; we are capable at one and the same time of imperial expansion in various directions, and of a complex energy of growth in our internal economy. The inspiration of great achievements throughout the world reacts upon the vitality of the British nation, rendering it capable of efforts of internal progress which would have been precluded by the ordinary course of smug insular self-development."

Now it is needless to argue the incompatibility of social reform with imperialism on any abstract principle regarding the quantity of national energy. Though limits of quantity exist underneath the finest economy of division of labour, as indeed is illustrated on the military plane by the limits which population imposes upon the combination of aggressive expansion and home defence, these limits are not always easy to discover and are sometimes capable of great elasticity. It cannot, therefore, be contended that the sound intellectual stuff which goes into our Indian Civil Service involves a corresponding loss to our home professions and official services, or that the adventurous energy of great explorers, missionaries, engineers, prospectors and other pioneers of empire could and would have found as ample a field and as sharp a stimulus for their energies within these islands. The issue we are considering—that of Imperialism—does not in its main political and social effects turn upon any such exact considerations of quantitative economy of energy, nor does the repudiation of Imperialism imply a confinement within rigid territorial limits of any individual or co-operative energy which may find better scope abroad. We are concerned with economy of governmental power, with Imperialism as a public policy. Even here the issue is not primarily one of quantitative economy, though, as we shall see, that is clearly involved. The antagonism of Imperialism and social reform is an inherent opposition of policy involving contradictory methods and processes of government. Some of the more obvious illustrations of this antagonism are presented by considerations of finance. Most important measures of social reform, the improvement of the machinery of public education, any large handling of the land and housing questions in town and country, the public control of the drink traffic, old-age pensions, legislation for improving the condition of the workers, involve considerable outlay of public money raised in taxation by the central or local authorities. Now Imperialism, through the ever-growing military expenditure it involves, visibly drains the public purse of the money which might be put to such purposes. Not only has the Exchequer not sufficient money to expend on public education, old-age pensions, or other State reforms ; the smaller units of local government are similarly crippled, for the taxpayers and the ratepayers are in the main the same persons, and when they are heavily mulcted by taxes for unproductive State purposes they cannot easily bear increased rates.

Every important social reform, even if it does not directly involve large public expenditure, causes financial disturbances and risks which are less tolerable at times when public expenditure is heavy and public credit fluctuating and embarrassed. Most social reforms involve some attack on vested interests, and these can best defend themselves when active Imperialism absorbs public attention. When legislation is involved, economy of time and of governmental interest is of paramount importance. Imperialism, with its " high politics," involving the honour and safety of the Empire, claims the first place, and, as the Empire grows, the number and complexity of its issues, involving close, immediate, continuous attention, grow, absorbing the time of the Government and of Parliament. It becomes more and more impossible to set aside parliamentary time for the full unbroken discussion of matters of most vital domestic importance, or to carry through any large serious measure of reform.

It is needless to labour the theory of this antagonism when the practice is apparent to every student of politics. Indeed, it has become a commonplace of history how Governments use national animosities, foreign wars and the glamour of empire-making, in order to bemuse the popular mind and divert rising resentment against domestic abuses. The vested interests, which, on our analysis, are shown to be chief prompters of an imperialist policy, play for a double stake, seeking their private commercial and financial gains at the expense and peril of the commonwealth. They at the same time protect their economic and political supremacy at home against movements of popular reform. The city ground landlord, the country squire, the banker, the usurer, and the financier, the brewer, the mine-owner, the ironmaster, the shipbuilder, and the shipping trade, the great export manufacturers and merchants, the clergy of the State Church, the universities, and great public schools, the legal trade unions and the services have, both in Great Britain and on the Continent, drawn together for common political resistance against attacks upon the power, the property, and the privileges which in various forms and degrees they represent. Having conceded under pressure the form of political power in the shape of elective institutions and a wide franchise to the masses, they are struggling to prevent the masses from gaining the substance of this power and using it for the establishment of equality of economic opportunities. The collapse of the Liberal party upon the Continent, and now in Great Britain, is only made intelligible in this way. Friends of liberty and of popular government so long as the new industrial and commercial forces were hampered by the economic barriers and the political supremacy of the *noblesse* and the landed aristocracy, they have come to temper their " trust " of the people by an ever-growing quantity of caution, until within the last two decades[1] they have either sought political fusion with the Conservatives or have dragged on a precarious existence on the strength of a few belated leaders with obsolescent principles. Where Liberalism preserves any real strength, it is because the older struggle for the franchise and the primary liberties has been delayed, as in Belgium and in Denmark, and a *modus vivendi* has been possible with the rising working-class party. In Germany, France, and Italy the Liberal party as a factor in practical politics has either disappeared or is reduced to impotence ; in England it now stands convicted of a gross palpable betrayal of the first conditions of liberty, feebly fumbling after programmes as a substitute for principles. Its leaders, having sold their party to a confederacy of stock gamblers and jingo sentimentalists, find themselves impotent to defend Free Trade, Free Press, Free Schools, Free Speech, or any of the rudiments of ancient Liberalism. They have alienated the confidence of the people. For many years they have been permitted to conduct a sham fight and to call it politics ; the people thought it real until the South African war furnished a

[1] Referring to the last twenty years of the nineteenth century.

decisive dramatic test, and the unreality of Liberalism became apparent. It is not that Liberals have openly abandoned the old principles and traditions, but that they have rendered them of no account by dallying with an Imperialism which they have foolishly and futilely striven to distinguish from the firmer brand of their political opponents. This surrender to Imperialism signifies that they have preferred the economic interests of the possessing and speculative classes, to which most of their leaders belong, to the cause of Liberalism. That they are not conscious traitors or hypocrites may be readily conceded, but the fact remains that they have sold the cause of popular reform, which was their rightful heritage, for an Imperialism which appealed to their business interests and their social pre-possessions. The mess of pottage has been seasoned by various sweeter herbs, but its " stock " is class selfishness. The majority of the influential Liberals fled from the fight which was the truest test of Liberalism in their generation because they were " hirelings," destitute of firm political principle, gladly abandoning themselves to whatever shallow and ignoble defences a blear-eyed, raucous " patriotism " was ready to devise for their excuse.

It is possible to explain and qualify, but this remains the naked truth, which it is well to recognise. A Liberal party can only survive as a discredited or feeble remnant in England, unless it consents definitely to dissever itself from that Imperialism which its past leaders as well as their opponents, have permitted to block the progress of domestic reforms.

There are individuals and sections among those who have comprised the Liberal party whose deception has been in large measure blind and involuntary, because they have been absorbed by their interest in some single important issue of social reform, whether it be temperance, land tenure, education, or the like. Let these men now recognize, as in honesty they can scarcely fail to do, that Imperialism is the deadly enemy of each of these reforms, that none of them can make serious advance so long as the expansion of the Empire and its satellite (militarism) absorb the time, the energy, the money of the State. Thus alone is it still possible that a strong rally of Liberals might, by fusion or co-operation with the political organisations of the working classes, fight Imperialism with the only effectual weapon, social reconstruction on the basis of democracy.

IV

The antagonism with democracy drives to the very roots of Imperialism as a political principle. Not only is Imperialism used to frustrate those measures of economic reform now recognized as essential to the effectual working of all machinery of popular government, but it operates to paralyse the working of that machinery itself. Representative institutions are ill adapted for empire, either as regards men or methods. The government of a great heterogeneous medley of lower races by departmental officials in London and their nominated emissaries lies outside the scope of popular knowledge and popular control. The Foreign, Colonial, and Indian Secretaries in Parliament, the permanent officials of the departments, the governors and staff who represent the Imperial Government in our dependencies, are not, and cannot be, controlled directly or effectively by the will of the people. This subordination of the legislative to the executive, and the concentration of executive power in an autocracy, are necessary consequences of the predominance of foreign over domestic politics. The process is attended by a decay of party spirit and party action, and an insistence on the part of the autocracy, whether it be a Kaiser or a Cabinet, that all effective party criticism is unpatriotic and verges on treason. An able writer, discussing the new foreign policy of Germany, summarises the point of view of the expansionists : " It is claimed by them that in foreign affairs the nation should stand as one man, that policies once entered upon by the Government should not be repudiated, and that criticism should be avoided as weakening the influence of the nation abroad. . . . It is evident that when the most important concerns of a nation are thus withdrawn from the field of party difference, party government itself must grow weak, as dealing no longer with vital affairs. . . . Thus, as the importance of the executive is enhanced, that of the legislative is lowered, and parliamentary action is looked down upon as the futile and irritating activity of unpractical critics. If the governmental measures are to be adopted inevitably, why not dispense with the irritating delay of parliamentary discussion ? "[1]

The Kaiser's speech at Hamburg, October 19, 1899, condenses the doctrine thus : " The face of the world has changed greatly during the last few years. What formerly required centuries is now accomplished in a few months. The task of Kaiser and Government has consequently grown beyond measure, and a solution will only be possible when the German people renounce party divisions. Standing in serried ranks behind the Kaiser, proud of their great fatherland, and conscious of their real worth, the Germans must watch the development of foreign States. They must make sacrifices for their position as a world-power, and, abandoning party spirit, they must stand united behind their prince and emperor."

Autocratic government in imperial politics naturally

[1] *World Politics*, by P. S. Reinsch, pp. 300, 301 (Macmillan & Co.).

reacts upon domestic government. The intricacy of the departmental work of the Home Office, the Board of Trade, of Education and other important offices has favoured this reaction, which has taken shape in government by administrative orders in accordance with large powers slipped into important statutes and not properly challenged or safeguarded amid the chaotic hurry in which most governments are driven in legislation. It is noticeable that in America a still more dangerous practice has sprung up, entitled " government by injunction," in which the judiciary is virtually empowered to issue decrees having the effect of laws with attendant penalties for specific acts.

In Great Britain the weakening of " party " is visibly attended by a decline of the reality of popular control. Just in proportion as foreign and colonial policy bulks more largely in the deliberative and administrative work of the State is government necessarily removed from the real control of the people. It is no mere question of economy of the time and energy of Parliament, though the dwindling proportion of the sessions devoted to consideration of domestic questions represents a corresponding decline of practical democracy. The wound to popular government penetrates far deeper. Imperialism, and the military, diplomatic, and financial resources which feed it, have become so far the paramount considerations of recent Governments that they mould and direct the entire policy, give point, colour and character to the conduct of public affairs, and overawe by continual suggestions of unknown and incalculable gains and perils the nearer and more sober processes of domestic policy. The effect on parliamentary government has been great, quick, and of palpable import, making for the diminution of the power of representative institutions. At elections the electorate is no longer invited to exercise a free, conscious, rational choice between the representatives of different intelligible policies; it is invited to endorse, or to refuse endorsement, to a difficult, intricate, and hazardous imperial and foreign policy, commonly couched in a few well-sounding general phrases, and supported by an appeal to the necessity of solidarity and continuity of national conduct—virtually a blind vote of confidence. In the deliberations of the House of Commons the power of the Opposition to oppose has been seriously and progressively impaired: partly by alteration in the rules of the House, which have diminished the right of full discussion of legislative measures in their several stages, and impaired the privileges of the Commons, viz., the right of discussing grievances upon votes of Supply, and of questioning ministers regarding the conduct of their offices; partly by a forcible encroachment of the Government upon the rights and privileges formerly enjoyed by private members in moving resolutions and in introducing bills. This diminution of the power of opposition is only the first of a series of processes of concentration of power. The Government now claims for its measures the complete disposal of the time of the House whenever it judges such monopoly to be desirable.

Within the Government itself the same centripetal forces have been operative. "There can," writes Mr. Bryce, "be no doubt that the power of the Cabinet as against the House of Commons has grown steadily and rapidly, and it appears (1901) to be still growing."[1]

So the Cabinet absorbs the powers of the House, while the Cabinet itself has been deliberately and consciously expanded in size so as to promote the concentration of real power in an informal but very real "inner Cabinet," retaining some slight selective elasticity, but virtually consisting of the Prime Minister and the Foreign and

[1] *Studies in History and Jurisprudence*, Vol. i, p. 177.

Colonial Secretaries and the Chancellor of the Exchequer. This process of centralisation of power, which tends to destroy representative government, reducing the House of Commons to be little more than a machine for the automatic registration of the decrees of an unelected inner Cabinet, is chiefly attributable to Imperialism.[1] The consideration of delicate, uncertain intelligence affecting our relations with foreign Powers, the accepted necessity of secrecy in diplomacy, and of expeditious, unobtrusive action, seem to favour and even to necessitate a highly centralised autocratic and bureaucratic method of government.

Amid this general decline of parliamentary government the " party system " is visibly collapsing, based as it was on plain cleavages in domestic policy which have little significance when confronted with the claims and powers of Imperialism. If the party system is destined to survive in British politics, it can only do so by the consolidation of all sections opposed to the " imperialist " practices to which Liberal as well as Conservative ministries have adhered during recent years. So long as Imperialism is allowed to hold the field, the only real political conflict is between groups representing the divergent branches of Imperialism, the men upon the spot and the Home Government, the Asiatic interests of India and China and the forward policy in Africa, the advocates of a German alliance or a Franco-Russian alliance.

[1] An experienced observer thus records the effect of these changes upon the character and conduct of members of Parliament : " For the most part, as in the country, so in the House, the *political* element has waned as a factor. The lack of interest in constitutional matters has been conspicuous. . . . The ' Parliament man ' has been disappearing ; the number of those desirous of furthering social and industrial reforms has been waning. On the other hand, those who have been anxious to grasp such opportunities of various kinds outside its work and duties as are afforded by membership of the House of Commons, and who are willing to support the Government in the division lobby without being called upon to do much more, came up in large numbers in 1895 and 1900, and now form a very large proportion, if not the majority, of the House of Commons " (Mr. John E. Ellis, M.P., *The Speaker*, June 7, 1902).

V

Imperialism and popular government have nothing in common: they differ in spirit, in policy, in method. Of policy and method I have already spoken; it remains to point out how the spirit of Imperialism poisons the springs of democracy in the mind and character of the people. As our free self-governing colonies have furnished hope, encouragement, and leading to the popular aspirations in Great Britain, not merely by practical successes in the arts of popular government, but by the wafting of a spirit of freedom and equality, so our despotically ruled dependencies have ever served to damage the character of our people by feeding the habits of snobbish subservience, the admiration of wealth and rank, the corrupt survivals of the inequalities of feudalism. This process began with the advent of the East Indian nabob and the West Indian planter into English society and politics, bringing back with his plunders of the slave trade and the gains of corrupt and extortionate officialism the acts of vulgar ostentation, domineering demeanour and corrupting largesse to dazzle and degrade the life of our people. Cobden, writing in 1860 of our Indian Empire, put this pithy question: " Is it not just possible that we may become corrupted at home by the reaction of arbitrary political maxims in the East upon our domestic politics, just as Greece and Rome were demoralised by their contact with Asia ? "[1]

Not merely is the reaction possible, it is inevitable. As the despotic portion of our Empire has grown in area, a larger and larger number of men, trained in the temper and methods of autocracy as soldiers and civil officials in our Crown colonies, protectorates, and Indian Empire, reinforced by numbers of merchants, planters, engineers, and overseers, whose lives have been those of a superior caste living an

[1] Morley, *Life of Cobden*, Vol. ii, p. 361.

artificial life removed from all the healthy restraints of ordinary European society, have returned to this country, bringing back the characters, sentiments, and ideas imposed by this foreign environment. The South and South-West of England is richly sprinkled with these men, many of them wealthy, most of them endowed with leisure, men openly contemptuous of democracy, devoted to material luxury, social display, and the shallower arts of intellectual life. The wealthier among them discover political ambitions, introducing into our Houses of Parliament the coarsest and most selfish spirit of " Imperialism," using their imperial experience and connexions to push profitable companies and concessions for their private benefits, and posing as authorities so as to keep the yoke of Imperialism firmly fixed upon the shoulders of the " nigger." The South African millionaire is the brand most in evidence : his methods are the most barefaced, and his success, social and political, the most redoubtable. But the practices which are writ large in Rhodes, Beit, and their parliamentary confederates are widespread on a smaller scale ; the South of England is full of men of local influence in politics and society whose character has been formed in our despotic Empire, and whose incomes are chiefly derived from the maintenance and furtherance of this despotic rule. Not a few enter our local councils, or take posts in our constabulary or our prisons : everywhere they stand for coercion and for resistance to reform. Could the incomes expended in the Home Counties and other large districts of Southern Britain be traced to their sources, it would be found that they were in large measure wrung from the enforced toil of vast multitudes of black, brown, or yellow natives, by arts not differing essentially from those which supported in idleness and luxury imperial Rome.

It is, indeed, a nemesis of Imperialism that the arts

and crafts of tyranny, acquired and exercised in our unfree Empire, should be turned against our liberties at home. Those who have felt surprise at the total disregard or the open contempt displayed by the aristocracy and the plutocracy of this land for infringements of the liberties of the subject and for the abrogation of constitutional rights and usages have not taken sufficiently into account the steady reflux of this poison of irresponsible autocracy from our " unfree, intolerant, aggressive " Empire.

The political effects, actual and necessary, of the new Imperialism, as illustrated in the case of the greatest of imperialist Powers, may be thus summarised. It is a constant menace to peace, by furnishing continual temptations to further aggression upon lands occupied by lower races and by embroiling our nation with other nations of rival imperial ambitions ; to the sharp peril of war it adds the chronic danger and degradation of militarism, which not merely wastes the current physical and moral resources of the nations, but checks the very course of civilization. It consumes to an illimitable and incalculable extent the financial resources of a nation by military preparation, stopping the expenditure of the current income of the State upon productive public projects and burdening posterity with heavy loads of debt. Absorbing the public money, time, interest and energy on costly and unprofitable work of territorial aggrandisement, it thus wastes those energies of public life in the governing classes and the nations which are needed for internal reforms and for the cultivation of the arts of material and intellectual progress at home. Finally, the spirit, the policy, and the methods of Imperialism are hostile to the institutions of popular self-government, favouring forms of political tyranny and social authority which are the deadly enemies of effective liberty and equality.

CHAPTER II

THE SCIENTIFIC DEFENCE OF IMPERIALISM

I

THOUGH it can hardly be denied that the ambitions of individuals or nations have been the chief conscious motives in Imperialism, it is possible to maintain that here, as in other departments of human history, certain larger hidden forces operate towards the progress of humanity. The powerful hold which biological conceptions have obtained over the pioneers in the science of sociology is easily intelligible. It is only natural that the laws of individual and specific progress so clearly discerned in other parts of the animal kingdom should be rigorously applied to man ; it is not unnatural that the deflections or reversals of the laws of lower life by certain other laws, which only attain importance in the higher psychical reaches of the *genus homo*, should be underrated, misinterpreted, or ignored. The biologist who enters human history often finds himself confronted by intellectual antagonists who regard him as an interloper, and seek to raise the barrier between human and animal development. Indeed, from the ranks of the biological profession itself, scientists of such eminence as Huxley and A. R. Wallace have lent themselves to this separatism, distinguishing the ethical or spiritual progress of the human race from the general cosmic process, and endowing men with qualities and with laws of action different in kind from those which obtain in the rest of the animal kingdom. A reaction against the abrupt dogmatism of this position has led many others to an equally abrupt and equally dogmatic assertion of the laws of the lower forms of physical struggle and selection which explain or describe progress in lower animals as sufficient for all purposes of sociology.

Sociologists have shown themselves in some cases eager to accept this view, and apply it to defend the necessity, the utility, and even the righteousness of maintaining to the point of complete subjugation or extermination the physical struggle between races and types of civilization.

Admitting that the efficiency of a nation or a race requires a suspension of intestine warfare, at any rate *à l'outrance*, the crude struggle on the larger plane must, they urge, be maintained. It serves, indeed, two related purposes. A constant struggle with other races or nations is demanded for the maintenance and progress of a race or nation; abate the necessity of the struggle and the vigour of the race flags and perishes. Thus it is to the real interest of a vigorous race to be " kept up to a high pitch of external efficiency by contest, chiefly by way of war with inferior races, and with equal races by the struggle for trade routes and for the sources of raw material and of food supply." " This," adds Professor Karl Pearson, " is the natural history view of mankind, and I do not think you can in its main features subvert it."[1]

Others, taking the wider cosmic standpoint, insist that the progress of humanity itself requires the maintenance of a selective and destructive struggle between races which embody different powers and capacities, different types of civilization. It is desirable that the earth should be peopled, governed, and developed, as far as possible, by the races which can do this work best, i.e. by the races of highest " social efficiency "; these races must assert their right by

[1] *National Life from the Standpoint of Science*, p. 44 (Black, 1901).

conquering, ousting, subjugating, or extinguishing races of lower social efficiency. The good of the world, the true cause of humanity, demands that this struggle, physical, industrial, political, continue, until an ideal settlement is reached whereby the most socially efficient nations rule the earth in accordance with their several kinds and degrees of social efficiency. This principle is clearly enunciated by M. Edmond Demolins, who describes it as being " as indisputable as the law of gravitation.

"When one race shows itself superior to another in the various externals of domestic life, it *inevitably* in the long run gets the upper hand in public life and establishes its predominance. Whether this predominance is asserted by peaceable means or feats of arms, it is none the less, when the proper time comes, officially established, and afterwards unreservedly acknowledged. I have said that this law is the only thing which accounts for the history of the human race, and the revolutions of empires, and that, moreover, it explains and justifies the appropriation by Europeans of territories in Asia, Africa, and Oceania, and the whole of our colonial development."[1]

The western European nations with their colonies represent the socially efficient nations, in various degrees. Some writers, American and English, such as Professor Giddings and Mr. Kidd, believe that the Teutonic races, and in particular the Anglo-Saxon branches, represent the highest order of efficiency, in which notion they are supported by a little group of Anglophil Frenchmen.

This genuine and confident conviction about " social efficiency " must be taken as the chief moral support of Imperialism. " Human progress requires the maintenance of the race struggle, in which the weakest races shall go under while the ' socially efficient ' races survive and flourish :

[1] *Boers or British?* p. 24.

we are the 'socially efficient' race." So runs the imperialist argument.

Now, thus closely stated, the meaning of the term "socially efficient" becomes evident. It is simply the antithesis of "weak," and is equivalent to "strong in the struggle of life." Taken at the first blush it suggests admitted moral and intellectual virtues of some broad general kind, and is afterwards taken to imply such qualities. But applied in the present "natural history" sense it signifies nothing more or less than capacity to beat other races, who, from their failure, are spoken of as "lower." It is merely a repetition of the phrase "survival of the fittest," the meaning of which is clear when the question is put, "Fittest to do what ?" and the answer follows, "Fittest to survive."

It is true that "social efficiency" seems to imply much more than mere fighting capacity in war and trade, and, if we were to take into account all qualities which go to make a good society, we should include much more ; but from our present "natural history" standpoint it is evident that these must be excluded and only those included which aid directly in the struggle.

Giving, then, the proper value to the terms, it simply comes to this. "In the history of man, as throughout nature, stronger races have continually trampled down, enslaved, and exterminated other races." The biologist says : "This is so rooted in nature, including human nature, that it must go on." He adds : "It has been the prime condition and mode of progress in the past, therefore it is desirable it should go on. It must go on, it ought to go on."

So easily we glide from natural history to ethics, and find in utility a moral sanction for the race struggle. Now, Imperialism is nothing but this natural history doctrine regarded from the standpoint of one's own nation. We represent the socially efficient nation, we have conquered and acquired dominion and territory in the past : we must go on, it is our destiny, one which is serviceable to ourselves and to the world, our duty.

Thus, emerging from natural history, the doctrine soon takes on a large complexity of ethical and religious finery, and we are wafted into an elevated atmosphere of " imperial Christianity," a " mission of civilization," in which we are to teach " the arts of good government " and " the dignity of labour."

II

That the power to do anything constitutes a right and even a duty to do it, is perhaps the commonest, the most "natural" of temperamental fallacies. Even Professor Pearson does not avoid it, when, after an able vindication of the necessity of intra-race selection and of race struggle, he speaks of " our right to work the unutilised resources of earth, be they in Africa or in Asia."[1]

This belief in a " divine right " of force, which teachers like Carlyle, Kingsley, Ruskin did so much to foster, is primarily responsible for the transmutation of a natural history law into a moral enthusiasm.

Elsewhere I have dwelt with so much insistence on the more sordid and calculating motives which direct Imperialism that I am anxious here to do justice to the nobler aspects of the sentiment of Imperialism, interpreted through a naïve rendering of science into a gospel of arduous chivalry. Such a revelation is conveyed in the charming nature and buoyant career of Hubert Hervey, of the British South African Chartered Company, as rendered by his fellow-adventurer, Earl Grey. In his career we have Imperialism at its best in action, and what is better for our purpose, a

[1] *National Life*, p. 46.

most ingenuous and instructive attempt to set forth the gist of the imperialist philosophy.

" Probably every one would agree that an Englishman would be right in considering his way of looking at the world and at life better than that of the Maori or Hottentot, and no one will object in the abstract to England doing her best to impose her better and higher view on those savages. But the same idea will carry you much farther. In so far as an Englishman differs in essentials from a Swede or Belgian, he believes that he represents a more perfectly developed standard of general excellence. Yes, and even those nations nearest to us in mind and sentiment—German and Scandinavian—we regard on the whole as not so excellent as ourselves, comparing their typical characteristics with ours. Were this not so, our energies would be directed to becoming what they are. Without doing this, however, we may well endeavour to pick out their best qualities and add them to ours, believing that our compound will be superior to the foreign stock.

" It is the mark of an independent nation that it should feel thus. How far such a feeling is, in any particular case, justified, history alone decides. But it is essential that each claimant for the first place should put forward his whole energy to prove his right. This is the moral justification for international strife and for war, and a great change must come over the world and over men's minds before there can be any question of everlasting universal peace, or the settlement of all international differences by arbitration. More especially must the difficulty caused by the absence of a generally recognised standard of justice be felt in the case of contact between civilized and uncivilized races. Is there any likelihood of the gulf between the white and the black man being bridged within any period of time that we can foresee ? Can there be any doubt that the white man must, and will, impose his superior civilization on the coloured races ? The rivalry of the principal European countries in extending their influence over other continents should lead naturally to the evolution of the highest attainable type of government of subject races by the superior qualities of their rulers."[1]

Here is the undiluted gospel of Imperialism, the fact of physical stuggle between white races, the fact of white subjugation of lower races, the necessity based upon these facts, the utility based upon the necessity, and the right or duty upon the utility. As a revelation of the purer spirit of Imperialism it is not to be bettered. The Englishman believes he is a more excellent type than any other man ; he believes that he is better able to assimilate any special virtues others may have ; he believes that this character gives him a right to rule which no other can possess. Mr. Hervey admits that the patriotic Frenchman, the German, the Russian feels in the same way his sense of superiority and the rights it confers on him ; so much the better (and here he is in line with Professor Pearson), for this cross-conviction and these cross-interests intensify the struggle of white races, and ensure the survival and progressive fitness of the fittest.

So long as we regard this Imperialism exclusively from the standpoint of the English, or any other single nation, its full *rationale* escapes us. It is essential to the maintenance of the struggle of nations, which is to quicken vigour and select the fittest or most efficient, that each competitor shall be stimulated to put forth his fullest effort by the same feelings regarding the superiority, the destiny, the rights and imperial duties of his country as the English imperialist entertains regarding England. And this is just what we seem to find.

[1] *Memoir of Hubert Hervey*, by Earl Grey (Arnold, 1899).

The Englishman is genuinely confident in the superior fitness of England for any work she may essay in the civilization of the world. This is the supreme principle of the imperialist statesman, so well expressed in Lord Rosebery's description of the British Empire as " the greatest secular agency for good the world has ever seen," and in Mr. Chamberlain's conviction[1] that " the Anglo-Saxon race is infallibly destined to be the predominant force in the history and civilization of the world." Of the superior competence of Englishmen for all purposes of government, quite irrespective of climatic, racial, or any other conditions, there is no touch of doubt in the average man. "Why, I suppose you imagine we could undertake to govern France better than Frenchmen can govern her ? " I heard put as an ironical poser in a discussion on British capacity. The triumphant retort, "Why, of course I do," was no rhetorical paradox, but a perfectly genuine expression of the real conviction of most Englishmen.

Now, the French Chauvinist, the German colonialist, the Russian Pan-Slavist, the American expansionist, entertain the same general conviction, with the same intensity, regarding the capacity, the destiny, the rights of their own nation. These feelings have, perhaps, come more clearly into the forefront of our national consciousness than in the case of any other nation, but events are rapidly educating the same imperial aspirations in all our chief industrial and political competitors.

"In our own day Victor Hugo declares France 'the saviour of nations,' and bursts out, ' Non, France, l'univers a besoin que tu vives ! Je le redis, la France est un besoin des hommes.' Villari, echoing the illustrious Gioberti, claims for Italy the primacy among nations. The Kaiser tells his people, ' Der alte gute Gott has always been on

[1] *Foreign and Colonial Speeches*, p. 6.

our side.' M. Pobyedonostseff points to the freedom of Russia from the shibboleths of a decadent civilization, and looks to the young and vigorous Slavonic stock as the residuary legatee of the treasures and conquests of the past. The Americans are not less confident than in the days of Martin Chuzzlewit that it is their mission to ' run this globe'."[1]

Nor are these barren sentiments ; in various parts of the world they have inspired young soldiers, politicians, and missionaries to a practical direction of the resources of France, Germany, Italy, Russia, the United States towards territorial expansion.

We are now in a position to restate and test the scientific basis of Imperialism regarded as a world-policy. The maintenance of a military and industrial struggle for life and wealth among nations is desirable in order to quicken the vigour and social efficiency of the several competitors, and so to furnish a natural process of selection, which shall give an ever larger and intenser control over the government and the economic exploitation of the world into the hands of the nation or nations representing the highest standard of civilization or social efficiency, and by the elimination or subjugation of the inefficient shall raise the standard of the government of humanity.

This statement withdraws the issue from the purely national—political, and from the distinctively ethical standpoints, referring it back to its scientific basis in the laws or analogies of biology.

Here we can profitably start from a statement of Professor K. Pearson. "History shows me one way, and one way only, in which a high state of civilization has been produced, namely, the struggle of race with race, and the survival of the physically and mentally fitter race. If men want to

[1] G. P. Gooch in *The Heart of the Empire*, p. 333

know whether the lower races of man can evolve a higher type, I fear the only course is to leave them to fight it out among themselves, and even then the struggle for existence between individual and individual, between tribe and tribe, may not be supported by that physical selection due to a particular element, on which, probably, so much of the Aryans' success depended."

Now, assuming that this is a true account of the evolution of civilization during the past, is it essential that the same methods of selection must dominate the future ? or are there any forces which have been coming into play during the later periods of human history that deeply modify, suspend, and even reverse the operations of selective forces that dominate the rest of nature ?

In the very work from which I quote, Professor Pearson furnishes a complete answer to his own contention for the necessity of this physical struggle between races.

In the last sentence of the passage given above, he seems to recognize the utility in lower races of the physical struggle for life between " individuals " in the same tribe. But his general position as a " socialist " is very different. In order that a tribe, a nation, or other society may be able to compete successfully with another society, the individual struggle for life within the society itself must be suspended. The conpetitive vigour, the social efficiency, of the nation requires a saving of the friction of individual competition for life or for the means of life. Now this is in itself a reversal of the generally recognized law of progress throughout the animal world, in which the struggle for food and other livelihood is held to be essential to the progress of the species, and this though every species is engaged in more or less direct competition for food, etc., with other species. Co-operation, social solidarity, is indeed recognized as an adjunct of progress in many of the higher species, but the struggle between individuals for a restricted supply of food or other necessaries is maintained as a leading instrument of progress by rejection of the physically unfit.

Now Professor Pearson justly recognizes and boldly admits the danger which attends the humanitarianism that has in large measure suspended the " struggle for life " among individuals, and has incited modern civilized nations to secure for all individuals born in their midst the food, shelter, and other necessaries enabling them to grow to maturity and to propagate their kind.

He sees quite clearly that this mere suspension of the individual struggle for life not only is not essential to the solidarity and efficiency of the nation, but that it impairs those virtues by burdening society with a horde of physical and moral weaklings, who would have been eliminated under earlier forms of the struggle for life. He rightly enforces the doctrine that a nation which is reproduced from its bad stock more than from its better stock is doomed to deterioration of physique and morale. It is as essential to the progress of man as to that of any other animal, as essential in the future as in the past, that reproduction shall be from the better stock and that the worst stock shall be eliminated. Humanitarianism and the sense of social solidarity by no means recognize, or even admit, that this condition should be sacrificed; they merely impose new methods on the process of selection.

Irrational nature selects wastefully and with the maximum of pain and misery, requiring innumerable individuals to be born in order that they may struggle and perish. Rational humanity would economize and humanize the struggle by substituting a rational, social test of parenthood for the destruction of children by starvation, disease, or weakness.

To prevent reproduction from bad stock, however difficult and dangerous it may be, is obviously the first duty of

M

an organized society, acting alike in its own self-defence and for the interests of its individual members. It is not necessary for the safety and progress of society that " unfit " children should die, it is necessary that they should not be born, and ultimately the society which prospers most in the character of its members will be the one which best fulfils this preventive duty.

Yet, when Professor Pearson passes from a society of individuals to the society of nations, which we call humanity, he insists upon retaining the older, cruder, irrational method of securing progress, the primitive struggle for physical existence. Why ? If it is profitable and consistent with progress to put down the primitive struggle for life among individuals with one another, the family and tribal feuds which survive even in fairly developed societies, and to enlarge the area of social internal peace until it covers a whole nation, may we not go farther and seek, with hope, to substitute international peace and co-operation, first among the more civilized and more nearly related nations, and finally throughout the complete society of the human race ? If progress is helped by substituting rational selection for the struggle for life within small groups, and afterwards within the larger national groups, why may we not extend the same mode of progress to a federation of European States, and finally to a world-federation ? I am not now concerned with the grave practical difficulties besetting such an achievement, but with the scientific theory.

Although a certain sort of individual efficiency is sacrificed by repressing private war within a tribe or nation, it is rightly judged that the gain in tribal or national unity and efficiency outweighs that loss. May not a similar biological and rational economy be subserved by substituting government for anarchy among nations ? We admit that a nation is strengthened by putting down internecine tribal warfare ;

what finality attaches to the arbitrary social group we term a " nation " which obliges us to reverse the economy applicable to tribes when we come to deal with nations ?

Two objections are raised against this idea of internationalism. One is historical in its nature; it consists in a denial that a society of nations does or can exist at the present time or in any future which concerns us. The physical and psychical relations which exist between nations, it is urged, have no real analogy with those existing between individuals or tribes within a nation. Society is dependent on a certain homogeneity of character, interests, and sympathies of those who form it. In the ancient world this was seldom found of sufficient strength save among close neighbours, and the city-state was the true social type ; the actual and positive relations of these city-states with one another were commonly those of war, modified by transitory compacts, which rarely led them into any truly national unity. In such a condition close-welded co-operation of citizens was essential as a condition of civic survival and progress, and a struggle for life between the several city-states was a means of progress in accordance with the biological law. The nation-state stands now where the city-state stood in ancient Greece or mediæval Italy ; there remains the same historical and even ethical necessity to retain the struggle between nations now as to retain the inter-civic struggle in earlier times.

Social psychologists attempt to fortify this position by laying emphasis upon the prime psychical condition of a national life. The possible area of a genuine society, a nation, is determined by the extension of a " consciousness of kind," an " ethical like-mindedness."[1] This may be applied as a limiting condition by a " little Englander " or as an expansive principle to justify imperial expansion,

[1] Professor Giddings, *Empire and Democracy*, pp. 10, 51.

according to the quantity and quality of like-mindedness taken as the basis of social unity in a "nation" or an "empire." The most precise statement of this doctrine in its application as a barrier to ethical and political internationalism is that of Dr. Bosanquet. "The nation-state is the widest organization which has the common experience necessary to found a common life."[2] He carries the finality of the national type of society so far as virtually to repudiate the ethical fact and the utility of the conception of humanity. "According to the current ideas of our civilization, a great part of the lives which are being lived and have been lived by mankind are not lives worth living, in the sense of embodying qualities for which life seems valuable to us. This being so, it seems to follow that *the object of our ethical idea of humanity is not really mankind as a single community*. Putting aside the impossibilities arising from succession in time, we see that no such identical experience can be pre-supposed in all mankind as is necessary to effective membership of a common society and exercise of a general will."[1] Though a subtle qualification follows, based on the duty of States to recognize humanity, not as a fact but as a type of life, "and in accordance with it to recognize and deal with the rights of alien individuals and communities," the real upshot of this line of thought is to emphasise the ethical self-sufficiency of a nation and to deny the validity of any practical standard of the conduct of nations towards one another, at any rate so far as the relations between higher and lower, or eastern and western, nations are concerned.

This view is stoutly supported by some sociologists and statesmen from the juridical standpoint. There can, we are told, be no real "rights" of nations because there exists no "sanction," no recognized tribunal to define and

---

[1] *The Philosophical Theory of the State*, p. 320.   [2] *Op. cit.* p. 329.

enforce rights.[1] The legal rigour of this position I am not greatly concerned to question. It may here suffice to say that the maintenance under ordinary conditions of treaty relations, international credit and exchange, a common postal, and within narrower limits, a common railway system, not to mention the actual machinery of conventions and conferences for concerted international action, and the whole unwritten law of war and international courtesies, embassies, consulates, and the like—all these things rest upon a basis of recognition of certain reciprocal duties, the neglect or violation of which would be punished by forfeiture of most favoured nations' treatment in the future, and by the reprobation and the possibly combined intervention of other States.

III

We have here at least a real beginning of effective international federation, with the rudiments of legal sanction for the establishment and enforcement of rights.

The studied ignoring of those vital facts in the more recent statecraft, and the reversion, alike of legal theorists and high politicians of the Bismarck school, to a nationalism which emphasises the exclusive rather than the inclusive aspect of patriotism and assumes the antagonism of nations as an all-important and a final fact, form the most dangerous and discreditable factor of modern politics. This conduct in politics we have already in part explained in our analysis of the economic driving forces that exhibit certain sectional interests and orders within the nation usurping the national will and enforcing their private advantages, which rest upon international antagonism, to the detriment of the national advantage, which is identical with that of other nations.

[1] On this point see the admirable chapter " International Rights " in L. T. Hobhouse's *Democracy and Reaction* (Unwin, 1904).

This obstinate halt in the evolution of such relations at the limit of political nationality now reached will be recognized as the most difficult of all present political phenomena for the future historian to explain. The community of interests between nations is so great, so multifarious, and so obvious, the waste, pain, and damage of conflicts so gross and palpable, that to those who do not understand the strong sectional control in every modern State it may well appear that some natural barriers, race, boundaries, or colour make any real extension of " society " outside the area of nationality impossible.

But to ascribe finality to nationalism upon the ground that members of different nations lack " the common experience necessary to found a common life " is a very arbitrary reading of modern history. Taking the most inward meaning of experience, which gives most importance to the racial and traditional characters that mark the divergences of nationality, we are obliged to admit that the fund of experience common to peoples of different nationality is growing with great rapidity under the numerous, swift, and accurate modes of intercommunication which mark the latest phases of civilization. It is surely true that the dwellers of large towns in all the most advanced European States, an ever-growing proportion of the total population, have, not merely in the externals of their lives, but in the chief formative influences of their reading, their art, science, recreation, a larger community of experience than existed a century ago among the more distant members of any single European nation, whether dwelling in country or in town. Direct intercommunication of persons, goods, and information is so widely extended and so rapidly advancing that this growth of " the common experience necessary to found a common life " beyond the area of nationality is surely the most mark-worthy feature of the age. Making, then, every due allowance for the subjective factors of national character which temper or transmute the same external phenomena, there surely exists, at any rate among the more conscious and more educated sections of the chief European nations, a degree of true "like-mindedness," which forms the psychical basis of some rudimentary internationalism in the field of politics. Indeed it is curious and instructive to observe that while some of those most insistent upon "like-mindedness" and "common experience," as the tests of a true social area, apply them in defence of existing nationalities and in repudiation of attempts to absorb alien nationalities, others, like Professor Giddings, apply them in the advocacy of expansion and Imperialism.

Surely there is a third alternative to the policy of national independence on the one hand, and of the right of conquest by which the more efficient nation absorbs the less efficient nation on the other, the alternative of experimental and progressive federation, which, proceeding on the line of greatest common experience, shall weave formal bonds of political attachment between the most "like-minded" nations, extending them to others as common experience grows wider, until an effective political federation is established, comprising the whole of "the civilized world," i.e. all those nations which have attained a considerable fund of that "common experience" comprised under the head of civilization.

This idea does not conflict with the preservation of what is really essential and valuable in nationalism, nor does it imply a suspension or abolition of any form of struggle by which the true character of a nation may express itself, in industry, in politics, in art or literature.

If it be objected that the requisite amount of "like-mindedness" or "common experience" does not exist even among the nations most subjected to modern assimilative influences, that the forces of racial and national antagonism even there preclude any truly effective union, I can only repeat that this is a matter for experiment, and that the experiment has never been tried. Racial and national antagonisms have been so fed, fostered, and inflamed, for the class and personal ends and interests which have controlled politics, that the deeper underlying sympathies and community of different peoples have never been permitted free expression, much less political assertion. The most potent and pervasive forces in the industrial, intellectual, and moral life of most European races, so far as the masses of the peoples are concerned, have so rapidly and closely assimilated during the last century as of necessity to furnish a large common body of thought and feeling, interests and aspirations which furnish a " soul " for internationalism.

The main economic conditions affecting the working life of the masses of the peoples, both in town and country, on the one hand, the matter and methods of education through the school, the church, the press upon the other, show features of similarity so much stronger and more numerous than those of difference as to make it a safe assertion that the " peoples " of Europe are far closer akin in actual interests than their governments, and that this common bond is already so strong as to furnish a solid and stable foundation for political federal institutions, if only the obstruction of class governments could be broken down and the real will of the peoples set in the seat of authority. To take the commonest of concrete instances, it is at least probable that the body of the workers in different countries who fight and pay for wars would refuse to fight and pay in the future if they were allowed to understand the real nature of the issues used to inflame them.

If this view is correct, the mere facts that wars still occur and that national animosities are continually flaring up must not be taken as proof that sufficient common sympathy and experience does not exist between the different nations to render impossible a suspension of physical conflict and the establishment of a political machinery required to maintain peace.

To hold this position it is not necessary to exaggerate the extent of this international community of interests. If any considerable amount of real community exists, it furnishes the spirit which should and might inform a body of political institutions. Here is the significance of the recent[1] Hague Conference, alike in its successes and its failure. Its success, the mere fact that it was held and the permanent nucleus of internationalism it created, attests a real and felt identity of interests among different nations in the maintenance of peace ; its failure and the open derision expressed by many politicians merely indicate the presence in high places of cliques and classes opposed in their interests and feelings to those of the peoples, and the necessity of dethroning these enemies of the people if the new cause of internationalism is to advance. Secure popular government, in substance and in form, and you secure internationalism : retain class government, and you retain military Imperialism and international conflicts.

IV

In following out the psychical argument against regarding nations as final social areas, I seem to have wandered very far from the biological basis, the alleged necessity of maintaining conflicts between nations for purposes of " natural selection." In reality I have come round precisely

[1] 1901.

to the point of divergence. Assuming it were possible to enthrone the will of the peoples and so to secure institutions of internationalism with a suspension of war, would the individuality of a nation suffer, would it lose vigour, become less efficient and perish ? Is the maintenance of physical conflict essential to the " natural selection " of nations ?

Turn to the suspension of the cruder physical struggle which takes place in the evolution of tribal or national solidarity. As such national organization becomes stronger and more skilful the ravages of intestine strife, starvation, and certain diseases cease to be selective instruments, and the kind of individual fitness which was tested by them is superseded ; the vast expenditure of individual energy formerly engaged in protecting life and in securing necessaries of life is reduced to insignificant dimensions ; but the struggle for individual life is not abated, it is simply shifted on to higher planes than that of bare animal existence, nourishment and propagation. Instead of struggling for these simpler vital ends, individuals now struggle with all the extra energy spared from the earlier struggles for other ends of an enlarged and more complex life, for comfort and wealth, for place and personal honour, for skill, knowledge, character, and even higher forms of self-expression, and for services to their fellow-men, with whom they have identified themselves in that expanded individuality we term altruism or public spirit.

Individuality does not suffer but greatly gains by the suppression of the lower struggle ; there is more energy, greater scope for its expression, a wider field of close competitors ; and higher and more varied forms of fitness are tested and evoked. It is not even true that the struggle ceases to be physical ; the strain and the support of the higher forms of struggle, even in the topmost intellectual and moral planes, are largely physical ; the health and nervous energy which take part in the struggles of the law or literature or on any intellectual arena are chief requisites if not the supreme determinant of success. In all the higher forms of struggle an elimination of the physically unfit is still maintained, though the criteria of physical unfitness are not quite the same as in the primitive human struggles. How arbitrary are the convenient distinctions between physical, intellectual, and moral qualities and defects is nowise better illustrated than in the elaborate methods which modern complex civilization evolves for the detection, degradation, and final extinction of bad stock whose " degeneracy " is attested not less by physical than by mental and moral stigmata. The struggle for physical fitness never flags, but the physical forms part of a higher and more complex test of character determined by a higher standard of social utility. The point is this : national government, or State socialism, using the term in its broad sense, as a coercive and educative force, does not, in so far as it is wisely exercised, diminish the individual struggle, repress individual vigour, reduce the arena for its display. It does just the opposite ; it quickens and varies the struggle ; by equalising certain opportunities it keeps a fairer ring, from which chance or other factors alien to personal fitness are excluded ; it admits on more equal terms a larger number of competitors, and so furnishes a better test of fitness and a more reliable selection of the fittest.

Professor Pearson rightly urges that truly enlightened national government will insist on mending the slow, painful, and irregular elimination of bad stock which goes on through progressive degeneracy by substituting some rational control of parentage, at least to the extent of preventing through public education, or if necessary by law, the propagation of certain surely recognized unfitnesses.

Does a nation thus firmly planted in rational self-government, with individual competition within its ranks conducted most keenly upon a wide variety of different fields, furnishing the keenest incentive to the education and display of every kind of personal originality, really require a maintenance of the crude form of physical struggle with other nations in order to maintain its character and progress ? If individuality does not disappear with the removal of the cruder struggle for life within the nation, why should the valid force of nationality disappear if a corresponding change takes place in the nature of international conflict ?

Biology furnishes no reason for believing that the competition among nations must always remain a crude physical struggle, and that the substitution of " rational " for " natural " selection among individual members of a nation cannot be extended to the selection of nations and of races.

V

The history of past nations indeed gives an appearance of natural necessity to imperial expansion and to the military policy which is its instrument, and many who deplore this necessity accept it. An American writer in a brilliant monograph[1] argues the perpetual necessity of wars of conquest and of the Imperialism which such wars express, as following from " the law of decreasing returns." A population on a limited area of land not only tends to grow but actually grows faster than the food supply that is available ; improvement in the arts of cultivation does not enable a people to obtain full subsistence for its growing population, hence a natural and necessary pressure for access to new rich land, and conflicts with and victories over neighbours who seek to hold their own, or are even

[1] " War and Economics," by Professor E. van Dyke Robinson, *Political Science Quarterly*, Dec. 1900.

actuated by the same needs of territorial expansion. Hunger is a necessary spur to migration, and where emigrants, planting themselves successfully upon new fertile lands, formerly unoccupied or occupied by people whom they have subjugated, desire to retain the political union with the mother country, an unlimited expansion of national areas ensues. Whether such expansion takes shape in genuine colonization or in what is here properly distinguished as Imperialism, involving centralized government and forcible control of " inferior races," matters little to this wide argument. The essence of this policy is the acquisition of an expanding area for food supply. A nation with growing population must either send a constant flow of population into other lands to grow food for themselves, or, failing this, it must produce at home an ever-growing surplus of manufactures which evade the law of decreasing returns and find markets for them, so as to obtain payment in food from foreign lands, which, in their turn, are thus forced more quickly to experience the pinch of the same natural law. As more nations pursue this course they either realize directly the pressure of the law driving them to find new lands for their surplus population, or they find themselves embroiled in an ever fiercer competition with rival manufacturing nations seeking a share in an overstocked or too slowly expanding market for manufactures. Imperialism lies in both directions, and cannot be avoided. " The cause of war is as permanent as hunger itself, since both spring from the same source, the law of diminishing returns. So long as that persists, war must remain, in the last analysis, a national business undertaking, designed to procure or preserve foreign markets, that is, the means of continued growth and prosperity. ' Chacun doit grandir ou mourir'. "[1]

[1] Robinson, *Political Science Quarterly*, p. 622.

Now the finality of this alleged necessity has often been subjected to incidental criticism, so far as Great Britain is concerned. Imperialism, it has been shown, is not in fact necessitated in order to obtain by trade an increased food supply which should keep pace with the growth of British population, nor has it chiefly been engaged in forwarding such trade; still less is it engaged in finding land upon which our surplus population may subsist and multiply.

But the validity of the whole argument from natural history is contestable. As man grows in civilization, i.e. in the art of applying reason to the adjustment of his relations with his physical and social environment, he obtains a corresponding power to extricate himself from the necessity which dominates the lower animal world. He can avoid the necessity of war and expansion in two ways, by a progressive mitigation of the law of diminishing returns in agriculture and the extractive arts, and by limiting the rate of growth of population. The tendency of rational civilization is to employ both methods. It may fairly be maintained that reason is educated in individual men, and is applied to further a co-operative policy, chiefly by acts of choice which are directed to avoid the hardships and perils of war and the expansive practices. In animal life, and in man just so far as he resembles other animals, war and extension of territory form the only means of providing for a growth of population which is determined by a mere interaction of sexual instincts and physical conditions of environment. But from very early times this dominion of irrational forces, which finds direct expression in " the law of diminishing returns," is qualified by two sets of checks. On the one hand, improvements in agriculture and the beginnings of trade increase the quantity of human life which a given piece of land is able to support; on the other, customs relating to marriage and maintenance of children, often of a degraded character, such as exposure or infanticide, are added to the " natural " checks upon increase of population. Both forces represent the crude beginnings of " reason " or conscious human policy in its struggle to overcome the play of the non-rational forces of nature. Throughout history, so far as it is known, these rational forces have been so slow and feeble in their application as only to moderate or postpone the operation of " the law of decreasing returns." But this need not always continue to be the case. There is some ground to believe that both sets of rational checks may in the future be amply adequate to suspend or overcome the limitations of matter so far as the food supply of a nation on a given area is concerned. Progress in agriculture even of the most progressive nations of the past was very slow : modern science, which has achieved such marvels in revolutionizing the manufacturing and transport industries, is beginning more and more to concentrate its power on agriculture in such wise that the pace of progress in this art may be vastly accelerated. When the sciences of agricultural chemistry and botany are adequately reinforced by mechanics, scientific method being duly guided and enriched by garnering the empirical wisdom of great agricultural races whose whole practical genius has been centred for countless ages on minute cultivation, like the Chinese, and when to such improved knowledge of agricultural arts is added a perfection of co-operative labour for those processes where this yields a true economy, the possibilities of intensive cultivation are virtually unlimited. These new conditions of a national policy of agriculture are themselves so important as to make it easily conceivable that a nation keenly set upon utilizing them might for a long time to come reverse the operation of " the law of diminishing returns " extracting from its own proper lands an increasing stock of food to meet its "natural" growth of population without a more than proportionate increase of labour engaged in agriculture. In face of recent experiments in intensive and scientific agriculture and the practical substitution of skilled gardening for unskilled farming, it is impossible to deny that such a triumph of the laws of mind over the laws of matter is probable in the most highly intelligent peoples. There are already manifested throughout Gteat Britain certain signs of such a set towards agriculture as took place in England during the middle of the eighteenth century and led them to relatively great improvements in crop growing and stock breeding. If a brief fashion and sportive interest on the part of a small well-to-do class could then produce what is not wrongly described as an " agricultural revolution," what might not be achieved now by vastly greater numbers, capital, and intelligence directed in a public policy and wielding the accumulated knowledge of modern science ? Many causes consciously contribute towards such a brilliant revival of British agriculture. The growing sense of the hygienic and military perils which attend a nation of town dwellers, whose powers of forcible resistance are impaired in just proportion as their dependence upon precarious foreign supplies of food increases, is driving the issue of restoring a people to the land into the forefront of politics. Modern scientific transport, hitherto centripetal in its main economy, now seems to tend more to become centrifugal, while the wider spread of culture does something, and may do much, to cause a moral and æsthetic revolt against the life and work of towns. A careful and drastic system of land reform which should aim at the net economy of individual enterprise and co-operative aid for agriculture is of course in Great Britain a prior condition to all rapid and effective progress. All these conditions are within the power of man, and belong to rational policy; once secured, it is at least probable that private incentives to gain, bringing brain and capital to bear upon the land, might in this or any other industrial country produce so vast an increase of the productiveness of the soil as to destroy completely all speciousness which history attaches to the necessity of expansion for purposes of food supply.

It is not necessary here to discuss the part played respectively by public policy and private initiative in the development of this economy of intensive cultivation. It is sufficient to insist that it furnishes the larger half of a complete answer to the alleged natural necessity of expansion. The other half has reference to a rational control of the growth of population, which must in any sound national economy tend more and more to replace the wasteful and cruel prodigality which nature unchecked by reason here as elsewhere displays. However difficult it may be, rational control of the quantity and quality of population is quite essential to the physical and moral progress of a species which has striven successfully to suspend or stay the cruel and wasteful checks which disease, famine, pestilence, internecine warfare, and early savage usages employed in the struggle for existence. To stay the " natural " checks, and to refuse to substitute " rational " checks, is to promote not merely the unrestricted growth of population, but the survival and multiplication of the physically and morally unfit, the least effective portion of the population, which is able to be born, reared, and to propagate its kind. How far the operation of the great public policy of preventing the propagation of certain definite forms of unfitness can best be left to the free play of individual interest and discretion, illuminated by the growing knowledge of biological science, or how far such private determination must be reinforced by public pressure, is a matter with which we need not here concern ourselves.

But there is every reason to believe that both quantitative and qualitative checks upon the "natural" growth of population are already operative in modern civilized communities, that they are already appreciably affecting the general growth of population, and that their operation is likely to continue in the future. With the spread of biological and moral education the methods of moderating the growth of population may be expected to come more truly "rational," and in particular the increasing economic liberty and enlightenment of women will contribute to the efficacy of this reasonable self-restraint. This second check upon the false necessity assigned to the law of decreasing returns is not unrelated to the first. It is, in fact, its true complement. Taken by itself the improvement in methods of obtaining food might not suffice to do more than to postpone or hold in check for a period the law of limitation of the food supply obtainable from a national area. But if the same forces of human reason which substitute intensive for extensive cultivation of the soil are at work imposing the same substitution in the cultivation of the species, checking the merely quantitative increase in order to secure a higher quality of individuation, this mutual reinforcement may secure the triumph of rational policy over the untamed forces of natural history.

I have laboured this issue at some length because it is required in order to bring home the distinctively rational character of that choice of national life against which Imperialism sins so fatally. There is no natural necessity for a civilized nation to expand the area of its territory, in order either to increase its production of food and other forms of material wealth, or to find markets for its increased products. Progress, alike for the nation and for the individual, consists in substituting everywhere an intensive or qualitative for an extensive or quantitative economy. The low-skilled farmer is given to spread his capital and labour over a large area of poorly cultivated land, wherever a large quantity of free or cheap land is available; the skilled, competent farmer obtains a larger net return by concentrating his productive power upon a smaller area scientifically cultivated, recognizing that the best use of his productive resources imposes a limit on the size of his farm. So with the economy of national resources—the craving and the necessity of expansion are signs of barbarism; as civilization advances and industrial methods become more highly skilled and better differentiated, the need for expansion of territory is weakened, the progress of the nation concerns itself more and more with the intensive or qualitative development of its national resources. Size of territory can never be eliminated as a condition of progress, but it becomes relatively less important with each step from barbarism to civilization, and the idea of indefinite expansion as necessary or good is opposed to reason and sane policy. This was recognized by the most profound of ancient thinkers. " There is," wrote Aristotle, " a certain degree of greatness fit for States as for all other things, living creatures, plants, instruments, for each has its proper virtue and faculty, when neither very little nor yet excessively great."[1] That the tendency has ever been to excess is the commonplace of history. The true greatness of nations has been educated by the concentrated skill in the detailed development of limited national resources which the contracted area of the State has developed in them. " It is to the burning vitality of compact, independent nations, the strong heart in the small body, to Judæa and to Athens, to Rome the republic, to the free cities of Italy, Germany,

[1] *Politics*, vii. 4.

and Flanders, to France, to Holland, and to England the island, that we owe the highest achievements in the things that make life most worth living."[1]

If imperial expansion were really nothing other than a phase of the natural history of a nation it would be as idle to protest against it as to argue with an earthquake. But the policy of civilized States differs from that of uncivilized States in resting more largely upon deliberate conscious choice, partaking more definitely of the character of conduct. The same growth of collective reason which makes it technically possible for a nation to subsist and prosper by substituting an intensive for an extensive economy of national resources enables it by deliberate exercise of will to resist the will of the older " destiny " by which nations attaining a certain degree of development were led by a debilitating course of Imperialism to final collapse.

VI

Thus met, the biological argument is sometimes turned on to another track.

" If these nations," it is argued, " are no longer called upon to struggle for food, and check their growth of population while they increase their control over their material supplies, they will become effete for purposes of physical struggle ; giving way to an easy and luxurious life, they will be attacked by lower races multiplying freely and maintaining their military vigour, and will succumb in the conflict." This is the danger indicated by Mr. C. H. Pearson in his interesting book *National Life and Character*. The whole argument, however, rests on a series of illusions regarding actual facts and tendencies.

It is not true that the sole object and result of the

[1] *Imperium et Libertas*, by Bernard Holland, p. 12.

stoppage of individual warfare has been to increase the efficiency of the nation for the physical struggle with other nations. As man has grown from barbarism towards civilization, the struggle to adapt his material and social environment to purposes of better livelihood and life has continuously tended to replace the physical struggle for the land and food supply of other nations. This is precisely the triumph of intensive over extensive cultivation : it implies a growing disposition to put that energy which formerly went to war into the arts of industry, and a growing success in the achievement. It is the need of peaceful, steady, orderly co-operation for this work, as the alternative to war, and not the needs of war itself, that furnishes the prime motive towards a suspension of internecine struggles, at any rate in most societies. This is a matter of pivotal importance in understanding social evolution. If the sole or main purpose of suspending individual conflict was to strengthen the purely military power of a tribe or nation, and the further evolution of society aimed at this sort of social efficiency, it might well be attended by the decay of individual freedom and initiative, by the sacrifice of individuality to a national life. The fact that this result has not occurred, that in modern civilized nations there exist far more individual freedom, energy, and initiative than in more primitive societies, attests the truth that military efficiency was not the first and sole object of social organization. In other words, the tendency of growing civilization on the national scale has been more and more to divert the struggle for life from a struggle with other nations to a struggle with environment, and so to utilize the fruits of reason as to divert a larger and larger proportion of energy to struggles for intellectual, moral, and æsthetic goods rather than for goods which tax the powers of the earth, and which, conforming to the law of diminishing returns are apt to bring them into conflict with other nations.

As nations advance towards civilization it becomes less needful for them to contend with one another for land and food to support their increasing numbers, because their increased control of the industrial arts enables them to gain what they want by conquering nature instead of conquering their fellow-men.

This truth does not indeed disclose itself readily with its full brilliancy to the eyes of modern civilized peoples, whose greed for foreign wealth and foreign lands seems as fruitful a source of war as in more primitive times. The illusion that it is necessary and advantageous to fight for new territory and distant markets, while leaving most imperfectly developed the land and markets of their own nation, is slow to be dispelled. Its sources have been already explored ; it has been traced to the dominance of class interests in national politics. Democracy alone, if it be attainable, will serve to fasten on the national mind the full economy of substituting the inner struggle with the natural environment for the outer struggle with other nations.

If, as seems possible, the civilized white nations, gradually throwing off the yoke of class governments whose interests make for war and territorial expansion, restrict their increase of population by preventing reproduction from bad stock, while they devote their energies to utilizing their natural resources, the motives of international conflict will wane, and the sympathetic motives of commerce and friendly intercourse will maintain permanent peace on a basis of international union.

Such a national economy would not only destroy the chief motives of war, it would profoundly modify the industrial struggle in which governments engage. Democracies chiefly concerned with developing their own markets would not need to spend men and money in fighting for the chance of inferior and less stable foreign markets. Such rivalry as was retained would be the rivalry not of nations but of individual manufacturers and merchants within the nation ; the national aspect of industrial warfare, by tariffs and bounties and commercial treaties, would disappear. For the dangers and hostilities of national commercial policies are due, as we have seen, almost entirely to the usurpation of the authority and political resources of the nations by certain commercial and financial interests. Depose these interests, and the deep, true, underlying harmonies of interest between peoples, which the prophets of Free Trade dimly perceived, will manifest themselves, and the necessity of permanent industrial warfare between nations will be recognized as an illusion analogous in nature and origin to the illusion of the biological necessity of war.

The struggle for life is indeed a permanent factor in social progress, selection of the physically fit is a necessity, but as men become more rational they rationalize the struggle, substituting preventive for destructive methods of selection, and raising the standard of fitness from a crudely physical robustness to one which maintains physical endurance as the raw material of higher psychical activities. Thus, while men no longer fight for food, their personal fitness is maintained, the struggle and the fitness are both raised to a higher plane. If this can take place in the struggle of individuals, it can take place in the struggle of nations. The economy of internationalism is the same as that of nationalism. As individuality does not disappear, but is raised and quickened by good national government, so nationality does not disappear but is raised and quickened by internationalism.

War and commercial tariffs are the crudest and most

wasteful forms of national struggles, testing the lowest forms of national fitness. Let international government put down wars and establish Free Trade, the truly vital struggles of national expression will begin. As in the case of individuals, so now of nations, the competition will be keener upon the higher levels ; nations having ceased to compete with guns and tariffs will compete with feelings and ideas.

Whatever there is of true original power and interest in the Celtic, the Teutonic, the various blends of Latin and Slavonic races can only bear its fruit in times of peace.

So far as nationality or race has any distinct character or value for itself and for the world, that value and character are expressed through work. Hitherto the absorption of so much national energy upon military, and in later times rude industrial occupations, has checked the higher forms of national self-expression ; while the permanent hostility of international relations has chilled the higher intercourse and prevented what is really great and characteristic in the national achievements of art, literature, and thought from penetrating other nations, and so by subtle educative processes laying the foundation of true feelings of humanity, based, as such feelings must be, not on vague imaginative sympathy, but upon common experience of life and a common understanding. Peaceful intercourse between nations is thus not merely the condition, but the powerful stimulus of national energy and achievement in the higher arts of life ; for the self-appreciation of national pride can never furnish so wholesome an incentive or so sound a criterion of human excellence as the impartial judgment of civilized humanity, no longer warped by baser patriotic prejudices, but testing what is submitted to it by the impartial universal standard of humanity. A few rare individual men of genius in art and literature, a few more in science and in religion, have broken the barriers of nationality and have become fertilizing, humanizing forces in other nations—such men as Jesus, Buddha, Mahomet, Homer, Shakespeare, Plato, Aristotle, Kant, Copernicus, Newton, Darwin. A larger number of great men have exercised some real and abiding influence upon the little world of science and letters which in the middle ages had attained an internationalism lost in the rise of militant nationalism and being slowly rediscovered in our own age.

But outside these conquests of personal genius the broad streams of national influence and achievement which might have fertilized the wide plains of the intellectual world have been confined within their narrow national channels. Nationalism as a restrictive and exclusive force, fostering political and industrial enmities and keeping down the competition of nationalities and races to the low level of military strife, has everywhere checked the free intercourse requisite for the higher kinds of competition, the struggle of languages, literatures, scientific theories, religious, political, and social institutions, and all the arts and crafts which are the highest and most important expressions of national as of individual life.

VII

This thought unearths the lowest root fallacy of the crude biological sociology, the assumption that there is one sort of national efficiency and that it is tested by a contest of military or commercial power. The only meaning that can be given to the " social efficiency " of a nation identifies it with the power it displays of adapting itself to its physical environment and of altering that environment to help the adaptation ; the attainments in religion, law, politics, intellectual life, industry, etc., are the expressions of this social efficiency. Bearing this in mind, it is evident that for concrete purposes of comparison there are many kinds of social efficiency, and that the notion that civilization is a single beaten track, upon which every nation must march, and that social efficiency, or extent of civilization, can be measured by the respective distances the nations have gone, is a mischievous delusion.

The true social efficiency, or civilization, of a nation only shows itself in its more complex achievements and activities. The biologist who understood his science would recognize that a true test of the efficiency of nations demanded that the conflict of nations should take place not by the more primitive forms of fight and the ruder weapons in which nations are less differentiated, but by the higher forms of fight and the more complex intellectual and moral weapons which express the highest degree of national differentiation. This higher struggle, conducted through reason, is none the less a national struggle for existence, because in it ideas and institutions which are worsted die, and not human organisms. The civilization of the world can only proceed upon the higher planes on condition that this struggle of national ideals and institutions is waged by a free field of competitors, and this struggle cannot be effectively maintained unless the lower military and industrial struggles cease.

Biology always demands as a condition of progress the competition of individuals, but as reason grows in the nation it closes the ring and imposes laws, not to stop the struggle, but to make it a fairer test of a fuller form of individual fitness. Biology demands as a condition of world-progress that the struggle of nations or races continue ; but as the world grows more rational it will in similar fashion rationalize the rules of that ring, imposing a fairer test of forms of national fitness.

The notion of the world as a cock-pit of nations in which round after round shall eliminate feebler fighters and leave in the end one nation, the most efficient, to lord it on the dung-hill, has no scientific validity. Invoked to support the claims of militant nationalism, it begins by ignoring the very nature and purposes of national life, assuming that uniformity of character and environment which are the negation of nationalism.

The belief that with the stoppage of war, could it be achieved, national vigour must decay, is based on a complete failure to recognize that the lower form of struggle is stopped for the express purpose and with the necessary result that the higher struggle shall become possible. With the cessation of war, whatever is really vital and valuable in nationality does not perish ; on the contrary, it grows and thrives as it could not do before, when the national spirit out of which it grows was absorbed in baser sorts of struggle.

Internationalism is no more opposed to the true purposes of nationalism than socialism within the nation, rightly guided, is hostile to individualism. The problem and its solution are the same. We socialize in order that we may individuate ; we cease fighting with bullets in order to fight with ideas.

All the essentials of the biological struggle for life are retained, the incentive to individual vigour, the intensity of the struggle, the elimination of the unfit and the survival of the fittest.

The struggle has become more rational in mode and purpose and result, and reason is only a higher form of nature.

VIII

The shortsightedness of this school of biological sociologists is nowhere more strikingly displayed than by the exclusive attention they pay to the simpler form of struggle, the direct conflict of individuals and species, to the exclusion of the important part played by " crossing " as a means of progress throughout organic life.

The law of the fertility of " crosses " as applied to civilization or " social efficiency " alike on the physical and psychical plane requires, as a condition of effective operation, internationalism. It is of course true that throughout history the " crossing " of national types has been largely achieved by means of war, conquest, and subjugation. But this, though subserving progress in the long run, has been a most wasteful, indirect, and unsafe method, the selection being determined by no clear view of the future or of any higher purpose of social efficiency. Just in proportion as internationalism promotes free intercourse between nations for higher purposes of peaceful interest, will blending of races by intermarriage be determined on grounds of affinity more fruitful of improved racial efficiency, and new modifications of species more numerous and more novel will compete with one another as factors in the civilization of the world, raising the character and intensity of the competition and enhancing the pace of human progress.

Nay, we may carry the biological analogy still farther, following the insistence of Professor Pearson regarding the necessity of bringing direct social pressure, of public opinion or of law, to prevent the fatal process of breeding from " bad stock." If the ordinary processes of physical degeneracy within the nation do not suffice for the elimination of bad stock, but must be supplemented by some direct prohibition of bad parentage, it might be necessary in the interests of humanity that similar measures should be enforced upon the larger scale by the mandates of organized humanity. As lower individuals within a society perish by contact with a civilization to which they cannot properly assimilate themselves, so " lower races " in some instances disappear by similar contact with higher races whose diseases and physical vices prove too strong for them. A rational stirpiculture in the wide social interest might, however, require a repression of the spread of degenerate or unprogressive races, corresponding to the check which a nation might place upon the propagation from bad individual stock. With the other moral and practical issues involved in such a proposal we need not here concern ourselves ; regarded exclusively from a biological standpoint, that course would seem to follow from the application of direct rational rejection of bad stock upon the smaller scale of national life. The importance of this consideration rests upon the fact that this rejection of unsound racial stock implies the existence of an international political organization which has put down war and has substituted this rational for the cruder national selection and rejection of races.

Whether a nation or a society of nations will ever proceed as far as this, or, going farther, will attempt the fuller art of stirpiculture, encouraging useful " crosses " of families or races, may be matter of grave doubt ; but if the maintenance and improvement of the national stock ever warranted such experiments, we are entitled to insist that logic would justify the application of the same rule in the society of nations.

Again, while it is questionable how far the law of the utility of cross-fertilization is transferable from the world of physical organisms to the psychical realm in its literal bearing, the more general applicability cannot be disputed. That scientific theories, religious, social, and political arts and institutions gain by free, friendly, vital intercourse with other theories, arts and institutions, undergoing serviceable accretions, excretions, and modifications, is a commonplace of intellectual life. Whether, therefore, we regard the contact of ideas and feelings and the arts they animate as a direct struggle for existence, in which the worse or falser perish and the better and truer survive, or as a friendly intercourse in which each selects and assimilates something from the others, internationalism is as essential to the efficiency of these processes as nationalism itself.

It is only when we realize the true nature of this spread and fertilization of ideas, arts, and institutions, the riper fruits of the spirit of a nation, that we realize the legitimate as distinguished from the illegitimate expansion, the valid significance of empire. When nations compete to take one another's lives or land or trade, the dominion which the conqueror establishes has no element of permanence; another turn of the military or commercial tide wipes out the victory and leaves scarce a ripple in the sands. But the influence exerted through acts of peace is more lasting, more penetrating, and more glorious. Shakespeare, Byron, Darwin, and Stevenson have done incomparably more for the influence of England in the history of the world than all the statesmen and soldiers who have won victories or annexed new provinces. Macaulay has well said it, " There is an empire exempt from all natural sources of decay—that empire is the imperishable empire of our art and our morals, our literature and our law." This antagonism between the extensive empire and the intensive empire is not rhetorical, it is grounded upon biological necessities.

The essential conditions of the lower struggle for the life and land and trade of others preclude the higher and more profitable competition of ideas by which the empire of the national mind is extended : it is not merely the economy of energy which determines that the national vigour cannot at the same time engage effectively in both struggles ; but, far more important, the very nature of the lower struggle drives each nationality to feed upon itself in insolent, exclusive pride, inhibiting the receptivity of other nations.

Effective internationalism is the only sound basis of competition and rational selection among nations. In the cruder form of the human struggle, accident, or numbers, or some primitive force or cunning, may secure the success of a people whose " social efficiency " is of a low order, impermanent and unproductive, while it stamps out or checks the growth of a people whose latent powers of achievement and capacities of progress are far superior. Only in proportion as racial or national selection is rationally guided and determined does the world gain security against such wastes and such calamities. An international government alone can furnish adequate protection to weak but valuable nationalities, and can check the insolent brutality of powerful aggressors, preserving that equality of oppotunities for national self-expression which is as essential to the commonwealth of nations as to the welfare of the several nations.

Only by raising the crude, fragmentary, informal, often insincere beginning of international government into a stronger, more coherent, and more complex authority can the struggle for life proceed upon the highest arena of competition, selecting the finest forms of social efficiency.

One further objection to the final efficacy of a federation of civilized nations demands consideration. Suppose a federal government of Western nations and their colonial offspring to be possible in such wise that internal conflicts were precluded, this peace of Christendom would be constantly imperilled by the " lower races," black and yellow, who, adopting the arms and military tactics now discarded by the " civilized races," would overwhelm them in barbarian incursions, even as the ruder European and Asiatic races overwhelmed the Roman Empire. We cannot get the whole world to the level of civilization which will admit it into the alliance ; the Powers outside will be a constant menace, and if the main purpose of federation is to eliminate militarism from the economy of national life, the attainment of this purpose will render effective resistance to such invaders no longer possible. This has been the universal fate of Empires in the past ; what talisman could this latest federal Empire possess enabling it to escape ? To this objection we may make this preliminary answer. Two factors in the older Empires have primarily contributed to weaken their powers of resistance against outside " barbarians," and to strengthen and stimulate the zeal of the invaders. There is first the habit of economic parasitism, by which the ruling State has used its provinces, colonies, and dependencies in order to enrich its ruling class and to bribe its lower classes into acquiescence. This bleeding of dependencies, while it enfeebles and atrophies the energy of the imperial people, irritates and eventually rouses to rebellion the more vigorous and less tractable of the subject races ; each repression of rebellion rankles in the blood, and gradually a force of gathering discontent is roused which turns against the governing Power.

The second factor, related to the first, consists in that form of " parasitism " known as employment of mercenary forces. This is the most fatal symptom of imperial infatuation, whereby the oppressor at once deprives himself of the habit and instruments of effective self-protection and hands them over to the most capable and energetic of his enemies.

This fatal conjunction of folly and vice has always contributed to bring about the downfall of Empires in the past. Will it prove fatal to a federation of Western States ?

Obviously it will, if the strength of their combination is used for the same parasitic purposes, and the white races, discarding labour in its more arduous forms, live as a sort of world-aristocracy by the exploitation of " lower races," while they hand over the policing of the world more and more to members of these same races. These dangers would certainly arise if a federation of European States were simply a variant of the older Empires, using a *pax Europæa* for similar purposes and seeking to maintain it by the same methods as those employed under the so-called *pax Romana*. The issue is a great one, furnishing, in fact, the supreme test of modern civilization.

Is it possible for a federation of civilized States to maintain the force required to keep order in the world without abusing her power by political and economic parasitism ?

CHAPTER III

MORAL AND SENTIMENTAL FACTORS

I

ANALYSIS of the actual course of modern Imperialism has laid bare the combination of economic and political forces which fashions it. These forces are traced to their sources in the selfish interests of certain industrial, financial, and professional classes, seeking private advantages out of a policy of imperial expansion, and using this same policy to protect them in their economic, political, and social privileges against the pressure of democracy. It remains to answer the question, " Why does Imperialism escape general recognition for the narrow, sordid thing it is ? " Each nation, as it watches from outside the Imperialism of its neighbours, is not deceived ; the selfish interests of political and commercial classes are seen plainly paramount in the direction of the policy. So every other European nation recognizes the true outlines of British Imperialism and charges us with hypocrisy in feigning blindness. This charge is false ; no nation sees its own shortcomings ; the charge of hypocrisy is seldom justly brought against an individual, against a nation never. Frenchmen and Germans believe that our zeal in promoting foreign missions, putting down slavery, and in spreading the arts of civilization is a false disguise conveniently assumed to cover naked national self-assertion. The actual case is somewhat different.

There exists in a considerable though not a large proportion of the British nation a genuine desire to spread Christianity among the heathen, to diminish the cruelty and other sufferings which they believe exist in countries less fortunate than their own, and to do good work about the world in the cause of humanity. Most of the churches contain a small body of men and women deeply, even passionately, interested in such work, and a much larger number whose sympathy, though weaker, is quite genuine. Ill-trained for the most part in psychology and history, these people believe that religion and other arts of civilization are portable commodities which it is our duty to convey to the backward nations, and that a certain amount of compulsion is justified in pressing their benefits upon people too ignorant at once to recognize them.

Is it surprising that the selfish forces which direct Imperialism should utilize the protective colours of these disinterested movements? Imperialist politicians, soldiers, or company directors, who push a forward policy by portraying the cruelties of the African slave raids or the infamous tyranny of a Prempeh or a Theebaw, or who open out a new field for missionary enterprise in China or the Soudan, do not deliberately and consciously work up these motives in order to incite British public. They simply and instinctively attach to themselves any strong, genuine elevated feeling which is of service, fan it and feed it until it assumes fervour, and utilize it for their ends. The politician always, the business man not seldom, believes that high motives qualify the political or financial benefits he gets : it is certain that Lord Salisbury really believed that the South African war, for which his Government was responsible, had been undertaken for the benefit of the people of South Africa, and would result in increased liberty and happiness ; it is quite likely that Earl Grey thought that the Chartered Company which he directed was animated by a desire to improve the material and moral condition of the natives of Rhodesia, and that it was attaining this object.

So Leopold, King of the Belgians, claimed for his government of the Congo—" Our only programme is that of the moral and material regeneration of the country." It is difficult to set any limit upon the capacity of men to deceive themselves as to the relative strength and worth of the motives which affect them : politicians, in particular, acquire so strong a habit of setting their projects in the most favourable light that they soon convince themselves that the finest result which they think may conceivably accrue from any policy is the actual motive of that policy. As for the public, it is only natural that it should be deceived. All the purer and more elevated adjuncts of Imperialism are kept to the fore by religious and philanthropic agencies : patriotism appeals to the general lust of power within a people by suggestions of nobler uses, adopting the forms of self-sacrifice to cover domination and the love of adventure. So Christianity becomes " imperialist " to the Archbishop of Canterbury, a " going out to all the world to preach the gospel " ; trade becomes " imperialist " in the eyes of merchants seeking a world market.

It is precisely in this falsification of the real import of motives that the gravest vice and the most signal peril of Imperialism reside. When, out of a medley of mixed motives, the least potent is selected for public prominence because it is the most presentable, when issues of a policy which was not present at all to the minds of those who formed this policy are treated as chief causes, the moral currency of the nation is debased. The whole policy of Imperialism is riddled with this deception. Although no candid student of history will maintain for a moment that

the entrance of British power into India, and the chief steps
leading to the present British Empire there, were motived
by considerations other than our own political and commercial aggrandisement, nothing is more common than to
hear the gains which it is alleged the natives of the country
have received from British rule assigned as the moral
justification of our Indian Empire. The case of Egypt
is a still more striking one. Though the reasons openly
assigned for the British occupation of Egypt were military
and financial ones affecting our own interests, it is now
commonly maintained that we went there in order to
bestow the benefits which Egyptians have received from
our sway, and that it would be positively wicked of us
to keep the pledge we gave to withdraw within a short
term of years from the country. When the ordinary
Englishman reads how " at no previous period of his
history has the fellah lived under a Government so careful
to promote his interests or to preserve his rights,"[1] he
instinctively exclaims, " Yes, that is what we went to
Egypt for," though, in point of fact, the play of " Imperialism " which carried us there was determined by quite other
considerations. Even if one supposes that the visible
misgovernment of Egypt, in its bearing on the life of the
inhabitants, did impart some unselfish element to our
conduct, no one would suggest that as an operative force
in the direction of our imperial policy such motive has ever
determined our actions.[2] Not even the most flamboyant

[1] *England in Egypt*, p. 97.

[2] How far the mystification of motives can carry a trained thinker upon politics
may be illustrated by the astonishing argument of Professor Giddings, who, in
discussing " the consent of the governed " as a condition of government, argues
that " if a barbarous people is compelled to accept the authority of a state more
advanced in civilization, the test of the rightfulness or wrongfulness of this
imposition of authority is to be found, not at all in any assent or resistance at the
moment when the government begins, but only *in the degree of probability* that,
after full experience of what the government can do to raise the subject population
to a higher plane of life, *a free and rational consent will be given* by those who have

Imperialist contends that England is a knight-errant, everywhere in search of a quest to deliver oppressed peoples from oppressive governments, regardless of her own interests and perils. Though perhaps not so inefficient, the Russian tyranny was quite as oppressive and more injurious to the cause of civilization than the government of the Khedive, but no one proposed that we should coerce Russia, or rescue Finland from her clutches. The case of Armenia, again, attests the utter feebleness of the higher motives. Both the Government and the people of Great Britain were thoroughly convinced of the atrocious cruelties of Turkey, public opinion was well informed and thoroughly incensed, Great Britain was expressly pledged by the Cyprus Convention to protect Armenia ; but the " cause of humanity " and the " mission of civilization " were powerless either for interference or for effective protest.

Aggressive Imperialism, as our investigation has shown, is virtually confined to the coercion by stronger or better-armed nations of nations which are, or seem to be, weaker and incapable of effective resistance ; everywhere some definite economic or political gain is sought by the imperial aggressor. The chivalrous spirit of Imperialism leads neither Great Britain nor any other Western nation to assail a powerful State, however tyrannous, or to assist a weak State reputed to be poor.

The blending of strong interested with weak disinterested forces is indeed characteristic of the age. It is the homage which Imperialism pays to humanity. But just as the

come to understand all that has been done " (*Empire and Democracy*, p. 265). Professor Giddings does not seem to recognize that the entire weight of the ethical validity of this curious doctrine of retrospective consent is thrown upon the act of judging *the degree of probability that a free and rational consent will be given*, that his doctrine furnishes no sort of security for a competent, unbiassed judgment, and that, in point of fact, it endows any nation with the right to seize and administer the territory of any other nation on the ground of a self-ascribed superiority and self-imputed qualifications for the work of civilization.

mixture known as " philanthropy and 5 per cent." is distrusted in the ordinary business world, so in the larger policy of nations the same combination is by right suspect. When business is harnessed with benevolence the former is commonly allowed to determine the direction and to set the pace. Doubtless it says something for the moral sensibility of a nation that a gainful course is rendered more attractive by a tincture of disinterestedness. But the theory and the practice in modern history often border so closely on hypocrisy that we cannot feel surprise that unfriendly foreigners apply the term to them. What, for example, can we say of the following frank description of Imperialism by Sir George now Lord Baden-Powell ? " The ultimate unit, the taxpayer—whether home or colonial —looks for two groups of results as his reward. On the one hand, he hopes to see Christianity and civilization *pro tanto* extended ; and, on the other, to see some compensating development of industry and trade. Unless he, or ' his servants the Government,' secure either or both these results, the question must be plainly asked, Has he the right, and is he right, to wage such wars ? "[1]

What is the mode of equating the two groups of results ? how much Christianity and civilization balance how much industry and trade ? are curious questions which seem to need an answer. Is not the ultimate unit in his capacity of taxpayer liable to lay more stress upon the asset which admits of monetary measurement, and to undervalue the one that evades arithmetic ?

" To combine the commercial with the imaginative " was the aim which Mr. Rhodes ascribed to himself as the key of his policy. The conjunction is commonly described by the word " speculation," a word whose meaning becomes more sinister when politics and private business are so

[1] Addendum to *The Downfall of Prempeh*.

inextricably interwoven as they were in the career of Mr. Rhodes, who used the legislature of Cape Colony to support and strengthen the diamond monopoly of De Beers, while from De Beers he financed the Raid, debauched the constituencies of Cape Colony, and bought the public press, in order to engineer the war, which was to win him full possession of his great " thought " the North.[1]

II

It may safely be asserted that, wherever " the commercial " is combined with " the imaginative " in any shape or sort, the latter is exploited by the former. There is a brand of " Christian Imperialist " much commended in certain quarters, the " industrial missionary," who is designed to float Christianity upon an ocean of profitable business, inculcating theological dogmas in the intervals of teaching the material arts and crafts. " To the sceptical Chinese the interest manifested by a missionary in business affairs would go far towards dispelling the suspicions which now attach to the presence in their midst of men whose motives they are unable to appreciate, and therefore condemn as unholy." " Immense services might be rendered to our commercial interests if only the members of the various missions in China would co-operate with our Consuls in the exploitation of the country, and the introduction of commercial as well as of purely theological ideas to the Chinese intelligence."[2] This revelation of the mercantile uses of Christianity by a British Consul leaves little to be desired in point of frankness. Its full significance is, however, only perceived when it is reinformed by the naïve confession of Lord Hugh Cecil. " A great many people

[1] " The North is my thought " (*Cecil Rhodes : His Political Life and Speeches*, p. 613.).

[2] Passages from a recent report of the British Consul at Canton.

were most anxious to go with their whole hearts into what might be called the imperial movement of the day, but had, as it were, a certain uneasiness of conscience whether, after all, this movement was quite as unpolluted by earthly considerations as they would desire it to be. He thought that by making prominent to our own minds the importance of missionary work we should to some extent sanctify the spirit of Imperialism."[1]

We are well aware that most British missionaries are quite untainted by admixture of political and commercial motives, and that they set about their work in a single spirit of self-sacrifice, eager to save the souls of the heathen, and not a whit concerned to push British trade or " sanctify the spirit of Imperialism." Indeed, it is quite evident that, just in proportion as the suspicions of worldly motives appear in missionary work, so the genuinely spiritual influence evaporates. The whole history of missionary work in China is one long commentary on this text. The early Catholic missionaries, relying on the authority of their holy lives and teaching, won not only security, but wide influence, both among the masses and in the governing circles, introducing not only Christianity, but the elements of Western science. Though they made no large numbers of converts, they constituted a powerful factor in the civilization of the great Eastern Empire. But the introduction in the nineteenth century of national and sectarian competition in missionary enterprise, each mission using freely the diplomatic and even the military resources of some European State for its defence or propagation, has inhibited the play of spiritual forces, generating suspicions which, only too well grounded, have changed the early receptiveness into a temper of fanatical hostility.

[1] An address at the annual meeting of the Society for the Propagation of the Gospel, May 4, 1900.

" It must be very difficult," writes an educated China-man, " for the mandarins to dissociate the missionaries from the secular power, whose gunboats seem ever ready to appear on behalf of their respective Governments. . . . The Chinese have watched with much concern the sequence of events—first the missionary, then the Consul, and at last the invading army. They had scarcely forgotten the loss of Annam in this way when the German action in Shan-tung created a profound sensation amongst all classes of the literati." " We cannot wonder that the Chinese officials should hate the missionaries. Their Church is an *imperium in imperio*, propagating a strange faith and alienating the people from that of their ancestors. The missionaries are not amenable to Chinese laws, and in some cases have acted in a high-handed manner in the protection of their converts. In this lies one of the secrets of the mysterious hatred entertained against ' the friends of China ' as the missionaries call themselves."[1]

How injurious to the cause " whose kingdom is not of this earth " is this alliance with politics and armaments might appear too obvious for discussion. Yet it is quite evident that sincere men are prepared to support the use of political and military force in order to open fields for missionary enterprise, and that the missionary, who is by turns trader, soldier, and politician, seems a most desirable instrument of civilization.

How close in motive and in conduct this combination really is may be thus illustrated from the history of the Soudan.

" Detachments of officers and men from every regiment, British and Egyptian, were conveyed across the Nile in the gunboats to take part in the Gordon memorial service, and to witness the hoisting of the British flag on the ruins

[1] *The Chinese Crisis from Within*, by Wen Ching, pp. 10, 12, 14 (Grant Richards).

of Khartoum. . . . Surrounded by the soldiers he had directed with terrible and glorious effect, the successful general ordered the flags to be hoisted. . . . The officers saluted, the men presented arms, and the band played the Egyptian National Anthem and our own. Then the Sirdar called for three cheers for Her Majesty. . . . The memorial service followed, and the solemn words of the English Prayer Book were read in that distant garden. . . . The bands played their dirge and Gordon's favourite hymn, ' Abide with Me ' ; a gunboat on the river crashed out the salute. . . . The Highlanders played a long lament, and thus the ceremony was duly fulfilled. Nine thousand of those who would have prevented it lay dead on the plain of Omdurman. Other thousands were scattered in the wilderness, or crawled wounded to the river for water."[1] While the writer of this passage omits the final touch, the deliberate shooting of wounded crawlers by troops under British commanders, the picture is profoundly suggestive, with its strange amalgam of the British flag, " Abide with Me," and the avenging of Gordon.

Yet it is evident that those who ascend to the misty heights of Imperialism are able to unite these diverse jarring factors in " a higher synthesis," and while deploring, often in earnest, the necessity of the maxim and the gun-boat, find a glorious justification in the higher ends of a civilization promoted by such means. The Western nations are, according to this gospel, rapidly realizing a beneficent control of the earth which will, in the near future, secure general peace and the industrial, scientific, and moral supremacy of Western arts.

> Fly, happy, happy sails, and bear the Press,
> Fly, happy with the mission of the Cross,
> Knit land to land, and blowing heavenward,
> Enrich the markets of the golden year.

[1] *The River War*, by Winston Churchill, vol. ii, pp. 204–206.

This is the benevolent theory. Let Sir Charles Dilke's estimate of our acquisitions in tropical Africa serve for commentary.

" If we cannot make the most fertile of the West India Islands pay, how can we expect to make countries which are far less healthy and less fertile in the very heart of Africa, return a profit ? Our people have been interested in Africa through their traditional desire to suppress the evils of the slave trade, and to pay conscience money in these days for the sins, in connexion with slavery, of their predecessors ; but it is probable that we have done more harm by promoting the partition of Africa and the creation, in the name of liberty, of such governments as that of the Congo Free State than the harm which our grandfathers did to Africa by their participation in African slavery and the slave trade."[1]

III

The psychical problem which confronts us in the advocates of the mission of Imperialism is certainly no case of hypocrisy, or of deliberate conscious simulation of false motives. It is partly the dupery of imperfectly realized ideas, partly a case of psychical departmentalism. Imperialism has been floated on a sea of vague, shifty, well-sounding phrases which are seldom tested by close contact with fact. " It is not in size and variety alone that English dominion is unique. Its crowning glory is its freedom,"[2] writes Mr. Henley, doubtless believing what he says. The suggestion of these words is that the " freedom " we enjoy in these isles is common to our fellow-subjects throughout the British Empire. This suggestion is false, as we have seen, but phrase-mongering Imperialism does not recognize its falsehood. The largest and most essential

[1] *The British Empire*, p. 114.   [2] *Imperialism*, p. 7.

facts of Imperialism, political, economic, moral, are commonly unknown to the average " educated " Briton. To him our Empire is composed of a number of free, self-governing States, which are in close and growing industrial relations with us; individual and racial freedom and equal justice prevail everywhere; Christianity and British moral ideals are rapidly winning their way over the vast populations of the lower races, which gladly recognize the superiority of our ideas and characters and the benefits which they receive from British rule. These vague, hasty notions are corrected by no close study of facts and figures : the only substance which they commonly possess is the assertion of some friends or relatives who are " on the spot " in some British possessions and whose individual testimony is made to sustain a pile of imperialist notions. How many persons, during the South African war, based their convictions regarding the " outlander grievances " and the character and motives of the Boer Government upon the impassioned statement of some single dweller in Johannesburg, who had virtually no contact with Boers and knew nothing of grievances, excepting through the Rhodesian press, which fashioned them !

To what extent Imperialism lives upon " masked words "[1] it is difficult to realize unless we turn to the language of diplomacy, the verbal armoury of Imperialism. Paramount power, effective autonomy, emissary of civilization, rectification of frontier, and a whole sliding scale of

[1] " There are masked words droning and skulking about us in Europe just now which nobody understands, but which everybody uses and most people will also fight for, live for, or even die for, fancying they mean this or that or the other of things dear to them. There never were creatures of prey so mischievous, never diplomatists so cunning, never poisons so deadly, as these masked words ; they are the unjust stewards of all men's ideas ; whatever fancy or favourite instinct a man most cherishes he gives to his favourite masked word to take care of for him ; the word at last comes to have an infinte power over him, and you cannot get at him but by its ministry " (Ruskin, *Sesame and Lilies*, p. 29).

terms from " hinterland " and " sphere of interest " to " effective occupation " and " annexation " will serve as ready illustrations of a phraseology devised for purposes of concealment and encroachment. The Imperialist who sees modern history through these masks never grasps the " brute " facts, but always sees them at several removes, refracted, interpreted, and glozed by convenient renderings. Some measure of responsibility for his ignorance he retains, for he must often be aware that the truth is not told him and that he is refusing to penetrate the disguises. This persistent evasion of naked truth endows him sometimes with an almost preternatural power of self-deceit. Mr. Lecky writes : " Of all forms of prestige, moral prestige is the most valuable, and no statesman should forget that one of the chief elements of British power is the moral weight that is behind it."[1] The vast majority of " educated " Englishmen genuinely believe that England's greatest gain from the Boer war is an enhancement of her " moral prestige " !

An error so monstrous is only made intelligible by reference to another curious psychical factor. Nowhere is the distrust of what is termed " logic " as a guide for public conduct, so firmly rooted as in England : a course of conduct which stands out sharply " logical " is in itself suspect. The practice of " party " government has so commonly made " compromises " a necessity that we have come to believe that our national progress is due to this necessity, and that if the sharper and more rapid application of " ideas " had been feasible, we should, by following them, have been led into false paths involving much trouble of retracing steps, or over the brink of some revolutionary peril. Though sound " compromise " is no wise illogical, but is simply logic applied within certain limits of time and environment, it easily degenerates into

[1] *The Map of Life.*

208

the opportunism of an idle policy of short-range utility. The complexity of modern politics in such a country as Great Britain, reacting on the exigencies and temptations of a party system, has driven the habit of " compromise " to such foolish extremes as to corrupt the political intelligence of the nation. Elsewhere the same tendency has been operative, but has been checked or modified by a narrow and more consciously definite policy on the part of a ruling monarch or a ruling class, by the limits of a written constitution, and, in some of the Latin nations, by an inherent and widespread belief in the value of ideas as operative forces in politics. In England, and indeed throughout Anglo-Saxondom, a sort of cheery optimism has commonly usurped the seat of intelligent direction, a general belief in " national destiny," which enables us " somehow to muddle through," and advises us " to do the best we can and not look too far ahead." Now, with the disdain of history and the neglect of sociological laws which this implies I am not here so much concerned as with the injurious reaction wrought upon the mind of the citizen confronted with some new event which challenges his judgment. Our rough-and-ready, hand-to-mouth, " take-what-you-can-get " politics have paralysed judgment by laming the logical faculty of comparison. Not being required to furnish to ourselves or others clear, consistent reasons for our short-range expediencies of public conduct, we have lost all habit of mental consistency, or, putting it conversely, we have developed a curious and highly dangerous aptitude for entertaining incompatible and often self-contradictory ideas and motives.

One or two extreme concrete instances will serve as illustrations of the damage done to the public intelligence by the absence of all sense of clear logical order in the conduct of affairs. At the beginning of the South African war the numerical insignificance of the Boers was regarded as an aggravation of their insolence in entering upon strife with the greatest Empire of the world. But the numerical smallness did not in the least interfere with the equally genuine belief and feeling that we were contending with a Power as large, numerically, as ourselves, which were required to support the sense of triumph when we won a victory, or to turn the edge of shame when our tiny adversary inflicted a defeat upon us. The shifts of detailed mendacity and curious invention to which we were driven in the course of the war by the necessity of keeping up this double and contradictory belief will doubtless attract the attention of the psychological historian, how the numbers alternately and automatically expanded and contracted according as it was sought to impress upon the nation the necessity of voting large supplies of troops and money, or else to represent the war as " nearly over " and as having lapsed into a trifling guerilla struggle. Or take another instance. It was possible for informed politicians to maintain at one and the same time that our conduct in providing food and shelter to the families whose property we had destroyed in South Africa was an act of unprecedented generosity, and to defend the right to sell by public auction their farms in order to defray the very cost of keep which was the ground for our self-commendation. These two contentions could be uttered in the House of Commons by the same minister and accepted by the nation without any recognition of their inconsistency. Why ? Simply from a practical inhibition of the faculty of comparison. A line of action is pursued from the felt pressure of some close expediency : afterwards some " reasons " must be found for it, some justification given : no attempt is made before or after the action to see it as a whole with its causes and its consequences, and so there is no clear comparison of actual motives and results. This genius of inconsistency, of holding conflicting ideas or feelings in the mind simultaneously, in watertight compartments, is perhaps peculiarly British. It is, I repeat, not hypocrisy ; a consciousness of inconsistency would spoil the play : it is a condition of the success of this conduct that it should be unconscious. For such inconsistency has its uses. Much of the brutality and injustice involved in " Imperialism " would be impossible without this capacity. If, for example, the British mind had been sufficiently consistent to have kept clearly before it the fact that 400 millions of people were contending with a body less than a quarter of a million, whatever view was held as to the necessity and justice of the war, much of its detailed barbarism and all the triumphant exultation on success would have been impossible.

There is of course much more than this in the psychology of Imperialism, but there are two main factors, the habit and capacity of substituting vague and decorative notions, derived through " masked words," for hard naked facts, and the native or acquired genius of inconsistency. Great Britain would be incapable of this policy if she realized in clear consciousness the actual play of motives and their results. Most of the men who have misled her have first been obliged to mislead themselves. There is no enthusiasm in hypocrisy, and even bare-faced greed furnishes no adequate stimulus to a long policy. Imperialism is based upon a persistent misrepresentation of facts and forces, chiefly through a most refined process of selection, exaggeration, and attenuation, directed by interested cliques and persons so as to distort the face of history.

The gravest peril of Imperialism lies in the state of mind of a nation which has become habituated to this deception and which has rendered itself incapable of self-criticism.

For this is the condition which Plato terms " the lie in the soul "—a lie which does not know itself to be a lie.

One of the marks of this diseased condition is a fatal self-complacency. When a nation has succumbed to it, it easily and instinctively rejects all criticism of other nations as due to envy and malice, and all domestic criticism is attributed to the bias of anti-patriotism. In more primitive nations the lusts of domination and material acquisition which underlie Imperialism express themselves freely and unconsciously : there is little self-complacency because there is little self-consciousness. But nations which have grown in self-consciousness as far as the Western European nations seek to stimulate and feed their instinctive lusts by conscious reflection. Hence the elaborate weaving of intellectual and moral defences, the ethics and sociology of empire which we have examined.

The controlling and directing agent of the whole process, as we have seen, is the pressure of financial and industrial motives, operated for the direct, short-range, material interests of small, able, and well-organized groups in a nation. These groups secure the active co-operation of statesmen and of political cliques who wield the power of "parties," partly by associating them directly in their business schemes, partly by appealing to the conservative instincts of members of the possessing classes, whose vested interest and class dominance are best preserved by diverting the currents of political energy from domestic on to foreign politics. The acquiescence, even the active and enthusiastic support, of the body of a nation in a course of policy fatal to its own true interests is secured partly by appeals to the mission of civilization, but chiefly by playing upon the primitive instincts of the race.

The psychology of these instincts is not easy to explore, but certain prime factors easily appear. The passion which a French writer describes as kilometritis,[1] or milo-mania,

[1] M. Novicov, *La Federation de l'Europe*, p. 158.

the instinct for control of land, drives back to the earliest times when a wide range of land was necessary for a food supply for men or cattle, and is linked on to the " trek " habit, which survives more powerfully than is commonly supposed in civilized peoples. The " nomadic " habit bred of necessity survives as a chief ingredient in the love of travel, and merges into " the spirit of adventure " when it meets other equally primitive passions. This " spirit of adventure," especially in the Anglo-Saxon, has taken the shape of " sport," which in its stronger or " more adventurous " forms involves a direct appeal to the lust of slaughter and the crude struggle for life involved in pursuit. The animal lust of struggle, once a necessity, survives in the blood, and just in proportion as a nation or a class has a margin of energy and leisure from the activities of peaceful industry, it craves satisfaction through " sport," in which hunting and the physical satisfaction of striking a blow are vital ingredients. The leisured classes in great Britain, having most of their energy liberated from the necessity of work, naturally specialize on " sport," the hygienic necessity of a substitute for work helping to support or coalescing with the survival of a savage instinct. As the milder expressions of this passion are alone permissible in the sham or artificial encounters of domestic sports, where wild game disappears and human conflicts more mortal than football are prohibited, there is an ever stronger pressure to the frontiers of civilization in order that the thwarted " spirit of adventure " may have strong, free play. These feelings are fed by a flood of the literature of travel and of imaginative writing, the security and monotony of the ordinary civilized routine imparting an ever-growing fascination to the wilder portions of the earth. The milder satisfactions afforded by sport to the upper classes in their ample leisure at home are imitated by the industrial masses, whose time and energy for recreation have been growing, and who, in their passage from rural to town conditions, have never abandoned the humbler sports of feudal country life to which from time immemorial they had been addicted. " Football is a good game, but better than it, better than any other game, is that of man-hunting."[1]

The sporting and military aspects of Imperialism form, therefore, a very powerful basis of popular appeal. The desire to pursue and kill either big game or other men can only be satisfied by expansion and militarism. It may indeed be safely said that the reason why our army is so inefficient in its officers, as compared with its rank and file, is that at a time when serious scientific preparation and selection are required for an intellectual profession, most British officers choose the army and undertake its work in the spirit of " sport." While the average " Tommy " is perhaps actuated in the main by similar motives, " science " matters less in his case, and any lack of serious professional purpose is more largely compensated by the discipline imposed on him.

But still more important than these supports of militarism in the army is the part played by " war " as a support of Imperialism in the non-combatant body of the nation. Though the active appeal of " sport " is still strong, even among townsmen, clear signs are visible of a degradation of this active interest of the participant into the idle excitement of the spectator. How far sport has thus degenerated may be measured by the substitution every-where of a specialized professionalism for a free amateur exercise, and by the growth of the attendant vice of betting, which everywhere expresses the worst form of sporting excitement, drawing all disinterested sympathy away

[1] Baden-Powell, *Aids to Scouting*, p. 124.

from the merits of the competition, and concentrating it upon the irrational element of chance in combination with covetousness and low cunning. The equivalent of this degradation of interest in sport is Jingoism in relation to the practice of war. Jingoism is merely the lust of the spectator, unpurged by any personal effort, risk, or sacrifice, gloating over the perils, pains, and slaughter of fellow-men whom he does not know, but whose destruction he desires in a blind and artificially stimulated passion of hatred and revenge. In the Jingo all is concentrated on the hazard and blind fury of the fray. The arduous and weary monotony of the march, the long periods of waiting, the hard privations, the terrible tedium of a prolonged campaign, play no part in his imagination ; the redeeming factors of war, the fine sense of comradeship which common personal peril educates, the fruits of discipline and self-restraint, the respect for the personality of enemies whose courage he must admit and whom he comes to realize as fellow-beings—all these moderating elements in actual war are eliminated from the passion of the Jingo. It is precisely for these reasons that some friends of peace maintain that the two most potent checks of militarism and of war are the obligation of the entire body of citizens to undergo military service and the experience of an invasion.

Whether such expensive remedies are really effectual or necessary we are not called on to decide, but it is quite evident that the spectatorial lust of Jingoism is a most serious factor in Imperialism. The dramatic falsification both of war and of the whole policy of imperial expansion required to feed this popular passion forms no small portion of the art of the real organizers of imperialist exploits, the small groups of business men and politicians who know what they want and how to get it.

Tricked out with the real or sham glories of military

heroism and the magnificent claims of empire-making, Jingoism becomes a nucleus of a sort of patriotism which can be moved to any folly or to any crime.

IV

Where this spirit of naked dominance needs more dressing for the educated classes of a nation, the requisite moral ans intellectual decorations are woven for its use; the church, the press, the schools and colleges, the political machine, the four chief instruments of popular education, are accommodated to its service. From the muscular Christianity of the last generation to the imperial Christianity of the present day is but a single step; the temper of growing sacerdotalism and the doctrine of authority in the established churches well accord with militarism and political autocracy. Mr. Goldwin Smith has rightly observed how " force is the natural ally of superstition, and superstition knows it well."[1] As for the most potent engine of the press, the newspaper, so far as it is not directly owned and operated by financiers for financial purposes (as is the case to a great extent in every great industrial and financial centre), it is always influenced and often dominated by the interests of the classes which control the advertisements upon which its living depends; the independence of a paper with a circulation so large and firm as to " command " and to retain advertisements in the teeth of a policy disliked by the advertising classes is becoming rarer and more precarious every year, as the cluster of interests which form the business nucleus of Imperialism becomes more consolidated and more conscious in its politics. The political machine is " an hireling,"

[1] Letter in *The Manchester Guardian*, October 14, 1900.

because it is a machine, and needs constant repair and lubrication from the wealthy members of the party; the machinist knows from whom he takes his pay, and cannot run against the will of those who are in fact the patrons of the party, the tightening of whose purse-strings will automatically stop the machine. The recent Imperialism both of Great Britain and America has been materially assisted by the lavish contributions of men like Rockefeller, Hanna, Rhodes, Beit to party funds for the election of "imperialist" representatives and for the political instruction of the people.

Most serious of all is the persistent attempt to seize the school system for Imperialism masquerading as patriotism. To capture the childhood of the country, to mechanize its free play into the routine of military drill, to cultivate the savage survivals of combativeness, to poison its early understanding of history by false ideals and pseudo-heroes, and by a consequent disparagement and neglect of the really vital and elevating lessons of the past, to establish a "geocentric" view of the moral universe in which the interests of humanity are subordinated to that of the "country" (and so, by easy, early, natural inference, that of the "country" to that of the "self"), to feed the always overweening pride of race at an age when self-confidence most commonly prevails, and by necessary implication to disparage other nations, so starting children in the world with false measures of value and an unwillingness to learn from foreign sources—to fasten this base insularity of mind and morals upon the little children of a nation and to call it patriotism is as foul an abuse of education as it is possible to conceive. Yet the power of Church and State over primary education is being bent consistently to this purpose, while the blend of clericalism and autocratic academicism which dominates the secondary education of

this country pours its enthusiasm into the same evil channel.[1]
Finally, our centres of highest culture, the universities,
are in peril of a new perversion from the path of free inquiry
and expression, which is the true path of intellectual life.
A new sort of "pious founder" threatens intellectual
liberty. Our colleges are, indeed, no longer to be the
subservient defenders of religious orthodoxy, repressing
science, distorting history, and moulding philosophy to
conserve the interests of Church and King. The academic
studies and their teachers are to employ the same methods
but directed to a different end: philosophy, the natural
sciences, history, economics, sociology, are to be employed
in setting up new earthworks against the attack of the
disinherited masses upon the vested interests of the plutocracy. I do not of course represent this perversion as
destructive of the educational work of the colleges: the
services rendered in defence of "conservatism" may even
be regarded in most cases as incidental: only perhaps in
philosophy and economics is the bias a powerful and
pervasive one, and even there the individuality of strong
independent natures may correct it. Moreover, it is needless to charge dishonesty against the teachers, who commonly
think and teach according to the highest that is in them.
But the actual teaching is none the less selected and
controlled, wherever it is found useful to employ the
arts of selection and control, by the business interests
playing on the vested academic interests. No one can
follow the history of political and economic theory during
the last century without recognizing that the selection and
rejection of ideas, hypothesis, and formulæ, the moulding
of them into schools or tendencies of thought, and the
propagation of them in the intellectual world, have been
plainly directed by the pressure of class interests. In political

[1] For striking illustrations *cf.* Spencer's *Facts and Comments*, pp. 126–7.

economy, as we might well suspect, from its close bearing upon business and politics, we find the most incontestable example. The "classical" economics in England were the barely disguised formulation of the mercantile and manufacturing interests as distinguished from, and opposed to, the landowning interest on the one hand, the labouring interest on the other, evoking in later years other class economics of "protection" and of "socialism" similarly woven out of sectional interests.

The real determinants in education are given in these three questions: "Who shall teach? What shall they teach? How shall they teach?" Where universities are dependent for endowments and incomes upon the favour of the rich, upon the charity of millionaires, the following answers will of necessity be given: "Safe teachers. Safe studies. Sound (i.e. orthodox) methods." The coarse proverb which tells us that "he who pays the piper calls the tune" is quite as applicable here as elsewhere, and no bluff regarding academic dignity and intellectual honesty must blind us to the fact.

The interference with intellectual liberty is seldom direct, seldom personal, though both in the United States and Canada some instances of the crudest heresy-hunting have occurred. The real danger consists in the appointment rather than in the dismissal of teachers, in the determination of what subjects shall be taught, what relative attention shall be given to each subject, and what text-books and other apparatus of instruction shall be used. The subservience to rank and money, even in our older English universities, has been evinced so nakedly, and the demands for monetary aid in developing new faculties necessarily looms so large in academic eyes, that the danger here indicated is an ever-growing one. It is not so much the weight of the "dead hand" that is to be feared as that of the living: a college so unfortunate as to harbour teachers who, in handling vital issues of politics or economics, teach truths deeply and obviously antagonistic to the interests of the classes from whom financial aid was sought, would be committing suicide. Higher education has never been economically self-supporting; it has hardly ever been fully organized from public funds; everywhere it has remained parasitic on the private munificence of wealthy persons. The peril is too obvious to need further enforcement: it is the hand of the prospective, the potential donor that fetters intellectual freedom in our colleges, and will do so more and more so long as the duty of organizing public higher education for a nation out of public funds fails of recognition.

The area of danger is, of course, far wider than Imperialism, covering the whole field of vested interests. But, if the analysis of previous chapters is correct, Imperialism stands as a first defence of these interests: for the financial and speculative classes it means a pushing of their private businesses at the public expense, for the export manufacturers and merchants a forcible enlargement of foreign markets and a related policy of Protection, for the official and professional classes large openings of honourable and lucrative employment, for the Church it represents the temper and practice of authority and the assertion of spiritual control over vast multitudes of lower people, for the political oligarchy it means the only effective diversion of the forces of democracy and the opening of great public careers in the showy work of empire-making.

This being so, it is inevitable that Imperialism should seek intellectual support in our seats of learning, and should use the sinews of education for the purpose. The millionaire who endows Oxford does not buy its men of learning outright, need not even stipulate what should be taught. But the practical pressure of Imperialism is such that when a professional appointment is made in history it is becoming more difficult for a scholar with the intellectual outlook of a John Morley, a Frederick Harrison, or a Goldwin Smith to secure election, or for a political economist with strong views on the necessity of controlling capital to be elected to a chair in economics. No formal tests are necessary; the instinct of financial self-preservation will suffice. The price which universities pay for preferring money and social position to intellectual distinction in the choice of chancellors and for touting among the million-aires for the equipment of new scientific schools is this subservience to the political and business interests of their patrons : their philosophy, their history, their economics, even their biology must reflect in doctrine and method the consideration that is due to patronage, and the fact that this deference is unconscious enhances the damage done to the cause of intellectual freedom.

Thus do the industrial and financial forces of Imperialism, operating through the party, the press, the church, the school, mould public opinion and public policy by the false idealization of those primitive lusts of struggle, domination and acquisitiveness, which have survived throughout the eras of peaceful industrial order, and whose stimulation is needed once again for the work of imperial aggression, expansion, and the forceful exploitation of lower races. For these business politicians biology and sociology weave thin convenient theories of a race struggle for the subjugation of the inferior peoples, in order that we, the Anglo-Saxon, may take their lands and live upon their labours ; while economics buttresses the argument by representing our work in conquering and ruling them as our share in the division of labour among nations, and history devises reasons why the lessons of past empire do not apply to ours while social ethics paints the motive of "Imperialism" as the desire to bear the "burden" of educating and elevating races of "children." Thus are the "cultured" or semi-cultured classes indoctrinated with the intellectual and moral grandeur of Imperialism. For the masses there is a cruder appeal to hero-worship and sensational glory, adventure and the sporting spirit: current history falsified in coarse flaring colours, for the direct stimulation of the combative instincts. But while various methods are employed, some delicate and indirect, others coarse and flamboyant, the operation everywhere resolves itself into an incitation and direction of the brute lusts of human domination which are everywhere latent in civilized humanity, for the pursuance of a policy fraught with material gain to a minority of co-operative vested interests which usurp the title of the commonwealth.

CHAPTER IV

IMPERIALISM AND THE LOWER RACES

I

THE statement, often made, that the work of imperial expansion is virtually complete is not correct. It is true that most of the " backward " races have been placed in some sort of dependence upon one or other of the " civilized " Powers as colony, protectorate, hinterland, or sphere of influence. But this in most instances marks rather the beginning of a process of imperialization than a definite attainment of empire. The intensive growth of empire by which interference is increased and governmental control tightened over spheres of influence and protectorates is as important and as perilous an aspect of Imperialism as the extensive growth which takes shape in assertion of rule over new areas of territory and new populations.

The famous saying, attributed to Napoleon, that " great empires die of indigestion " serves to remind us of the importance of the imperialist processes which still remain after formal " expansion " has been completed. During the last twenty years of the last century Great Britain, Germany, France, and Russia had bitten off huge mouthfuls of Africa and Asia which are not yet chewed, digested, or assimilated. Moreover, great areas still remain whose independence, though threatened, is yet unimpaired.[1]

Vast countries in Asia, such as Persia, Thibet, Siam,

[1] The reader is reminded that this and ensuing remarks relate to the situation at the beginning of the century.

223

Afghanistan, are rapidly forging to the front of politics as likely subjects of armed controversy between European Powers with a view to subjugation ; the Turkish dominions in Asia Minor, and perhaps in Europe, await a slow, precarious process of absorption ; the paper partition of Central Africa teems with possibilities of conflict. The entrance of the United States into the imperial struggle throws virtually the whole of South America into the arena ; for it is not reasonable to expect that European nations, with settlements and vast economic interests in the southern peninsula, will readily leave all this territory to the special protection or ultimate absorption of the United States, when the latter, abandoning her old consistent isolation, has plunged into the struggle for empire in the Pacific.

Beyond and above all this looms China. It is not easy to suppose that the lull and hesitancy of the Powers will last, or that the magnitude and manifest risks of disturbing this vast repository of incalculable forces will long deter adventurous groups of profit-seekers from driving their Governments along the slippery path of commercial treaties, leases, railway and mining concessions, which must entail a growing process of political interference.

It is not my purpose to examine here the entanglement of political and economic issues which each of these cases presents, but simply to illustrate the assertion that the policy of modern Imperialism is not ended but only just begun, and that it is concerned almost wholly with the rival claims of Empires to dominate " lower races " in tropical and sub-tropical countries, or in other countries occupied by manifestly unassimilable races.

In asking ourselves what are the sound principles of world policy and of national policy in this matter, we may at first ignore the important differences which should affect our conduct towards countries inhabited by what appear to be definitely low-typed unprogressive races, countries whose people manifest capacity of rapid progress from a present low condition, and countries like India and China, where an old civilization of a high type, widely differing from that of European nations, exists.

Before seeking for differences of policy which correspond to these conditions, let us try to find whether there are any general principles of guidance in dealing with countries occupied by " lower " or unprogressive peoples.

It is idle to consider as a general principle the attitude of mere *laissez faire*. It is not only impracticable in view of the actual forces which move politics, but it is ethically indefensible in the last resort.

To lay down as an absolute law that " the autonomy of every nation is inviolable " does not carry us very far. There can no more be absolute nationalism in the society of nations than absolute individualism in the single nation. Some measure of practical internationality, implying a " comity of nations," and some relations of " right " and " duty " between nations, are almost universally admitted. The rights of self-government, implied by the doctrine of autonomy, if binding in any sense legal or ethical on other nations, can only possess this character in virtue of some real international organization, however rudimentary.

It is difficult for the strongest advocate of national rights to assert that the people in actual occupation or political control over a given area of the earth are entitled to do what they will with " their own," entirely disregarding the direct and indirect consequences of their actions upon the rest of the world.

It is not necessary to take extreme cases of a national policy which directly affects the welfare of a neighbouring State, as where a people on the upper reaches of a river like the Nile or the Niger might so damage or direct the flow as to cause plague or famine to the lower lands belonging to another nation. Few, if any, would question some right of interference from without in such a case. Or take another case which falls outside the range of directly other-regarding actions. Suppose a famine or flood or other catastrophe deprives a population of the means of living on their land, while unutilized land lies in plenty beyond their borders in another country, are the rulers of the latter entitled to refuse an entrance or a necessary settlement? As in the case of individuals, so of nations, it will be generally allowed that necessity knows no laws, which, rightly interpreted, means that the right of self-preservation transcends all other rights as the prime condition of their emergence and exercise.

This carries us on an inclined plane of logic to the real issue as ably presented by Mr. Kidd, Professor Giddings, and the " Fabian " Imperialists. It is an expansion of this plea of material necessity that constitutes the first claim to a control of the tropics by " civilized " nations. The European races have grown up with a standard of material civilization based largely upon the consumption and use of foods, raw materials of manufacture, and other goods which are natural products of tropical countries. The industries and the trade which furnish these commodities are of vital importance to the maintenance and progress of Western civilization. The large part played in our import trade by such typically tropical products as sugar, tea, coffee, indiarubber, rice, tobacco, indicates the dependence of such countries as Great Britain upon the tropics. Partly from sheer growth of population in temperate zones, partly from the rising standard of material life, this dependence of the temperate on the tropical countries must grow. In order to satisfy these growing needs larger and larger tracts of tropical country must be cultivated, the cultivation must be better and more regular, and peaceful and effective trade relations with these countries must be maintained. Now the ease with which human life can be maintained in the tropics breeds indolence and torpor of character. The inhabitants of these countries are not " progressive people "; they neither develop the arts of industry at any satisfactory pace, nor do they evolve new wants or desires, the satisfaction of which might force them to labour. We cannot therefore rely upon the ordinary economic motives and methods of free exchange to supply the growing demand for tropical goods. The resources of the tropics will not be developed voluntarily by the natives themselves.

" If we look to the native social systems of the tropical East, the primitive savagery of Central Africa, to the West Indian Islands in the past in process of being assisted into the position of modern States by Great Britain, or the black republic of Hayti in the present, or to modern Liberia in the future, the lesson seems everywhere the same ; it is that there will be no development of the resources of the tropics under native government." [1]

We cannot, it is held, leave these lands barren ; it is our duty to see that they are developed for the good of the world. White men cannot " colonize " these lands and, thus settling, develop the natural resources by the labour of their own hands ; they can only organize and superintend the labour of the natives. By doing this they can educate the natives in the arts of industry and stimulate in them a desire for material and moral progress, implanting new " wants " which form in every society the roots of civilization.

It is quite evident that there is much force in this presentation of the case, not only on material but on moral grounds ; nor can it be brushed aside because it is liable

[1] Kidd, *The Control of the Tropics*, p. 53 (Macmillan & Co.).

to certain obvious and gross abuses. It implies, however, two kinds of interference which require justification. To step in and utilize natural resources which are left undeveloped is one thing, to compel the inhabitants to develop them is another. The former is easily justified, involving the application on a wider scale of a principle whose equity, as well as expediency, is recognized and enforced in most civilized nations. The other interference whereby men who prefer to live on a low standard of life with little labour shall be forced to harder or more continuous labour, is far more difficult of justification.

I have set the economic compulsion in the foreground, because in point of history it is the *causa causans* of the Imperialism that accompanies or follows.

In considering the ethics and politics of this interference, we must not be bluffed or blinded by critics who fasten on the palpable dishonesty of many practices of the gospel of " the dignity of labour " and " the mission of civilization." The real issue is whether, and under what circumstances, it is justifiable for Western nations to use compulsory government for the control and education in the arts of industrial and political civilization of the inhabitants of tropical countries and other so-called lower races. Because Rhodesian mine-owners or Cuban sugar-growers stimulate the British or American Government to Imperialism by parading motives and results which do not really concern them, it does not follow that these motives under proper guidance are unsound, or that the results are undesirable.

There is nothing unworthy, quite the contrary, in the notion that nations which, through a more stimulative environment, have advanced further in certain arts of industry, politics, or morals, should communicate these to nations which from their circumstances were more backward, so as to aid them in developing alike the material resources of their land and the human resources of their people. Nor is it clear that in this work some " inducement, stimulus, or pressure " (to quote a well-known phrase) or in a single word, " compulsion," is wholly illegitimate. Force is itself no remedy, coercion is not education, but it may be a prior condition to the operation of educative forces. Those, at any rate, who assign any place to force in the education or the political government of individuals in a nation can hardly deny that the same instrument may find a place in the civilization of backward by progressive nations.

Assuming that the arts of " progress," or some of them, are communicable, a fact which is hardly disputable, there can be no inherent natural right in a people to refuse that measure of compulsory education which shall raise it from childhood to manhood in the order of nationalities. The analogy furnished by the education of a child is prima facie a sound one, and is not invalidated by the dangerous abuses to which it is exposed in practice.

The real issue is one of safeguards, of motives, and of methods. What are the conditions under which a nation may help to develop the resources of another, and even apply some element of compulsion in doing so ? The question, abstract as it may sound, is quite the most important of all practical questions for this generation. For that such development will take place, and such compulsion, legitimate or illegitimate, be exercised, more and more throughout this new century in many quarters of this globe, is beyond the shadow of a doubt. It is the great practical business of the country to explore and develop, by every method which science can devise, the hidden natural and human resources of the globe.

That the white Western nations will abandon a quest on which they have already gone so far is a view which does not deserve consideration. That this process of development may be so conducted as to yield a gain to world-civilization, instead of some terrible *débâcle* in which revolted slave races may trample down their parasitic and degenerate white masters, should be the supreme aim of far-sighted scientific statecraft.

II

To those who utter the single cry of warning, "*laissez faire*, hands off, let these people develop their resources themselves with such assistance as they ask or hire, undisturbed by the importunate and arrogant control of foreign nations," it is a sufficient answer to point out the impossibility of maintaining such an attitude.

If organized Governments of civilized Powers refused the task, they would let loose a horde of private adventurers, slavers, piratical traders, treasure hunters, concession mongers, who, animated by mere greed of gold or power, would set about the work of exploitation under no public control and with no regard to the future ; playing havoc with the political, economic, and moral institutions of the peoples, instilling civilized vices and civilized diseases, importing spirits and firearms as the trade of readiest acceptance, fostering internecine strife for their own political and industrial purposes, and even setting up private despotisms sustained by organized armed forces. It is unnecessary to revert to the buccaneering times of the sixteenth century, when a " new world " was thrown open to the plunder of the old, and private gentlemen of Spain or England competed with their Governments in the most gigantic business of spoliation that history records. The story of Samoa, of Hawaii, and a score of South Sea Islands in quite recent years, proves that, at a time when every sea is a highway, it is impossible for the most remote land to escape the intrusion of "civilized" nations, represented by precisely their most reckless and debased specimens, who gravitate thither in order to reap the rapid fruits of licence. The contact with white races cannot be avoided, and it is more perilous and more injurious in proportion as it lacks governmental sanction and control. The most gigantic modern experiment in private adventure slowly yielded its full tale of horrors in the Congo Free State, while the handing over of large regions in Africa to the virtually unchecked government of Chartered Companies has exposed everywhere the dangers of a contact based on private commercialism.[1]

To abandon the backward races to these perils of private exploitation, it is argued forcibly, is a barbarous dereliction of a public duty on behalf of humanity and the civilization of the world. Not merely does it leave the tropics to be the helpless prey of the offscourings of civilized nations ; it opens grave dangers in the future, from the political or military ambitions of native or imported rulers, who, playing upon the religious fanaticism or the combative instincts of great hordes of semi-savages, may impose upon them so effective a military discipline as to give terrible significance to some black or yellow " peril." Complete isolation is no longer possible even for the remotest island ; absolute self-sufficiency is no more possible for a nation than for an individual : in each case society has the right and the need to safeguard its interests against an injurious assertion of individuality.

[1] Chartered Company government is not necessarily bad in its direct results. It is, in fact, little else than private despotism rendered more than usually precarious in that it has been established for the sake of dividends. A " managing director " may be scrupulous and far-sighted, as Sir G. T. Goldie in the Niger Company, or unscrupulous and short-sighted, as Mr. Rhodes in the South African Chartered Company. The unchecked tyranny of the managing director may be illustrated by the evidence of the Duke of Abercorn, tendered to the South African Committee. " Mr. Rhodes had received a power of attorney to do precisely what he liked without consultation with the Board, he simply notifying what was done."

Again, though there is some force in the contention that the backward natives could and would protect themselves against the encroachments of private adventurers, if they had the assurance that the latter could not call upon their Government for assistance or for vengeance, history does not lead us to believe that these powers of self-protection however adequate against forcible invasions, would suffice to meet the more insidious wiles by which traders, prospectors, and political adventurers insinuate their poisons into primitive societies like that of Samoa or Ashanti.

So far, we have established two tentative principles. First, that all interference on the part of civilized white nations with " lower races " is not prima facie illegitimate. Second, that such interference cannot safely be left to private enterprise of individual whites. If these principles be admitted, it follows that civilized Governments *may* undertake the political and economic control of lower races—in a word, that the characteristic form of modern Imperialism is not under all conditions illegitimate.

What, then, are the conditions which render it legitimate ? They may be provisionally stated thus : Such interference with the government of a lower race must be directed primarily to secure the safety and progress of the civilization of the world, and not the special interest of the interfering nation. Such interference must be attended by an improvement and elevation of the character of the people who·are brought under this control. Lastly, the determination of the two preceding conditions must not be left to the arbitrary will or judgment of the interfering nation, but must proceed from some organized representation of civilized humanity.

The first condition is deduced directly from the principle of social utility expanded to its widest range, so as to be synonymous with " the good of humanity." Regarding the conduct of one nation towards another we can find no other standard. Whatever uncertainty or other imperfection appertains to such a standard, regarded as a rule for international policy, any narrower standard is, of necessity, more uncertain and more imperfect. No purely legal contentions touching the misapplication of the term " right " to international relations, in the absence of any form of " sanction," affects our issue. Unless we are prepared to re-affirm in the case of nations, as the all-sufficient guide of conduct, that doctrine of " enlightened selfishness " which has been almost universally abandoned in the case of individuals, and to insist that the unchecked self-assertion of each nation, following the line of its own private present interest, is the best guarantee of the general progress of humanity, we must set up, as a supreme standard of moral appeal, some conception of the welfare of humanity regarded as an organic unity. It is, however, needless to insist upon the analogy between the relation of an individual to the other individuals of his society, and that of one society towards another in the commonwealth of nations. For, though cynical statesmen of the modern Macchiavelli school may assert the visible interest of their country as the supreme guide of conduct, they do not seriously suggest that the good of humanity is thus attained, but only that this wider end has no meaning or appeal for them. In the light of this attitude all discussion of general principles " justifying " conduct is out of place, for " just " and " justice " are ruled out *ab initio*. The standard here proposed would not, however, in point of fact, be formally rejected by any school of political thinkers who were invited to find a general law for the treatment of lower races. No one would assert in so many words that we had a right to sacrifice the good of any other nation, or of the world at large, to our own private national gain.

In England, certainly, Lord Rosebery's declaration that the British Empire is " the greatest secular agency for good known to the world " would everywhere be adopted as the fundamental justification of empire.

Lord Salisbury expressly endorsed the principle, asserting that " the course of events, which I should prefer to call the acts of Providence, have called this country to exercise an influence over the character and progress of the world such as has never been exercised in any Empire before " ; while the Archbishop of Canterbury propounded a doctrine of " imperial Christianity " based upon the same assumptions. It may, then, fairly be understood that every act of " Imperialism " consisting of forcible interference with another people can only be justified by showing that it contributes to " the civilization of the world."

Equally, it is admitted that some special advantage must be conferred upon the people who are the subject of this interference. On highest ground of theory, the repression, even the extinction, of some unprogressive or retrogressive nation, yielding place to another more socially efficient and more capable of utilizing for the general good the natural resources of the land, might seem permissible, if we accepted unimpaired and unimproved the biological struggle for existence as the sole or chief instrument of progress. But, if we admit that in the highest walks of human progress the constant tendency is to substitute more and more the struggle with natural and moral environment for the internecine struggle of living individuals and species, and that the efficient conduct of this struggle requires the suspension of the lower struggle and a growing solidarity of sentiment and sympathy throughout entire humanity, we shall perceive two important truths. First, " expansion," in order to absorb for the more " progressive " races an ever larger portion of the globe, is not the "necessity" it once appeared, because progress will take place more and more upon the qualitative plane, with more intensive cultivation alike of natural resources and of human life. The supposed natural necessity for crowding out the lower races is based on a narrow, low, and purely quantitative analysis of human progress.

Secondly, in the progress of humanity, the services of nationality, as a means of education and of self-development, will be recognized as of such supreme importance that nothing short of direct physical necessity in self-defence can justify the extinction of a nation. In a word, it will be recognized that "le grand crime internationnel est de détruire une nationalité."[1] But even those who would not go so far in their valuation of the factor of nationality will agree that it is a sound practical test of conduct to insist that interference with the freedom of another nation shall justify itself by showing some separate advantage conferred upon the nation thus placed in an inferior position : partly, because it seems obvious that the gain to the general cause of civilization will chiefly be contained in or compassed by an improvement in the character or condition of the nation which is the subject of interference ; partly, because the maxim which recognizes the individual person as an end, and requires State government to justify itself by showing that the coercion it exercises does in reality enlarge the liberty of those whom it restrains, is applicable also to the larger society of nations. Without unduly pressing the analogy of individual and nation as organisms, it may safely be asserted that imperial interference with a "lower race" must justify itself by showing that it is acting for the real good of the subject race. Mr. Chamberlain is no sentimentalist, and his declaration may

[1] M. Brunetière, quoted *Edinburgh Review*, April, 1900.

rank as a *locus classicus* upon this matter. " Our rule over the territories [native] can only be justified if we can show that it adds to the happiness and prosperity of the people."

The moral defence of Imperialism is generally based upon the assertion that in point of fact these two conditions are fulfilled, viz. that the political and economic control forcibly assumed by " higher " over " lower races " does promote at once the civilization of the world and the special good of the subject races. The real answer, upon which British Imperialists rely in defending expansion, is to point to actual services rendered to India, Eygpt, Uganda, etc., and to aver that other dependencies where British government is less successful would have fared worse if left either to themselves or to another European Power.

Before considering the practical validity of this position, and the special facts that determine and qualify the work of " civilizing " other races, it is right to point out the fundamental flaw in this theory of " Imperialism," viz. the non-fulfilment of the third condition laid down above. Can we safely trust to the honour, the public spirit, and the insight of any of the competing imperial races the subordination of its private interests and ends to the wider interests of humanity or the particular good of each subject race brought within its sway ?

No one, as we point out, contends that so perfect a natural harmony exists that every nation, consciously following its own chief interest, is " led " as " by an invisible hand " to a course of conduct which necessarily subserves the common interest, and in particular the interest of the subject race. What security, then, can possibly exist for the practices of a sound Imperialism fulfilling the conditions laid down ? Does any one contend that the special self-interest of the expanding and annexing

nation is not a chief, or indeed the chief conscious determinant in each step of practical Imperialism ? Prima facie
it would seem reasonable to suppose that many cases would
occur in which the special temporary interests of the
expanding nation would collide with those of the world-
civilization, and that the former would be preferred. It
is surely unreasonable to take as proof of the fulfilment of
the conditions of sane Imperialism the untested and
unverified *ipse dixit* of an interested party.

III

While it is generally agreed that the progress of world-
civilization is the only valid moral ground for political
interference with " lower races," and that the only valid
evidence of such progress is found in the political, industrial,
and moral education of the race that is subjected to this
interference, the true conditions for the exercise of such
a " trust " are entirely lacking.

The actual situation is, indeed, replete with absurdity.
Each imperialist nation claims to determine for itself what
are the lower races it will take under its separate protection,
or agrees with two or three neighbours to partition some
huge African tract into separate spheres of influence ; the
kind of civilization that is imposed is never based on any
sober endeavour to understand the active or latent progressive forces of the subject race, and to develop and
direct them, but is imported from Europe in the shape of
sets arts of industry, definite political institutions, fixed
religious dogmas, which are engrafted on alien institutions.
In political government progress is everywhere avowedly
sacrificed to order, and both alike are subservient to the
quick development of certain profitable trading industries,
or to the mere lust of territorial aggrandisement. The

recurrent quarrels of the armed white nations, each insisting on his claim to take up the white man's burden in some fresh quarter of the globe ; the trading companies seeking to oust each other from a new market, the very missionaries competing by sects and nationalities for " mission fields," and using political intrigue and armed force to back their special claims, present a curious commentary upon the " trust for civilization " theory.[1]

It is quite evident that this self-assertive sway lacks the first essentials of a trust, viz. security that the " trustee " represents fairly all the interested parties, and is responsible to some judicial body for the faithful fulfilment of the terms of the trust. Otherwise what safeguard exists against the abuse of the powers of the trustee ? The notorious fact that half the friction between European nations arises from conflicting claims to undertake the office of " trustee for civilization " over lower races and their possessions augurs ill alike for the sincerity of the profession and the moral capacity to fulfil it. It is surely no mark of cynicism to question closely this extreme anxiety to bear one another's burdens among the nations.

This claim to justify aggression, annexation, and forcible government by talk of duty, trust, or mission can only be made good by proving that the claimant is accredited by a body genuinely representative of civilization, to which it acknowledges a real responsibility, and that it is in fact capable of executing such a trust.

---

[1] From *The Times*, February 24, 1902—

" Hong-Kong, February 22.

" The German missionaries who escaped after the mission house at Frayuen was destroyed by Chinese have returned. It is reported from Canton that the French bishop intends to protect the natives who destroyed the Berlin mission station. The first information showed that hostility existed on the part of the Catholics towards the native Protestants, but it is believed that the aggressors assumed Catholicism as a subterfuge. If the bishop defends them, the situation of the missions in Kwang-tung will become complicated."

In a word, until some genuine international council exists, which shall accredit a civilized nation with the duty of educating a lower race, the claim of a " trust " is nothing else than an impudent act of self-assertion. One may well be sceptical about the early feasibility of any such representative council; but until it exists it would be far more honest for " expanding " nations to avow commercial necessity or political ambition as the real determinant of their protection of lower races than to feign a " trust " which has no reality. Even were international relations more advanced, and the movement begun at the Hague Conference solidified in a permanent authoritative body, representative of all the Powers, to which might be referred not only the quarrels between nations, but the entire partition of this " civilizing " work, the issue would still remain precarious. There would still be grave danger lest the " Powers," arrogating to themselves an exclusive possession of " civilization," might condemn to unwholesome and unjust subjection some people causing temporary trouble to the world by slow growth, turbulence or obnoxious institutions, for which liberty might be the most essential condition of progress. Apart from such genuine misapprehensions, there would exist the peril of the establishment of a self-chosen oligarchy among the nations which, under the cloak of the civilizing process, might learn to live parasitically upon the lower races, imposing upon them " for their own good " all the harder or more servile work of industry, and arrogating to themselves the honours and emoluments of government and supervision.

Clear analysis of present[1] tendencies points indeed to some such collusion of the dominant nations as the largest and gravest peril of the early future. The series of treaties and conventions between the chief European Powers,

[1] Relates to the period in which this book was written, 1903.

beginning with the Berlin African Conference of 1885, which fixed a standard for the "amicable division" of West African territory, and the similar treaty in 1890, fixing boundaries for English, German and Italian encroachments in East Africa, doubtless mark a genuine advance in the relations of the European Powers, but the objects and methods they embody throw a strange light upon the trust theory. If to the care of Africa we add that of China, where the European Powers took common action in "the interests of civilization," the future becomes still more menacing. While the protection of Europeans was the object in the foreground, and imposed a brief genuine community of policy upon the diverse nations, no sooner was the immediate object won than the deeper and divergent motives of the nations became manifest. The entire history of European relations with China in modern times is little else than one long cynical commentary upon the theory that we are engaged in the civilization of the Far East. Piratical expeditions to force trade upon a nation whose one principle of foreign policy was to keep clear of foreigners, culminating in a war to compel the reception of Indian opium ; abuse of the generous hospitality given for centuries to peaceful missionaries by wanton insults offered to the religious and political institutions of the country, the forcible exaction of commercial and political "concessions" as punishment for spasmodic acts of reprisal, the cold-blooded barter of murdered missionaries for the opening of new treaty ports, territory at Kiao Chow, or a new reach of the Yang-Tse for British trading vessels ; the mixture of menace, cajolery, and bribery by which England, Russia, Germany, France, and Japan laboured to gain some special and separate railway or mining concessions, upon terms excluding or damaging the interest of the others ; the definite assumption by Christian bishops and missionaries of political authority, and the arrogant and extensive use of the so-called right of " extra-territoriality," whereby they claim, not only for themselves but for their alleged converts and protégés, immunity from the laws of the land— all these things sufficiently expose the hollowness in actual history of the claims that considerations of a trust for civilization animate and regulate the foreign policy of Christendom, or of its component nations. What actually confronts us everywhere in modern history is selfish, materialistic, short-sighted, national competition, varied by occasional collusion. When any common international policy is adopted for dealing with lower races it has partaken of the nature, not of a moral trust, but of a business " deal."

It seems quite likely that this policy of " deals " may become as frequent and as systematic in the world of politics as in the world of commerce, and that treaties and alliances having regard to the political government and industrial exploitation of countries occupied by lower races may constitute a rude sort of effective internationalism in the early future.

Now, such political arrangements fall short in two important respects of that genuine trust for civilization which alone could give moral validity to a " civilized " control of lower peoples. In the first place, its assignment of a sphere of interest or a protectorate to England, to Germany, or Russia, is chiefly determined by some particular separate interest of that country by reason of contiguity or other private convenience, and not by any impartial considera- tion of its special competence for the work of civilization. If, for example, European Powers were really animated by the desire to extend Western civilization to China for her own good and that of the world, they might more favourably essay this task by promoting the influence of Japan than by inserting their own alien occidentalism.

But no one proposes to delegate to Japan this "trust"; every nation thinks of its own present commercial interests and political prestige.

Secondly, the civilization of the lower races, even according to accepted Western lights, is nowhere adopted as the real aim of government. Even where good political order is established and maintained, as in Egypt or India, its primary avowed end, and its universally accepted standard of success, are the immediate economic benefits attributed thereto. The political government of the country is primarily directed everywhere to the rapid, secure, effective development of the national resources, and their profitable exploitation by native labour under white management. It is maintained and believed that this course is beneficial to the natives, as well as to the commerce of the controlling power and of the world at large. That Indians or Egyptians are better off to-day than they were before our autocratic sway, not merely in economic resources but in substantial justice, may be quite true; it may even be accredited to us that many of our governors and officials have displayed some disinterested concern for the immediate well-being of the races committed (by ourselves) to our trust. But it can nowhere be sincerely contended that either we or any other Christian nation are governing these lower races upon the same enlightened principles which we profess and sometimes practise in governing ourselves. I allude here not to methods of government, but to ends. In the more enlightened European States and their genuine colonies, though present economic considerations bulk largely enough, they do not absorb the present and the future of public policy; provision is made for some play of non-economic forces, for the genuine culture of human life and character, for progress alike in individual growth and in the social growth which comes by free processes of self-government. These are regarded as essential conditions of the healthy growth of a nation. They are not less essential in the case of lower nations, and their exercise demands more thought and more experiment. The chief indictment of Imperialism in relation to the lower races consists in this, that it does not even pretend to apply to them the principles of education and of progress it applies at home.

IV

If we or any other nation really undertook the care and education of a " lower race " as a trust, how should we set about the execution of the trust ? By studying the religions, political and other social institutions and habits of the people, and by endeavouring to penetrate into their present mind and capacities of adaptation, by learning their language and their history, we should seek to place them in the natural history of man ; by similar close attention to the country in which they live, and not to its agricultural and mining resources alone, we should get a real grip upon their environment. Then, carefully approaching them so as to gain what confidence we could for friendly motives, and openly discouraging any premature private attempts of exploiting companies to work mines, or secure concessions, or otherwise to impair our disinterested conduct, we should endeavour to assume the position of advisers. Even if it were necessary to enforce some degree of authority, we should keep such force in the background as a last resort, and make it our first aim to understand and to promote the healthy free operations of all internal forces for progress which we might discover.

Natural growth in self-government and industry along tropical lines would be the end to which the enlightened policy of civilized assistance would address itself.

Now, what are the facts ? Nowhere has any serious organized attempt been made, even by Great Britain, by far the largest of the trustees, to bring this scientific disinterested spirit of inquiry to bear upon the races whose destiny she dominates.[1] The publications of the Aborigines Protection Society, and the report of the Native Races Committee, dealing with South Africa, indicate the vast range of unexplored knowledge, and the feeble fumblings which have hitherto taken the place of ordered investigations.[2] It is natural that this should be so. White pioneers in these countries are seldom qualified to do the work required ; the bias of the trader, the soldier, or the professional traveller, is fatal to sober, disinterested study of human life, while the missionary, who has contributed more than the rest, has seldom been endowed with a requisite amount of the scientific spirit or the scientific training.

Even the knowledge which we do possess is seldom utilized for light and leading in our actual government of native races. There have indeed been signs of an awakening intelligence in certain spots of our Empire ; administrators like Sir George Grey, Lord Ripon, and Sir Marshall Clarke brought sympathy and knowledge to the establishment of careful experiments in self-government. The forms of protectorate exercised over Basutoland and Khama's Country in South Africa, the restoration of the province of Mysore to native government, and the more careful abstention from interference with the internal policy of feudatory States in India, were favourable signs of a more enlightened policy.

In particular, the trend of liberal sentiment regarding

[1] The formation of an African Society, in memory of Miss Mary Kingsley for the study of the races of that continent, was a move in the right direction.

[2] No slight is here intended upon the excellent work of the Society and the Committee here named. They have handled well and accurately their material. It is the work of original research that is so lacking.

government of lower races was undergoing a marked change. The notion that there exists one sound, just, rational system of government, suitable for all sorts and conditions of men, embodied in the elective representative institutions of Great Britain, and that our duty was to impose this system as soon as possible, and with the least possible modifications, upon lower races, without any regard to their past history and their present capabilities and sentiments, was tending to disappear in this country, though the new headstrong Imperialism of America was still exposed to the taunt that " Americans think the United States has a mission to carry ' canned ' civilization to the heathen." The recognition that there may be many paths to civilization, that strong racial and environmental differences preclude a hasty grafting of alien institutions, regardless of continuity and selection of existing agencies and forms—these genuinely scientific and humane considerations are beginning to take shape in a demand that native races within our Empire shall have larger liberty of self-development assured to them. and that the imperial Government shall confine its inter- ference to protection against enemies from without, and preservation of the elements of good order within.

The true " imperial " policy is best illustrated in the case of Basutoland, which was rescued in 1884 from the aggressive designs of Cape Colony, stimulated by industrial exploiters.

Here British imperial government was exercised by a Commissioner, with several British magistrates to deal with grave offences against order, and a small body of native police under British officers. For the rest, the old political and economic institutions are preserved—government by chiefs, under a paramount chief, subject to the informal control or influence of public opinion in a national assembly ; ordinary administration, chiefly consisting in allotment of land, and ordinary jurisdiction are left to the chiefs.

" As far back as 1855 Moshesh forbade the ' smelling-out ' of witches, and now the British authorities have suppressed the more noxious or offensive kinds of ceremonies practised by the Kaffirs. Otherwise, they interfere as little as possible with native ways, trusting to time, peace, and the missionaries to secure the gradual civilization of the people." " No Europeans are allowed to hold land, and a licence is needed even for the keeping of a store. Neither are any mines worked. European prospectors are not permitted to come in and search for minerals, for the policy of the authorities has been to keep the country for the natives, and nothing alarms the chiefs so much as the occasional appearance of these speculative gentry, who, if admitted, would soon dispossess them."[1]

These sentences serve to point the path by which most of our Imperialism has diverged from the ideal of a " trust for civilization."

The widest and ultimately the most important of the struggles in South Africa is that between the policy of Basutoland and that of Johannesburg and Rhodesia ; for there, if anywhere, we lay our finger on the difference between a " sane " Imperialism, devoted to the protection, education, and self-development of a " lower-race," and an " insane " Imperialism, which hands over these races to the economic exploitation of white colonists who will use them as " live tools " and their lands as repositories of mining or other profitable treasure.

V

It is impossible to ignore the fact that this " saner " Imperialism has been vitiated in its historic origins in almost every quarter of the globe. Early Imperialism had two

[1] Mr. Bryce, *Impressions of South Africa*, p. 422.

main motives, the lust of "treasure" and the slave trade.

Gold and silver, diamonds, rubies, pearls, and other jewels, the most condensed forms of portable and durable wealth by which men in a single hazardous adventure, by fortune, fraud, or force, might suddenly enrich themselves —these from the ancient days of Tyre and Carthage have directed the main current alike of private and national exploration, and have laid the foundation of white dominion over the coloured races. From Ophir, Golconda, and the Orinoco to Ashanti, Kimberley, Klondike, the Transvaal and Mashonaland it is the same story : to the more precious metals, tin and copper were early added as motives of nearer and less hazardous trading ventures, and the machine economy of recent generations has lifted coal and iron deposits to the rank of treasures worth capture and exploitation by civilized nations. But gold still holds its own as the dramatic centre of gravitation for Imperialism.

But along with these motives, and of even wider operation, has been the desire to obtain supplies of slave or serf labour. The earliest, the most widely prevalent, and the most profitable trade in the history of the world has been the slave trade. Early forms of imperial expansion were directed less to any permanent occupation and government of foreign countries than to the capture of large supplies of slave labour to be transmitted to the conquering country. The early Imperialism of the Greek States and of Rome was largely governed by this same motive. Greeks and Romans did not often effect large permanent settlements among the barbarians they conquered, but, contenting themselves with keeping such military and magisterial control as sufficed to secure order and the payment of tribute, drafted large numbers of slaves into their countries in order to utilize their labour. The Greek cities were mostly maritime, commercial, and industrial, and the slaves they drew from Eastern trade or from the Scythian and Thracian "hinterlands" they employed upon their ships and docks, in their mines, and as artisans and labourers in their towns : Rome, the capital of an agricultural State, used her slaves on a "plantation system," ousting by this cheap forced labour the peasantry, who, driven into Rome, were subsisted chiefly upon public charity, defrayed out of the tribute of their foreign conquests.[1]

Now modern Imperialism in its bearing on the "lower races" remains essentially of the same type : it employs other methods, other and humaner motives temper the dominance of economic greed, but analysis exposes the same character at bottom. Wherever white men of "superior races" have found able-bodied savages or lower races in possession of lands containing rich mineral or agricultural resources, they have, whenever strong enough, compelled the lower race to work for their benefit, either organizing their labour on their own land, or inducing them to work for an unequal barter, or else conveying them as slaves or servants to another country where their labour-power could be more profitably utilized. The use of imperial force to compel "lower races" to engage in trade is commonly a first stage of Imperialism ; China is here the classic instance of modern times, exhibiting the sliding scale by which sporadic trade passes through "treaties," treaty ports, customs control, rights of inland trading, mining and railway concession, towards annexation and general exploitation of human and natural resources.

The slave trade or forcible capture and conveyance of natives from their own to a foreign land has in its naked form nearly disappeared from the practice of Western nations (save in the case of Belgium in the Congo), as also

[1] *Cf.* Mr. Gilbert Murray in *Liberalism and the Empire*, pp. 126–129 (Brimley Johnson).

the working of conquered people as slaves in their own country.

The entire economic basis of the industrial exploitation of inferior races has shifted with modern conditions of life and industry. The change is a twofold one : the legal status of slave has given place to that of wage-labourer, and the most profitable use of the hired labour of inferior races is to employ them in developing the resources of their own lands under white control for white men's profit.

" In ancient times the employer would not, if he could, go away from his own country to employ Libyans or Scythians in their native places. If he left home, it was not so easy to come back. He was practically in exile. In the second place, he was not sufficiently master of his slaves in their own country. If they were all of one nation and all at home, they might rebel or break loose. If a strong Government prevented that, it was at any rate much easier for individual slaves to escape—a consideration always of the utmost importance. In modern times, the increasing ease of communication has enabled white men to go abroad to all parts of the earth without suffering much real exile and without losing the prospect of returning home at will. Our Governments, judged by ancient standards, are miraculously strong ; our superior weapons make rebellions almost impossible. Consequently we do not attempt to import blacks, coolies, and Polynesians into Great Britain. The opposition of the working classes at home would be

[1] In the British Protectorate of Zanzibar and Pemba, however, slavery still (1902) exists (notwithstanding the Sultan's decree of emancipation in 1897) and British courts of justice recognize the status. Miss Emily Hutchinson, who was associated with the Friends' Industrial Mission at Pemba, said it was five years since the legal status of slavery was abolished in Zanzibar and Pemba. Every one, including those who were most anxious that the liberation should proceed slowly, was dissatisfied with the present state of affairs. Out of an estimated population of 25,000 slaves in Pemba less than 5,000 had been liberated so far under the decree (Anti-Slavery Society Annual Meeting, April 4, 1902).

furious; and, even if that obstacle were overcome, the coloured men would die too fast in our climate. The whole economic conditions are in favour of working the coloured man in his own home."[1]

This conclusion, however, requires some considerable qualification in the case of European colonies. Though " imperial " nations do not introduce the subject races into their home labour-markets, they induce an ever-growing stream of labour to flow between different parts of the subject portions of this Empire. The practice of indentured immigration is largely in vogue. The British Colony of Queensland and the French New Caledonia have been fed with labour from Polynesia; the trade and agriculture of Natal has been largely absorbed by Indian " coolie " labour; Chinese labour, free or indentured, has found its way into the Straits Settlements, Burma, Borneo, New Guinea, and parts of Australia, America, Oceania, and tropical Africa, a startling illustration of the movement being afforded by the Chinese indentured labour system adopted for the working of the Transvaal mines. Still, it is true that the general modern tendency is to work the coloured man in his own home, or in some neighbouring country to whose climatic and other natural characters he can easily adapt himself.

The chief economic condition which favours this course is not, however, the greater willingness of modern white men to sojourn for a while abroad, but the ever-growing demand for tropical goods, and the abundant overflow of capital from modern industrial States, seeking an investment everywhere in the world where cheap labour can be employed upon rich natural resources.

The ancients carried off the lower races to their own country, because they could use their labour but had little

[1] Murray, *Liberalism and the Empire*, p. 141.

use for their land; we moderns wish the lower races to exploit their own lands for our benefit. The tastes for tropical agricultural products, such as rice, tea, sugar, coffee, rubber, etc., first aroused by trade, have grown so fast and strong that we require larger and more reliable supplies than trade with ill-disciplined races can afford us; we must needs organize the industry by Western science and Western capital, and develop new supplies. So likewise with the vast mineral resources of lands belonging to lower races; Western capital and Western exploiting energy demand the right to prospect and develop them. The real history of Imperialism as distinguished from Colonization clearly illustrates this tendency. Our first organized contact with the lower races was by means of trading companies, to which some powers of settlement and rights of government were accorded by charter as incidental to the main purpose, viz., that of conducting trade with native inhabitants. Such small settlement as took place at first was for trade and not for political expansion or genuine colonization of a new country. This was the case even in America with the London and Plymouth Companies, the Massachusetts Bay Company, and the Hudson's Bay Company, though other colonizing motives soon emerged; our first entrance into the West Indies was by a trading settlement of the London Company in Barbados; the foundation of our great Eastern Empire was laid in the trading operations of the East India Company, while the Gold Coast was first touched by the Royal Africa Company in 1692. Holland and France were moved by the same purpose, and the tropical or sub-tropical settlements which later passed from their hands into ours were mostly dominated by commercialism and a government based avowedly on commercial exploitation.[1]

As we approach more recent times, investment of capital

[1] *Cf.* Morris, *The History of Colonisation*, vol. ii, p. 60, etc.

and organization of native labour on the land, the plantation system, play a more prominent part in the policy of new companies, and the British North Borneo Company, the Sierra Leone Company, the Royal Niger Company, the East Africa Company, the British South Africa Company, are no longer chiefly trading bodies, but are devoted more and more to the control and development of agricultural and mining resources by native labour under white management to supply Western markets. In most parts of the world a purely or distinctively commercial motive and conduct have furnished the nucleus out of which Imperialism has grown, the early trading settlement becoming an industrial settlement, with land and mineral concessions growing round it, an industrial settlement involving force, for protection, for securing further concessions, and for checking or punishing infringements of agreement or breaches of order; other interests, political and religious, enter in more largely, the original commercial settlement assumes a stronger political and military character, the reins of government are commonly taken over by the State from the Company and a vaguely defined protectorate passes gradually into the form of a colony. Sierra Leone, Uganda, and, at no distant date, Rhodesia, will serve for recent instances of this evolution.

VI

The actual history of Western relations with lower races occupying lands on which we have settled throws, then, a curious light upon the theory of a " trust for civilization." When the settlement approaches the condition of genuine colonization, it has commonly implied the extermination of the lower races, either by war or by private slaughter, as in the case of Australian Bushmen,

African Bushmen and Hottentots, Red Indians, and Maoris, or by forcing upon them the habits of a civilization equally destructive to them.[1] This is what is meant by saying that "lower races" in contact with "superior races" naturally tend to disappear. How much of "nature" or "necessity" belongs to the process is seen from the fact that only those "lower races" tend to disappear who are incapable of profitable exploitation by the superior white settlers, either because they are too "savage" for effective industrialism or because the demand for labour does not require their presence.

Whenever superior races settle on lands where lower races can be profitably used for manual labour in agriculture, mining, and domestic work, the latter do not tend to die out, but to form a servile class. This is the case, not only in tropical countries where white men cannot form real colonies, working and rearing families with safety and efficiency, and where hard manual work, if done at all, must be done by "coloured men," but even in countries where white men can settle, as in parts of South Africa and of the southern portion of the United States.

As we entered these countries for trade, so we stay there for industrial exploitation, directing to our own profitable purposes the compulsory labour of the lower races. This is the root fact of Imperialism so far as it relates to the control of inferior races ; when the latter are not killed out they are subjected by force to the ends of their white superiors.

With the abolition of the legal form of slavery the

[1] Mr. Bryce (Romanes Lecture, 1902, p. 32) says : " I was told in Hawaii that the reduction of the native population, from about 300,000 in Captain Cook's time to about 30,000 in 1883, was largely due to the substitution of wooden houses for the old wigwams, whose sides, woven of long grass, had secured natural ventilation, and to the use of clothes, which the natives, accustomed to nothing more than a loin cloth, did not think of changing or drying when drenched with rain."

economic substance has not disappeared. It is no general question of how far the character of slavery adheres in all wage labour that I am pressing, but a statement that Imperialism rests upon and exists for the sake of " forced labour," i.e. labour which natives would not undertake save under direct or indirect personal compulsion issuing from white masters.

There are many methods of " forcing " labour.

Wherever the question of industrial development of tropical or sub-tropical lands for agricultural or mining purposes comes up, the same difficulty confronts the white masters. The Report of the Select Committee of the House of Commons in 1842 on the state of the West Indies, subsequent to the emancipation of slaves, states the problem most succinctly : " The labourers are enabled to live in comfort and to acquire wealth without, for the most part, labouring on the estates of the planters for more than three or four days in a week, and from five to seven hours in a day, so that they have no sufficient stimulus to perform an adequate amount of work." The reason of this inadequate amount of work (how many white men in the West Indies put in a five to seven hours' working-day ?) is that they can get high wages, and this is attributed " to the easy terms upon which the use of land has been obtainable by negroes." In a word, the Committee considered " that the cheapness of land has been the main cause of the difficulties which have been experienced, and that this cheapness is the natural result of the excess of fertile land beyond the wants of the existing population."

The negro would only put in a five to seven hours' day at high pay because he had the option of earning his livelihood on fertile land of his own. The same trouble confronts the white master everywhere where the lower races are in possession of agricultural land sufficient for their low and unprogressive standard of comfort; they either will not work at all for wages, or will not work long enough or for low enough pay.

" The question, in a few words," writes Professor Ireland, " is this—What possible means are there of inducing the inhabitants of the tropics to undertake steady and continuous work if the local conditions are such that from the mere bounty of nature all the ambitions of the people can be gratified without any considerable amount of labour ? "[1]

There are only two genuinely economic forces which will bring such labour more largely into the labour market : The growth of population with increased difficulty in getting a full easy subsistence from the soil is one ; the pressure of new needs and a rising standard of consumption is the other.

These may be regarded as the natural and legitimate inducements to wage labour, and even in most tropical countries they exercise some influence, especially where white settlements have taken up much of the best land. In the lowest races, where the increase of population is kept down by high mortality, aggravated by war and infanticide, and where new wants are slowly evolved, these inducements are feeble ; but in more progressive peoples they have a fair amount of efficacy. Unfortunately, these natural forces are somewhat slow, and cannot be greatly hastened ; white industrialists are in a hurry to develop the country, and to retire with large, quick profits. The case of South Africa is typical. There many of the Bantu races are fairly educable in new needs, and are willing to undertake wage labour for their satisfaction ; many of them, notably the Basutos, are becoming overcrowded on their reserved lands, and are willing to go far for good wages. But the demands of a vast mining industry, growing within

[1] *Tropical Colonization*, p. 155 (The Macmillan Co.).

a few years to gigantic proportions, cannot await the working of these natural stimuli; the mine-owners want an unnatural accession to the labour market. The result is frantic efforts to scour the continents of Africa and Asia, and bring in masses of Zanzibari, Arabs, Indian coolies, or Chinese, or else to substitute for natural economic pressure various veiled modes of political or private compulsion.

The simplest form of this compulsion is that of employing armed force upon individual natives to " compel them to come in," as illustrated by the methods of the South Africa Chartered Company before 1897,[1] which, when the chiefs failed to provide labour, sent out native police to " collect the labour." Save its illegal character, there is nothing to distinguish this from the *corvée* or legalized forced labour imposed on natives in Natal, or the Compulsory Labour Ordinance passed by the Gold Coast Legislature in December 1895, reviving the lapsed custom under which it was " obligatory on persons of the labouring class to give labour for public purposes on being called out by their chiefs or other native superiors," and authorizing the Government to compel native chiefs to furnish as many carriers as were needed for the projected expedition to Kumasi.[2]

Military service, borrowing a semblance of " civilized " usage from the European system of conscription, is utilized, not merely for emergencies, as in the Kumasi expedition,

---

[1] Sir Richard Martin in his report states his conviction " that the Native Commissioners, in the first instance, endeavoured to obtain labour through the Indunas, but failing that, they procured it by force."

Howard Hensman, defending the administration of the Company in his *History of Rhodesia* (Blackwood & Sons), admits the practice, thus describing it: " In Rhodesia a native who declined to work " (i.e. for wages) " was taken before the Native Commissioners and sent off to some mine or public work close at hand, paid at what, to him, were very high rates, fed and housed, and then at the end of three months he was allowed to return to his kraal, where he was permitted to remain for the rest of the year " (p. 257).

[2] *Cf. Whites and Blacks in South Africa*, by H. R. Fox Bourne, p. 63.

and in our South African campaign, where native labour had everywhere been " pressed," when ordinary economic motives failed, but for regular industrial labour. The classical instance is that of the Congo Free State, where a " militia " levy was made upon the population, nominally for defence, but really for the State and Chartered Company service in the " rubber " and other industries.

In face of unrepealed decrees according " une protection speciale aux noirs," and prescribing that " l'esclavage, même domestique, ne saurait être reconnu officialement," a system of " voluntary " and " militia " levies has been instituted to be used " in the establishment of plantations and the construction of works of public utility." The accuracy of Mr. Fox Bourne's commentary is attested by numerous witnesses. " The ' force publique ' with its ' agriculteurs soldats ' and others subordinate to it, when not employed on military expeditions, are used as overseers of what are virtually slave-gangs or as collectors of ' tribute ' from the luckless aborigines, whose right to live in their own country, without paying heavily for the privilege, is denied."[1]

So far as " forced labour " is designed merely as a mode of revenue to the State, a system of " taxation in kind," it cannot be condemned as essentially unjust or oppressive, however liable it may be to abuses in practice. All taxation is " forced labour," whether the tax be levied in money, in goods, or in service. When such " forced labour " is confined to the needs of a well-ordered government, and is fairly and considerately administered, it involves no particular oppression. Such " servitude " as it involves is concealed under every form of government.

The case is quite different where governmental regulations and taxation are prostituted to purposes of commercial

[1] *Slavery and its Substitutes in Africa*, p. 11.

profit ; where laws are passed, taxes levied, and the machinery
of public administration utilized in order to secure a large,
cheap, regular, efficient, and submissive supply of labourers
for companies or private persons engaged in mining,
agricultural, or other industries for their personal gain.

Where white settlers find " lower races " in occupation
of lands rich in agricultural, mineral, or other resources,
they are subject to a double temptation. They want
possession of the land and control of a cheap native supply
of labour to work it under their control and for their gain.
If the " natives " are of too low an order or too untamable
to be trained for effective labour they must be expelled or
exterminated, as in the case of the " lower nomads " the
Bushmen of Australia and South Africa, the Negritos,
Bororos, Veddahs, etc., and even the Indians of North
America. War, murder, strong drink, syphilis and other
civilized diseases are chief instruments of a destruction
commonly couched under the euphemism " contact with
a superior civilization." The land thus cleared of natives
passes into white possession, and white men must work
it themselves, or introduce other lower industrial peoples
to work it for them, as in the case of slave labour introduced
into the United States and West Indies, or indentured
labour into Natal, British Guiana, etc.

But where the " lower races " are capable of being set
to profitable labour on their own land, as agriculturists,
miners, or domestics, self-interest impels the white to
work a " forced-labour " system for their private ends.
In most tropical or sub-tropical countries the natives can
by their own labour and that of their families get a tolerably
easy subsistence from the land. If they are to be induced
to undertake wage labour for white masters, this must be
put a stop to. So we have pressure brought upon government to render it impossible for the natives to live as

formerly upon the land. Their land and, when they are a pastoral people, their cattle are objects of attack.

The Torrens Act, by which in 1852 the doctrine of "eminent domain" was applied to South Australia in such wise as to make all the country virtually Crown land, though not ill-meant, has furnished a baneful precedent, not only for encroachment of British settlers, but for the still more flagrant abuses of Belgian adventurers on the Congo. White settlers or explorers, sometimes using legal instruments, sometimes private force or fraud, constantly encroach upon the fertile or mineralized lands of natives, driving them into less fertile lands, crowding them into reserves, checking their nomadic habits, and otherwise making it more difficult for them to obtain a livelihood by the only methods known to them.

A chief object and a common result of this policy is to induce or compel natives to substitute wage labour, altogether or in part, for the ancient tribal life upon the land. Those ignorant of the actual conditions involved often suppose that the alienation of lands or mineral rights, or the contracts for labour, are negotiated in accordance with ordinary methods of free bargain.

The modern history of Africa, however, is rich in instances to the contrary.

The history of competitive knavery and crime, by which Lobengula was inveigled into signing away "rights" which he neither owned nor understood to the Chartered Company, cannot yet be written completely, but its outlines are plain and profitable reading.

A "free contract," implying voluntary action, full knowledge and approximate equality of gain to both parties, is almost unknown in the dealings of superior with inferior races. How political treaties and industrial concessions are actually obtained may be described for us by

Major Thruston,[1] who was sent to negotiate treaties in 1893 in Uganda.

"I have been instructed by Colonel Colvile to make a treaty with Kavalli, by which he should place himself under British protection ; in fact, I had a bundle of printed treaties which I was to make as many people sign as possible. This signing is an amiable farce, which is supposed to impose on foreign Governments, and to be the equivalent of an occupation. The *modus operandi* is somewhat as follows : A ragged, untidy European, who in any civilized country would be in danger of being taken up by the police as a vagrant, lands at a native village ; the people run away, he shouts after them to come back, holding out before them a shilling's worth of beads. Someone, braver than the rest, at last comes up ; he is given a string of beads, and is told that if the chief comes he will get a great many more. Cupidity is, in the end, stronger than fear ; the chief comes and receives his presents ; the so-called interpreter pretends to explain the treaty to the chief. The chief does not understand a word of it, but he looks pleased as he receives another present of beads ; a mark is made on a printed treaty by the chief, and another by the interpreter ; the vagrant, who professes to be the representative of a great Empire, signs his name. The chief takes the paper, but with some hesitation, as he regards the whole performance as a new and therefore dangerous piece of witchcraft. The boat sails away, and the new ally and protégé of England or France immediately throws the treaty into the fire."

This cynical bit of realistic humour expresses with tolerable accuracy the formal process of " imperial expansion " as it operates in the case of lower races. If these are the methods of political agents, it may well be understood that the methods of private " concession-mongers "

[1] *Personal Experiences in Egypt and Unyoro* (Murray).

are not more scrupulous. Indeed, " political protectorate " and " land concession " are inextricably blended in most instances where some adventurer, with a military or other semi-official commission, pushes across the frontier into a savage country, relying upon his Government to endorse any profitable deal he may accomplish.

But since, in the case of England at any rate, political expansion is commonly subordinate to industrial exploitation, a treaty or concession, giving rights over land or minerals, is of little value without control of labour. Enclosure of lands, while it facilitates a supply of native labour by restricting free land for native agriculture or pasture, does not commonly suffice. Various devices are adopted for bringing pressure to bear upon individual labourers to " contract " for wage labour. The simplest, apart from direct compulsion, is to bribe chieftains to use their " influence " with members of their tribe. Such was the system devised by the philanthropic Earl Grey to procure labour for the mines in Rhodesia.[1]

Such bargaining, either with " headmen " or with individual natives, is usually conducted by professional labour touts, who practise every form of craft and falsehood so as to induce ignorant natives to enter a labour contract. In the case of the Transvaal mines this abuse had become so monstrous as to " spoil the labour market," obliging the mine-owners to go ever farther afield for their labour, and eventually compelling them to petition the Government for assistance in putting down the system of private labour touts and substituting authorized respon-

---

[1] " We propose to give to the big chiefs, when they have proved themselves worthy of trust, a salary of £5 a month and a house. . . . The indunas will then be responsible to the Government for the conduct of their people." This, Earl Grey supposes, " is the best way to secure a considerable revenue in the future in the shape of hut tax, and to obtain a fair supply of labour for the mines " (*Times*, November 28, 1896).

sible officials. Alike in the Boer Republics and in Cape Colony, the seizures of land and labour have been chief motives of the border warfare constantly recurring in the history of South Africa. The encroachments of Boers or British colonists upon native territory or reserves, or the seizure of cattle on border land by one party or the other, had led to punitive expeditions, the result of which has been further confiscation of land and capture of prisoners, who, formerly held as slaves, have in more recent times been kept to labour as " apprentices " or indentured labourers.

The case of Bechuanaland in 1897 affords a serviceable illustration. A small local riot got up by a drunken native sub-chief on a trifling grievance, and involving armed resistance on the part of a few hundred Kaffirs, easily put down by a small body of armed volunteers, was exaggerated into a " rebellion," and was made a pretext for driving some 8,000 natives from the lands " inalienably " secured to them by the Bechuanaland Annexation Act of 1895, and for confiscating these lands for British occupation, while the rest of the population, some 30,000, were to be gradually removed from their settlements, and given " equivalent land " in some other district. In the speech introducing the confiscation measure in the Cape Parliament, Sir Gordon Sprigg explained that this was " very valuable land, and probably would be cut up into very small farms, so that there might be a considerable European population established in that part of the country." There was no pretence that most of those who were deprived of their lands or deported were proved to have taken part in the " rebellion." The sequel of this clearing is most significant. What was to become of the people taken from their land? They were offered a choice between prosecution " on a charge of sedition " and " service in the colony upon such conditions and with such rates of wages as the Government might arrange for a term of five years." The Government, in thus proposing to compound a felony, was well aware of the extreme difficulty of proving " sedition " in a court of justice, and, in point of fact, in two cases which were put on trial the Public Prosecutor declined to bring the case before a jury. The object of the threat of trial was to coerce into the acceptance of " indentured labour," and in fact 584 men, with three times as many women and children were handed over to serve under colonial farmers, wages being fixed at 10s. a month for able-bodied men and 7s. 6d. for women.

Thus did covetous colonials kill two birds with one stone, obtaining the land and the labour of the Bechuana " rebels."[1] It is not necessary to suppose that such incidents are deliberately planned : where empire is asserted over lower races in the form of protectorate, the real government remaining in native hands, offences must from time to time arise, local disturbances which can by rash or brutal treatment be fanned into " rebellion," and form the pretext for confiscation and a forcing of the landless rebels into " labour."

---

[1] The details of this business, recorded in *Blue-book* C. 8,797, relating to native disturbances, are most instructive to the student, of Imperialism.

The inspector of Native Locations in his report of the affair distinctly asserts : " That it was not a general rising of the Mashowing people is certain, because there were not more than 100 natives engaged in the Kobogo fight." Yet the whole of the Mashowing territory was confiscated and all the population treated as rebels.

While only some 450 men were taken with arms, 3,793 men, women, and children were arrested and deported, 1,871 being afterwards " indentured " in the colony. Seven-eighths of the prisoners were women, children, or unarmed men. Even of the men who were taken in arms at the Langeberg Sir A. Milner wrote (January 5, 1898) : " I am inclined to think that in many other cases, if the prisoners had chosen to stand their ground, the same difficulty (as in two cases taken to trial) would have been found in establishing legal evidence of treason. It is probable that, of the men who surrendered at the Langeberg, some had never fought against the Government at all, while many others had done so reluctantly. To bring home treasonable intent to any large number of them would, I conceive, have been a difficult matter " (p. 48).

Among African tribes the most vulnerable point is the cattle, which form their most important, often their only, property. To encroach upon this is a sure way of provoking hostility. The Bechuana riot seems to have arisen from an injudicious handling of precautions needed to deal with the rinderpest. The second Matabele war, with its murders of white settlers and the wholesale slaughter in reprisal, was directly instigated by the seizure of cattle belonging to the tribesmen, on the unproven theory that all cattle belonged to the king and thus came into the possession of the Chartered Company. As a sequel of the first Matabele war large quantities of cattle had been stolen by white settlers to stock the farms which had just been pegged out for them in the land they had taken, and the further threat of a wholesale confiscation of cattle, though not carried into full effect, lay at the root of the subsequent rebellion.[1]

Everywhere these attacks upon the land and cattle of lower races, provoking reprisals, followed by further confiscation and a breaking-up of the old tribal life upon the soil, have as a related secondary object the provision of a supply of cheap labour for the new white masters, to be employed in farming, on mines, or for military service.

---

[1] Here is the account of a Rhodesian writer, defending the British policy :—

" Seeing that Lobengula only allowed his followers to own cattle on sufferance as it were, all the herds in the country might be said to be the property of the late king, and that was the view which the British South Africa Company took. The number of cattle in the country at this time was estimated at not less than a quarter of a million head, and the indunas were ordered at once to drive in the cattle from the districts over which they had control to Buluwayo. Some of the indunas duly complied with this demand, in which they saw nothing more than what was to be expected as the outcome of the war ; but others, and those chiefly who had not taken any part in the fighting, declined to do so, and hid the cattle away out of reach of the Native Commissioners. As the cattle did not come in in such numbers as they ought to have done, the Government ordered the Native Commissioners to collect and send in each month a certain number of cattle. . . . This step proved a highly unpopular one among the natives " (*History of Rhodesia*, by H. Hensman, p. 165).

Such labour commonly preserves a semblance of free contract, engagements " voluntarily " entered into for a fixed period at agreed wages. The amount of real freedom depends partly upon the amount of personal pressure brought to bear by the chief through whom bargains are commonly struck, still more on the amount of option which remains to get a living from the land.

This last is the vital matter in an understanding of " forced labour." In one sense all labour is " forced " or " unfree," where it is not open to the " proletariat " to get a living by cultivation of the soil : this is the normal condition of the vast majority of the people in Great Britain and in some other white man's countries. What is peculiar to the system of " forced labour," as here used, is the adoption by a white ruling race of legal measures designed expressly to compel the individual natives to whom they apply to quit land, which they occupy and by which they can live, in order to work in white service for the private gain of the white man. When lands formerly occupied by natives are confiscated, or otherwise annexed for white owners, the creation of a labour supply out of the dis-possessed natives is usually a secondary object. But this " forcing " becomes a system when measures are devised by Government for the express purpose of " compelling " labour.

VII

The simplest method, that of " slavery," is generally abolished by European nations. *Corvée*, the Congo and former Rhodesian methods are seldom openly advocated or defended ; but the adoption of various forms of public compulsion in order to drive natives into private service is generally approved by " colonials," and is sanctioned by imperialist statesmen. A chief instrument of this indirect compulsion is taxation. There is nothing essentially un-reasonable in imposing a hut or a poll-tax upon natives to assist in defraying the expenses of government, provided that care is taken in the modes of assessment and collection, and due allowance made for the fluctuating economic circumstances of agricultural populations with narrow markets and small use of money. But these taxes are not infrequently applied so as to dispossess natives of their land, force them to work for wages and even to drive them into insurrections which are followed by wholesale measures of confiscation.

The case of the risings in Sierra Leone during 1898 attests the nature of this impolicy, and the following passage from the report of the Special Commissioner, Sir David Chalmers, deserves attention. His conclusions as to the causes of the insurrection are thus summarized :—

" The hut-tax, together with the measures used for its enforcement, were the moving causes of the insurrection. The tax was obnoxious to the customs and feelings of the people. A peremptory and regularly recurring impost is unknown in their own practices and tradition. The English Government has not as yet conferred any such benefits as to lead to a burden of a strange and portentous species being accepted willingly. There was a widespread belief that it was a means of taking away their rights in their country and in their property."[1] " The amount of the tax is higher than the people, taken together, can pay, and the arrangements by which liability is primarily placed

[1] Miss Mary Kingsley regards this " widespread belief " as justified.

" It has been said that the Sierra Leone hut-tax war is a ' little Indian Mutiny ' ; those who have said it do not seem to have known how true the statement is, for these attacks on property in the form of direct taxation are, to the African, treachery on the part of England, who, from the first, has kept on assuring the African that she does not mean to take his country from him, and then, as soon as she is strong enough, in his eyes, deliberately starts doing so " (West African Studies, p. 372 ; Macmillan & Co.).

on the chiefs to make good definite amounts on demand are unworkable." "The mode of enforcing payment provided by the law would probably prove abortive, whether used to meet inability or unwillingness to pay." "Repugnance to the tax was much aggravated by the sudden, uncompromising and harsh methods by which it was endeavoured to be brought into operation not merely by the acts of native policemen, but in the whole scheme adopted by the colonial authorities."

Here Sir. D. Chalmers condenses all the familiar grievances of monetary taxes imposed by strong expensive white Governments upon poor "native" races. White government, if good, is expensive, hence taxation tends to be heavy in amount ; fixed in amount, it must be paid out of very fluctuating industries ; levied in money, it forces self-subsisting families or tribes to find markets for their goods or labours ; collected, as it must be, by native authorities, it breeds extortion, corruption, and cruelty. But Sir D. Chalmers lays his finger on the central vice when he names " a widespread belief that it was a means of taking away their rights in their country and in their property."[1]

Where there exists a large growing demand for native labour this method of compelling natives to pay money taxes is seen to have a new importance. They can only earn money by undertaking labour contracts. Hence a system of direct taxation imposed by hut, poll, or labour-taxes is devised. Everywhere, as we have seen, under free popular government, the tendency is to subordinate direct to indirect taxation. "Imperialism" alone favours

[1] Compare the pathetic plaint of the natives in Rhodesia, as voiced by Sir Richard Martin in his official report. "The natives practically said : ' Our country is gone and our cattle ; we have nothing to live for. Our women are deserting us ; the white man does as he likes with them. We are the slaves of the white man ; we are nobody, and have no rights or laws of any kind ' " (Cd. 8547).

direct taxation of the working classes. It does not, however, propose a general system of direct taxation applicable alike to white and blacks. The direct taxes with which we are here concerned are applied exclusively to the " subject " races.

In South Africa their chief avowed aim is, not to provide revenue, but to compel labour. The hut and labour taxation is not strongly developed in Cape Colony or in Natal, because the break-up of old tribal life, and the substitution of individual economic family life favouring wage labour, have hitherto furnished a sufficient supply of labour to countries, mainly agricultural, thinly peopled by white settlers, and only in one district, that of Kimberley, developing a considerable centralized demand for native labour. The hut-tax in these colonies has, therefore, not proved an oppressive burden. Only when the diamond fields found difficulties in obtaining a ready supply of native labour, and wages rose, did Mr. Rhodes, a chief proprietor, use his public position as Cape Premier to procure an Act designed to assist De Beers in obtaining cheap labour. By this statute, the Glen Grey Act, it was enacted that every male native in districts where the Act was adopted, should pay a " labour-tax " of 10s. per annum, unless he could prove that during three months of each year " he has been in service or employment beyond the borders of the district." No secret was made of the fact that this measure was designed, not to provide revenue, but to compel to labour. " If they could make these people work they would reduce the rate of labour in the country," said Mr. Rhodes ; and in another speech in Parliament : " It was wrong that there should be a million natives in that country, and yet that they should be paying a sum equal to about £1 a week for their labour, while that labour was absolutely essential for the proper development of the country."

The "labour-tax" has not, however, operated oppressively in Cape Colony; for the diamond industry, being limited in output, has not demanded more native labour than could be easily supplied by ordinary economic inducements.

It is in the Transvaal and Rhodesia that taxation of natives ripens into a plan for forcing labour. The mine-owners of the Transvaal are agreed as to their right and their need to compel the natives to undergo the dignity of labour, and they regard taxation as one important instrument. The testimony of witnesses before the Industrial Commission in 1897 was unanimous in favouring such compulsion, and Mr. Rudd, of the Consolidated Goldfields, stated the demand very plainly at the annual meeting of his company.[1] " If we could only call upon one-half of the natives to give up three months of the year to work, that would be enough. We should try some cogent form of inducement, or practically compel the native through taxation or in some other way, to contribute his quota to the good of the community, and to a certain extent he should then have to work." The general feeling of the " Outlanders " in the Transvaal has favoured the oppressive hut-tax of £2, imposed by the Republic in 1895, and has only complained of its inadequate enforcement.

Similarly, in Rhodesia, where mines require a larger supply of labour than can be obtained from natives by ordinary economic motives, an increase of the hut-tax and a labour-tax are an integral part of the public policy. Earl Grey, recent administrator and director of the Chartered Company, thus states the case : " Means have to be found to induce the natives to seek, spontaneously (sic !), employment at the mines, and to work willingly for long terms of more or less continuous employment. An incentive to labour must be provided, and it can only be provided by the

[1] November 19, 1899.

imposition of taxation. I look forward to the imposition of a hut-tax of £1 per hut in conformity with the practice which exists in Basutoland, and I also hope that we may, with the permission of the imperial authorities, be able to establish a labour-tax, which those able-bodied natives should be required to pay who are unable to show a certificate of four months' work."

It remains to add that one "imperial authority" of some importance has expressly endorsed this policy of using public finance for private profit-making purposes. In a speech in the House of Commons dealing with the Chartered Company[1] Mr. Chamberlain said : " When you say to a savage people who have hitherto found their chief occupation in war, ' You shall no longer go to war ; tribal war is forbidden,' you have to bring about some means by which they may earn their living in place of it, and you have to induce them to adopt the ordinary means of earning a livelihood by the sweat of their brow. But with a race of this kind I doubt very much whether you can do it merely by preaching. I think that something in the nature of an inducement, stimulus or pressure is absolutely necessary if you are to secure a result which is desirable in the interests of humanity and civilization."

A far more thorough and logical application of the policy of taking natives from their life upon the land in order to perform wage labour is devised by the Transvaal mine-owners. The native labour problem there differs widely from the case of Kimberley, where only some 12,000 natives under strict control are required for the diamond industry. The intention of working out, with the utmost rapidity, the gold of the Rand can only be accomplished by securing a vast and a growing supply of native labour on the spot. In 1899, with great difficulty and at heavy expense, less than 100,000

[1] May 7, 1898.

natives were secured for work upon the mines. If twice or thrice this number are to be procured and at lower prices, this can only be accomplished by using taxation, coercion and persuasion to induce large numbers of Kaffirs to come and settle down with their families upon locations in the mining districts, where the amount of land provided does not enable them to get a living from agriculture, and where they will consequently be dependent on wage labour at the mines, and will breed a permanent supply of young labour on the spot. The wages paid will be determined, not by competition, but by the Chamber of Mines ; the houses they will occupy will be the property of the mines, as also the shops where they will be compelled to deal. This has been the policy advocated by the chief mining experts.

Break up the tribal system which gives solidarity and some political and economic strength to native life ; set the Kaffir on an individual footing as an economic bargainer, to which he is wholly unaccustomed, take him by taxation or other " stimulus " from his locality, put him down under circumstances where he has no option but to labour at the mines—this is the plan which mine-owners propose and missionaries approve.[1]

[1] This has been the policy of the Glen Grey Act, and the following passage from the official report of a resident magistrate in a district of Cape Colony (Mr. W. T. Brownlie of Butterworth) makes its main economic motive transparent : " I have long held and still hold that the labour question and the land question are indissolubly bound together. In my opinion it is of little use framing enactments to compel unwilling persons to go out to work. It is like the old saw about leading a horse to the water ; you can take him there, but you cannot make him drink. In the same way you may impose your labour-tax, but you cannot make your unwilling persons leave work. Create a healthy thirst in your horse and he will drink fast enough. Similarly create the necessity for the native to work and he will work, and none better.

" Hitherto, under our commercial-tenure system, there has been little absolute necessity for our young natives to leave their homes to work. The land supplies them with food, and a few shillings will buy a blanket, and as soon as the young man marries he is entitled to receive his lot of arable land ; but once this is stopped—and it will be stopped by the survey and individual tenure—a young man before he marries a wife will have to be in a position to support a wife, and

This system of " native locations," fortified by hut and labour-taxes, and by pass laws which interfere with freedom of travel and practically form a class of *ascripti glebæ*, was the method devised before the war by the missionaries for dealing with the labour problem in the Transvaal mines[1]: it is the method still advocated by the South African Native Affairs Commission, reporting in 1905[2]. To limit the access of the growing Kaffir population to the land and to impose taxes with the object of compelling them to wage labour, still remains the sheet-anchor of the South African labour policy. The drafting in of large numbers of Chinese is supplementary to this policy, used partly to afford an increased supply, partly to give mine-owners a better pick of Kaffir labour at a reduced price.

VIII

The introduction of large numbers of Chinese into the Transvaal mines under the Labour Ordinance of 1904, has given great prominence to the indentured labour system which is widely operative in our tropical dominions.

As regards the actual conditions of employment, there is reason to believe that where this system is practised under imperial protection as applied to Indian coolie labour it

to obtain this he must work, and once having married her he must still work to maintain her and himself, and once the necessity of work is created there will be no lack of men ready and willing to work " (*Blue-book on Native Affairs*, C. 31, p. 75).

[1] *Cf.* the Report of the Chamber of Mines for 1898 (quoted *Cd.* 9,345, p. 31), and the Report of the Industrial Commission, Johannesburg, 1897, *passim*.

[2] The gist of the " economic " recommendations of this Commission is that " squatting " of natives upon unoccupied public lands be stopped, that existing native locations for agriculture should be defined and that no more land should be reserved for the use of the growing population of natives ; that outside these restricted areas no land should be purchased or leased by natives, that a minimum poll tax of £1 per head should be imposed on all adult male natives except those employed in wage labour or paying rates in towns.

has been free from the worst abuses of " forced labour."
British Guiana, Mauritius, and Trinidad are the West
Indian possessions where the system of importing Indian
coolie labour has been most practised, and where the system
is being tested.

The law[1] governing indentured labour in British Guiana
provided against most of the abuses which beset the
economic relations of white employers towards " lower
races," and appears to be well administered. Here the
Imperial Government in India approves all contracts with
immigrants, and these contracts not only contain a full
statement of time, wages, and other conditions of labour
and of living for the immigrant and his family, but provide
for his return, if necessary at the public expense, at the end
of his time. During the term of his indenture in British
Guiana he is under the protection of authorities appointed
and controlled by the governor alone. An immigration
agent-general, with a staff of agents, who visit all plantations
where indentured labourers are employed, hear privately
all complaints, and bring them, if necessary, into the courts,
retaining counsel and acting in all cases as the principals.
Employers of indentured labour are obliged to keep and
produce full and accurate books of accounts under heavy
penalties, and are forbidden to pay wages below a certain
sum or to overwork their labourers. No punishment of any
kind can be imposed by employers without recourse to the
courts. It is contended by Professor Ireland, who has had
long experience as an overseer, that this system operates
with remarkable success both economically and socially[2]
in British Guiana and in other West Indian islands ; and
in Natal, though " coolies " are regarded with anything

[1] As existing in 1903.
[2] *Tropical Colonization*, chap. v, by Professor Ireland, gives a full and detailed
account of the theory and practice of indentured labour in British Guiana.

but favour by large sections of the population, substantially the same protective legislation is in force, and there is every reason to suppose that indentured labourers are well protected as regards wages and other economic conditions.

But the very encomium passed upon this well-administered system of indenture shows how defective is the grasp of the magnitude and the real nature of the issues involved in the control of tropical labour.

It seems a light and natural thing that large bodies of men, with or without their families, should be driven by economic pressure to quit their native soil in our Indian Empire or in China, and absent themselves for ten years at a time in some unknown and remote colony. Migration to, and colonization of, sparsely peopled lands by inhabitants of thickly peopled lands is a natural and wholly beneficial movement, but the break-up of settled life, implied by long periods of alienation, is fraught with grave injuries to both countries alike. A country which relies for its economic development on continual influxes of foreign labourers who will not settle is impaired in its natural process of industrial and political self-development by this mass of unassimilated sojourners, while the country which they have abandoned suffers a corresponding injury.

Why is it necessary or desirable that large bodies of our Indian fellow-subjects should desert their native land, removing for long periods their industrial services in order to develop another country which is not theirs ? If India is over-populated, permanent colonization is surely the remedy ; if it is not, this practice of " indentured labour " seems to testify to misgovernment and bad husbandry of our Indian resources. To break up considerable areas of Indian society, and remove its able-bodied males for ten years at a time, in order that these men may bring back some " savings " at the end of their term, seems at best a wanton sacrifice of the stability and normal progress of Indian society to a narrow consideration of purely monetary gain. History teaches, in fact, that a peasant people living on soil which they own will not consent thus to alienate themselves for purposes of slight economic gain, unless they are compelled by excessive taxation on the part of Government, or by extortions of money-lenders, which deprive them in large measure of the enjoyment of the fruits of their labour on their land.

However well administered this system of indentured labour may be, it seems vitiated in origin by its artificial character and its interference with normal processes of self-development. It involves a subordination of wider social considerations to purposes of present industrial exploitation. What is true of the system, as applied in the West Indies and elsewhere for agricultural work, is still more true of industrial labour in mining processes. When " civilized " Kaffirs choose to quit their individual farms in the Transkei, or elsewhere, in order to earn extra money by three months' service in the mines, no particular harm may offset their monetary gain ; but when labour agents are employed to break up tribal life and tempt " raw " Kaffirs away from their kraals and the restraints of their habitual life into the utterly strange and artificial life upon the mines, the character of the Kaffir goes to pieces ; he becomes a victim to drink if he can get it, and often succumbs to the vices of the crowded, laborious, unhealthy life to which he has sold himself, while the arbitrary restrictions under which he works and lives, however justified, degrade and damage his personality. According to the evidence of most experienced and competent investigators, he returns home a " damaged " man, and often by his example a damage to his neighbours.[1]

[1] Cf. *Cape Colony Blue-books on Native Affairs*, G. 31, 1899, pp. 5, 9, 72, 75, 91, etc. ; G. 42, 1898, pp. 13, 14, 58, 82.

The least reflection will expose the dangers which must arise from suddenly transferring men from a semi-savage, tribal, agricultural life to a great modern, elaborate, industrial business like that of diamond and gold mining.

What is true of the uncivilized Kaffir is equally true of the more highly developed Chinaman. These men are introduced into the Transvaal as mere economic machines, not as colonists to aid the industrial and social development of a new country. Their presence is regarded as a social danger ; they are kept in " compounds," denied the right to acquire property or even to remain in the country as free settlers on the termination of their service. Hordes of able-bodied males, without any women, huddled in close barracks, rigorously guarded during work and at leisure, kept continually at hard routine manual labour, deprived of all the educative influences of self-direction in a free civilized society, however well-fed, however highly paid, these men are inevitably degraded in morals by the conditions of this service, and damage the society to which they return.

Nor is this all. The effect upon the Transvaal is to substitute for a normal gradual and natural development, a hasty artificial abnormal development, to complicate the already grave racial and economic problems of the country by introducing a new factor of dangerous character and dimensions, a supply of cheap labour designed expressly to diminish the demand for white settlers and for black wage-earners. It is difficult to overestimate the gravity of the case in its bearing on the future of South Africa.

The mining industry of the Transvaal is by far the most important industry in the whole country ; so far as British interests are concerned, the whole future depends on husbanding and developing these resources so as to keep a large growing number of permanent British colonists in the country. Now the cheapest and most profitable exploitation of the mines involves a minimum employment of white British labour and a short period of over-stimulated industrial activity. Although it is clearly the interest and the intention of the mine-owners, in defiance of the conditions in the ordinance, to displace by skilled Chinese labour most of the white labour formerly required for working the mines, it is possible that a considerable though fluctuating demand for British labour in other industrial and commercial undertakings may be furnished during this artificially shortened life of the richer mines. But upon such an economic foundation no secure fabric of industrial and political civilization can be erected : after a single generation of feverish gold-getting, in which British supremacy is maintained by a constantly changing majority of temporary town residents, the industrial strength of the country must steadily and surely decline, returning not to the more primitive condition of wholesome agriculture from which it temporarily emerged, but to a prolonged miserable struggle of trade and manufactures in a country strewn with the decaying wreckage of disused mines and rotting towns. Hebrew mining speculators, American and Scotch engineers, Chinese miners, German traders will evacuate the country they have sacked, leaving behind them a population of Boers spoiled in large part by their contact with a gambling and luxuriant European civilization, and a host of Kaffirs broken from their customary life of agriculture and hanging around the cities of South Africa—a chronic pest of vagabonds and unemployed.

Such are some of the reactions of the indentured labour system in South Africa. The legitimate and wholesome means of developing a country is by utilizing the labour-power of its inhabitants, inducing them by ordinary economic stimuli to settle where remunerative employment is afforded.

If such a country is under-peopled, emigration is rightly encouraged from more thickly-peopled lands. But such emigration should bring genuine colonists, people intending to become citizens of their adopted country, social as well as economic units. In such fashion, by free flow of populations from less desirable to more desirable regions, the civilization of the world is forwarded, and the social safety and future prosperity of the newly developed countries are best subserved. An indentured labour system, however well administered, sins against the fundamental laws of civilization because it treats the labourers primarily as instruments and not as men. Badly operated, without proper safeguards of impartially administered law,[1] it is a source of grave damage to the political, social and industrial prosperity of the country where it is applied.

It may well be doubted whether there is a net gain to the civilization of the world by increasing the supply of gold and diamonds at such a price.

IX

It may be said: " Whatever the motives of employers may be, it is surely a good thing to take natives, by persuasion or even by force, from a life of idleness and habituate them to labour, which educates their faculties, brings them under civilizing influences, and puts money into their pockets."

Now while the statement that such Kaffirs, West Africans, and other tropical or semi-tropical men, left to themselves, lead an idle life, is commonly a gross exaggeration, due largely to the fact that their work is more irregular and capricious than that of their women, it must be admitted

---

[1] The worst of many evil features in the Chinese Indentured Labour System of the Transvaal is that here alone within the dominions of Great Britain a large body of residents are deprived of the right of appeal to the common law as administered in the Courts of Justice.

that the repression of internecine warfare and the restriction of hunting do set free a large quantity of male energy which it is really desirable should be utilized for industrial purposes. But for whose industrial purposes ? Surely it is far better that the " contact with civilization " should lead these men to new kinds of industry on their own land, and in their own societies, instead of dragging them off to gang-labour on the lands or mining properties of strangers. It can do this in two ways : by acquainting them with new wholesome wants it can apply a legitimate stimulus, and by acquainting them with new industrial methods applicable to work in their own industries it can educate them to self-help. Where native peoples are protected from the aggressive designs of white profit-mongers, this salutary evolution operates. In large districts of Basutoland and in certain reserves of Zululand the substitution of the plough for the primitive hoe or pick has led to the introduction of male labour into the fields ;[1] every encouragement in stock-raising, dairy-farming, or other occupations connected with animals enhances male employment among natives ; the gradual introduction of new manufacturing industries into village life leads to men's taking a larger share in those industries in or near the kraal which were formerly a monopoly of women.

So far as Imperialism seeks to justify itself by sane civilization of lower races, it will endeavour to raise their industrial and moral status on their own lands, preserving as far as possible the continuity of the old tribal life and institutions, protecting them against the force and deceit of prospectors, labour touts, and other persons who seek to take their land and entice away their labour. If under the gradual teaching of industrial arts and the general educational

[1] Cf. *Report of South African Native Races Commission*, p. 52, etc. ; also *The Labour Question in South Africa*, by Miss A. Werner (*The Reformer*, December 1901).

influences of a white protectorate many of the old political, social, and religious institutions decay, that decay will be a natural wholesome process, and will be attended by the growth of new forms, not forced upon them, but growing out of the old forms and conforming to laws of natural growth in order to adapt native life to a changed environment.

But so long as the private, short-sighted, business interests of white farmers or white mine-owners are permitted, either by action taken on their own account or through pressure on a colonial or Imperial Government, to invade the lands of " lower peoples," and transfer to their private profitable purposes the land or labour, the first law of " sane " Imperialism is violated, and the phrases about teaching " the dignity of labour " and raising races of " children " to manhood, whether used by directors of mining companies or by statesmen in the House of Commons, are little better than wanton exhibitions of hypocrisy. They are based on a falsification of the facts, and a perversion of the motives which actually direct the policy.

X

In setting forth the theory which sought to justify Imperialism as the exercise of forcible control over lower races, by regarding this control as a trust for the civilization of the world, we pointed out three conditions essential to the validity of such a trust: first, the control must be directed to the general good, and not to the special good of the " imperialist " nation; secondly, it must confer some net advantage to the nation so controlled; lastly, there must exist some organization representative of inter-national interests, which shall sanction the undertaking of a trust by the nation exercising such control.

The third condition, which is fundamental to the validity of the other two, we saw to be unfulfilled, inasmuch as each nation claiming to fulfil the trust of governing lower races assumed this control upon its own authority alone.

The practice of Imperialism, as illustrated in a great variety of cases, exhibits the very defects which correspond with the unsound theory. The exclusive interest of an expanding nation, interpreted by its rulers at some given moment, and not the good of the whole world, is seen to be the dominant motive in each new assumption of control over the tropics and lower peoples; that national interest itself commonly signifies the direct material self-interest of some small class of traders, mine-owners, farmers, or investors who wish to dispose of the land and labour of the lower peoples for their private gain. Other more disinterested motives woven in may serve to give an attractive colouring to each business in hand, but it is impossible to examine the historic details in any important modern instance without recognizing the supremacy of economic forces. At best it is impossible to claim more than this, that some consideration is taken of justice and humanity in the exercise of the authority assumed, and that incidentally the welfare of the lower race is subserved by the play of economic and political forces not primarily designed to secure that end.

Everywhere, in the white administration of these lower races, considerations of present order are paramount, and industrial exploitation of the land and labour under private management for private immediate gain is the chief operative force in the community, unchecked, or inadequately checked, by imperial or other governmental control. The future progress of the lower race, its gradual education in the arts of industrial and political self-government, in most instances do not at all engage the activity of imperial government, and nowhere are such considerations of the welfare of the governed really paramount.

The stamp of "parasitism" is upon every white settlement among these lower races, that is to say, nowhere are the relations between white and coloured people such as to preserve a wholesome balance of mutual services. The best services which white civilization might be capable of rendering, by examples of normal, healthy, white communities practising the best arts of Western life, are precluded by climatic and other physical conditions in almost every case : the presence of a scattering of white officials, missionaries, traders, mining or plantation overseers, a dominant male caste with little knowledge of or sympathy for the institutions of the people, is ill-calculated to give to these lower races even such gains as Western civilization might be capable of giving.

The condition of the white rulers of these lower races is distinctively parasitic ; they live upon these natives, their chief work being that of organizing native labour for their support. The normal state of such a country is one in which the most fertile lands and the mineral resources are owned by white aliens and worked by natives under their direction, primarily for their gain : they do not identify themselves with the interests of the country or its people, but remain an alien body of sojourners, a " parasite " upon the carcass of its " host," destined to extract wealth from the country and retiring to consume it at home. All the hard manual or other severe routine work is done by natives ; most of the real labour of administration, or even of aggression, is done by native overseers, police and soldiery. This holds of all white government in the tropics or wherever a large lower population is found. Even where whites can live healthily and breed and work, the quantity of actual work, physical or mental, which they do is very small, where a large supply of natives can be made to work for them. Even in the parts of South Africa where whites thrive best, the life they lead, when clearly analyzed, is seen to be parasitic. The white farmer, Dutch or British, does little work, manual or mental, and tends everywhere to become lazy and " unprogressive " ; the trading, professional or official classes of the towns show clear signs of the same laxity and torpor, the brief spasmodic flares of energy evoked by dazzling prospects among small classes of speculators and business men in mushroom cities like Johannesburg serving but to dazzle our eyes and hide the deep essential character of the life.

If this is true of South Africa, much more is it true of countries where climate inhibits white settlement and white energy, the general condition of those countries which represent the expansion of modern Imperialism.

Nowhere under such conditions is the theory of white government as a trust for civilization made valid ; nowhere is there any provision to secure the predominance of the interests, either of the world at large or of the governed people, over those of the encroaching nation, or more commonly a section of that nation. The relations subsisting between the superior and the inferior nations, commonly established by pure force, and resting on that basis, are such as preclude the genuine sympathy essential to the operation of the best civilizing influences, and usually resolve themselves into the maintenance of external good order so as to forward the profitable development of certain natural resources of the land, under " forced " native labour, primarily for the benefit of white traders and investors, and secondarily for the benefit of the world of white Western consumers.

This failure to justify by results the forcible rule over alien peoples is attributable to no special defect of the British or other modern European nations. It is inherent in the nature of such domination. " The government of a people by itself has a meaning and a reality, but such a thing as government of one people by another does not and cannot exist. One people may keep another as a warren or preserve for its own use, a place to make money in, a human cattle-farm, to be worked for the profits of its own inhabitants ; but if the good of the governed is the proper business of a government, it is utterly impossible that a people should directly attend to it."[1]

[1] J. S. Mill *Representative Government*, p. 326.

CHAPTER V

IMPERIALISM IN ASIA

I

THE great test of Western Imperialism is Asia, where vast peoples live, the inheritors of civilizations as complex as our own, more ancient and more firmly rooted by enduring custom in the general life. The races of Africa it has been possible to regard as savages or children, " backward " in their progress along the same general road of civilization in which Anglo-Saxondom represents the vanguard, and requiring the help of more forward races. It is not so easy to make a specious case for Western control over India, China, and other Asiatic peoples upon the same ground. Save in the more recent developments of the physical sciences and their application to industrial arts, it cannot be contended that these peoples are " backward," and though we sometimes describe their civilizations as " arrested " or " unprogressive," that judgment either may imply our ignorance of the pace at which civilizations so much older than our own must continue moving, or it may even afford unconscious testimony to a social progress which has won its goal in securing a well-nigh complete adjustment between human life and its stable environment.

The claim of the West to civilize the East by means of political and military supremacy must rest ultimately upon the assumption that civilizations, however various in their surface growths, are at root one and the same, that they have a common nature and a common soil. Stripped of metaphor, this means that certain moral and intellectual qualities, finding embodiment in general forms of religion, law, customs, and arts of industry, are essential to all local varieties of civilization, irrespective of race, colour, climate, and other conditions; that Western nations, or some of them, possess these qualities and forms of civilization in a pre-eminent degree, and are able to impart them to Eastern nations by government and its accompanying political, religious, and industrial education. It certainly seems as if " humanity " implies such common factors. The ethics of the Decalogue appears to admit of a wide common application; certain rights of the individual, certain elements of social justice, embodied in law and custom, appear capable of universal appeal; certain sorts of knowledge and the arts of applying them appear useful to all sorts and conditions of men. If Western civilization is richer in these essentials, it seems reasonable to suppose that the West can benefit the East by imparting them, and that her government may be justified as a means of doing so.

The British Empire in India may be taken as the most serviceable test. We did not, indeed, go there in the first instance for the good of the Indians, nor have our various extensions of political power been motived primarily by this consideration; but it is contended that our government of India has in point of fact conferred upon the people the benefits arising from our civilization, and that the conferring of these benefits has of later years played a larger and a larger part in our conscious policy. The experiment has been a long and varied one, and our success in India is commonly adduced as the most convincing argument in favour of the benefits accruing to subject races from Imperialism.

The real questions we have to answer are these : " Are we civilizing India ? " and " In what does that civilization consist ? " To assist in answering there exists a tolerably large body of indisputable facts. We have established a wider and more permanent internal peace than India had ever known from the days of Alexander the Great. We have raised the standard of justice by fair and equal administration of laws; we have regulated and probably reduced the burden of taxation, checking the corruption and tyranny of native princes and their publicans. For the instruction of the people we have introduced a public system of schools and colleges, as well as a great quasi-public missionary establishment, teaching not only the Christian religion but many industrial arts. Roads, railways, and a network of canals have facilitated communication and transport, and an extensive system of scientific irrigation has improved the productiveness of the soil; the mining of coal, gold, and other minerals has been greatly developed; in Bombay and elsewhere cotton mills with modern machinery have been set up, and the organization of other machine industries is helping to find employment for the population of large cities. Tea, coffee, indigo, jute, tobacco, and other important crops have been introduced into Indian agriculture. We are gradually breaking down many of the religious and social superstitions which sin against humanity and retard progress, and even the deeply rooted caste system is modified wherever British influence is felt. There can be no question that much of this work of England in India is well done. No such intelligent, well-educated, and honourable body of men has ever been employed by any State in the working of imperial government as is contained in the Civil Service of India. Nowhere else in our Empire has so much really disinterested and thoughtful energy been applied in the work of government. The same may be said of the line of great statesmen sent out from England to preside over our government in India.

Our work there is the best record British Imperialism can show. What does it tell us about the capacity of the West to confer the benefits of her civilization on the East ?

Take first the test of economic prosperity. Are the masses of the people under our rule wealthier than they were before, and are they growing wealthier under that rule ? There are some who maintain that British government is draining the economic life-blood of India and dragging her population into lower and more hopeless poverty. They point to the fact that one of the poorest countries in the world is made to bear the cost of a government, which, however honestly administered, is very expensive ; that one-third of the money raised by taxation flows out of the country without return ; that India is made to support an army admittedly excessive for purposes of self-defence, and even to bear the cost of wars in other parts of the Empire, while nearly the whole of the interest on capital invested in India is spent out of the country. The statistical basis of this argument is too insecure for much reliance to be placed on it : it is probably untrue that the net cost of British government is greater than the burden of native princes which it has largely[1] superseded, though it is certainly true that the extortionate taxation under native rule was expended in the country on productive work or unproductive native services. Whether the increasing drain of wheat and other food-stuffs from India exceeds the gain from improved irrigation, and whether the real income of the " ryot " or other worker is increasing or diminishing, cannot be established, so far as the whole country is concerned, by any accurate measure. But it is generally admitted, even by British officials strongly favourable to our rule, that we have not succeeded in giving any considerable economic

[1] About three-eighths of the country is still under native government, with British supervision.

prosperity to India. I quote from a source strongly favourable to our rule :

" The test of a people's prosperity is not the extension of exports, the multiplication of manufactures or other industries, the construction of cities. No. A prosperous country is one in which the great mass of the inhabitants are able to procure, with moderate toil, what is necessary for living *human* lives, lives of frugal and assured comfort. Judged by this criterion, can India be called prosperous ?

" Comfort, of course, is a relative term. . . . In a tropical country, like India, the standard is very low. Little clothing is required there. Simple diet suffices. Artificial wants are very few, and, for the most part are not costly. The Indian Empire is a peasant Empire. Ninety per cent. of the people live upon the land. . . . An unfailing well of water, a plot of land, and a bit of orchard—that will satisfy his heart's desire, if indeed you add the cattle needful to him, ' the ryot's children,' as they are called in many parts. Such is the ryot's ideal. Very few realize it. An acre may stand for the *modus agri*, the necessary plot of ground. A man to an acre, or 640 men to the square mile, is the utmost density of population which India can comfortably support, except near towns or in irrigated districts. But millions of peasants in India are struggling to live on half an acre. Their existence is a constant struggle with starvation, ending too often in defeat. Their difficulty is not to live *human* lives—lives up to the level of their poor standard of comfort— but to live at all and not die. . . . We may truly say that in India, except in the irrigated tracts, famine is chronic— endemic."[1]

A century of British rule, then, conducted with sound ability and goodwill, had not materially assisted to ward off the chronic enemy, starvation, from the mass of the

[1] *India and its Problems*, by W. S. Lilly, pp. 284, 285 (Sands & Co.).

people. Nor can it be maintained that the new industrialism of machinery and factories, which we have introduced, is civilizing India, or even adding much to her material prosperity. In fact, all who value the life and character of the East deplore the visible decadence of the arts of architecture, weaving, metal work and pottery, in which India had been famed from time immemorial. "Architecture, engineering, literary skill are all perishing out, so perishing that Anglo-Indians doubt whether Indians have the capacity to be architects, though they built Benares; or engineers, though they dug the artificial lakes of Tanjore; or poets, though the people sit for hours or days listening to the rhapsodists as they recite poems, which move them as Tennyson certainly does not move our common people."[1] The decay or forcible supersession of the native industrial arts is still more deplorable, for these always constitute the poetry of common life, the free play of the imaginative faculty of a nation in the ordinary work of life.

Sir George Birdwood, in his great work on *The Industrial Arts of India*, written more than twenty years ago[2], gives a significant judgment upon the real meaning of a movement which has ever since been advancing at an accelerating pace: "If, owing to the operation of certain economic causes, machinery was to be gradually introduced into India for the manufacture of its great traditional handicrafts, there would ensue an industrial revolution which, if not directed by an intelligent and instructed public opinion and the general prevalence of refined taste, would inevitably throw the traditional arts of the country into the same confusion of principles, and of their practical application to the objects of daily necessity, which has for three generations been the destruction of decorative

[1] *Asia and Europe*, by Meredith Townsend, p. 102 (Constable & Co.).
[2] Now (1938) more than fifty years ago.

art and of middle-class taste in England and North-Western Europe and the United States of America. The social and moral evils of the introduction of machinery into India are likely to be greater." Then follows a detailed account of the free picturesque handicrafts of the ordinary Indian village, and the author proceeds : " But of late these handicraftsmen, for the sake of whose works the whole world has been ceaselessly pouring its bullion into India, and who, for all the marvellous tissue they have wrought, have polluted no rivers, deformed no pleasing prospects, nor poisoned any air ; whose skill and individuality the training of countless generations has developed to the highest perfection—these hereditary handicraftsmen are being everywhere gathered from their democratic village communities in hundreds and thousands into the colossal mills of Bombay, to drudge in gangs for tempting wages, at manufacturing piece goods, in competition with Manchester, in the production of which they are no more intellectually and morally concerned than the grinder of a barrel organ in the tunes turned out from it."

Even from the low standpoint of the world-market this hasty destruction of the native arts for the sake of employing masses of cheap labour in mills is probably bad policy ; for, as the world becomes more fully opened up and distant countries are set in closer communication with one another, a land whose industries had so unique and interesting a character as those of India would probably have found a more profitable market than by attempting to undersell Lancashire and New England in stock goods.

But far more important are the reactions of these changes on the character of the people. The industrial revolution in England and elsewhere has partaken more largely of the nature of a natural growth, proceeding from inner forces, than in India, and has been largely coincident with a liberation of great popular forces finding expression in scientific education and in political democracy: it has been an important phase of the great movement of popular liberty and self-government. In India, and elsewhere in the East, there is no such compensation.

An industrial system, far more strongly set and more closely interwoven in the religious and social system of the country than ever were the crafts and arts in Europe, has been subjected to forces operating from outside, and unchecked in their pace and direction by the will of the people whose life they so vitally affected. Industrial revolution is one thing when it is the natural movement of internal forces, making along the lines of the self-interests of a nation and proceeding *pari passu* with advancing popular self-government; another thing when it is imposed by foreign conquerors looking primarily to present gains for themselves, and neglectful of the deeper interests of the people of the country. The story of the destruction of native weaving industry[1] for the benefit of mills started by the Company will illustrate the selfish, short-sighted economic policy of the late eighteenth and early nineteenth centuries. "Under the pretence of Free Trade, England has compelled the Hindus to receive the products of the steam-looms of Lancashire, Yorkshire, Glasgow, etc., at mere nominal duties; while the hand-wrought manufactures of Bengal and Behar, beautiful in fabric and durable in wear, have had heavy and almost prohibitive duties imposed on their importation to England."[2] The effect of this policy, rigorously maintained during the earlier decades of the nineteenth century, was the irreparable ruin of many of the most valuable and characteristic arts of Indian industry.

[1] *Cf.* the careful summary of official evidence in Mr. Romesh Dutt's *Economic History of British India*, chap. xv. (Kegan Paul).

[2] *Eastern India*, by Montgomery Martin (London, 1838), vol. iii. Introd. (quoted Romesh Dutt, p. 290).

" In India the manufacturing power of the people was stamped out by Protection against her industries, and then Free Trade was forced on her so as to prevent a revival."[1]

When we turn from manufacture to the great industry of agriculture, which even now occupies nine-tenths of the population, the difficulty of alien administration, with whatever good intention, is amply illustrated. Not a few of our greatest Indian statesmen, such as Munro, Elphinstone, and Metcalfe, have recognized in the village community the true embodiment of the spirit of Eastern civilization.

" The village communities," wrote Sir C. Metcalfe,[2] " are little republics, having nearly everything that they can want within themselves, and almost independent of any foreign relations. They seem to last where nothing else lasts. Dynasty after dynasty tumbles down ; revolution succeeds to revolution ; Hindu, Pathan, Moghul, Mahratta, Sikh, English, are masters in turn ; but the village communities remain the same." " The union of the village communities, each one forming a separate little State in itself, has, I conceive, contributed more than any other cause to the preservation of the people of India through all revolutions and changes which they have suffered, and it is in a high degree conducive to their happiness and to the enjoyment of a great portion of freedom and independence. I wish, therefore, that the village constitutions may never be disturbed, and I dread everything which has a tendency to break them up."

Yet the whole efforts of British administration have been directed to the destruction of this village self-government in industry and politics. The substitution of the individual ryot for the community as the unit of revenue throughout

[1] Romesh Dutt, p. 302.
[2] Letter to the Board of Revenue, April, 1838 (quoted Romesh Dutt, p. 386).

Bombay and Madras struck a fatal blow at the economic life of the village, while the withdrawal of all real judicial and executive powers from the zemindars or headmen, and their concentration in British civil courts and executive officers, virtually completed the destruction of the strongest and most general institution of India—the self-governing village.

Both these important steps were taken in furtherance of the new Western idea of individual responsibility as the only sound economic basis, and centralized government as the most efficacious mode of political machinery. The fact that it should be considered safe and profitable suddenly to subvert the most ancient institutions of India, in order thus to adapt the people to English modes of life, will be taken by sociologists as one of the most amazing lessons of incompetence in the art of civilization afforded by modern history. Indeed the superior prosperity of a large part of Bengal, attributable in part at any rate to the maintenance of a local landlord class, who served as middlemen between the State and the individual cultivators, and mitigated the mechanical rack-rent of the land-tax, is a sufficiently remarkable testimony to the injury inflicted upon other parts of India by sudden ill-advised application of Western economic and political methods.[1]

II

When we turn from industry to the administration of justice and the general work of government in which the ability and character of British officialism finds expression, we are led to further questioning. Is Great Britain able

[1] The prosperity of districts under the Bengal settlement, as compared with other parts of British India, must however be imputed largely to the fact that this settlement enables Bengal to evade its full proportion of contribution to the revenue of India, and throws therefore a disproportionate burden upon other parts.

to Anglicize the government of India, is she doing so, and is she thereby implanting Western civilization in India? How much a few thousand British officials, endowed with the best ability and energy, can achieve in stamping British integrity and efficiency upon the practical government of three hundred million people of alien race and character it is difficult to judge. Numbers are not everything, and it is probable that these diffused units of British authority exercise directly and indirectly a considerable influence upon the larger affairs of government, and that this influence may sometimes permeate far down among native official circles. But it must be kept in mind that those few British officials are rarely born in India, have seldom any perfect understanding of the languages of the people, form a close " caste," never mingling in free social intercourse with those whom they govern, and that the laws and regulations they administer are largely foreign to the traditionary institutions of the Indian peoples. When we remember how large a share of real government is the personal administration of detail, the enforcement of law or regulation upon the individual citizen, and that in the overwhelming majority of cases this work must always be left to native officials, it is evident that the formal virtues of British law and justice must admit much elasticity and much perversion in the actual processes of administration.

" No one can deny that this system of civil and criminal administration is vastly superior to anything which India ever possessed under former rulers. Its defects arise chiefly from causes extraneous to it. The unblemished integrity and unswerving devotion to duty of the officials, whether English or Indian, who occupy the higher posts, no one will call in question. The character of the subordinate officials is not always so entirely above suspicion, and the course of justice is too often perverted by a lamentable characteristic of the Oriental mind. ' Great is the rectitude of the English, greater is the power of a lie ' is a proverbial saying throughout India. Perhaps the least satisfactory of the government departments is the police. A recent writer says, ' It is difficult to imagine how a department can be more corrupt.' This, too, may be an over-statement. But, taken on the whole, the rank and file of the Indian police are probably not of higher integrity and character than those of New York."[1] Now one sentence of this statement deserves special attention. " Its defects arise chiefly from causes extraneous to it." This is surely incorrect. It is an essential part of our system that the details of administration shall be in native hands : no one can contemplate any considerable displacement of lower native officials by English ; the latter could not do the work and would not if they could, nor could the finances, always precarious, possibly admit of so huge an increase of expenditure as would be involved by making the government of India really British in its working. The tendency, in fact, is all the other way, and makes for the more numerous employment of natives in all but the highest grades of the public service. If it is true that corruption and mendacity are deeply rooted in all Eastern systems of government, and that the main moral justification of our rule consists in their correction by British character and administration, it is pretty clear that we cannot be performing this valuable work, and must in the nature of the case be disabled from even understanding where and how far we fall short of doing so. The comment made by Mr. Lilly upon Indian police is chiefly significant because this is the one department of detailed practical government where special scandals are most likely to reveal the failure of our excellent intentions as embodied in criminal codes and judicial procedure.

[1] *India and its Problems*, p. 182.

One would wish to know whether the actual native officer who collects the land-tax or other dues from the individual ryot practises the integrity of his British superior official or reverts to the time-honoured and universal practice of the East.

How much can a handful of foreign officials do in the way of effectual check and supervision of the details of government in a country which teems with populations of various races, languages, creeds, and customs ? Probably not very much, and *ex hypothesi* they, and so we, cannot know their failures.

The one real and indisputable success of our rule in India, as indeed generally through our Empire, is the maintenance of order upon a large scale, the prevention of internecine war, riot, or organized violence. This, of course, is much, but it is not everything ; it is not enough in itself to justify us in regarding our imperial rule as a success. Is British justice, so far as it prevails, and British order good for India ? will seem to the average Briton a curious question to ask. But Englishmen who have lived in India, and who, on the whole, favour the maintenance of our authority, sometimes ask it. It must, in the first place, be remembered that some of the formal virtues of our laws and methods which seem to us most excellent may work out quite otherwise in practice. The rigorous justice in the exaction of the land-tax and in the enforcement of the legal claims of userers is a striking instance of misapplied notions of equity. Corrupt as the practice of Eastern tax-gatherers has ever been, tyrannical as has been the power of the userer, public opinion, expediency, and some personal consideration have always qualified their tyranny ; the mechanical rigour of British law is one of the greatest sources of unpopularity of our government in India, and is probably a grave source of actual injury.

There is even some reason to suspect that Indians resent less the illegal and irregular extortion of recognized native autocrats, whose visible authority is familiarly impressed on their imaginations, than the actually lighter exactions of an inhuman, irresistible and immitigable machine, such as the British power presents itself to them.

It is pretty clear that, so far as the consent of the governed in any active sense is a condition of success in government, the British Empire in India has not succeeded. We are deceived by Eastern acquiescence, and our deception may even be attended by grave catastrophe unless we understand the truth. Mr. Townsend, who has brought close thought to bear upon the conditions of our hold of India, writes thus :—

" Personal liberty, religious liberty, equal justice, perfect security—these things the Empire gives; but then are these so valued as to overcome the inherent and incurable dull distaste felt by the brown men to the white men who give them ? I doubt it greatly."[1]

The reasons he gives for his doubt are weighty. The agricultural populace, whom we have, he holds, materially benefited, is an inert mass : the active classes endowed with initiative, political ambition, patriotism, education, are silently but strongly hostile to our rule. It is natural this should be so. We have spoiled the free career open to these classes under native government ; the very order we have imposed offends their instincts and often thwarts their interests. The caste system, which it is the boast of our more liberal laws and institutions to moderate or disregard, is everywhere consciously antagonistic to us in self-defence, and deeply resents any portion of our educative influences which impairs its hold upon the minds of the people. This force is well illustrated by the almost

[1] *Asia and Europe*, p. 101.

complete failure of our energetic Christian missions to make converts out of any members of the higher castes. The testimony of one of the most devoted of Roman Catholic missionaries after thirty years of missionary labours deserves attention :—

" During the long period I have lived in India in the capacity of a missionary, I have made, with the assistance of a native missionary, in all between two and three hundred converts of both sexes. Of this number two-thirds were Pariahs or beggars, and the rest were composed of Sudras, vagrants and outcasts of several tribes, who, being without resources, turned Christians in order to form connexions, chiefly for the purpose of marriage, or with some other interested views."[1]

This view is borne out in the general treatment of Christian missions in Mr. Barrie's report on the census in 1891. " The greatest development (of Christianity) is found where the Brahmanic caste system is in force in its fullest vigour, in the south and west of the Peninsula, and among the hill tribes of Bengal. In such localities it is naturally attractive to a class of the population whose position is hereditarily and permanently degraded by their own religion."

If British Christianity and British rule were welcomed by large bodies of the ryots and the low-caste and Pariah populations, the opposition of the native " classes " might seem a strong testimony to the beneficence of our rule, as an instrument for the elevation of the poorer working people who always form the great majority. Unfortunately no such result can seriously be pretended. There is no reason to suppose that we hold the allegiance of any large section of the people of India by any other bond than that of fear and respect for our external power. Mr. Townsend

[1] Quoted Lilly, *India and its Problems*, p. 163.

puts the matter in a nutshell when he affirms : " There is no corner in Asia where the life of a white man, if unprotected by force, either actual or potential, is safe for an hour; nor is there an Asiatic State which, if it were prudent, would not expel him at once and for ever."[1] There are, according to this view, no psychical roots to the civilization we are imposing upon India : it is a superficial structure maintained by force, and not grafted on to the true life of the nation so as to modify and educate the soul of the people. Mr. Townsend is driven with evidently deep reluctance to the conclusion that " the Empire hangs in air, supported by nothing but the minute white garrison and the unproved assumption that the people of India desire it to continue to exist."[2] It was indeed pointed out by Professor Seeley, and is generally admitted, that our Empire in India has only been rendered possible by the wide cleavages of race, language, religion and interests among the Indian populations, first and foremost the division of Mohammedan and Hindu.

But it may be fairly contended that the forcible foundation of our rule and the slowness and reluctance of the natives to appreciate its benefits are no proof that it is not beneficial, or that in process of time we may not infuse the best principles of Western civilization into their life.

Are we doing this ? Is the nature of our occupation such as to enable us to do it ? Apart from the army, which is the aspect of the Empire most in evidence, there is a British population of some 135,000,[1] less than 1 to every 2,000 of the natives, living neither the normal life of their own country nor that of the foreign country which they occupy, in no sense representative units of British civilization, but exotics compelled to live a highly artificial life and unable to rear British families or to create British society

[1] *Asia and Europe*, p. 98.　　[2] *Asia and Europe*, p. 89.　　[3] At about 1900.

of such a sort as to embody and illustrate the most valuable contents of our civilization.

It is certain that the machinery of government, however excellent, can of itself do little to convey the benefits of civilization to an alien people. The real forces of civilization can only be conveyed by contact of individual with individual. Now the conditions of free, close, personal contact between British and Indians are virtually non-existent. There is no real, familiar, social intercourse on equal terms, still less is there inter-marriage, the only effective mode of amalgamating two civilizations, the only safeguard against race hatred and race domination. "When inter-marriage is out of the question," writes Dr. Goldwin Smith, "social equality cannot exist; without social equality political equality is impossible, and a republic in the true sense can hardly be."[1]

The vast majority of whites admittedly live their own life, using natives for domestic and industrial service, but never attempting to get any fuller understanding of their lives and character than is required to exact these services from them or to render official services in return. The few who have made some serious attempt to penetrate into the Indian mind admit their failure to grasp with any adequacy even the rudiments of a human nature which differs, in its fundamental valuations and its methods of conduct, so radically from our own as to present for its chief interest a series of baffling psychological puzzles. It is indeed precisely from these students that we come to understand the impossibility of that close, persistent, interactive contact of mind with mind which is the only method by which that "mission of civilization" which we profess is capable of fulfilment. Even those English writers who seem to convey most forcibly what is called

[1] *Commonwealth or Empire* (Macmillan & Co.).

the spirit of the East as it shows forth in the drama of modern life, writers such as Mr. Kipling and Mrs. Steel, hardly do more than present a quaint alluring atmosphere of un-intelligibility; while study of the great Indian literature and art which may be taken as the best expression of the soul of the people exhibits the hitherto unbridgeable divergence of the British conception of life from the Indian. The complete aloofness of the small white garrison is indeed in no small measure due to an instinctive recognition of this psychical chasm and of their inability to enter into really vital sympathy with these members of an "inferior" race. They are not to blame, but rather the conditions which have brought them there and imposed on them a task essentially impossible, that of implanting genuine white civilization on Asiatic soil. It must clearly be understood that it is not a question of the slowness of a process of adaptation: the really vital process of change is not taking place. We are incapable of implanting our civilization in India by present methods of approach: we are only capable of disturbing their civilization.[1] Even the external life of the vast bulk of the population we hardly touch; the inner life we do not touch at all. If we are deceived by the magnitude of the area of our political control and the real activity of the machinery of government into supposing that we are converting the Indian peoples

[1] The effects of this disturbance, however, may be of considerable importance. If, as is maintained by some Hindoo politicians of the new school, our influence is sensibly undermining the antagonism between Hindoo and Mohammedan, and is gradually breaking down the rigour of "caste" among Hindoos, it is tolerably manifest that we are sapping the sources of our political rule, by removing the most powerful obstacles to the growth of "nationalism" in India. If the levelling influence of our Western ideas, operating through religious, literary, political and social institutions on the minds of the people, goes beyond a certain distance in breaking down the racial, religious and linguistic barriers which have always divided and subdivided India, the rise of a national self-consciousness upon a basis of common interests and common antagonisms may raise the demand of "India for the Indians" above the margin of vague aspiration into a region of organized political and military endeavour.

to British Christianity, British views of justice, morality, and to the supreme value of regular intense industry, in order to improve the standard of material comfort, the sooner we face the facts the better. For that we are doing none of these things in an appreciable degree is plain to most British officials. Of the nearest approaches to such success they are openly contemptuous, condemning outright the Eurasian and ridiculing the " stucco civilization of the baboo." The idea that we are civilizing India in the sense of assisting them to industrial, political, and moral progress along the lines either of our own or their civilization is a complete delusion, based upon a false estimate of the influence of superficial changes wrought by government and the activity of a minute group of aliens. The delusion is only sustained by the sophistry of Imperialism, which weaves these fallacies to cover its nakedness and the advantages which certain interests suck out of empire.

This judgment is not new, nor does it imply the spirit of a " little Englander." If there is one writer who, more than another, is justly accredited with the stimulation of large ideas of the destiny of England, it is the late Professor Seeley. Yet this is his summary of the value of the " imperial " work which we have undertaken in India :—

" At best we think of it as a good specimen of a bad political system. We are not disposed to be proud of the succession of the Grand Mogul. We doubt whether, with all the merits of our administration, the subjects of it are happy. We may even doubt whether our rule is preparing them for a happier condition, whether it may not be sinking them lower in misery ; and we have our misgivings that perhaps a genuine Asiatic Government, and still more a national Government springing up out of the Hindu population itself, might, in the long run, be more beneficial, because more congenial, though perhaps less civilized, than such a foreign, unsympathetic Government as our own."[1]

III

While India presents the largest and most instructive lesson in distinctively British Imperialism, it is in China that the spirit and methods of Western Imperialism in general are likely to find their most crucial test. The new Imperialism differs from the older, first in substituting for the ambition of a single growing empire the theory and the practice of competing empires, each motived by similar lusts of political aggrandisement and commercial gain; secondly, in the dominance of financial or investing over mercantile interests.

The methods and motives of the European Powers are not open to serious dispute. The single aim of Chinese policy from time immemorial had been to avoid all dealings with foreigners which might lead to the establishment of inter-governmental relations with them. This did not imply, at any rate until recently, hostility to individual foreigners or a reluctance to admit the goods or the ideas which they sought to introduce. Arabs and other Asiatic races of the West had traded with China from very early times. Roman records point to intercourse with China as early as Marcus Aurelius. Nor were their relations with the outside world confined to trade. Christianity was introduced some fifteen hundred years ago by the Nestorians, who propagated their religious views widely in the Central Kingdom ; Buddhist foreign missionaries were well received, and their teaching found wide acceptance. Indeed few nations have displayed so much power of assimilating foreign religious notions as the Chinese. Roman Catholic

[1] *The Expansion of England*, pp. 273, 274.

missionaries entered China during the Mongol dynasty, and later in the Ming dynasty.[1] Jesuits not only propagated Christianity, but introduced Western science into Pekin, attaining the climax of their influence during the latter part of the seventeenth century. Not until the arrival of the Dominicans introduced an element of religious faction, attended by political intrigue, did Christianity come into disrepute or evoke any sort of persecution. With the introduction of Protestant missions during the nineteenth century, the trouble has grown apace. Though the Chinese as a nation have never displayed religious intolerance, they have naturally mistrusted the motives of Westerns who, calling themselves Christians, quarrelled amongst themselves, and by their tactless zeal often caused local rioting which led to diplomatic or armed interference for their protection. Almost all lay European authorities in China bear out the following judgment of Mr. A. J. Little :—

"The riots and consequent massacres resulting from mission work throughout Indo-China may be justified by the end; but it is certain our relations with the Chinese would be far more cordial than they are, were we not suspected of an insidious design to wean them from such habits of filial piety and loyalty as they possess, to our advantage."[1]

The main outlines of Chinese policy are quite intelligible. Though not averse from incidental contact with Europeans or with other Asiatics, traders, travellers, or missionaries, they have steadily resisted all attempts to disturb their political and economic system by organized pressure of foreign Powers. Possessing in their enormous area of territory, with its various climatic and other natural conditions, its teeming industrial population, and its

[1] A.D. 1138 to 1644.
[1] *Through the Yang-Tse Gorges*, edition 1888, p. 334.

ancient, well-developed civilization, a full material basis of self-sufficiency, the Chinese, following a sound instinct of self-defence, have striven to confine their external relations to a casual intercourse. The successful practice of this policy for countless centuries has enabled them to escape the militarism of other nations; and though it has subjected them to a few forcible dynastic changes, it has never affected the peaceful customary life of the great mass of little self-sufficing industrial villages of which the nation is composed. The sort of politics of which Western history is mainly composed has meant virtually nothing to the Chinese. It is the organized attempt of Western nations to break through this barrier of passive resistance, and to force themselves, their wares, their political and industial control, on China that gives importance to Imperialism in the Far East. It is not possible here to trace, even in bare outlines, the history of this pressure, how quarrels with traders and missionaries have been utilized to force trade with the interior, to establish treaty ports, to secure special political and commercial rights for British or other European subjects, to fasten a regular system of foreign political relations upon the central government, and at the conclusion of the nineteenth century to drive China into wars, first with Japan, next with a confederacy of European Powers, which threaten to break up the political and industrial isolation of forty centuries, and to plunge China into the great world-competition.

The conduct of European Powers towards China will rank as the clearest revelation of the nature of Imperialism. Until late in the nineteenth century Great Britain, with France as a poor second, had made the pace in pursuit of trade, covering this trading policy with a veneer of missionary work, the real relative importance of the two being put to a crucial test by the opium war. The entrance of Germany and America upon a manufacturing career, and the occidentation of Japan, enhanced the mercantile competition, and the struggle for the Far Eastern markets became a more definite object of national industrial policy. The next stage was the series of forceful moves by which France, Russia, Germany, Great Britain, and Japan have fastened their political and economic fangs into some special portion of the body of China by annexation, sphere of influence, or special treaty rights, their policy at this stage culminating in the ferocious reprisals of the recent[1] war, and the establishment of a permanent menace in the shape of international political and financial conditions extorted from a reluctant and almost impotent central government by threats of further violence.

It is now hardly possible for any one who has carefully followed these events to speak of Europe undertaking "a mission of civilization" in China without his tongue in his cheek.[2] Imperialism in the Far East is stripped nearly bare of all motives and methods save those of distinctively commercial origin. The schemes of territorial acquisition and direct political control which Russia, Germany, and France developed, the "sphere of influence" which has oscillated with "an open door" in our less coherent policy, are all manifestly motived by commerce and finance.

China seems to offer a unique opportunity to the Western business man. A population of some four hundred millions

[1] "recent" in 1903.

[2] The *Times* correspondent, in describing the forcible entrance of the allied troops into Pekin, affords this glimpse into Christianity *a la mode* in China. "The raising of the siege was signalized by the slaughter of a large number of Chinese who had been rounded up into a *cul-de-sac* and who were killed to a man, the Chinese Christian converts joining with the French soldiers of the relieving force, who lent them bayonets, and abandoned themselves to the spirit of revenge. Witnesses describe the scene as a sickening sight, but in judging such acts it is necessary to remember the provocation, and these people had been sorely tried" (The *Times*, October 16, 1900).

endowed with an extraordinary capacity of steady labour, with great intelligence and ingenuity, inured to a low standard of material comfort, in occupation of a country rich in unworked minerals and destitute of modern machinery of manufacture or of transport, opens up a dazzling prospect of profitable exploitation.

In our dealings with backward races capable of instruction in Western industrial methods there are three stages. First comes ordinary commerce, the exchange of the normal surplus produce of the two countries. Next, after Great Britain or some other Western Power has acquired territory or invested capital in the foreign country with the aim of developing the resources, she enjoys a period of large export trade in rails, machinery, and other forms of capital, not necessarily balanced by the import trade since it really covers the process of investment. This stage may continue long, when capital and business capacity cannot be obtained within the newly developed country. But a third stage remains, one which in China at any rate may be reached at no distant period, when capital and organizing energy may be developed within the country, either by Europeans planted there or by natives. Thus fully equipped for future internal development in all the necessary productive powers, such a nation may turn upon her civilizer, untrammelled by need of further industrial aid, undersell him in his own market, take away his other foreign markets and secure for herself what further developing work remains to be done in other undeveloped parts of the earth. The shallow platitudes by which the less instructed Free Trader sometimes attempts to shirk this vital issue have already been exposed. It is here enough to repeat that Free Trade can nowise guarantee the maintenance of industry or of an industrial population upon any particular country, and there is no consideration, theoretic or practical, to prevent British capital from transferring itself to China, provided it can find there a cheaper or more efficient supply of labour, or even to prevent Chinese capital with Chinese labour from ousting British produce in neutral markets of the world. What applies to Great Britain applies equally to the other industrial nations which have driven their economic suckers into China. It is at least conceivable that China might so turn the tables upon the Western industrial nations, and, either by adopting their capital and organizers or, as is more probable, by substituting her own, might flood their markets with her cheaper manufactures, and refusing their imports in exchange might take her payment in liens upon their capital, reversing the earlier process of investment until she gradually obtained financial control over her quondam patrons and civilizers. This is no idle speculation. If China in very truth possesses those industrial and business capacities with which she is commonly accredited, and the Western Powers are able to have their will in developing her upon Western lines, it seems extremely likely that this reaction will result.

IV

The inner significance of the joint attack of Western Powers in China lies here. It is the great speculative coup of international capitalism not fully ripened for international co-operation, but still hampered by the necessity under which the groups of capitalists lie, of using national feelings and policies to push their special interests. So long as it is necessary to use diplomatic pressure and armed force in order to secure some special field of investment in railroads, mining rights, or other developments, the peace of Europe is endangered by national intrigues and bickering. Though certain areas may be considered as more or less definitely allocated, Manchuria to Russia, the southern provinces of Tonking, with Hainan to France, Shan-tung to Germany, Formosa and Fokien to Japan, for industrial exploitation and for political control, there are large areas where the industrial and future political control, as spheres of influence, is likely to cause grave discord. Yunnan and Quan-tung on the southern boundary are disputed territory between England and France, the Chinese Government having given to each of these Powers a similar assurance that these provinces should not be alienated to any other Power. Great Britain's claim to the vast indefinite area known as the Yang-Tse basin as her separate sphere of influence for industrial concessions and political dominance is now exposed to the serious avowed encroachments of Germany, while Corea remains an open sore between Russia and Japan. The United States, whose interest in China for investment and for trade is developing faster than that of any European Power, will certainly insist upon an open door, and will soon be in a position to back her claim by strong naval force. The present[1] epoch, therefore, is one of separate national policies and special alliances, in which groups of financiers and capitalists urge their Governments to obtain leases, concessions, or other preferences over particular areas. It is quite possible that the conflicts of national Imperialism thus provoked, skilfully used for self-defence by the Chinese Government, may retard for a long time any effective opening up of China by Western enterprise, and that China may defend herself by setting her enemies to fight among themselves.

But it is idle to suppose that the industrial attack on China can be ultimately evaded. Unless China can be roused quickly from the sleep of countless centuries of peace and can transform herself into a powerful military

[1] The author writes of 1903.

nation, she cannot escape the pressure of the external powers. To suppose that she can do this, because her individual citizens show a capacity for drill and discipline, is to mistake the issue. The whole genius of the Chinese peoples, so far as it is understood, is opposed to militant patriotism and to the strongly centralized government required to give effect to such a policy. The notion of China organizing an army of six millions under some great general, and driving " the foreign devil " out of the country, or even entering herself upon a career of invasion and conquest, ignores the chief psychological and social factors of Chinese life. At any rate this is the least likely of all early issues in the Far East.

Far more reasonable is it to suppose that capitalism, having failed to gain its way by national separatist policies issuing in strife of Western peoples, may learn the art of combination, and that the power of international capitalism, which has been growing apace, may make its great crucial experiment in the exploitation of China. The driving force of the competing Imperialism of Western nations has been traced to the interests of certain small financial and industrial groups within each nation, usurping the power of the nation and employing the public force and money for their private business ends. In the earlier stage of development, where the grouping of these forces is still distinctively national, this policy makes for wars in pursuit of " national " markets for investments and trade. But the modern science of militarism renders wars between " civilized " Powers too costly, and the rapid growth of effective internationalism in the financial and great industrial magnates, who seem destined more and more to control national politics, may in the future render such wars impossible. Militarism may long survive, for that, as has been shown, is serviceable in many ways to the maintenance of a plutocracy. Its expenditure furnishes a profitable support to certain strong vested interests, it is a decorative element in social life, and above all it is necessary to keep down the pressure of the forces of internal reform. Everywhere the power of capital in its more concentrated forms is better organized than the power of labour, and has reached a further stage in its development; while labour has talked of international co-operation, capital has been achieving it. So far, therefore, as the greatest financial and commercial interests are concerned, it seems quite probable that the coming generation may witness so powerful an international union as to render wars between the Western nations almost impossible. Notwithstanding the selfish jealousies and the dog-in-the-manger policies which at present weaken European action in the Far East, the real drama will begin when the forces of international capitalism, claiming to represent the civilization of united Christendom, are brought to bear on the peaceful opening up of China. It is then that the real " yellow peril " will begin. If it is unreasonable to expect that China can develop a national patriotism which will enable her to expel the Western exploiters, she must then be subjected to a process of disintegration, which is more aptly described as " the break-up " of China than by the term " development."

Not until then shall we realize the full risks and folly of the most stupendous revolutionary enterprise history has known. The Western nations may then awaken to the fact that they have permitted certain little cliques of private profit-mongers to engage them in a piece of Imperialism in which every cost and peril of that hazardous policy is multiplied a hundred-fold, and from which there appears no possibility of safe withdrawal. The light-hearted, casual mood in which the nations have been drawn on to the opening up of a country with a population almost

as large as that of Europe, nineteen-twentieths of whom
are perfectly unknown to us, is the crowning instance of
irrational government. In large measure such an enterprise must rank as a plunge in the dark. Few Europeans
even profess to know the Chinese, or to know how far the
Chinese they do know are representative of the nation as
a whole. The only important fact upon which there is
universal agreement is that the Chinese are of all the
" lower races " most adaptable to purposes of industrial
exploitation, yielding the largest surplus product of labour
in proportion to their cost of keep. In a word the investors
and business managers of the West appear to have struck
in China a mine of labour power richer by far than any of
the gold and other mineral deposits which have directed
imperial enterprise in Africa and elsewhere ; it seems so
enormous and so expansible as to open up the possibility
od raising whole white populations of the West to the
position of " independent gentlemen," living, as do the small
white settlements in India or South Africa, upon the
manual toil of these laborious inferiors. For a parasitic
exploit so gigantic the competing groups of business men
who are driving on their respective Governments might
even abate their competition and co-operate in the forceful
steps required in starting their project. Once encompass
China with a network of railroads and steamer services,
the size of the labour market to be tapped is so stupendous
that it might well absorb in its development all the spare
capital and business energy the advanced European countries
and the United States can supply for generations. Such
an experiment may revolutionize the methods of Imperialism ; the pressure of working-class movements in politics
and industry in the West can be met by a flood of China
goods, so as to keep down wages and compel industry, or,
where the power of the imperialist oligarchy is well set,

by menaces of yellow workmen or of yellow mercenary troops, while collaboration in this huge Eastern development may involve an understanding between the groups of business politicians in the Western States close enough and strong enough to secure international peace in Europe and some relaxation of militarism.

This would drive the logic of Imperialism far towards realization ; its inherent necessary tendencies towards unchecked oligarchy in politics, and parasitism in industry, would be plainly exhibited in the condition of the " imperialist " nations. The greater part of Western Europe might then assume the appearance and character already exhibited by tracts of country in the South of England, in the Riviera, and in the tourist-ridden or residential parts of Italy and Switzerland, little clusters of wealthy aristocrats drawing dividends and pensions from the Far East, with a somewhat larger group of professional retainers and tradesmen and a large body of personal servants and workers in the transport trade and in the final stages of production of the more perishable goods : all the main arterial industries would have disappeared, the staple foods and manufactures flowing in as tribute from Asia and Africa.[1] It is, of course, idle to suppose that the industrialization of China by Western methods can be achieved without effective political control, and just in proportion as Western Europe became dependent economically upon China would the maintenance of that joint imperial control react upon Western politics, subordinating all movements of domestic reform to the need of maintaining the Empires, and check-

---

[1] Mr. Bryce, in his Romanes Lecture, p. 9, seems to hint at the probability of such a development. " It is hardly too much to say that for economic purposes all mankind is fast becoming one people, in which the hitherto backward nations are taking a place analogous to that which the unskilled workers have held in each one of the civilized nations. Such an event opens a new stage in world history."

mating the forces of democracy by a skilful use of a highly centralized bureaucracy and army.

How far the advent of Japan into the status of a first rank political and industrial power will affect the problem of Imperialism in Asia is a question which presses ever more vigorously upon the consideration of Western nations. It is, however, impossible to deny that the recent manifestation of Japan as an Eastern nation equipped with all the effective practical arts of Western civilization is likely to alter profoundly the course of Asiatic history in the near future.

Regarding as the most important issue the economic development of China upon Western lines, we cannot fail to see that Japan has great advantages over Western powers for doing this work and securing the profits which it will yield. These advantages are partly derived from certain energies of mind which the Japanese exhibit, partly from the geographical and racial factors in the situation. Summarizing the acknowledged facts, the Japanese, as a people, seem to have assimilated within two generations all those mechanical and political sciences of the West which contribute to the military, commercial and social strength of a nation, while they can operate these instruments of civilization quite as accurately and more economically from the standpoint of the common good than any of the nations which have been their teachers. If this is " imitation " it is thoroughly intelligent imitation, for it is admitted that the Japanese have exercised fine judgment in selecting the weapons, machines, laws and customs which they have adopted, and that they work their political, social and economic institutions easily and efficiently. The wonderful success of Japan appears to be in large measure due to two inner sources of economy. In the first place they appear to be able to give out a great quantity of mental energy in the complex operations of modern life without sustaining the amount of nervous waste perceptible in Western peoples : they appear to do more easily a larger quantity of cerebral work. Secondly, a more widely diffused, a more intense and a more sustained public spirit appears to produce a better co-operation of individual activities for the common good than is found in any Western people : there is less waste from indolence, corruption and other diseases of officialism, while a high consideration of public service pervades the popular mind. This intense patriotism and self-sacrifice may be only a psychical survival from an old social order which is passing away, but so long as it endures, it supplies a great operative force for further activity.

The proximity of Japan to North China, the associations of race, language, religion, literature, modes of life must give Japan an immense advantage over any European race in the economic development of China. If, as seems likely, the peace following the Russo-Japanese war opens an era of rapid commercial expansion for Japan, and capitalism advances swiftly within her islands, China will be the natural outlet for the investment of her capital and for the employment of her organizing energy in business and in the public services. Whether Japan will be dominated by the same spirit of territorial aggrandisement and political empire as European nations have exhibited depends in large measure upon the part played by the latter in the opening up of China. If the Western powers keep their political and military hands off China, content to encourage private companies to build railways, start mining and manufacturing operations and open up commercial inter-course with the interior, keeping the policy of " an open door," Japan will play this same game, but more successfully because of the better cards she holds, and the prestige of her successful war will stand her in good stead. If, on the other hand, there is closing of doors, ear-marking, and further political absorption of chosen areas by the Western powers, Japan will be driven to enter this sort of competition, and with her better understanding of the conditions of success, and her superior faculty for managing the Chinese, is likely to get the better of her European and American competitors.

Should European nations resent the growing industrial or perhaps political, supremacy of Japan in China and adopt some concerted action to defend their " spheres of influence " or their extorted " concessions," it is not wholly improbable that Japan may organize a great military and naval power in which she will utilize the latent force of China to drive the Western nations out of the China seas.

Such an opportunity for playing a great new part in imperial history may be open to Japan : if so, her temporary alliances with European powers are not likely to divert her from a course which will seem to her people as plain an instance of " manifest destiny " as any of the exploits of imperialism in the annals of England or the United States.

In speculating on the chances of this new chapter of world-history, a great deal depends upon how far Japan maintains her financial independence and is enabled to avoid becoming a catspaw of cosmopolitan capitalism in the great work of developing China. Should the future industrialization of Japan and China be conducted in the main out of their own resources of capital and organizing skill, passing quickly through a short period of dependence upon Europe for capital and instruction, the great industrial power of the Far East may quickly launch itself upon the world-market as the biggest and most effective competitor in the great machine industries, taking to itself first the trade of Asia and the Pacific, and then swamping the markets of the West and driving these nations to a still more rigorous Protection with its corollary of diminished production. Lastly, it is conceivable that the powerful industrial and financial classes of the West, in order better to keep the economic and political mastery at home, may combine to reverse the policy which has hitherto been gaining ground in the United States and in our white colonies, and may insist upon the free importation of yellow labour for domestic and industrial service in the West. This is a weapon which they hold in reserve, should they need to use it in order to keep the populace in safe subjection.

Those who regard with complacency the rapid development of China, because of a general conviction that the liberation of these great productive forces must by ordinary processes of commercial intercourse be beneficial to the Western nations, entirely miss the issue. The peaceful, equitable distribution over the industrial world of the increase of world-wealth rising from the development of China implies a successful movement of industrial democracy in the Western nations, yielding not merely increased productivity of their national resources, but a continual rise in standard of consumption of the peoples. Such a condition might, by securing ordinary processes of world-exchange, enrich the nations with a legitimate share of the prosperity of China. But the economic *raison d'être* of Imperialism in the opening up of China is, as we see, quite other than the maintenance of ordinary commerce : it consists in establishing a vast new market for Western investors, the profits of which will represent the gains of an investing class and not the gains of whole peoples. The normal healthy processes of assimilation of increased world-wealth by nations are inhibited by the nature of this Imperialism, whose essence consists in developing markets for investment, not for trade, and in using the superior economies of cheap foreign production to supersede the industries of their own nation, and to maintain the political and economic domination of a class.

V

So far the influence of the " opening " or " break-up " of China upon the Western world has been the subject of inquiry. Let us now ask what this " break-up " means for China. Certain plain features stand out in the structure of Chinese society. China has never been a great Empire, or had any strong national existence in the European sense. The central government has always been very slight, virtually confined to a taxing power exercised through the provincial government, and to a small power of appointment of high officials. Even the provincial government has, in ordinary times, touched the actual life of the mass of the people lightly and at few points. China may be described properly as a huge nest of little free village communes, self-governing, and animated by a genuine spirit of equality. Mr. Colquhoun names the faculty of local self-government as " a main source of national vitality." " Groups of families constitute villages, which are self-governing, and the official who ventures to trench on their immemorial rights to the point of resistance is, according to an official code not confined to China, disavowed by his superiors, and generally finds a change of scene imperative. " The family system, with its extension to village and town groups, is the cheapest form of government extant, for it dispenses with police, while disposing effectually of offenders against the peace or respectability of the community."[1] Similarly the great German explorer Richthofen : " No people in the world are more exempt from official interference."

" The great fact," says Colquhoun, " to be noted as between the Chinese and the Government is the almost

[1] *Transformation in China*, by A. R. Colquhoun, p. 176.

unexampled liberty which the people enjoy, and the infinitesimally small part which Government plays in the scheme of national life."[1]

The family is the political, economic, and moral unit of society, the village commune being either a direct enlargement of a single family or a group of closely related families. Sometimes communal ownership is maintained, but usually a division takes place with each growth of family, and the operative principle in general vogue is an occupying ownership of small proprietors, paying a low land-tax to the State, the sole landlord, in return for a lease in perpetuity. The land-tax is based on profitable use, and unoccupied lands revert to the community. Patrimonial institutions prevent accumulation of large properties. Numerous provisions of law and custom provide against land-grabbing and monopoly. "Nowhere in China would it be possible for a rich man to take possession of a spring and convey its water to his pond by subterranean drains, leaving dry the fields under which it passed. Water is as indispensable to life as air and land. No individual has the right to say ' It is mine, it belongs to me.' This feeling is very strongly rooted in China."[2]

A family council, partly elective, partly hereditary, settles most important issues, punishing crimes, collecting the taxes, and settling divisions of property; recourse to legal processes is rare, the moral authority of the family commonly sufficing to preserve order.

This moral factor is, indeed, the one great vital principle in Chinese life. It not only governs economic relations, and presents a substitute for wider politics, but it figures prominently in the education and the religious or ethical system of the people. " Life seems so little worth living to a man outlawed from family and home that even capital

[1] *Transformation in China*, by A. R. Colquhoun, p. 296.   [2] Colquhoun.

sentences are executed by consent " ;[1] and where growth of population drives male members to seek employment in the towns, the closest family associations are retained. The reverence for family history and for the moral obligations it entails constitutes the kernel of national culture and the great stimulus to individual education and ambition in life.

Upon this basis is built one of the most extraordinary civilizations the world has known, differing in certain very vital matters from the civilization of the West.

Two points merit particular attention, because they drive down into the roots of Chinese civilization. The first is the general recognition of that " dignity of labour " which in the West has degenerated into a cant phrase so far as the common forms of work are concerned. Manual labour is not only a necessary means of livelihood, but a genuinely absorbing personal interest for the entire body of the nation ; with simple tools, and scarcely any use of machinery, minute personal skill is applied to agriculture and the manufactures ; most workers have some considerable variety of occupation, and see and enjoy the useful results of their toil. The whole economic system stands on a broad basis of " bread labour," applied in intensive cultivation of the land ; destitute of Western science or Western machinery, the detailed empirical study of agriculture has been carried farther than in any other country, and this " gardening " life is the most prominent factor in the external civilization of the country.

The second point is the wide diffusion of some sort of literary education and a genuine reverence for " things of the mind." The high respect in which a narrow conservative and pedantic literary system is held, the extraordinary importance attached to verbal memory and trivialities of ritual in their culture, have not unnaturally aroused much

[1] Simcox, *Primitive Civilizations*, vol. II.

astonishment and some contempt among educated Westerns. But the general prevalence of schools and libraries, the democratization of the machinery of education, the opening of the highest offices of State to a free competition of the people, conducted on an intellectual test, are indicative of a standard of valuation which entitles China to rank high among the civilizations of the world. In no Western nation do the man of learning and the gardener rank higher in the common regard of the people than the soldier. These valuations, economic and intellectual, lie firmly rooted in the Chinese mind, and have helped through countless generations to mould the social institutions of the people. The civilization, sprung up under these conditions, manifests some serious defects, compared with the best standards of the West. Life and conduct seem unduly cramped by detailed conventions; outside officialism there seems little scope for individual distinction; beyond the range of family, emotional life appears attenuated; the fine arts have never flourished, literature is conventional, morals are closely practical; the rigorous economy of material life seems attended by a less sensitive, nervous organization than that of any Western nation, and individual life seems to run upon a somewhat lower level of consciousness, and to be valued proportionately less.

But it should be recognized that the merits of this civilization are better attested than the defects, for the fruits of Chinese industry, honesty, orderly behaviour, and high regard for learning, are easily discernible by foreigners, while the more serious defects might vanish or be deeply modified by a more intimate understanding of Chinese psychology than any foreigner is likely to possess. The " barbarities " which have commonly won for China an ill-fame in Western lands, the savage punishments inflicted on criminals, the exposure of female infants, the brutal assaults on foreigners, are no normal part of the conduct of the nation, but rather sporadic survivals of brute habits and instincts, not more to be regarded as final tests of the civilization of China than negro-lynching of that of America or wife-kicking of that of England.

If this brief conspectus of the essential features of Chinese civilization is substantially correct, it is evident that " the break-up " brought about by the forces of Western nations will destroy the very foundations of the national order.

Its first fruits have been to impair security of life, peaceful industry and property over large areas of territory, to arouse a disorderly spirit of guerilla, to erect large public debts and so to enhance the burden of central government upon the body of the people, diminishing their communal independence. As the Western economic forces make further way, they must, partly by increased taxation needed for an expensive central government with armies, elaborate civil services and military debts, partly by the temptation of labour agents, draw large numbers of the workers from the position of independent little farmers into that of town wage-earners. This drain of population into industrial cities and mining districts, and the specialization of agriculture for large markets, will break up the communal land system with its fixed hereditary order and will sap the roots of family solidarity, introducing those factors of fluidity, minute subdivision, and concentration of labour which are the distinctive characteristics of Western industry. The economic and social equality which belongs to ordinary Chinese life will disappear before a new system of industrial caste which capitalism will entail. The decay of morals, which is so noticeable in the *declassés* Chinese, will spread with the decay of the family power, and an elaborate judicial and punitory machinery will replace the rule of the self-governing family. This collapse of local status will

X

react upon the habit of commercial integrity attested throughout China by the inviolability of business pledges; the new credit system of elaborate Western commerce will involve a network of commercial law and an education in that habit of litigiousness which exercises so dangerous a fascination over some other Asiatic peoples. The increase of wealth which this new industrialism would bring would either flow in economic tribute to the West, or would go to the endowment of a new powerful capitalist caste in China itself, who, following the Western lines, would ally themselves with imperialist politics in order to protect their vested interests. Capitalism, centralized government, militarism, protection, and a whole chain of public regulations to preserve the new order against the rising of old conservative traditional forces—such would be the inevitable outcome. The changes of external environment which have come with dangerous rapidity on Europe during the nineteenth century, forced still more rapidly on China by foreign profit-seekers, would produce reactions of incalculable peril upon the national life and character.

It would seem to imply no less than the destruction of the existing civilization of China and the substitution in its place of what? There has been no serious pretence that European nations can impose or inculcate the essentials of their civilization on China. The psychology of the Chinese is a *terra incognita*: the most experienced European residents are those who are the frankest in declaring their inability to grapple with the mysteries of Chinese character and Chinese morality; where less discreet writers venture on generalizations, their pages are riddled with the wildest contradictions and inconsistencies. What is, however, pretty clear is this: the Chinaman who detaches himself from the family bond and its moral associations and adopts European manners is distrusted alike by his fellow-countrymen and by his new patrons; Christianity makes no way among "respectable" Chinese, the educated classes presenting no ground of appeal for any form of supernaturalism; though Western science may hope in time to make a legitimate impression upon the intellectual life of China, the process will be one of slow absorption from within and cannot be imposed by alien instruction from without.

That the squabbles of European potentates for territorial expansion, the lusts of merchants or financiers, the ludicrously false expectations of missionaries, the catchwords of political parties in European elections, should be driving European nations to destroy the civilization of a quarter of the human race without possessing the ability or even recognizing the need to provide a substitute, ought surely to give pause to those Imperialists who claim to base their policy on reason and the common good.

No thinking man can seriously question the immense importance of free intercourse between the West and the East, or doubt the gain that would accrue to the civilization of the world by a wise communication to the Eastern mind of those arts which peculiarly represent Western civilization, the laborious, successful study of the physical sciences and their application to the arts of industry, the systematic development of certain definite principles and practices of law and government, and the thought and literature which are the conscious flowering of this growth of practical achievement.

That Europe could in this way render an invaluable service to Asia is certain.

"Some strange fiat of arrest, probably due to mental exhaustion, has condemned the brown men and the yellow men to eternal reproduction of old ideas."[1] To revivify the mind of Asia, to set it working again along new lines of rich

[1] *Asia and Europe*, p. 9.

325

productivity, this might be the boon of Europe. And for this service she too might take a rich reward. The brooding mind of Asia gave to sluggish Europe in past ages the great momenta in religion and philosophy and in the mathematics; even in its sleep, or what appears to us the sleep of many centuries, it may have had its noble and illuminative dreams. The reason of the West may yet need the insight of the East. A union so profitable in the past may not be barren for the future. It is the right condition of this wholesome intercourse which is of supreme importance to the cause of civilization. Now one thing at least is certain. Force and the pushful hand of material greed inhibit the free interaction of mind and mind essential to this intercourse. The ancient civilizations of India and China, whose duration bears testimony to inherent qualities of worth, have not been directed chiefly to the attainment of progress in the arts of material wealth, though the simpler industries have in parts of China and India attained a high perfection, but rather to the maintenance of certain small types of orderly social life, with a strong hierarchy of social and industrial ranks in India, with a fundamentally democratic character in China.

The energy spared from political and industrial struggles, and in China from military practises, has gone, partly to the cultivation of certain simple qualities of domestic life and personal conduct, partly to the wide diffusion of a certain real life of the soul, animated by profound religious and philosophic speculations and contemplations in India, or by the elaboration of a more practical, utilitarian wisdom in China. These Eastern civilizations alone have stood the test of time; the qualities which have enabled them to survive ought surely to be matter of deep concern for the mushroom civilizations of the West. It may even be true that the maintenance of these younger and more unstable civilizations depends upon unlocking the treasure-house of the wisdom of the East. Whether this be so or not, the violent breaking down of the characteristic institutions of Asia to satisfy some hasty lust of commerce, or some greed of power, is quite the most fatally blind misreading of the true process of world-civilization that it is possible to conceive. For Europe to rule Asia by force for purposes of gain, and to justify that rule by the pretence that she is civilizing Asia and raising her to a higher level of spiritual life, will be adjudged by history, perhaps, to be the crowning wrong and folly of Imperialism. What Asia has to give, her priceless stores of wisdom garnered from her experience of ages, we refuse to take ; the much or little which we could give we spoil by the brutal manner of our giving. This is what Imperialism has done, and is doing, for Asia.

CHAPTER VI

IMPERIAL FEDERATION

I

THE imperial policy of Great Britain after 1870, and more particularly after 1885, was almost entirely absorbed in promoting the subjugation and annexation of tracts of territory where no genuine white settlement of any magnitude was contemplated. This policy, as we have seen, differs essentially from colonization ; and from the standpoint of government it implies a progressive diminution of freedom in the British Empire by constantly increasing the proportion of its subjects who are destitute of real power of self-government.

It is important to consider how this new Imperialism reacts, and is likely in the future to react, upon the relations between Great Britain and her self-governing colonies. Will it stimulate these colonies to an assertion of growing independence and final formal severance from the mother country, or will it lead them to form a closer political union with her upon a basis, no longer of Empire, but of a Federation of equal States ? This is a vital issue, for it is quite certain that the present[1] relations will not be maintained.

Hitherto the tendency has been towards a steady consistent increase of self-government, and a growing relaxation of Empire in the shape of control exercised by the

[1] 1903.

home Government. In Australasia, North America, and South Africa seventeen self-governing colonies have been established, endowed with reduced types of the British constitution. In the case of Australia and of Canada the growth of self-government has been formally and actually advanced by acts of federation, which have, in fact, especially in Australia, compensated the restriction of the power of the federated States by a more than equivalent increase of governing power vested in the federal Government.

Great Britain has in the main learned well the lesson of the American Revolution ; she has not only permitted but favoured this growing independence of her Australian and American colonies. During the very period when she has been occupied in the conscious policy of extending her Empire over lands which she cannot colonize and must hold by force, she has been loosening her " imperial " hold over her white colonies. While 1873 removed the last bond of economic control which marked the old " plantation " policy, by repealing the Act of 1850 which had forbidden Australian colonies from imposing differential duties as between the colonies and foreign countries, and permitting them in future to tax one another's goods, the Australian Commonwealth Act of 1900 has, by the powers accorded to its Federal Judicature, reduced to the narrowest limits yet attained the constitutional control of the Privy Council, and has by the powers enabling the Federal Government to raise a central armed force for defence obtained a new substantial basis for a possible national independence in the future. Though it is unlikely for some time to come that the federal Government which is contemplated for British South Africa will be accorded powers equivalent to those of the Australian or even the Canadian Federations, the same tendency to increase self-government has in the past steadily prevailed in Cape Colony and Natal, and it is tolerably certain that, if the racial animosities between the two white races are abated, a South African Commonwealth would soon be found in possession of a far larger measure of real self-government than the British colonies which enter it have hitherto possessed.[1]

But while the trend of British colonialism has uniformly been towards increased self-government or practical independence, and has been appreciably strengthened by the process of federating colonial States, it is evident that the imperial statesmen who have favoured most this federation policy have had in view some larger recasting of the political relations with the mother country, which should bind parent and children in closer family bonds, not merely of affection or of trading intercourse, but of political association. Though imperial federation for British purposes is no modern invention, Lord Carnarvon was the first Colonial Secretary to set it before him as a distinct object of attainment, favouring federation in the various groups of colonies as the first step in a process which should federate the Empire. The successful completion in 1873 of the process of federation which formed the Dominion of Canada doubtless stimulated Lord Carnarvon, entering office the next year, to further experiments along similar lines. Unfortunately he laid hands upon South Africa for his forcing process, and suffered a disastrous failure. Twenty years later Mr. Chamberlain resumed the task, and, confronted by the same essential difficulties, the forcible annexation of the two Dutch Republics, and the coercion of Cape Colony, carried his federation policy in South Africa on the road towards completion, while the establishment of the Australian Commonwealth marks another and a safer triumph of the federation principle.

[1] This relates to the situation in 1903.

The process of federation, as bearing on the relations of the federating colonies, is of course a triumph for the centripetal forces ; but, by securing a larger measure of theoretical and practical independence for the federal Governments, it has been centrifugal from the standpoint of the Imperial Government. The work of securing an effective political imperial federation implies, therefore, a reversal of hitherto dominant tendencies.

It is quite evident that a strong and increasing desire for imperial federation was growing among a large number of British politicians. So far as Mr. Chamberlain and some of his friends were concerned, it dates back to the beginning of the struggle over Mr. Gladstone's Home Rule for Ireland policy. Speaking on Mr. Gladstone's Home Rule Bill in 1886, Mr. Chamberlain said : " I should look for the solution in the direction of the principle of federation. My right honourable friend has looked for his model to the relations between this country and her self-governing and practically independent colonies. I think that is of doubtful expediency. The present connexion between our colonies and ourselves is no doubt very strong, owing to the affection which exists between members of the same nation. But it is a sentimental tie, and a senti-mental tie only. . . . It appears to me that the advantage of a system of federation is that Ireland might under it really remain an integral part of the Empire. The action of such a scheme is centripetal and not centri-fugal, and it is in the direction of federation that the democratic movement has made most advances in the present century."

Now, it is quite true that the democratic movement, both now and in the future, seems closely linked with the formation of federal States, and the federation of the parts of the British Empire appears to suggest, as a next step and logical outcome, the federation of the whole.

Holding, as we must, that any reasonable security for good order and civilization in the world implies the growing application of the federation principle in international politics, it will appear only natural that the earlier steps in such a process should take the form of unions of States most closely related by ties of common blood, language, and institutions, and that a phase of federated Britain or Anglo-Saxondom, Pan-Teutonism, Pan-Slavism, and Pan-Latinism might supervene upon the phase already reached. There is perhaps a suspicion of excessive logic in such an order of events, but a broad general view of history renders it plausible and desirable enough. Christendom thus laid out in a few great federal Empires, each with a retinue of uncivilized dependencies, seems to many the most legitimate development of present tendencies and one which would offer the best hope of permanent peace on an assured basis of inter-Imperialism. Dismissing from our mind the largest aspect of this issue, as too distant for present profitable argument, and confining our attention to British imperial federation, we may easily agree that a voluntary federation of free British States, working peacefully for the common safety and prosperity, is in itself eminently desirable, and might indeed form a step towards a wider federation of civilized States in the future.

The real issue for discussion is the feasibility of such a policy, and, rightly stated, the question runs thus : " What forces of present or prospective self-interest are operative to induce Great Britain and her colonial groups to reverse the centrifugal process which has hitherto been dominant ? " Now, there are many reasons for Great Britain to desire political federation with her self-governing colonies, even upon terms which would give them a voice proportionate to their population in a Parliament or other council charged

with the control of imperial affairs, provided the grace
difficulties involved in the establishment of such a representative, responsible, governing body could be overcome.
The preponderance of British over colonial population
would enable the mother country to enforce her will where
any conflict of interest or judgment arose in which there
was a sharp line of division between Great Britain and the
colonies : the distribution of imperial burdens and the
allocation of imperial assistance would be determined by
Great Britain. If the Crown colonies and other non-self-
governing parts of the Empire were represented in the
imperial council, the actual supremacy of the mother
country would be greater still, for these representatives,
either nominated by the Crown (the course most consonant
with Crown colony government), or elected on a narrow
franchise of a small white oligarchy, would have little in
common with the representatives of self-governing colonies,
and would inevitably be more amenable to pressure from
the home Government. A chief avowed object of imperial
federation is to secure from the colonies a fair share of
men, ships, and money for imperial defence, and for
those expansive exploits which in their initiation almost
always rank as measures of defence. The financial basis
of imperial defence in 1903 is one which, on the face of
it, seems most unfair ; Great Britain is called upon to
support virtually the whole cost of the imperial navy,
and, with India, almost the whole cost of the imperial
army, though both these arms are at the service of any
of our self-governing colonies that is threatened by external
enemies or internal disorders. In 1899, while the population of these colonies was close upon one-third of that of
the United Kingdom, their revenue nearly one-half, and the
value of their sea-borne commerce one-fifth of the entire
commerce of the Empire, the contribution they were

making to the cost of the naval defence of the Empire was less than one-hundredth part.[1] These colonies raised in 1903 no regular or irregular military force available for the general defence of the Empire, though they have supported small contingents of imperial troops quartered upon them by the Imperial Government, and have maintained considerable militia and volunteer forces for home defence. The colonial contingents taking part in the South African war, though forming a considerable volunteer force, fell far short of an imperial levy based upon proportion of population, and their expenses were almost entirely borne by the United Kingdom. From the standpoint of the unity of the British Empire, in which the colonies are presumed to have an interest equivalent to that of the United Kingdom, it seems reasonable that the latter should be called upon to bear their fair share of the burden of imperial defence ; and an imperial federation which was a political reality would certainly imply a provision for such equal contribution. Whatever were the form such federation took, that of an Imperial Parliament, endowed with full responsibility for imperial affairs under the Crown, or of an Imperial Council, on which colonial representatives must sit to consult with and advise the British ministry, who still retained the formal determination of imperial policy, it would certainly imply a compulsory or quasi-compulsory contribution on the part of the colonies proportionate to that of the United Kingdom.

[1] 1899.	Population.	Revenue.	Trade.	Naval Contribution.
United Kingdom } Self-govern-ing Colonies }	39,000,000 12,000,000	£104,000,000 46,000,000	£766,000,000 222,000,000	£24,734,000 177,000

Now it is quite evident that the self-governing colonies will not enter such an association, involving them in large new expenses, out of sentimental regard for the British Empire. The genuineness and the warmness of the attachment to the British Empire and to the mother country are indisputable, and though they were not called upon to make any considerable self-sacrifice in the South African campaign, it is quite evident that their sentiments are such as would lead them voluntarily to expend both blood and money where they thought the existence, the safety, or even the honour of the Empire was at stake. But it would be a grave error to suppose that the blaze of enthusiastic loyalty evinced at such a period of emergency can be utilized in order to reverse the general tendency towards independence, and to " rush " the self-governing colonies into a closer formal union with Great Britain, involving a regular continuous sacrifice. If the colonies are induced to enter any such association, they must be convinced that it is essential to their individual security and prosperity. In 1903 they get the protection of the Empire with out paying for it ; as long as they think they can get adequate protection on such terms it is impossible to suppose they would enter an arrangement which required them to pay, and which involved an entire recasting of their system of revenue. The temper of discussions in the Australian and Canadian Parliaments, amid all the enthusiasm of the South African war, makes it quite clear that no colonial ministry could in time of peace persuade the colonists to enter such a federation as is here outlined unless they had been educated to the conviction that their individual colonial welfare was to be subserved. Either Australia and Canada must be convinced that imperial defence of Australia or Canada upon the present[1] basis is becoming more inadequate,

[1] 1903.

335

and that such defence is essential to them, or else they must be compensated for the additional expense which federation would involve by new commercial relations with the United Kingdom which will give them a more profitable market than they possess already.

Now the refusal of the self-governing colonies hitherto to consider any other contribution to imperial defence than a small voluntary one has been based upon a conviction that the virtual independence they hold under Great Britain is not likely to be threatened by any great Power, and that, even were it threatened, though their commerce might suffer on the sea, they would be competent to prevent or repel invasion by their own internal powers of self-defence. The one exception to this calculation may be said to prove the rule. If Canada were embroiled in war with her great republican neighbour, she is well aware that though the British navy might damage the trade and the coast towns of the United States, she could not prevent Canada from being over-run by American troops, and ultimately from being subjugated.

But, it may at least be urged, the importance of maintaining a British navy adequate to protect their trade will at least be recognized; the colonies will perceive that in face of the rising wealth and naval preparations of rival Empires, in particular Germany, France, and the United States, the United Kingdom cannot bear the financial strain of the necessary increase of ships without substantial colonial assistance. This is doubtless the line of strongest pressure for imperial federation. How far is it likely to prove effective? It is certain to educate colonial politicians to a closer consideration of the future of their colony; it will force them to canvass most carefully the net advantages or disadvantages of the imperial connexion. Such consideration seems at least as likely to lead them towards that definite future severance from Great Britain which, until now, in 1903, none of them has seriously contemplated, as it is to bring them into a federation. This consummation, if it ultimately comes about, will arise from no abatement of natural good feeling and affection towards the United Kingdom, but simply from a conflict of interests.

If the movement towards imperial federation fails, and the recent drift towards independence on the part of the self-governing colonies is replaced by a more conscious movement in the same direction, the cause will be Imperialism. A discreet colonial statesman, when invited to bring his colony closer to Great Britain, and to pay for their common support while leaving to Great Britain the virtual determination of their common destiny, is likely to put the following pertinent questions : Why is Great Britain obliged to increase her expenditure in armaments faster than the growth of trade or income, so that she is forced to call upon us to assist ? Is it because she fears the jealousy and the hostility of other Powers ? Why does she arouse these ill feelings ? To these questions he can hardly fail to find an answer ? " It is the new Imperialism that is wholly responsible for the new perils of the Empire, and for the new costs of armaments." He is then likely to base upon this answer further questions. Do we self-governing colonies benefit by this new Imperialism ? If we decide that we do not, can we stop it by entering a federation in which our voices will be the voices of a small minority ? May it not be a safer policy for us to seek severance from a Power which so visibly antagonizes other Powers, and may involve us in conflict with them on matters in which we have no vital interest and no determinant voice, and either to live an independent political life, incurring only those risks which belong to us, or (in the case of Canada) to seek admission within the powerful republic of the United States ?

However colonial history may answer these questions, it is inevitable that they will be put. Imperialism is evidently the most serious obstacle to " imperial federation," so far as the self-governing colonies are concerned. Were it not for the presence of these unfree British possessions and for the expansive policy which has continually increased them, a federation of free British States throughout the world would seem a reasonable and a most desirable step in the interests of world-civilization. But how can the white democracies of Australasia and North America desire to enter such a hodge-podge of contradictory systems as would be presented by an imperial federation, which might, according to one authority,[1] be compiled in the following fashion : first a union of Great Britain, Ireland, Canada, West Indies, Australia, Tasmania, New Zealand, Newfoundland, Mauritius, South Africa, Malta, to be followed later by the admission of Cyprus, Ceylon, India, Hong-Kong, and Malaysia, with an accompaniment of semi-independent States such as Egypt, Afghanistan, Natal, Bhutan, Jehore, and perhaps the kingdoms of Uganda and of Barotse, each with some sort of representation on an Imperial Council and some voice in the determination of the imperial destiny ?

Is it likely that the great rising Australian Commonwealth or the Dominion of Canada will care to place her peaceful development and her financial resources at the mercy of some Soudanese forward movement or a pushful policy in West Africa ?

An imperial federation comprising all sorts and conditions of British States, colonies, protectorates, veiled protectorates and nondescripts would be too unwieldy, and too prolific of frontier questions and of other hazards,

[1] Sir H. H. Johnston, *Nineteenth Century*, May 1902.

to please our more isolated and self-centred free colonies;
while, if these former were left without formal representation
as special protégés of the United Kingdom, their existence
and their growth would none the less hang like a mill-stone
round the neck of the federal Government, constantly
compelling the United Kingdom to strain the allegiance
of her confederates by using her technical superiority of
voting power in what she held to be their special interest
and hers.

The notion that the absence of any real strong identity
of interest between the self-governing colonies and the
more remote and more hazardous fringes of the Empire
can be compensated by some general spirit of loyalty
towards and pride in " the Empire " is a delusion which
will speedily be dispelled. The detached colonies of
Australasia may not unreasonably argue that the very
anxiety of British statesmen to draw them into federation
is a confession of the weakening of that very protection
which constitutes for them the chief value of the present
connexion. " The United Kingdom," they may say,
" asks us to supply men and ships and money in a binding
engagement in order to support her in carrying farther
the very imperialist policy which arouses the animosity
of rival Powers and which disables her for future reliance
on her own resources to sustain the Empire. For our
increased contribution to the imperial resources we shall
therefore receive in return an increase of peril. Is it not
something like asking us, out of pure chivalry, to throw
in our lot with a sinking vessel ? " It will doubtless be
replied that a firmly federated Empire will prove such a
tower of strength as will enable her to defy the increased
jealousy of rival Powers. But this tempting proposition
will be submitted to cool calculation in our colonies, which
will certainly refuse to be " rushed " into a change of

policy implying a reversal of the general tendency of half a century. Admitting the obvious political and military gain of co-operative action in the face of an enemy, the colonists will ask whether this gain is not offset by an increased likelihood of having to face enemies, and when they reflect that they are really invited to federate, not merely with the England whom they love and admire, but with an ever-growing medley of savage States, the balance of judgment seems likely to turn against federation, unless other special inducements can be applied.

II

There are two special inducements which might bring the self-governing colonies, or some of them, to favour a closer political union with Great Britain. The first is a revision of the commercial and financial policy of the mother country, so as to secure for the colonies an increased market for their produce in Great Britain and in other parts of the British Empire. In discussion of this issue it is customary to begin by distinguishing the proposal to establish an Imperial Zollverein, or Customs Union, from the proposal for a preferential tariff. But very little reflection suffices to perceive the futility of the former without the latter as an appeal to the self-interest of the colonies. Will these colonies assimilate their financial policy to that of Great Britain, abolishing their protective tariffs and entering a full Free Trade career ? The most sanguine Free Trader suggests no such possibility, nor indeed would such a course afford any real guarantee of increasing the commercial inter-dependence of the Empire. It would simply force the colonies upon processes of direct taxation repugnant to their feelings. Is Free Trade within the

Empire, with a maintenance of the *status quo* as regards foreign countries, really more feasible ? It would simply mean that the colonies gave up the income they obtained from taxing the goods of one another and of Great Britain, each getting in return a remission of tariffs from the other colonies with which its trade is small and no remission from Great Britain, which would continue to receive its goods free as before.

It is now admitted that the colonies will not, and indeed cannot remit or greatly reduce their taxes upon imported goods from Great Britain and from one another. They are prepared to give British goods a preferential treatment upon two conditions : first, that such preference does not involve any net reduction of their income from customs ; secondly, that it does not make British goods to compete more effectively with their own manufactures. A preferential tariff constructed under these conditions implies that any net reductions of the duty upon classes of British imports must be compensated by a general rise of the tariff in regard to other imports, and that where British imports compete with colonial products there can be no reduction of the duty, but only an increased tax in foreign as compared with British goods.

If it does not cost anything to the exchequer of the Dominion and the Commonwealth, or considerably raise prices to colonial consumers, Canada and Australia are willing to oust foreign goods in favour of British, but the tendency will be to do this by raising the duty against foreigners, and not by lowering it against Great Britain. Moreover, the nature of British imports into these countries (i.e. highly manufactured goods) generally involves some amount of competition with home products, so that any actual reduction of duty is inconsistent with protection of home industries. Thus the principles of Canadian protection oblige her to maintain a higher average duty upon British goods than upon American and other foreign goods, many of which are raw materials or semi-manufactured goods which do not compete appreciably with Canadian products. Thus, though the preferences given by Canada to the mother country in 1897 and 1900 have checked the rapid decline in the growth of British as compared with foreign imports into Canada, they have not prevented foreign trade from increasing at a slightly faster pace than British, while the importation (largely of free raw materials) from the United States continues to grow faster than the importation from Great Britain. Moreover, the powerful organized opposition of Canadian manufacturers against favoured British competition is a factor of increasing importance now that Canada is putting more of her own and American capital into manufacturing industry. The tendency will be more and more towards an encouragement of Canadian manufactures by higher duties upon imports, so that a show of British preference can only be maintained by a general raising of duties on imported manufactures. What holds of Canada holds also of Australia. Both nations look forward to a great manufacturing future which will give them that self-sufficing character which is the protectionist ideal; more and more will their desire to favour the mother country conflict with their higher sense of duty towards their own manufactures. The notion that they will abstain from setting up any manufacture which they can successfully establish out of consideration for the English manufacturers who have hitherto supplied these goods is puerile. These being the conditions, such preferences as they give to British imports must be slight and temporary.

To purchase this small boon, Great Britain must give in return preferential treatment involving, first, a reversal of our Free Trade policy; secondly, taxes upon foreign food and raw materials. Grain and flour, cattle and meat, wool, timber, and iron would form the chief commodities which, in the supposed interests of our colonies, would be taxed first. Unless this preference raised prices it could have no effect in enabling colonial producers to displace foreign producers : the tariff, to be operative at all, must remove all profit from some portion of foreign goods previously imported, and, by preventing such goods from entering our markets in the future, reduce the total supply : this reduction of supply acts of necessity in raising the price for the whole market. This well-recognized automatic operation of the law of supply and demand makes it certain that English consumers would pay in enhanced prices a new tax, part of which would be handed over to colonists in payment for their new " loyalty," part would go to the British exchequer, part to defray expenses of collection, and the rest in enhanced rent to British landowners.

Nor is this all, or perhaps the worst. By this very method of binding our colonies closer to us we take the surest way of increasing the resentment of those very nations whose political and military rivalry impels us to abandon Free Trade. The vast and increasing trade we have with France, Germany, Russia, and the United States is the most potent guarantee of peace which we possess. Reduce the volume and the value of our commerce with these nations, by means of the re-establishment of a tariff avowedly erected for the purpose, and we should convert the substantial goodwill of the powerful financial, mercantile, and manufacturing interests in these countries into active and dangerous hostility. It would be far better for us that we had never been a Free Trade country than that we relapsed into a protective system motived by the desire to weaken our commercial bonds with the political and commercial Powers whose rivalry we have most to fear. By the statistics of an earlier chapter[1] it has been shown that not merely is our trade with these foreign nations far greater than the trade with the self-governing colonies, but that it is growing at a faster rate. To offend and antagonize our better customers in order to conciliate our worse is bad economy and much worse politics.

The shrewder politicians in our colonies might surely be expected to look such a gift-horse in the mouth. For the very bribe which is designed to win them for federation is one which enhances for them enormously and quite incalculably the perils of a new connexion by which they throw in their lot irrevocably with that of Great Britain. A monopoly of the imperial market for their exports may be bought too dear, if it removes the strongest pledge for peace which England possesses, at a time when that pledge is needed most. Nor would these colonies share only the new peril of England; their own discriminative tariffs would breed direct ill-feeling against them on the part of foreigners, and would drag them into the vortex of European politics. Finally, by distorting the more natural process of commercial selection, which, under tariffs equally imposed, has in the past been increasing the proportion of the trade done by these colonies with foreign countries, and reducing the proportion done with Great Britain, we shall be forcing them to substitute a worse for a better trade, a course by which they will be heavy losers in the long run.

III

In face of such facts it will be impossible for Great Britain to offer the self-governing colonies a sufficient commercial

[1] *Cf.* Part I, chap. ii.

inducement to bring them into imperial federation. Is there any other possible inducement or temptation ? There is, I think, one, viz., to involve them on their own account in Imperialism, by encouraging and aiding them in a policy of annexation and the government of lower races. Independently of the centralized Imperialism which issues from Great Britian, these colonies have within themselves in greater or less force all the ingredients out of which an Imperialism of their own may be formed. The same conspiracy of powerful speculators, manufacturing interests and ambitious politicians, calling to their support the philanthropy of missions and the lust for adventure which is so powerful in the new world, may plot the subversion of honest, self-developing democracy, in order to establish class rule, and to employ the colonial resources in showy enterprises of expansion for their own political and commercial ends.

Such a spirit and such a purpose was plainly operative in South Africa for many years. That which appears to us as an achievement of British Imperialism, viz., the acquisition of the two Dutch Republics and the great North, is and always has appeared something quite different to a powerful group of business politicians in South Africa. These men at the Cape, in the Transvaal and in Rhodesia, British or Dutch, have fostered a South African Imperialism, not opposed to British Imperialism, willing when necessary to utilize it, but independent of it in ultimate aims and purposes. This was the policy of " colonialism " which Mr. Rhodes espoused so vehemently in his earlier political career, seeking the control of Bechuanaland and the North for Cape Colony and not directly for the Empire. This has been right through the policy of an active section of the Africander Bond, developing on a large scale the original " trek " habit of the Dutch. This was the policy to which Sir Hercules

Robinson gave voice in his famous declaration of 1889 regarding Imperialism: "It is a diminishing quantity, there being now no longer any permanent place in the future of South Africa for direct imperial rule on any large scale." A distinctively colonial or South African expansion was the policy of the politicians, financiers, and adventurers up to the failure of the Jameson Raid; reluctantly they sought the co-operation of British Imperialism to aid them in a definite work for which they were too weak, the seizure of the Transvaal mineral estates; their absorbing aim hereafter will be to relegate British Imperialism to what they conceive to be its proper place, that of an *ultima ratio* to stand in the far background while colonial Imperialism manages the business and takes the profits. A South African federation of self-governing States will demand a political career of its own, and will insist upon its own brand of empire, not that of the British Government, in the control of the lower races in South Africa.

Such a federal State will not only develop an internal policy regarding the native territories different from, perhaps antagonistic to, that of British Imperialism, but its position as the "predominant" State of South Africa will develop an ambition and a destiny of expansion which may bring it into world politics on its own account.

Australasia similarly shows signs of an Imperialism of her own. She has recently taken over New Guinea, and some of her sons are hankering after a "Monroe doctrine" applicable throughout the South Pacific, the opening step of which would consist of the assignation of our Pacific Islands to Australia and New Zealand for administrative purposes. "The same principle," it is suggested, "is applicable to the connexion between Canada and the British West Indies. Economically the latter are important to Canada, as furnishing a tropical market of the kind which the United States possess within their own borders, and also in their newly acquired dependencies. Strategically, also, the islands are becoming important to Canada as a base for the protection of her growing interests, especially in connexion with the Panama Canal, so that here the privilege of administration would enforce the sense of responsibility for naval defence."[1]

If Great Britain is prepared to guarantee to Australasia, Canada and South Africa a special imperial career of their own, placing the entire federal resources of the Empire at the disposal of the colonial federal States, to assist them in fulfilling an ambition or a destiny which is directed and determined by their particular interests and will, such a decentralization of Imperialism might win the colonies to a closer federal union with the mother country. For Great Britain herself it would involve great and obvious dangers, and some considerable sacrifice of central imperial power; but it might win the favour and support of ambitious colonial politicians and capitalists desirous to run a profitable Imperialism of their own and to divert the democratic forces from domestic agitation into foreign enterprises.

If Australasia can get from Great Britain the services of an adequate naval power to enforce her growing " Monroe doctrine " in the Pacific without paying for it, as British South Africa has obtained the services of our land forces, she will not be likely to enter closer formal bonds which will bind her to any large financial contribution towards the expenses of such a policy. But if Great Britain were willing to organize imperial federation upon a basis which in reality assigned larger independence to Australia and Canada than they have at present, by giving them a call upon the imperial resources for their own private imperial

[1] *Colonial Nationalism*, by Richard Jebb, pp. 306–7.

347

career in excess of their contribution towards the common purse, business instincts might lead them to consider favourably such a proposal.

How fraught with peril to this country such imperial federation would be it is unnecessary to prove. Centralized Imperialism, in which the Government of Great Britain formally reserves full control over the external policy of each colony, and actually exercises this control, affords some considerable security against the danger of being dragged into quarrels with other great Powers : the decentralized Imperialism, involved in imperial federation, would lose us this security. The nascent local Imperialism of Australasia, Canada and South Africa would be fed by the consciousness that it could not be checked or overruled in its expansive policy as it is now ; and the somewhat blatant energy of self-expression in the Australasian Governments would be likely to entangle us continually with Germany, Japan and the United States in the Pacific, while Canada and Newfoundland would possess a greatly enhanced power to embroil us with France and the United States. If it be urged that after all no serious steps in Australian, Canadian or South African " Imperialism " could be taken without the direct conscious consent of Great Britain, who would, by virtue of population and prestige, remain the predominant partner, the answer is that the very strengthening of the imperial bond would give increased efficacy to all the operative factors in Imperialism. Even as matters stand now there exists in Great Britain a powerful organized business interest which is continually inciting the Imperial Government to a pushful policy on behalf of our colonies : these colonies, the Australasian in particular, are heavily mortgaged in their land and trade to British financial companies ; their mines, banks, and other important commercial assets are largely owned in Great Britain; their enormous public debts[1] are chiefly held in Great Britain. It is quite evident that the classes in this country owning these colonial properties have a stake in colonial politics, different from and in some cases antagonistic to that of the British nation as a whole : it is equally evident that they can exercise an organized pressure upon the British Government in favour of their private interests that will be endowed with enhanced efficacy under the more equal conditions of an imperial federation.

Whether the bribe of a preferential tariff, or of a delegated Imperialism, or both, would suffice to bring the self-governing colonies into a closer formal political federation with Great Britain may, however, well be doubted. Still more doubtful would be their permanent continuance in such a federation. It is at least conceivable that the colonial democracies may be strong and sane enough to resist temptation to colonial Imperialism, when they perceive the dangerous reaction of such a course. Even were they induced to avail themselves of the ample resources of the Empire to forward their local imperial policy, they would, in Australia as in South Africa, be disposed to break away from such a federation when they had got out of it what advantages it could be made to yield, and they felt strong enough for an independent Empire of their own.

It is no cynical insistence upon the dominance of selfish

---

[1] In 1900 the public debts of the Australasian colonial Governments amounted to £194,812,289, for a population of 3,756,894 ; while the New Zealand debt was £46,930,077 for a population of 756,510 *Statesman's Year Book*, 1901).

New South Wales							£65,332,993
Victoria							48,774,885
Queensland							34,338,414
South Australia							26,156,180
West Australia							11,804,178
Tasmania							8,395,639
							£194,812,289

interests which leads us to the conviction that the historic drift towards independence will not be reversed by any sentiments of attachment towards Great Britain. " My hold of the colonies," wrote Burke, " is the close affection which grows from common names, from kindred blood, from similar privileges, and equal protection. These are ties which, though light as air, are as strong as links of iron."[1] But in these ties, save the last only, there is nothing to demand or to ensure political union. The moral bonds of community of language, history and institutions, maintained and strengthened by free social and commercial intercourse, this true union of hearts, have not been weakened by the progress towards political freedom which has been taking place in the past, and will not be weakened if this progress should continue until absolute political independence from Great Britain is achieved.

It is quite certain that the issue must be determined in the long run by what the colonies consider to be their policy of net utility. That utility will be determined primarily by the more permanent geographical and economic conditions. These have tended in the past, so far as they have had free play, towards political independence : they will have a freer play in the future, and it seems, therefore, unlikely that their tendency will be reversed. Though the element of distance between the parts of an Empire is now less important than formerly as a technical difficulty in representation, the following pithy summary of American objections to schemes of imperial federation in the eighteenth century, as recorded by Pownall, still has powerful application :—

" The Americans also thought that legislative union would be unnecessary, inexpedient, and dangerous, because—

" (1) They had already sufficient legislatures of their own.

[1] *Conciliation with America.*

" (2) If the colonies were so united to England they would share the burden of British taxes and debt.

" (3) Representatives in England would be too far from their constituents, and the will of the colonies would, therefore, be transferred out of their power, and involved in that of a majority in which the proportion of their representatives would hold no balance."[1]

While then it is conceivable, perhaps possible, that, for a time at any rate, the self-governing colonies might be led into an imperial federation upon terms which should secure their private industrial and political ambitions as colonies, it is far more reasonable to expect that Canada would drift towards federation with her southern neighbour, and Australasia and South Africa towards independent political entities, with a possible future re-establishment of loose political relations in an Anglo-Saxon federation.

It is no aspersion on the genuineness and the strength of the " loyalty " and affection entertained by the colonies towards England to assert that these sentiments cannot weigh appreciably in the determination of the colonial " destiny " against the continuous pressure of political, industrial, and financial forces making towards severance. Though a few politicians, or even a party in these colonies, may coquet with the notion of close federation on an equal basis, the difficulties, when the matter is resolved, as it must be, into financial terms, will be found insuperable. The real trend of colonial forces will operate in the same direction as before, and more persistently, when the nature of the burdens they are invited to undertake is disclosed to them.

The notion that one great result of the South African war has been to generate a large fund of colonial feeling which will materially affect the relations of the colonies

[1] Holland, *Imperium et Libertas*, p. 82.

with Great Britain is an amiable delusion based upon childish psychology. While the rally of sentiment has been genuine, so has been the discovery of the perils of the mother country which have made colonial assistance so welcome and caused it to be prized so highly that imperial statesmen essay to turn the tide of colonial development by means of it.

Reflection, which follows every burst of sentiment, cannot fail to dwell upon the nature of the peril which besets an empire so vast, so heterogeneous, and so dispersed as the British Empire. When the glamour of war has passed away, and history discloses some of the brute facts of this sanguinary business which have been so carefully kept from the peoples of Australia, New Zealand and Canada, their relish for the affair will diminish : they will be more suspicious in the future of issues whose character and magnitude have been so gravely misrepresented to them by the Imperial Government.[1] But the discovery likely to weigh most with the colonial democracies is the unsubstantial assets of the new Imperialism. It is one thing to enter a federation of free self-governing States upon an equal footing, quite another to be invited to contribute to the maintenance and acquisition of an indefinitely large and growing number of dependencies, the property of one of the federating States. The more clearly the colonies recognize the precarious nature of the responsibilities they are asked to undertake, the more reluctant will they show themselves. Unless the democratic spirit of these colonies can be broken and they can be driven to " Imperialism " upon their own account, they will refuse to enter a federation which,

[1] Public feeling in Australia and New Zealand was of a particularly simple manufacture in the autumn of 1899. Mr. Chamberlain communicated the " facts " of the South African war to the Premiers of the colonies and they served them out to the press. This official information was not checked by any really independent news.

whatever be the formal terms of entrance, fastens on them perils so incalculable. The new Imperialism kills a federation of free self-governing States : the colonies may look at it, but they will go their way as before.

The sentimental attractions which the idea may at first present will not be void of practical results. It may lead them to strengthen their preparation for internal defence, and to develop, each of them, a firmer national spirit of their own. The consciousness of this gain in defensive strength will not the more dispose them to closer formal union with Great Britain ; it is far more likely to lead them to treat with her upon the terms of independent allies. The direction in which the more clear-sighted colonial statesmen are moving is and always has been tolerably clear. It is towards a slighter bond of union with Great Britain, not a stronger. The near goal is one clearly marked out for the American colonies by Jefferson as early as 1774, and one which then might have been attained if England had exercised discretion. Jefferson thus describes his plan in the draft of instructions to delegates sent by Virginia to Congress : " I took the ground that from the beginning I had thought the only one orthodox or tenable, which was that the relation between Great Britain and those colonies was exactly the same as that of England and Scotland after the accession of James and until after the Union, and the same as the present relation with Hanover, having the same executive chief, but no other necessary political connexion."[1] This same project, that of narrowing down the imperial connexion to the single tie of a common monarchy, was avowed by the " Reformers " who in Upper Canada usually made a majority of the Legislative Assembly during 1830–40, and underlies the conscious or unconscious policy of all our

[1] Quoted *Imperium et Libertas*, p. 70.

self-governing colonies when subject to normal influences. Brief, temporary set-backs to this movement under the stress of some popular outburst of enthusiasm or some well-engineered political design are possible, but unless the real forces of colonial democracy can be permanently crushed they will continue to drive colonial policy towards this goal. Whether they will drive still farther, to full formal severance, will depend upon the completeness with which Great Britain has learnt during the last century and a half the lesson of colonial government which the American Revolution first made manifest. At present, owing to our liberal rendering of the term "responsible self-government," there exists no powerful set of conscious forces making for complete independence in any of our colonies, save in South Africa, where our exceptional policy has given birth to a lasting antagonism of economic interests, which, working at present along the lines of race cleavage, must in the not distant future arouse in the people of a federated South Africa a demand for complete severance from British control as the only alternative to a control which they, British and Dutch, will regard as an intolerable interference with their legitimate rights of self-government.

This forcible interference of the Imperial Government with the natural evolution of a British South Africa, accompanied by a direct attack upon colonial liberties and a substitution of mechanical stimulation for organic growth in the process of a South African federation, will come home later to the other self-governing colonies through its reaction upon British policy. The legacy of this disastrous imperial exploit is enhanced militarism for Great Britain, and the rapacious dominance of armaments over public finance. These considerations almost inevitably goad public policy in Great Britain to make eager overtures to the colonies which will be rightly understood as an invitation to share risks and burdens in large excess of all assured advantages. The endeavours on our part to secure the closer political connexion of the colonies are more likely than any other cause to bring about a final disruption; for the driving force behind these endeavours will be detected as proceeding from national rather than imperial needs. Australia, New Zealand, Canada have had no voice in determining recent expansion of British rule in Asia and Africa; such expansion serves no vital interest of theirs; invited to contribute a full share to the upkeep and furtherance of such Empire, they will persistently refuse, preferring to make full preparation for such self-defence as will enable them to dispense with that protection of the British flag, which brings increasing dangers of entanglement with foreign Powers.

The new Imperialism antagonizes colonial self-government, tends to make imperial federation impracticable, and furnishes a disruptive force in the relations of Great Britain with the self-governing colonies.

CHAPTER VII

THE OUTCOME

I

IF Imperialism may no longer be regarded as a blind inevitable destiny, is it certain that imperial expansion as a deliberately chosen line of public policy can be stopped ? We have seen that it is motived, not by the interests of the nation as a whole, but by those of certain classes, who impose the policy upon the nation for their own advantage. The amalgam of economic and political forces which exercises this pressure has been submitted to close analysis. But will the detection of this confederacy of vicious forces destroy or any wise abate their operative power ? For this power is a natural outcome of an unsound theory in our foreign policy. Put into plain language, the theory is this, that any British subject choosing, for his own private pleasure or profit, to venture his person or his property in the territory of a foreign State can call upon this nation to protect or avenge him in case he or his property is injured either by the Government or by any inhabitant of this foreign State. Now this is a perilous doctrine. It places the entire military, political, and financial resources of this nation at the beck and call of any missionary society which considers it has a peculiar duty to attack the religious sentiments or observances of some savage people, or of some reckless explorer who chooses just those spots of earth known to be inhabited by hostile peoples ignorant of British power ; the speculative trader or the mining prospector gravitates naturally towards dangerous and unexplored countries, where the gains of a successful venture will be quick and large. All these men, missionaries, travellers, sportsmen, scientists, traders, in no proper sense the accredited representatives of this country, but actuated by private personal motives, are at liberty to call upon the British nation to spend millions of money and thousands of lives to defend them against risks which the nation has not sanctioned. It is only right to add that unscrupulous statesmen have deliberately utilized these insidious methods of encroachment, seizing upon every alleged outrage inflicted on these private adventurers or marauders as a pretext for a punitive expedition which results in the British flag waving over some new tract of territory. Thus the most reckless and irresponsible individual members of our nation are permitted to direct our foreign policy. Now that we have some four hundred million British subjects, any one of whom in theory or in practice may call upon the British arms to extricate him from the results of his private folly, the prospects of a genuine *pax Britannica* are not particularly bright.

But these sporadic risks, grave though they have sometimes proved, are insignificant when compared with the dangers associated with modern methods of international capitalism and finance. It is not long since industry was virtually restricted by political boundaries, the economic intercourse of nations being almost wholly confined to commercial exchanges of goods. The recent habit of investing capital in a foreign country has now grown to such an extent that the well-to-do and politically powerful classes in Great Britain to-day derive a large and ever larger proportion of their incomes from capital invested outside the British Empire. This growing stake of our wealthy classes in countries over which they have no political control is a revolutionary force in modern politics ; it means a constantly growing tendency to use their political power as citizens of this State to interfere with the political condition of those States where they have an industrial stake.

The essentially illicit nature of this use of the public resources of the nation to safeguard and improve private investments should be clearly recognized. If I put my savings in a home investment, I take into consideration all the chances and changes to which the business is liable, including the possibilities of political changes of tariff, taxation, or industrial legislation which may affect its profits. In the case of such investment, I am quite aware that I have no right to call upon the public to protect me from loss or depreciation of my capital due to any of these causes. The political conditions of my country are taken into calculation at the time of my investment. If I invest in consols, I fully recognize that no right of political interference with foreign policy affecting my investment is accorded to me in virtue of my interest as a fund-holder. But, if I invest either in the public funds or in some private industrial venture in a foreign country for the benefit of my private purse, getting specially favourable terms to cover risks arising from the political insecurity of the country or the deficiencies of its Government, I am entitled to call upon my Government to use its political and military force to secure me against those very risks which I have already discounted in the terms of my investment. Can anything be more palpably unfair ?

It may be said that no such claim of the individual investor upon State aid is admitted. But while the theory may not have been openly avowed, recent history shows a growth of consistent practice based upon its tacit acceptance. I need not retrace the clear chain of evidence, consisting chiefly of the admissions of the mining capitalists, by which this claim to use public resources for their private profit has been enforced by the financiers who seduced our Government and people into our latest and most costly exploit. This is but the clearest and most dramatic instance of the operation of the world-wide forces of international finance. These forces are commonly described as capitalistic, but the gravest danger arises not from genuine industrial investments in foreign lands, but from the handling of stocks and shares based upon these investments by financiers. Those who own a genuine stake in the natural sources or the industry of a foreign land have at least some substantial interest in the peace and good government of that land ; but the stock speculator has no such stake : his interest lies in the oscillations of paper values, which require fluctuation and insecurity of political conditions as their instrument.

As these forms of international investment and finance are wider spread and better organized for economic and political purposes, these demands for political and military interference with foreign countries, on the ground of protecting the property of British subjects, will be more frequent and more effective ; the demands of investors will commonly be backed by personal grievances of British outlanders, and we shall be drawn into a series of inter-ferences with foreign Governments, which, if we can conduct them successfully, will lead to annexation of territory as the only security for the lives and property of our subjects.

That this policy marks a straight road to ruin there can be no doubt. But how to stop it ? What principle of safety can we lay down ? Only one—an absolute repudiation of the right of British subjects to call upon their Government to protect their persons or property from injuries or dangers incurred on their private initiative. This principle is just and expedient. If we send an emissary on a public mission into a foreign country, let us support and protect him by our public purse and arms; if a private person, or a company of private persons, place their lives or property in a foreign land, seeking their own ends, let them clearly understand that they do so at their own risk, and that the State will not act for their protection.

If so complete a reversal of our consistent policy be regarded as a counsel of perfection involving a definite abandonment of domiciliary, trading, and other rights secured by existing treaties or conventions with foreign States, upon the observance of which we are entitled to insist, let us at any rate lay down two plain rules of policy. First, never to sanction any interference on the part of our foreign representatives on general grounds of foreign misgovernment outside the strict limits of our treaty rights, submitting interpretation of such treaty rights to arbitration. Secondly, if in any case armed force is applied to secure the observance of these treaty rights, to confine such force to the attainment of the specific object which justifies its use.

II

Analysis of Imperialism, with its natural supports, militarism, oligarchy, bureaucracy, protection, concentration of capital and violent trade fluctuations, has marked it out as the supreme danger of modern national States. The power of the imperialist forces within the nation to use the national resources for their private gain, by operating the instrument of the State, can only be overthrown by the establishment of a genuine democracy, the direction of public policy by the people for the people through representatives over whom they exercise a real control. Whether this or any other nation is yet competent for such a democracy may well be matter of grave doubt, but until and unless the external policy of a nation is " broad-based upon a people's will " there appears little hope of remedy. The scare of a great recent war may for a brief time check the confidence of these conspirators against the commonwealth, and cause them to hold their hands, but the financial forces freshly generated will demand new outlets, and will utilize the same political alliances and the same social, religious, and philanthropic supports in their pressure for new enterprises. The circumstances of each new imperialist exploit differ from those of all preceding ones : whatever ingenuity is requisite for the perversion of the public intelligence, or the inflammation of the public sentiment, will be forthcoming.

Imperialism is only beginning to realize its full resources, and to develop into a fine art the management of nations : the broad bestowal of a franchise, wielded by a people whose education has reached the stage of an uncritical ability to read printed matter, favours immensely the designs of keen business politicians, who, by controlling the press, the schools, and where necessary the churches, impose Imperialism upon the masses under the attractive guise of sensational patriotism.

The chief economic source of Imperialism has been found in the inequality of industrial opportunities by which a favoured class accumulates superfluous elements of income which, in their search for profitable investments, press ever farther afield : the influence on State policy of these investors and their financial managers secures a national alliance of other vested interests which are threatened by movements of social reform : the adoption of Imperialism thus serves the double purpose of securing private material benefits for favoured classes of investors and traders at the public cost, while sustaining the general cause of conservatism by diverting public energy and interest from domestic agitation to external employment.

The ability of a nation to shake off this dangerous usurpation of its power, and to employ the national resources in the national interest, depends upon the education of a national intelligence and a national will, which shall make democracy a political and economic reality. To term Imperialism a national policy is an impudent falsehood : the interests of the nation are opposed to every act of this expansive policy. Every enlargement of Great Britain in the tropics is a distinct enfeeblement of true British nationalism. Indeed, Imperialism is commended in some quarters for this very reason, that by breaking the narrow bounds of nationalities it facilitates and forwards internationalism. There are even those who favour or condone the forcible suppression of small nationalities by larger ones under the impulse of Imperialism, because they imagine that this is the natural approach to a world-federation and eternal peace. A falser view of political evolution it is difficult to conceive. If there is one condition precedent to effective internationalism or to the establishment of any reliable relations between States, it is the existence of strong, secure, well-developed, and responsible nations. Internationalism can never be subserved by the suppression or forcible absorption of nations ; for these practices react disastrously upon the springs of internationalism, on the one hand setting nations on their armed defence and stifling the amicable approaches between them, on the other debilitating the larger nations through excessive corpulence and indigestion. The hope of a coming internationalism enjoins above all else the maintenance and natural growth of independent nationalities, for without such there could be no gradual evolution of internationalism, but only a series of unsuccessful attempts at a chaotic and unstable cosmopolitanism. As individualism is essential to any sane form of national socialism, so nationalism is essential to internationalism : no organic conception of world-politics can be framed on any other supposition.

Just in proportion as the substitution of true national governments for the existing oligarchies or sham democracies becomes possible will the apparent conflicts of national interests disappear, and the fundamental co-operation upon which nineteenth-century Free Trade prematurely relied manifest itself. The present class government means the severance or antagonism of nations, because each ruling class can only keep and use its rule by forcing the antagonisms of foreign policy : intelligent democracies would perceive their identity of interest, and would ensure it by their amicable policy. The genuine forces of internationalism, thus liberated, would first display themselves as economic forces, securing more effective international co-operation for postal, telegraphic, railway, and other transport services, for monetary exchange and for common standards of measurement of various kinds, and for the improved intercommunication of persons, goods, and information. Related and subsidiary to these purposes would come a growth of machinery of courts and congresses, at first informal and private, but gradually taking shape in more definite and more public machinery : the common interests of the arts and sciences would everywhere be weaving an elaborate network of intellectual internationalism, and both economic and intellectual community of needs and interests would contribute to the natural growth of such political solidarity as was required to maintain this real community.

It is thus, and only thus, that the existing false antagonisms of nations, with their wastes and perils and their retardation of the general course of civilization, can be resolved. To substitute for this peaceful discovery and expression of common interests a federal policy proceeding upon directly selfish political and military interests, the idea which animates an Anglo-Saxon alliance or a Pan-Teutonic empire, is deliberately to choose a longer, more difficult, and far more hazardous road to internationalism. The economic bond is far stronger and more reliable as a basis of growing internationalism than the so-called racial bond or a political alliance constructed on some short-sighted computation of a balance of power. It is, of course, quite possible that a Pan-Slav, Pan-Teutonic, Pan-British, or Pan-Latin alliance might, if the federation were kept sufficiently voluntary and elastic, contribute to the wider course of internationalism. But the frankly military purpose commonly assigned for such alliances bodes ill for such assistance. It is far more likely that such alliances would be formed in the interests of the "imperialist" classes of the contracting nations, in order the more effectively to exploit the joint national resources.

We have foreshadowed the possibility of even a larger alliance of Western States, a European federation of great Powers which, so far from forwarding the cause of world-civilization, might introduce the gigantic peril of a Western parasitism, a group of advanced industrial nations, whose upper classes drew vast tribute from Asia and Africa, with which they supported great tame masses of retainers, no longer engaged in the staple industries of agriculture and manufacture, but kept in the performance of personal or minor industrial services under the control of a new financial aristocracy. Let those who would scout such a theory as undeserving of consideration examine the economic and social condition of districts in Southern England to-day which are already reduced to this condition, and reflect upon the vast extension of such a system which might be rendered feasible by the subjection of China to the economic control of similar groups of financiers, investors, and political and business officials, draining the greatest potential reservoir of profit the world has ever known, in order to consume it in Europe. The situation is far too complex, the play of world-forces far too incalculable, to render this or any other single interpretation of the future very probable : but the influences which govern the Imperialism of Western Europe to-day are moving in this direction, and, unless counteracted or diverted, make towards some such consummation.

If the ruling classes of the Western nations could realize their interests in such a combination (and each year sees capitalism more obviously international), and if China were unable to develop powers of forcible resistance, the opportunity of a parasitic Imperialism which should reproduce upon a vaster scale many of the main features of the latter Roman Empire visibly presents itself.

Whether we regard Imperialism upon this larger scale or as confined to the policy of Great Britain, we find much that is closely analogous to the Imperialism of Rome.

The rise of a money-loaning aristocracy in Rome, composed of keen, unscrupulous men from many nations, who filled the high offices of States with their creatures, political " bosses " or military adventurers, who had come to the front as usurers, publicans, or chiefs of police in the provinces, was the most distinctive feature of later imperial Rome. This class was continually recruited from returned officials and colonial millionaires. The large incomes drawn in private official plunder, public tribute, usury and official incomes from the provinces had the following reactions upon Italy. Italians were no longer wanted for working the land or for manufactures, or even for military service. " The later campaigns on the Rhine and the Danube," it is pointed out, " were really slave-hunts on a gigantic scale."[1]

[1] Adams, *Civilization and Decay*, p. 38.

The Italian farmers, at first drawn from rural into military life, soon found themselves permanently ousted from agriculture by the serf labour of the *latifundia*, and they and their families were sucked into the dregs of town life, to be subsisted as a pauper population upon public charity. A mercenary colonial army came more and more to displace the home forces. The parasitic city life, with its lowered vitality and the growing infrequency of marriage, to which Gibbon draws attention,[1] rapidly impaired the physique of the native population of Italy, and Rome subsisted more and more upon immigration of raw vigour from Gaul and Germany. The necessity of maintaining powerful mercenary armies to hold the provinces heightened continually the peril, already manifest in the last years of the Republic, arising from the political ambitions of great proconsuls conspiring with a moneyed interest at Rome against the Commonwealth. As time went on, this moneyed oligarchy became an hereditary aristocracy, and withdrew from military and civil service, relying more and more upon hired foreigners : themselves sapped by luxury and idleness, and tainting by mixed servitude and licence the Roman populace, they so enfeebled the State as to destroy the physical and moral vitality required to hold in check and under government the vast repository of forces in the exploited Empire. The direct cause of Rome's decay and fall is expressed politically by the term " over-centralization," which conveys in brief the real essence of Imperialism as distinguished from national growth on the one hand and colonialism upon the other. Parasitism, practised through taxation and usury, involved a constantly increasing centralization of the instruments of government, and a growing strain upon this government, as the prey became more impoverished by the drain and showed signs of restive-

[1] Chap. xii.

ness. " The evolution of this centralized society was as logical as every other work of nature. When force reached the stage where it expressed itself exclusively through money, the governing class ceased to be chosen because they were valiant or eloquent, artistic, learned or devout, and were selected solely because they had the faculty of acquiring and keeping wealth. As long as the weak retained enough vitality to produce something which could be absorbed, this oligarchy was invariable ; and, for very many years after the native peasantry of Gaul and Italy had perished from the land, new blood, injected from more tenacious races, kept the dying civilization alive. The weakness of the moneyed class lay in this very power, for they not only killed the producer but in the strength of their acquisitiveness they failed to propagate themselves."[1]

This is the largest, plainest instance history presents of the social parasitic process by which a moneyed interest within the State, usurping the reins of government, makes for imperial expansion in order to fasten economic suckers into foreign bodies so as to drain them of their wealth in order to support domestic luxury. The new Imperialism differs in no vital point from this old example. The element of political tribute is now absent or quite subsidiary, and the crudest forms of slavery have disappeared : some elements of more genuine and disinterested government serve to quality and mask the distinctively parasitic nature of the later sort. But nature is not mocked : the laws which, operative throughout nature, doom the parasite to atrophy, decay, and final extinction, are not evaded by nations any more than by individual organisms. The greater complexity of the modern process, the endeavour to escape the parasitic reaction by rendering some real but quite unequal and inadequate services to " the host," may retard but cannot

[1] Adams, *Civilization and Decay*, p. 44.

finally avert the natural consequences of living upon others. The claim that an imperial State forcibly subjugating other peoples and their lands does so for the purpose of rendering services to the conquered equal to those which she exacts is notoriously false : she neither intends equivalent services nor is capable of rendering them, and the pretence that such benefits to the governed form a leading motive or result of Imperialism implies a degree of moral or intellectual obliquity so grave as itself to form a new peril for any nation fostering so false a notion of the nature of its conduct. " Let the motive be in the deed, not in the event," says a Persian proverb.

Imperialism is a depraved choice of national life, imposed by self-seeking interests which appeal to the lusts of quantitative acquisitiveness and of forceful domination surviving in a nation from early centuries of animal struggle for existence. Its adoption as a policy implies a deliberate renunciation of that cultivation of the higher inner qualities which for a nation as for an individual constitutes the ascendency of reason over brute impulse. It is the besetting sin of all successful States, and its penalty is unalterable in the order of nature.

APPENDIX I

AREA AND POPULATION OF THE BRITISH EMPIRE, 1933-4.

	Area (sq. miles).	Population.
DOMINIONS, COLONIES, AND PROTECTORATES—		
Europe	30,709	3,589,000
Asia	2,113,679	364,012,000
Africa	3,093,949	51,583,000
America	4,008,214	13,091,000
Australasia	3,188,405	8,887,000
Total	12,434,956	441,162,000
MANDATED TERRITORIES—		
Asia	9,000	1,036,000
Africa	726,325	6,412,000
Australasia	90,512	768,000
Total	825,837	8,216,000
Grand Total . . .	13,270,793	449,378,000

Compiled from the *Statesman's Year Book* for 1934.

APPENDIX II

	Area in Square Miles.		Population.	
	Mother Country.	Dependencies.	Mother Country.[1]	Dependencies.[2]
Great Britain .	94,633	13,270,793	46,610,000	449,378,000
France . .	212,750	4,617,514	41,880,000	65,179,000
Germany .	181,822	—	65,350,000	—
Netherlands .	13,128	791,907	8,290,000	60,971,000
Austria . .	32,434	—	6,750,000	—
Hungary .	35,909	—	8,841,000	—
Denmark .	16,603	121,395	3,640,000	41,000
Italy . .	119,696	906,213[3]	42,217,000	2,393,000[3]
Portugal .	35,699	807,637	7,090,000	8,426,000
Spain . .	194,216	10,993	24,242,000	1,000,000
Czechoslovakia	54,056	—	15,020,000	—
United States	3,026,200	711,726[4]	126,000,000	15,014,000[4]

[1] Estimates for 31.xii.33. [2] Estimates for as near the above date as possible.
[3] Excluding Abyssinia. [4] Including Alaska.

Figures from the *Statesman's Year Book* for 1935, the *Armaments Year Book* for 1935, and the *League of Nations Year Book* for 1934-5.

APPENDIX III

	Total Overseas Trade. (millions of £'s.)	Value per Head of the Population. (£'s.)		Total Overseas Trade. (millions of £'s.)	Value per Head of the Population. (£'s.)
1910 .	1,117		1925 .	2,103	
11 .	1,143		26 .	1,906	
12 .	1,241		27 .	1,939	
13 .	1,306		28 .	1,928	
14 .	1,133		29 .	1,960	
Average	1,188	28·0	Average	1,967	43·3
1915 .	1,238		1930 .	1,619	
16 .	1,460		31 .	1,255	
17 .	1,597		32 .	1,068	
18 .	1,825		33 .	1,044	
19 .	2,436		34 .	1,130	
Average	1,711	42·0	Average	1,223	26·5
1920 .	3,279				
21 .	1,790				
22 .	1,727				
23 .	1,870				
24 .	2,085				
Average	2,150	48·6			

APPENDIX IV

TRADE OF THE UNITED KINGDOM : PERCENTAGES OF TOTAL VALUES.

	Imports from		Exports to	
	Foreign Countries.	British Empire.	Foreign Countries.	British Empire.
1913 . . .	75·1	24·9	67·1	32·9
Average 1924–9 .	69·4	30·6	59·1	40·9
1931 . . .	71·2	28·8	58·9	41·1
1933 . . .	63·1	36·9	58·2	41·8

APPENDIX V

	Percentages of Imports into British Empire from United Kingdom.	Percentages of Exports from British Empire into United Kingdom.
1913–4	47·2	40·4
Average 1924–9 . . .	35·6	33·6
1933–4	36·1	39·3

Figures from *Statistical Abstract for the United Kingdom* for 1934, and Sir George Schuster, "Empire Trade Before and After Ottawa," *Economist*, November 3rd, 1934.

APPENDIX VI

BRITISH, IMPERIAL AND FOREIGN TRADE, 1934–35.

	Imports from		Exports to	
	Value (£'s).	Percentage.	Value (£'s).	Percentage.
	£		£	
Foreign Countries . .	460,129,000	62·72	210,412,000	53·15
British India . . .	42,102,000	5·74	36,675,000	9·30
Australasia . .	90,368,000	12·30	37,681,000	9·50
South Africa[1] . .	16,446,000	2·24	32,509,000	8·20
Canada . . .	50,390,000	6·90	19,726,000	5·00
Other British Dependencies	74,102,000	10·10	58,982,000	14·85
Total . . .	733,537,000	100·00	395,985,000	100·00

[1] Including Rhodesia.
Figures from *Statistical Abstract for the United Kingdom* for 1934.

APPENDIX VII

	Percentage of Imports by Value from United Kingdom.			Percentage of Exports by Value to United Kingdom.		
	1913–4	Average. 1924–9	1933–4	1913–4	Average. 1924–9	1933–4
India	65·4	48·9	41·2	23·5	22·7	31·8
Self Governing Dominions	39·0	36·5	41·9	54·1	46·0	50·2
Other Parts of British Empire[1] .	45·0	23·6	22·8	42·2	20·2	21·4

[1] Including Crown Colonies Sudan, Southern Rhodesia, and Malaya and Hong Kong (except 1913–4).
Figures from *Statistical Abstract for the United Kingdom* for 1934, and Sir George Schuster, "Empire Trade Before and After Ottawa," *Economist*, November 3rd, 1934.

APPENDIX VIII

VALUE OF EXPORTS FROM GREAT BRITAIN (U.K.) IN £'s.

Year.			Dominions.	India.	Other British Possessions.
1904	.	.	.	52,094,444	40,641,277	19,687,997
1905	.	.	.	52,204,632	42,996,388	19,016,423
1906	.	.	.	56,923,891	45,181,307	19,904,287
1907	.	.	.	64,104,666	52,027,221	22,011,879
1908	.	.	.	56,422,882	49,418,713	20,923,432
1909	.	.	.	61,585,480	43,581,501	22,071,103
1910	.	.	.	75,401,799	45,998,500	25,902,643
1911	.	.	.	80,585,992	52,245,604	26,012,488
1912	.	.	.	90,183,258	57,626,101	29,283,279
1913	.	.	.	91,287,754	70,273,145	33,745,909
1914	.	.	.	79,268,272	62,888,506	29,472,720
1915	.	.	.	69,923,562	45,603,792	32,892,330
1916	.	.	.	89,116,567	52,787,920	44,271,384
1917	.	.	.	64,521,497	59,965,373	48,170,946
1918	.	.	.	70,879,622	49,180,830	58,301,670
1919	.	.	.	71,143,432	70,860,991	63,618,037
1920	.	.	.	180,971,372	181,239,634	139,259,417
1921	.	.	.	109,843,563	108,868,548	79,904,522
1922	.	.	.	125,769,446	92,104,778	67,694,500
1923	.	.	.	133,686,453	86,246,488	80,669,685
1924	.	.	.	139,356,994	90,577,148	107,530,219
1925	.	.	.	141,365,824	86,047,757	107,700,581
1926	.	.	.	140,286,071	81,755,046	94,810,310
1927	.	.	.	140,350,373	85,044,842	101,254,995
1928	.	.	.	140,910,867	83,900,440	102,856,595
1929	.	.	.	143,172,986	78,227,208	103,051,301
1930	.	.	.	105,145,131	52,944,447	90,255,381
1931	.	.	.	68,131,620	32,288,579	70,252,593
1932	.	.	.	64,895,734	34,088,361	66,528,185
1933	.	.	.	71,686,278	33,402,404	58,428,581
1934	.	.	.	87,626,611	36,674,581	61,271,842

VALUE OF IMPORTS INTO GREAT BRITAIN (U.K.) IN £'s.

Year.				Dominions.	India.	Other British Possessions.
1904	.	.	.	70,526,674	42,704,004	12,916,861
1905	.	.	.	77,158,417	36,039,789	20,212,314
1906	.	.	.	88,431,030	37,722,235	22,940,401
1907	.	.	.	94,511,293	43,912,588	25,110,466
1908	.	.	.	80,177,264	29,588,187	22,977,771
1909	.	.	.	91,593,058	35,430,771	24,398,063
1910	.	.	.	103,726,165	42,763,715	32,250,753
1911	.	.	.	99,517,676	45,423,316	34,585,783
1912	.	.	.	103,660,165	52,148,731	39,294,383
1913	.	.	.	113,179,193	48,420,490	41,902,295
1914	.	.	.	107,622,853	43,348,176	42,301,442
1915	.	.	.	129,282,519	62,213,614	81,981,097
1916	.	.	.	143,646,423	72,366,184	91,940,009
1917	.	.	.	195,276,511	66,836,578	103,014,290
1918	.	.	.	213,262,757	88,541,217	128,294,040
1919	.	.	.	313,699,316	108,213,961	172,193,212
1920	.	.	.	283,339,215	95,721,420	288,075,222
1921	.	.	.	198,587,225	44,307,742	89,022,436
1922	.	.	.	188,242,235	47,719,039	85,832,351
1923	.	.	.	167,332,394	66,950,068	98,316,894
1924	.	.	.	196,411,435	78,872,953	119,087,035
1925	.	.	.	227,230,222	80,099,083	129,421,942
1926	.	.	.	199,924,304	57,638,068	127,808,804
1927	.	.	.	185,073,001	65,840,065	125,056,495
1928	.	.	.	189,694,151	64,472,793	116,135,592
1929	.	.	.	182,271,186	62,844,796	121,903,815
1930	.	.	.	152,502,896	51,044,435	103,248,648
1931	.	.	.	127,339,016	36,711,288	81,290,012
1932	.	.	.	142,099,520	32,308,273	74,376,155
1933	.	.	.	146,444,670	37,351,929	65,431,482
1934	.	.	.	153,991,428	42,102,298	76,533,361

This includes Straits Settlements and Dependencies as well as British India.

APPENDIX IX

NUMBER OF OUTWARD-BOUND BRITISH PASSENGERS FROM THE UNITED KINGDOM
TO THE FOLLOWING COUNTRIES.

	United States.	Canada and Newfoundland.	Union of South Africa.	Other Parts of the British Empire.	Total.
1912 ·	117,310	186,147	28,216	116,700	448,373
13 ·	129,169	196,278	25,855	99,317	450,619
14 ·	92,808	94,482	21,124	70,409	278,823
15 ·	37,763	19,434	11,699	30,675	99,571
16 ·	28,884	18,953	7,905	17,309	73,051
17 ·	3,981	6,415	2,794	6,508	19,698
18 ·	3,445	3,218	2,374	7,518	16,555
19 ·	32,765	89,102	7,761	39,794	169,422
1920 ·	90,811	134,079	29,019	83,532	337,441
21 ·	67,499	84,145	28,138	76,269	256,051
22 ·	61,826	69,690	21,414	81,371	234,301
23 ·	101,063	121,941	18,938	78,904	320,846
24 ·	39,057	99,717	22,452	85,055	246,281
25 ·	54,898	70,810	21,144	83,921	230,773
26 ·	59,535	83,886	22,958	98,309	264,688
27 ·	58,243	89,571	22,213	87,214	257,241
28 ·	56,508	95,307	22,569	74,144	248,528
29 ·	64,188	107,772	23,870	62,810	258,640
1930 ·	59,390	69,281	21,816	49,426	199,913
31 ·	27,320	38,003	19,491	37,927	122,741
32 ·	23,731	33,911	16,707	37,689	112,038
33 ·	22,189	28,391	19,714	39,966	110,260
34 ·	26,449	30,621	22,878	43,945	123,893

Figures compiled from the *Statistical Abstract for the United Kingdom* for 1934, and Willcox and Ferenczi, *International Migration*, Volume I.

APPENDIX X

	(a) £ooo's From Public (Governmental and Municipal) Loans to Empire and Foreign Countries.	(b) £ooo's Income from all British Investments Overseas (excluding undistributed profits).
1929 . . .	64,661	212,365
1930 . . .	64,676	192,175
1931 . . .	65,920	155,513
1932 . . .	62,377	144,118
1933 . . .	61,126	138,274

APPENDIX XI

TOTAL (NOMINAL) BRITISH INVESTMENTS OVERSEAS.

	(a) £ooo's Imperial Public (Governmental and Municipal) Loans.	(b) £ooo's Foreign Public (Governmental and Municipal) Loans.	(c) £ooo's Total (Nominal) Investments Overseas— Public and Private.
1929 .	1,061,000	351,000	3,438,000
1930 .	1,080,000	357,000	3,425,000
1931 .	1,104,000	337,000	3,410,000
1932 .	1,109,000	323,000	3,355,000
1933 .	1,147,000	333,000	3,386,000

From Sir R. Kindersley, " Britain's Overseas Investments," *Economic Journal,* 1931 and 1935.

375

APPENDIX XII

					Armaments and War.	Colonial Trade : Import and Export Trade with the Empire.
					£000's	£000's
1904	.	.	.	.	66,055	238,571
05	.	.	.	.	62,150	247,628
06	.	.	.	.	59,199	271,103
07	.	.	.	.	58,256	301,678
08	.	.	.	.	59,028	259,508
09	.	.	.	.	63,043	278,660
1910	.	.	.	.	67,835	326,044
11	.	.	.	.	70,507	338,371
12	.	.	.	.	72,432	372,196
13	.	.	.	.	86,028	398,809
14	.	.	.	.	361,156	364,902
15	.	.	.	.	1,001,330	421,897
16	.	.	.	.	1,414,281	494,128
17	.	.	.	.	1,767,550	537,785
18	.	.	.	.	1,977,751	608,460
19	.	.	.	.	959,192	799,729
1920	.	.	.	.	386,491	1,072,885
21	.	.	.	.	178,300	630,536
22	.	.	.	.	118,000	607,369
23	.	.	.	.	112,400	633,213
24	.	.	.	.	116,900	731,921
25	.	.	.	.	121,500	773,351
26	.	.	.	.	117,400	704,449
27	.	.	.	.	118,600	705,004
28	.	.	.	.	115,700	699,771
29	.	.	.	.	115,000	693,620
1930	.	.	.	.	112,700	556,984
31	.	.	.	.	111,400	420,833

Figures from the *Statistical Abstract for the United Kingdom* for 1914, 1922, and 1934.

APPENDIX XIII

Yearly average or year.	Total.	Crude materials.	Crude food-stuffs.	Manu-factured foodstuffs.	Semi-manu-factures.	Finished manu-factures.
1871–1875	486,128	218,449	75,206	95,282	22,681	74,509
1876–1880	663,650	213,989	158,853	161,915	30,174	98,719
1881–1885	774,607	261,645	162,714	197,457	37,044	115,747
1886–1890	725,685	276,703	108,708	181,521	40,023	118,730
1891–1895	876,326	295,087	150,846	238,580	55,343	136,470
1896–1900	1,136,039	296,664	214,778	272,759	109,500	242,338
1901–1905	1,427,020	432,027	173,972	316,226	161,206	343,589
1906–1910	1,750,980	554,754	155,828	317,374	249,134	473,890
1911	2,013,549	720,611	103,402	282,017	309,152	598,368
1912	2,170,320	731,164	99,899	318,839	348,150	672,268
1913	2,428,506	740,290	181,907	321,204	408,807	776,297
1914	2,329,684	799,838	137,495	293,219	374,224	724,908
1915	2,716,178	591,282	506,993	454,575	355,862	807,466
1916	5,422,642	815,693	421,284	648,039	912,262	2,625,364
1917	6,169,617	832,827	508,762	806,941	1,315,242	2,705,845
1918	6,047,875	972,107	547,436	1,405,820	1,053,270	2,069,242
1919	7,749,816	1,623,085	678,363	1,962,616	922,246	2,563,505
1920	8,080,481	1,882,530	917,991	1,116,605	958,497	3,204,858
1921	4,378,928	983,553	673,334	685,025	410,167	1,626,849
1922	3,765,091	988,456	458,611	587,987	437,730	1,292,307
1923	4,090,715	1,208,468	257,478	583,292	563,718	1,477,759
1924	4,497,649	1,332,746	392,691	573,492	610,668	1,588,052
1925	4,818,722	1,422,058	317,894	573,753	661,683	1,843,334
1926	4,711,721	1,261,325	335,063	503,005	655,547	1,956,781
1927	4,758,864	1,192,776	421,107	463,299	699,727	1,981,955
1928	5,030,099	1,293,257	294,677	465,811	716,352	2,260,002
1929	5,157,083	1,142,352	269,590	484,304	729,013	2,531,823
1930	3,781,172	829,098	178,533	362,650	512,802	1,898,089
1931	2,377,982	566,791	127,072	246,814	317,647	1,119,657
1932	1,576,151	513,659	89,419	152,118	196,727	624,228

APPENDIX XIV

EXPENDITURE OF THE GREAT POWERS ON DEFENCE, 1934.

	In millions of £'s
Great Britain . .	114·2
France . . .	90·0
Germany . . .	43·8
Italy . . .	46·4
Russia . . .	242·6
United States . .	145·2

From the *Peace Year Book* for 1935.

APPENDIX XV

GREAT BRITAIN—MILITARY AND OTHER EXPENDITURE, 1904-1931.

	Military.	Munitions.	Military and Munitions.	Cost of Collection.	Education.	Grants to Local Authorities.	National Debt (and Sinking Fund).	Civil Services	Total (excl. P.O.)
1904	66,055,000			3,093,000	15,574,513	12,126,112	31,367,086	7,959,289	136,175,000
1905	62,150,000			3,148,000	16,396,481	12,214,826	32,433,925	8,091,768	134,435,000
1906	59,199,000			3,179,000	16,946,419	12,536,891	35,936,574	5,256,116	133,054,000
1907	58,256,000			3,222,000	17,359,203	11,155,379	38,707,765	5,584,853	134,285,000
1908	59,028,000			3,320,000	17,368,771	9,824,286	34,911,999	9,725,944	134,179,000
1909	63,043,000			3,342,000	17,907,467	9,445,395	26,368,797	19,145,341	139,252,000
1910	67,835,000			3,919,000	18,744,175	9,881,709	29,246,397	22,688,719	152,315,000
1911	70,507,000			3,951,000	18,983,036	9,636,399	31,104,783	23,815,782	157,998,000
1912	72,432,000			4,200,000	19,530,615	9,653,299	34,858,760	24,923,326	165,598,000
1913	86,027,992			4,578,227	19,169,647	9,734,128	24,500,000	38,924,916	182,934,910
1914	361,156,272			4,810,774	20,031,043	9,529,134	22,668,896	114,028,326	532,224,445
1915	754,609,463	246,720,787	1,001,330,250	4,752,177	20,284,996	9,756,851	60,249,311	525,283,334	1,561,405,608
1916	854,840,831	559,439,949	1,414,280,780	5,143,704	20,092,095	9,895,466	127,250,493	692,639,473	2,269,302,011
1917	1,052,449,272	715,101,222	1,767,550,494	5,839,189	24,702,215	9,730,538	189,851,086	948,480,714	2,946,154,216
1918	1,415,523,534	562,227,196	1,977,750,730	6,817,049	25,719,344	9,680,811	269,964,650	813,305,071	3,103,237,655
1919	766,348,663	192,843,559	959,192,222	10,123,896	42,610,904	10,746,142	332,033,708	635,083,836	1,989,790,708
1920	353,568,648	32,922,770	386,491,418	12,749,648	58,318,053	10,785,504	349,598,616	449,409,267	1,267,343,506
1921	178,300,000			12,900,000	53,700,000	9,400,000	328,900,000	413,600,000	996,800,000
1922	118,000,000			10,700,000	47,400,000	10,100,000	321,300,000	264,200,000	771,700,000
1923	112,400,000			10,300,000	46,300,000	13,300,000	344,300,000	224,300,000	750,600,000
1924	116,900,000			10,300,000	46,600,000	13,600,000	353,700,000	206,900,000	748,000,000
1925	121,500,000			10,700,000	47,100,000	14,100,000	354,300,000	226,700,000	774,400,000
1926	117,400,000			10,900,000	48,400,000	14,200,000	374,300,000	219,200,000	784,400,000
1927	118,600,000			11,100,000	48,700,000	15,700,000	374,000,000	214,200,000	782,300,000
1928	115,700,000			11,600,000	47,800,000	16,400,000	369,000,000	202,200,000	762,700,000
1929	115,400,000			11,500,000	48,200,000	31,500,000	359,800,000	205,200,000	771,600,000
1930	112,700,000			12,000,000	53,500,000	45,700,000	360,000,000	241,200,000	825,100,000
1931	111,400,000			11,500,000	56,800,000	46,200,000	354,900,000	245,900,000	826,700,000

Obtained from *British Budgets* (Mallet & George) 1887–1913, 1913–1921, 1921–1931.

NOTES

1 *Imperialism, A Study* was first published in 1902 by Nisbet (London), the second edition in 1905 by Constable (London) and the third in 1938 by Allen & Unwin (London). This last edition was published with a substantial preface by the author, which is published here for the first time since 1938. (The 1938 edition will be referred to in the text unless otherwise stated.) *Imperialism* consisted of articles published elsewhere, in *The Speaker*, the *Contemporary Review*, the *Political Science Quarterly* and the *British Friend*. See Porter, 1968, pp. 215—16. A number of Hobson's other books were compiled in a similar fashion.

2 See, for example, G. P. Gooch's essay in Masterman, 1901, G. H. Perris's in Coit, 1900, F. W. Hirst's, J. L. Hammond's and G. Murray's essays, in *Liberalism and Empire*, 1900, and Robertson, 1899. These works do not have either the originality, breadth or penetration.

3 Campbell-Bannerman said *Imperialism* was the 'most trenchant thing that I have seen for many a day'; Spender, 1923, Vol. II, p. 87. See H. N. Brailsford's *War of Steel and Gold* (1914), J. Strachey's *The End of Empire* (1959), L. S. Woolf's *Empire and Commerce in Africa* (1920) and Lenin's *Imperialism, The Highest Stage of Capitalism* (1917). See also Koebner and Schmidt, 1965, p. 271 and Etherington, 1984, pp. 99—102.

4 The fullest accounts of Hobson's life are Lee, 1972, pp. 176—81, and Allett, 1981, pp. 3—46. Hobson's own *Confessions of an Economic Heretic*, 1938, although even less personally revealing than Mill's *Autobiography*, is also useful.

5 The 'Introductory', written by William Clarke, in the first edition of the *Progressive Review* (vol. 1, no. 1, October 1896, pp. 1—9) is the best summary of the Rainbow Circle's thinking at this time and can be seen almost as Hobson's own political credo in this period.

6 Works that provide a useful background to the Liberal Party and Hobson's thought in this period are: Butler, 1968, Clarke, 1978, Emy, 1973, Poirier, 1958, Scally, 1975, Searle, 1971, Semmel, 1960, Stansky, 1964, Weiler, 1982, and Wood, 1983. Two doctoral dissertations have been written on Hobson, by Lee, 1970 and Townshend, 1973.

7 H. D. Lloyd seems to have articulated this theoretical and practical compromise between liberalism and state socialism some time before Hobson; see Townshend, 1973, p. 97. In general the American in-

fluences on Hobson's thought have been underplayed by most commentators.

8 For a fuller discussion of Hobson's views on this, see Townshend, 1973, pp. 227–39. Others felt the same way as Hobson about the Liberal Party in this period: for example, William Clarke, Edward Pease, John Morley and Richard Haldane.

9 John Morley also supported this position; see Auld, 1975, p. 96.

10 For an account of the discussion that took place see Townshend, 1973, pp. 244–53.

11 See note 2 for those who advanced similar Cobdenite arguments.

12 Hobson, under the pseudonym of 'Nemo', wrote an obituary of Clarke: 'He hated with a most holy hatred the rampant Imperialism of the time, and inspired many others with his passionate detestation of its manifestations both in England and in America' (Hobson, 1901d, p. 314). An anthology of Clarke's writings, edited by Herbert Burrows and Hobson (1908), demonstrates, at least in print, how many of Clarke's thoughts either prefigured or were similar to Hobson's, for example, on significance of monopoly (pp. 3–23), the privileging of qualitative values as opposed to quantitative values (pp. 24–43), the social and economic decline of Britain (pp. 44–58), the connection between imperialism and undemocratic government (pp. 44–58), the connection between imperialism and finance (pp. 76–89), the difficulties of imperial federation (pp. 76–89), the link between jingoism and capitalism (pp. 108–17) and the notion that retribution would be facing Britain as a result of its imperialist deeds (p. xix). See Etherington, 1984, ch. 3, for an interesting but extravagant interpretation of the impact of the American socialist W. G. Wilshire on Hobson's thinking. Whilst containing an element of truth as far as Hobson's account of US imperialism is concerned, Etherington's precise estimation of Wilshire's impact on Hobson is unclear. Moreover, Etherington's analysis ignores the influence of Clarke and the American progressivists such as H. D. Lloyd in the 1890s in making Hobson aware of the significance of trusts and monopolies. For a rebuttal of Etherington which sets Hobson within the wider radical British tradition see Cain, 1985b.

13 cf. Morley, 1881, Vol. II, p. 100.

14 cf. Cobden, 1886, pp. 324 and 375.

15 cf. Morley, 1881, Vol. II, p. 361.

16 Cain, 1978, provides a useful discussion of Hobson's autarkic tendencies, although I believe he overstates his case.

17 Koebner and Schmidt, 1965, pp. 235 and 254, were the first to note this change, but they do not follow up the implications of this for Hobson's Cobdenite faith in the pacific effect of international trade and investment, a belief which he held until the First World War.

18 The exact proposals in *Imperialism* are vague, but some idea of what he had in mind can be gleaned from what he said later. Apart from abo-

lishing the House of Lords veto, the House of Commons could also be democratized. 'By securing an extended franchise, shorter parliaments and adequate reforms of electoral machinery, representatives might at least become a genuine expression of popular will' (Hobson, 1909, p. 117).

19 See Freeden, 1978, and Jones, 1980 for useful accounts of the relationship between liberalism and Social Darwinism.

20 Hobson substituted 'can' for 'shall', emphasizing his attempt to 'biologize' his moral theory.

21 The economic aspects of this argument were developed earlier. See Hobson, 1894, pp. 364–73.

22 His concern with biological explanation also possibly accounted for his racial stereotyping. He referred to the Jews as a 'peculiar race' (*Imperialism*, p. 57) and as for blacks, he stated: 'A certain quickness of memory and assimilative power in childhood is found among blacks, but in concentration, reflection, and reasoning, they are inferior, and early puberty checks their general development' (Hobson, 1929, p. 360).

23 The view that Hobson was a cultural relativist can be exaggerated; see, for example, Porter, 1968, pp. 234–5; Cain, 1979, p. 417; Allett, 1981, pp. 140–1. He did not extend this appreciation to African and other cultures of the 'lower races', who were deemed to be 'children' and could therefore be legitimately 'educated', with safeguards, by Western powers. This logically implies that either these races possessed no culture or, if they did, it was of an inferior kind. See *Imperialism*, pp. 224, 229, 285, and Townshend, 1982.

24 The changes that he made to the different editions were not particularly significant to his line of argument. The greatest modifications were in the 1905 edition. (1) pt I, ch. ii. In response to criticism he conceded in the form of changes in statistical comparisons that foreign trade was more important than he had originally argued, but he still held to his former position that this trade was diminishing in importance (pp. 23–31, cf. Clarke, 1981, pp. 308–12). (2) pt II, ch. iv. He added in the light of events in South Africa an attack on the use of Chinese indentured labour in the Transvaal (pp. 243–5). (3) pt II, ch. v. Probably as a result of its victory over Russia in 1905, he contemplated Japan ousting the West in its domination of China (pp. 227–9). (4) pt II, ch. vi. Possibly due to his trip to Canada in 1905, Hobson added the observation that local manufacturing interests in Canada and Australia would oppose Imperial Federation which was based on preferential treatment to British manufactures (pp. 300–2). In the 1938 edition he made few changes, but wrote an introduction to clarify (and modify) his explanation of imperialism and demonstrate its continuing relevance.

25 See pt I, chs i and vi, *passim*.

26 See Hobson, 1938a, p. xv. This absolves him from the charge of crude economic determinism.

27 For a discussion of the theoretical changes that Hobson made after *Imperialism*, see Cain, 1978, Kruger, 1955, Townshend, 1982.

28 cf. *The Chronicle*, 1 November 1902, *Yorkshire Post*, 19 November 1902, *Glasgow Herald*, 17 October 1902.

29 A line pursued in greater depth by Porter, 1968, p. 225.

30 See p. 28 of this introduction.

31 *The Great Illusion* was published in 1909 and by 1911 it had run into three new editions and five reprints. Hobson's second edition of *Imperialism* was published with the help of a subsidy.

32 For example, those who see little theoretical indebtedness, Owen and Sutcliffe, 1972, p. 315, Stokes, 1969, p. 295, and those who take the opposite line, Allett, 1981, p. 157, Arrighi, 1978, p. 24. Kemp, 1967, p. 82, takes a middle position.

33 For an extended Leninist critique of Hobson, see Kemp, 1967, ch. iii, *passim*.

34 For criticisms of this view see Cain, 1985a, and Townshend, 1973, pp. 416−19.

35 Since Hobson was primarily concerned to attack the finance capitalists for their speculative activities in the stock exchange and related institutions, figures showing that actual investments were not made in newly acquired territories are insufficient proof that Hobson was wrong on this question.

36 It is interesting to note in the twentieth century the huge increase of trade both in absolute and relative terms with 'Other British Possessions' in comparison with the Dominions and India (*Imperialism*, p. 372).

37 See, for example, the attempt by Cain, 1985a, to validate some of Hobson's observations on the British socioeconomic structure in the 1870−1914 period.

38 cf. Lloyd, 1972, pp. 145−6.

REFERENCES

Allett, J. (1981), *New Liberalism, the Political Economy of J. A. Hobson* (Toronto: University of Toronto Press).

Angell, N. (1909), *The Great Illusion* (London: Heinemann).

Arrighi, G. (1978), *The Geometry of Imperialism* (London: New Left Books).

Auld, J. (1975), 'The Liberal pro-Boers', *Journal of British Studies*, vol. XIV, no. 2, pp. 78–99.

Baran, P. A. and Sweezy, P. M. (1966, 1968), *Monopoly Capital* (Harmondsworth: Penguin).

Baumgart, W. (1982), *Imperialism: The Idea and Reality of British and French Colonial Expansion, 1880–1914* (Oxford: Oxford University Press).

Bleaney, M. F. (1976), *Underconsumptionist Theories* (London: Lawrence & Wishart).

Brailsford, H. N. (1914), *War of Steel and Gold* (London: Bell).

Brailsford, H. N. (1948), 'The life-work of J. A. Hobson', L. T. Hobhouse Memorial Trust Lecture, no. 17 (Oxford: Oxford University Press).

Brewer, A. (1980), *Marxist Theories of Imperialism. A Critical Survey* (London: Routledge & Kegan Paul).

Brown, M. B. (1963, 1970), *After Imperialism* (London: Merlin).

Brunschwig, H. (1964), 'The origins of the new French empire', in G. Nadel and P. Curtis, *Imperialism and Colonialism* (London: Macmillan), pp. 111–12.

Burrows, H. and Hobson, J. A. (1908), *William Clarke, A Collection of His Writings* (London: Sonnenschein).

Butler, J. E. (1968), *The Liberal Party and the Jameson Raid* (Oxford: Clarendon).

Cain, P. J. (1978), 'J. A. Hobson, Cobdenism, and the radical theory of economic imperialism, 1898–1914', *Economic History Review*, second series, XXXI, pp. 565–84.

Cain, P. J. (1979), 'International trade and economic development in the work of J. A. Hobson before 1914', *Journal of the History of*

REFERENCES

Political Economy, vol. XI, pp. 406–24.

Cain, P. J. (1985a), 'J. A. Hobson, financial capitalism and imperialism in late Victorian and Edwardian England', *Journal of Commonwealth History*, vol. 13, pp. 1–27.

Cain, P. J. (1985b), 'Hobson, Wilshire and the capitalist theory of capitalist imperialism', *History of Political Economy*, vol. 17, no. 3, pp. 455–60.

Cairncross, A. K. (1967), 'Did foreign investments pay?', in D. K. Fieldhouse (ed.), *The Theory of Capitalist Imperialism*, pp. 154–9.

Clarke, P. (1978), *Liberals and Social Democrats* (Cambridge: Cambridge University Press).

Clarke, P. (1981), 'Hobson, free trade and imperialism', *Economic History Review*, second series, XXXIV, pp. 308–12.

Cobden, R. (1886), *Political Writings*, 2nd edn (London: Cassell).

Coit, S. (ed.) (1900), *Ethical Democracy* (London: Richards).

Courtney, L. (1903), 'What is the advantage of foreign trade?', *Nineteenth Century*, vol. LIII, pp. 806–12.

Emy, H. V. (1973), *Liberals, Radicals and Social Politics, 1892–1914* (Cambridge: Cambridge University Press).

Etherington, N. (1984), *Theories of Imperialism* (London: Croom Helm).

Fieldhouse, D. K. (1961), "Imperialism": an historiographical revision', *Economic History Review*, second series, XIV, pp. 187–209.

Fieldhouse, D. K. (ed.) (1967), *The Theory of Capitalist Imperialism* (London: Longman).

Frankel, S. H. (1967), 'Investments in Africa', in Fieldhouse (ed.), op. cit., pp. 151–3.

Freeden, M. (1978), *The New Liberalism* (Oxford: Clarendon).

Gann, L. H. and Duignan, P. (1968), *Burden of Empire* (London: Pall Mall).

Gollwitzer, H. (1969), *Europe in the Age of Imperialism, 1880–1914* (London: Thames & Hudson).

Hamer, D. A. (1972), *Liberal Politics in the Age of Gladstone and Rosebery* (London: Oxford University Press).

Hirst, F. W., Murray, G., Hammond, J. L. (1900), *Liberalism and Empire* (London: Johnson).

Hobson, J. A. (1890–1), 'The law of three rents', *Quarterly Journal of Economics*, vol. V, pp. 363–88.

Hobson, J. A. (1894, 1906), *The Evolution of Modern Capitalism* (London: Scott).

Hobson, J. A. (1898), 'Free trade and foreign policy', *Contemporary Review*, vol. 74, pp. 167−80.

Hobson, J. A. (1900a), *The War in South Africa* (London: Nisbet).

Hobson, J. A. (1900b), 'Capitalism and imperialism in South Africa', *Contemporary Review*, vol. 77, pp. 1−17.

Hobson, J. A. (1900c), *The Economics of Distribution* (New York: Macmillan).

Hobson, J. A. (1901a), 'The crisis of trade unionism', *New Age*, vol. xiii, 616−17.

Hobson, J. A. (1901b), *The Social Problem* (London: Nisbet).

Hobson, J. A. (1901c), *The Psychology of Jingoism* (London: Richards).

Hobson, J. A. (1901d), 'William Clarke', *New Age*, vol. xiii, p. 314.

Hobson, J. A. (1902), *Imperialism, A Study* (London: Nisbet).

Hobson, J. A. (1904), 'Herbert Spencer', *South Place Magazine*, vol. 9, pp. 49−55.

Hobson, J. A. (1905), *Imperialism, A Study*, 2nd edn (London: Constable).

Hobson, J. A. (1909), 'After the destruction of the veto', *English Review*, vol. 4, pp. 111−21.

Hobson, J. A. (1911a), *An Economic Interpretation of Investment* (London: Financial Review of Reviews).

Hobson, J. A. (1911b), *The Science of Wealth* (London: Home University Library).

Hobson, J. A. (1917), *Democracy After the War* (London: Allen).

Hobson, J. A. (1919), *Richard Cobden, International Man* (New York: Holt).

Hobson, J. A. (1920), 'Why the war came as a surprise', *Political Science Quarterly*, vol. XXXV, pp. 337−59.

Hobson, J. A. (1921), *Problems of a New World* (London: Allen & Unwin).

Hobson, J. A. (1926), *Free Thought in the Social Sciences* (London: Allen & Unwin).

Hobson, J. A. (1929), *Wealth and Life* (London: Macmillan).

Hobson, J. A. (1934), *Democracy in a Changing Civilisation* (London: Bodley Head).

Hobson, J. A. (1938a), *Imperialism, A Study*, 3rd edn (London: Allen & Unwin).

Hobson, J. A. (1938b), *Confessions of an Economic Heretic* (London: Allen & Unwin).

Jones, G. (1980), *Social Darwinism in English Thought* (Brighton: Harvester).

REFERENCES

Kautsky, K. (1970), 'Ultra-Imperialism', *New Left Review*, no. 59, pp. 39–46.

Kemp, T. (1967), *Theories of Imperialism* (London: Dobson).

Keynes, J. M. (1936), *The General Theory of Employment, Interest and Money* (London: Macmillan).

Koebner, R. (1949), 'The concept of economic imperialism', *Economic History Review*, second series, vol. II, pp. 1–29.

Koebner, R. and Schmidt, R. D. (1965), *Imperialism* (Cambridge: Cambridge University Press).

Kruger, D. H. (1955), 'Hobson, Lenin and Schumpeter on imperialism', *Journal of the History of Ideas*, vol. XVI, pp. 252–9.

Langer, W. L. (1935), *The Diplomacy of Imperialism*, 2 vols (New York: Knopf).

Le Bon, G. (1896), *The Crowd. A Study of the Popular Mind* (London: Unwin).

Le Bon, G. (1899), *The Psychology of Peoples* (London: Unwin).

Lee, A. J. F. (1970), 'A study of the social and economic thought of J. A. Hobson', PhD thesis, University of London.

Lee, A. J. F. (1972), 'Hobson', in M. Bellamy and J. Saville (eds), *Dictionary of Labour Biography*, Vol. 1 (London: Macmillan), pp. 176–81.

Lenin, V. I. (1968), *Collected Works*, Vol. 39 (Moscow: Progress Publishers).

Lenin, V. I. (1917, 1966), *Imperialism, The Highest Stage of Capitalism* (Moscow: Progress Publishers).

Lloyd, T. (1972), 'Africa and Hobson's Imperialism', *Past and Present*, no. 55, pp. 130–53.

'Lucian' (Hobson, J. A.) (1918), *1920: Dips into the Near Future* (London: Headley).

MacKillop, I. (1986), *The British Ethical Societies* (Cambridge: Cambridge University Press).

Masterman, C. F. G. (ed.) (1901), *The Heart of the Empire* (London: Unwin).

Matthew, H. C. G. (1973), *The Liberal Imperialists* (London: Oxford University Press).

Mommsen, W. J. (1981), *Theories of Imperialism* (London: Weidenfeld & Nicolson).

Morley, J. (1881), *Life of Richard Cobden*, 2 vols (London: Chapman & Hall).

Muirhead, J. H. (1942), *Reflections of a Journeyman in Philosophy* (London: Allen & Unwin).

Mummery, A. F. and Hobson, J. A. (1889), *The Physiology of Industry* (London: Murray).

Nemmers, E. E. (1967), 'Underconsumptionist evaluated', in Fieldhouse (ed.), op. cit., pp. 120–4.

Nevinson, H. W. (1925), *More Changes, More Chances* (London: Nisbet).

Nurske, R. (1967), 'Capital export as the product of trade', in Fieldhouse (ed.), op. cit., pp. 160–2.

Owen, R. and Sutcliffe, R. (eds) (1972), *Studies in the Theories of Imperialism* (London: Longman).

Poirier, P. P. (1958), *The Advent of Labour* (London: Allen & Unwin).

Porter, B. (1968), *Critics of Empire* (London: Macmillan).

Ricci, D. M. (1969), 'Fabian socialism: a theory of rent as exploitation', *Journal of British Studies*, vol. 9, pp. 105–21.

Robertson, J. M. (1899), *Patriotism and Empire*, (London: Richards).

Robinson, R. E. and Gallagher, J. (1953), 'The imperialism of free trade', *Economic History Review*, second series, VI, pp. 1–15.

Robinson, R. E. and Gallagher J. (1961), *Africa and the Victorians, the official mind of imperialism* (London: Macmillan).

Scally, R. J. (1975), *The Origins of the Lloyd George Coalition* (Princeton: Princeton University Press).

Searle, G. R. (1971), *The Quest for National Efficiency* (Oxford: Blackwell).

Semmel, B. (1960), *Imperialism and Social Reform* (London: Allen & Unwin).

Spender, J. A. (1923), *The Life of the Right Hon. Sir Henry Campbell-Bannerman, GCB* , 2 vols (London: Hodder & Stoughton).

Staley, E. (1967), 'Capitalists and others', in Fieldhouse (ed.), op. cit., pp. 146–50.

Stansky, P. (1964), *Ambitions and Strategies* (Oxford: Clarendon).

Stokes, E. (1969), 'Late nineteenth century colonial expansion and the attack on the theory of economic imperialism: a case of mistaken identity?', *Historical Journal*, vol. XII, pp. 285–301.

Strachey, J. (1959), *The End of Empire* (London: Gollancz).

Taylor, A. J. P. (1967), 'Hobson's misapplication of the theory', in Fieldhouse (ed.), op. cit., pp. 125–9.

Townshend, J. A. (1973), 'J. A. Hobson and the crisis of liberalism', PhD thesis, University of Southampton.

Townshend, J. A. (1982), 'J. A. Hobson: anti-imperialist?', *International Review of History and Political Science*, vol. XIX, pp. 28–41.

REFERENCES

Wallas, G. (1908), *Human Nature and Politics* (London: Constable).

Weiler, P. (1974), 'William Clarke: the making and unmaking of a Fabian socialist', *Journal of British Studies*, vol. XIV, pp. 77–108.

Weiler, P. (1982), *The New Liberalism: Liberal Social Theory in Great Britain, 1889–1914* (New York: Garland).

Winslow, E. M. (1931), 'Marxian, liberal and sociological theories of imperialism', *Journal of Political Economy*, vol. 39, pp. 713–58.

Woolf, L. S. (1920), *Empire and Commerce in Africa* (London: Allen & Unwin).

Wood, J. C. (1983), *British Economists and the Empire* (London: Croom Helm).

INDEX

INDEX

INDEX

INDEX